Elders on Trial

Florida A&M University, Tallahassee
Florida Atlantic University, Boca Raton
Florida Gulf Coast University, Ft. Myers
Florida International University, Miami
Florida State University, Tallahassee
University of Central Florida, Orlando
University of Florida, Gainesville
University of North Florida, Jacksonville
University of South Florida, Tampa
University of West Florida, Pensacola

Elders on Trial

Age and Ageism in the American Legal System

Howard Eglit

University Press of Florida
Gainesville/Tallahassee/Tampa/Boca Raton
Pensacola/Orlando/Miami/Jacksonville/Ft. Myers

Copyright 2004 by Howard Eglit
Printed in the United States of America on recycled, acid-free paper

09   08   07   06   05   04   6   5   4   3   2   1

A record of cataloging-in-publication data is available from
the Library of Congress.

ISBN 0-8130-2765-9

The University Press of Florida is the scholarly publishing agency
for the State University System of Florida, comprising Florida A&M
University, Florida Atlantic University, Florida Gulf Coast University,
Florida International University, Florida State University, University
of Central Florida, University of Florida, University of North Florida,
University of South Florida, and University of West Florida.

University Press of Florida
15 Northwest 15th Street
Gainesville, FL 32611-2079
http://www.upf.com

This book is dedicated to the most important people in my life:

Barbara, Susan, Michael, and Daniel

It also is dedicated to Dr. Bernice Neugarten, a friend and a scholar who never settled for less than the best in her own work or the work of others.

Contents

Acknowledgments

My thanks are due to my colleague Professor Nancy Marder for her comments regarding the chapter of the book addressing the jury, and my colleague Keith Stiverson, director of the Chicago-Kent Information Center, for her comments regarding the entire manuscript. I am also indebted to Professor Rebecca Morgan, of Stetson University College of Law, for her insights regarding the initial draft of this book. I also want to express my appreciation to Joe Mitzenmacher for putting his librarian skills to expert use in locating source materials for me.

Howard Eglit
May 10, 2004

1

Demographics, Destiny, and the American Legal System

I grow old . . . I grow old
I shall wear the bottom of
my trousers rolled.
—T. S. Eliot, "The Love Song of J. Alfred Prufrock"

It took such a long time to get here, but it went so fast.
—Comedian Victor Borge, musing on being 87 years old

All would live long, but none would be old.
—Benjamin Franklin

Demographics and the Legal System

The United States is in the midst of a "demographic revolution."[1] Steadily increasing numbers of older men and women populate most communities in most states, and there are more to come.[2] Indeed, the statistical data are daunting. Fifty years ago there were 12.4 million men and women over the age of 64 living in the United States; they constituted 8.1 percent of the population.[3] By mid-2004 the number of elders had tripled to about 36 million.[4] By mid-2030, it is estimated, there will be more than 70 million such individuals—20 percent of the projected American populace (and more than the present-day populations of Great Britain or France).[5] Thereby they will exceed the percentage of those who will be under age 18.[6] (This enormous increase in the numbers of elders is not unique to the United States; rather, the tremendous growth of the elderly population is a worldwide phenomenon,[7] both in developed and Third World countries.)[8]

This morphing, so to speak, of its demographic profile promises both profound consequences and new demands for American society. We will need, for example, increased venues and opportunities for advanced education;[9] new or modified systems for the financing, delivery, and allocation of health care resources;[10] an expanded supply of affordable and supportive elder-friendly housing;[11] and innovative efforts to satisfy public transportation requirements for oldsters decreasingly able to manage without assistance their own travel needs.[12] It no doubt also is correct—and directly to the point here—to predict that alteration, accommodation, and innovation will be required of the multi-layered American legal system—an amalgam of statutes, ordinances, regulations, executive orders, and judicial rulings that are daily invoked, manipulated, modified, interpreted, and/or promulgated by hundreds of thousands of litigants, legislators, bureaucrats, police officers, judges, and more.[13]

This is not to say, of course, that until now the significant rise in the number of oldsters—a rise that already was occurring in post–World War II America—went unnoted. In the past 30 or so years, both Congress and state legislatures, as well as federal and state courts, increasingly addressed through legislative enactments and judicial rulings concerns of special relevance for the elderly[14] and the near-elderly. Reformatory statutes were aimed at particular age-associated issues, such as discrimination in employment[15] and in credit eligibility.[16] Considerable legislative attention, spurred both by a very impressive body of scholarly literature and by revelatory hearings and government studies,[17] was directed in the past two decades or so to enhancing and adding protective procedures and standards as predicates to the imposition of guardianships on allegedly cognitively impaired seniors.[18] Beset by recurring instances of abuse and inadequate care,[19] long-term care facilities (commonly known as nursing homes) have been the targets over the past 20-plus years of expanding statutory and regulatory controls.[20] During this same period governmental programs were created or modified to afford various types of assistance and benefits to oldsters.[21] Moreover, the past quarter century was marked by notable private sector initiatives responsive to legal problems affecting elders.[22] Add to all this the fairly recent appearance on the scene of elder law attorneys, who hold themselves out as specialists in the various legal issues confronting older women and men.[23]

This impressive array of public and private sector efforts notwithstanding, the demographic revolution that is barreling forward, with the first cohort of baby boomers turning 65 in 2011,[24] promises to demand even more numerous and more intense responses from the American legal system and its participants. There likely will be occasion for the enactment of new or refined legislation. New programmatic endeavors are almost certain—for example, technological and infrastructural aids to enable people of diminished mobility to gain access to the courts.[25]

But challenges of a different sort, and their correlative responses, are my concern here. Rather than espousing prescriptive or proscriptive laws, or large-scale programs for spending and allocating money, and rather than proposing doctrinal changes (such as elevating age classifications to a level of special constitutional status),[26] my aim is to focus on the role of age in the interplay among the actors who populate the American legal system. My concerns are human interactions and responses, rather than matters of infrastructure or formal legislative enterprises.

For example, how do jurors respond to older plaintiffs, defendants, and witnesses—of whom we certainly can expect many more in the next 30 years than we saw in previous decades? And what of judges? What can we realistically predict regarding the attitudes and responses of jurists to growing cadres of older attorneys, claimants, jurors, and witnesses? Assessment of the ways in which younger attorneys interact with older clients also is very much in order. In addition, apart from the matter of how a legal system participant of a given age responds to another participant of a given age, there is the separate issue of how age affects the performance of these participants. Are older witnesses less reliable than younger ones? Do older jurors need aids in carrying out their roles that the young do not need? Aged judges pose another concern.

Such issues hitherto have received only occasional attention. Moreover, the data are unsettled and therefore unsettling. There is a perception, for example, among the employment bar that the composition of federal court juries is skewed toward the elderly, and because of this it is thought by some that plaintiffs in age discrimination in employment cases unduly benefit by reason of the sympathies of their age-contemporary juror peers.[27] Hardly any solid research has been done, however, to test the accuracy of this perception. Numerous courthouse philosophers, to cite another example of conflicting information, long have identified various alleged biases of older jurors, but their anecdotally based opinions are disputed by scholars.[28]

Given the demographic tidal wave lapping at the doors of lawyers' offices and judges' chambers, there is little time left to examine, analyze, explicate, and try to resolve the issues generated by a burgeoning population of older Americans intersecting with the pervasive American legal enterprise.[29]

Age Bias

Arguably, the very need for attention to the foregoing concerns already is waning by virtue of the very demographic phenomenon—a ballooning older population—that I rely upon as impetus for addressing the play of the age factor. In other words, one legitimately might predict that the cultural weight of expanding numbers of older men and women will lead of its own force to the discarding of outmoded stereotypes and pejorative thinking hitherto directed against them. Thus, this reasoning would go, the impact of the age factor for elders in the courts will disappear or at least decline in the natural order of things. Accordingly, an investment of energy and time in examining the age factor is unnecessary: time alone will soon ameliorate whatever problems may exist. I think, however, that this argument is flawed.

The argument fails because embedded in American culture is a diffuse bias that, depending upon the individuals involved and depending further on the context—that is, the workplace, the courtroom, the community (neighborhood, nursing home, assisted living center), and so on—generally works to the detriment of older men and women. Ageism, as this bias is termed, entails a collection of negative notions, beliefs, and attitudes—both consciously and unconsciously held—about the elderly: notions entailing perceptions of physical decay, intellectual decline, psychological and social lassitude, lack of creativity and initiative, and more.

And so, even as the numbers and percentage of older folks markedly increase, the still very large majority of the populace will be, in absolute numbers, nonelderly people. By virtue of *their* numbers they will continue to control and shape dominant societal perceptions, values, and attitudes.[30] Thus, no quick demise for ageism legitimately can be forecast. Moreover, the harboring of bias toward the elderly is not a phenomenon characterizing just the non-old. We all are indoctrinated through both overt and subtle means to subscribe to negative attitudes regarding old age, and so older people themselves often maintain—consciously or unconsciously—negative views about the status of being old and the competencies of oldsters.[31] For example, it has been pointed out that "elderly subjects themselves are even more likely than college students—as well as than [sic] lawyers, judges, and other randomly selected potential jurors—to hold a negative stereotype about elderly witnesses' ability to give accurate testimony."[32] Similarly, in a study using drawings of attractive and unattractive faces, there was found to be a strong association between perceptions of older age and unattractiveness not only by the younger respondents (i.e., those under age 30) but also on the part of the older ones (those over age 56).[33] What is more, data suggest that people who are the objects of negative stereotypes actually conform their behavior to correlate with those stereotypes![34] Finally, while adversity for older men and women may decline by reason of their increased numbers, it correlatively may well increase for younger individuals—those on the wrong end of graying America's age profile.

In brief, an aging America portends problems and issues for our legal system and for those who function within it. The enormous imminent increase in oldsters in and of itself makes urgent the need for both study and action. Ageist bias makes such study and action essential if the legal system, and those who make it run—judges, lawyers, plaintiffs, defendants, witnesses, and juries—are to act fairly and are themselves to be treated fairly.

Theses and Conclusions

My broad (and admittedly unremarkable) thesis is that with vastly expanded numbers of older people in our society, it logically follows that the legal system's occasions for encountering older people as plaintiffs, defendants, witnesses, jurors, judges, and lawyers will greatly increase (albeit not necessarily in each and every possible legal setting). My narrower, more worrying, thesis (again, admittedly not an entirely novel one)—a thesis that in many of its particulars cries out, I readily acknowledge, for solid empirical research—is that the age factor can work to the disadvantage of individuals caught up in the legal system.[35] Older men and women increasingly confront the risk of being impeded, discounted, and disrespected because they are old. On the other hand, young individuals also may be disadvantaged because of the increasing prevalence of older decision makers. In either case, the possibilities of detrimental consequences will greatly expand in the next two or three decades as the number of oldsters involved in some way in the legal system burgeons.

And the conclusions that ensue?

- First, ageism is prevalent throughout American society, although the levels of ageist bias will vary from individual to individual and from context to context. More importantly here, age bias is obviously present in the interactions that, in the aggregate, make up the American legal system. The interactions between judges and jurors, jurors and litigants, clients and lawyers, lawyers and jurors, and so on, all are infected by stereotypes—stereotypes (not all of which are pernicious) that sometimes are mitigated by fact-based knowledge and sometimes not.
- Second, and particularly insofar as the American legal system is concerned, we need more study and more information. There is an urgent need for intensive analysis directed to such issues as the sources of ageism, the impact of ageist bias on the various facets of the legal system, and the effect of age on the performance of the participants in that system, that is, judges, lawyers, jurors, and witnesses (and court administrative personnel, as well).
- Third, there are a number of concrete steps that can be taken today— even without more study and more research—to address and mitigate age bias and age-related problems in the American legal system.

And so to the task at hand.[36] But first, a necessary (or at least useful) preface to exploring the roles of the age factor in our legal system is a focused review of the phenomenon of age as a mediating cultural, political, and social force throughout American society.

2

Age and Ambivalence

It is doubtful that there has ever been a society in which old people as a whole have been as politically influential, as materially well-off, and probably as happy as they are in modern American society, although they are not revered.
—Judge Richard A. Posner, U.S. Court of Appeals for the Seventh Circuit, *Aging and Old Age*

There is . . . a deep and profound prejudice against the elderly which is found to some degree in all of us.
—Robert A. Butler, M.D., first director of the National Institute on Aging, *Why Survive? Being Old in America*

The Ubiquitous Age Factor

Age matters. It matters in every society, from primitive to advanced. So I emphasized in an earlier work:

"Every known society," it has been observed, "has a named social category of people who are old—chronologically, physiologically, or generationally". . . . And the same authors further note that "[i]n every case these people have different rights, duties, privileges, and burdens from those enjoyed or suffered by their juniors". . . . The American experience reveals no departure from this universal cultural phenomenon: in a number of respects, older people in the United States are treated as a distinct subset of the population, and age-based differentiations accordingly are utilized in a variety of contexts. Age is used, sometimes in statutory or regulatory provisions, sometimes in private sector entities' policies and rules, and sometimes more informally, for allocating public and private resources, for extending or denying public benefits, for imposing or relaxing legal responsibilities, and for distributing or restricting various types of opportunities.[1]

In terms of efficiency, convenience, and even fairness, there are clearly discernible advantages—both for individuals and for societies—that derive from utilizing age as a lever for making decisions, dispensing rights, and imposing obligations:

> An administrator of an age-defined program can avoid engaging in a time-consuming and perhaps financially burdensome effort to determine a given applicant's satisfaction of a need-based program's terms. Instead, the bureaucrat can simply rely on a readily ascertainable, and typically indisputable, fact: the age of the person involved. Thereby, presumably at least some individual program applicants benefit, by virtue of being insulated from potential abuses of bureaucratic discretion. Moreover, they further enjoy the benefit of eligibility determinations that likely are more speedily made than otherwise would be the case. . . .
>
> The use of age as a basis for decision making may also produce societal benefits of a larger dimension. So long as a system operates consistently by dispassionately relying on the objective fact of age as the determinant for decision making, both the appearance of impartiality and perhaps even actual justice, to some extent, are obtained.[2]

Given these integral functions that the age factor can, and does, serve, it is hardly surprising that age-based benchmarks and classifications are widespread in the United States (and throughout every other society, as well).

Often, a particular age demarcation is explicitly utilized. For example, age can be, and has been, used as the basis for designating both those who are too young to be enrolled in elementary school[3] and those who are too old to enroll in college,[4] for defining crimes,[5] for setting appropriate prison sentences,[6] for establishing eligibility for social welfare programs, such as Medicare,[7] and for authorizing expedited judicial proceedings.[8] The age factor is used by states to separate those who may drive from those who may not,[9] by the U.S. Constitution to establish eligibility for election to federal office,[10] and by private enterprises to set premiums for automobile liability insurance.[11] And more examples readily can be mustered.[12]

Age also functions informally as a powerful normative device for influencing—and sometimes even dictating—attitudes and conduct.[13] Thus we see age used as a lever for defining appropriate roles and behaviors.[14] "Act your age" is a common admonition reflecting this phenomenon, and departures by older folks, in particular, from its dictate can elicit scorn and even ridicule.[15] We snicker in response to the 60-year-old woman who wears a bikini at the beach, and we chuckle at the notion of an elderly couple attending a Britney Spears concert. In the same vein, May-December romances raise figurative eyebrows (particularly when the woman is the older partner).[16] Why these expressions of disapprobation for "inappropriate" behavior? Because these folks are not comporting themselves in ways society deems fitting for people who are no longer young![17]

Other instances of age's normative force can be readily identified. There is the common experience of children emulating their older siblings and schoolmates. In the workplace older workers may bridle at reporting to younger supervisors: the usual, perhaps even innate, ordering of hierarchy by age is amiss.[18] Age can play significant, albeit not formally prescribed, roles in judges' sentencing of criminal offenders, even when consideration of the age factor is not expressly dictated by statute or rule.[19] Age also may be used, typically within the context of loose formal statutory prescriptions, as a factor in determining whether the best interests of proposed adoptee children are served by placement with older adults.[20]

Age and Ambivalence

Most uses of age, whether formal or informal, occasion little thought.[21] Most prominently, in pretty much all instances the *lack* of age is dealt with consistently and unreflectively in every society. The United States, and seemingly every other society as well,[22] is characterized by a system of age-grading dictating that those who lack some level of specific or generalized chronological and/or physical maturity are both denied rights that older individuals enjoy and excused from bearing responsibilities that older individuals shoulder.[23] Admittedly, within this system there may be a little bit of flexibility: the age of consent to marry, for example, may be 16 in one state and 17 in another. Nonetheless, the overall conclusion is still valid: age is a ubiquitous factor that in some instances disables, and in some instances advantages, the young, but that rarely in any event is accorded any second thought.

With regard to the elderly, however, the anthropological and sociological data reveal more variation. Elders in preindustrial village societies enjoyed (and continue to enjoy in such of those societies that survive today) higher status, power, authority, and security than they did, or do, in industrialized societies.[24] Indeed, Leo Simmons, the leading student of the role of age in so-called primitive societies, observed in 1945: "The most striking fact about respect for old age is its widespread occurrence," and he continued: "Some degree of prestige for the aged seems to have been practically universal," at least until a final stage of superannuation.[25] In contrast, in Western industrialized societies—and more particularly, in the United States—old age plays a much more checkered role, producing both positive and negative visions and consequences.[26]

On the positive side, we see in the United States that at a very general level old people are depicted as in some sense cultural icons: avuncular white-haired oldsters who lavish selfless, nonjudgmental affection on loving extended families, while imparting to young folks pithy nuggets of native wisdom earned during their years of hard, honest work.[27] Cheery white-bearded Santa Clauses—along with Norman Rockwell reprints—reinforce this paradigmatic image. On a much more concrete level, political choices have been made in the United States to expend enormous sums of money for government programs that primarily, or even exclusively, benefit older men and women. Of course, the prime example is Medicare, which accounted for the expenditure of $212 billion in fiscal year 2000[28] and which utilizes attainment of age 65 as the usual trigger for eligibility.[29] Add to all this the fact that in significant measure the levers of political power in the United States are controlled by individuals (the great majority of whom are male) who are well into their 60s, 70s, 80s, and even on rare occasion their 90s.[30]

But there also exist grimmer scenarios regarding the treatment, status, and roles—both public and private—of the elderly. Often, old age is seen and experienced, both by the young and the old, as a stage of life devoid of quality, purpose, and meaning.[31] More than that, evidence abounds of a frequent distaste for, and demeaning of, the old—again by the young and even by the old themselves. Dr. Robert Butler, the first director of the federal government's National Institute on Aging, recited a litany of the dishearteningly negative images and characterizations often associated with older adults in a seminal work published in 1975:

An older person thinks and moves slowly. He does not think as he used to, nor as creatively. He is bound to himself and to his past and can no longer change or grow. He can neither learn well nor swiftly, and even if he could, he would not wish to. Tied to his personal traditions and growing conservatism, he dislikes innovations and is not disposed to new ideas. Not only can he not move forward, he often moves backwards. He enters a second childhood, caught often in increasing egocentricity and demanding more from his environment than he is willing to give to it. Sometimes he becomes more like himself, a caricature of a lifelong personality. He becomes irritable and cantankerous, yet shallow and enfeebled. He lives in his past. He is behind the times. He is aimless and wandering of mind, reminiscing and garrulous. Indeed, he is a study in decline. He is the picture of mental and physical failure. He has lost and cannot replace friends, spouse, jobs, status, power, influence, income. He is often stricken by diseases which in turn restrict his movement, his enjoyment of food, the pleasures of well-being. His sexual interest and activity decline. His body shrinks; so, too, does the flow of blood to his brain. His mind does not utilize oxygen and sugar at the same rate as formerly. Feeble, uninteresting, he awaits his death, a burden to society, to his family, and to himself.[32]

Dr. Butler titled this dreary depiction of the old *ageism*,[33] a term that since has come to have wide currency. Unfortunately, his exposition is all too easily buttressed by readily available evidence. For example, some sense of the breadth and depth of the negative attitudes inflicted upon the elderly is afforded by taking stock of the plethora of pejorative nouns and adjectives commonly applied to identify and characterize older adults: *old bag, old bat, battle ax, biddy, cantankerous, codger, coot, crank, crotchety, curmudgeon, dirty old man, dotard, dotty, eccentric, fogy, old fool, forgetful, fossil, gaffer, geezer, hag, old fart, ornery, senile, witch,* and *wizened* are just a few.[34] The ease with which such epithets are accepted and used reveals just how ingrained and accepted negative notions of old people are.[35] More troubling, perhaps, is the fact that while one's attitudes and perceptions influence the words and phrases one uses to articulate those attitudes and perceptions, the words and phrases themselves can in turn influence attitudes and perceptions—even the views of those who are the victims of such negativism. "If negative words are used in labeling individuals, eventually those persons [subjected to that labeling] may come to believe that those words reflect who and what they are."[36] Pejorative language thus takes on a force of its own that engenders more negative thoughts and conceptions in a spiraling process of negativism.

Epithets aside, it is readily apparent that in magazines, on television, in the movies, in consumer advertising, and in dialogues both public and private, the American populace is relentlessly instructed to aspire to those qualities typically associated with youthfulness: smooth skin, silky hair, sleekly muscled bodies, athleticism, sexual prowess, mental acuity.[37] Physical attractiveness is in fact a virtually impossible characteristic for the elderly to be seen as possessing.[38]

For the most part, the popular visual and print media dwell almost exclusively on the doings of the non-old: their romances, their avocations, their homes, their opinions, and so on. The sports events that entrance millions of spectators each week further convey the message—incidentally but nonetheless powerfully—that almost all our hero athletes share at least one trait: they are not old.[39] (Indeed, when the rare older athlete—40-year-old baseball player Cal Ripken or mid-40s baseball player Nolan Ryan, or even 39-year-old basketball star Michael Jordan or 39-year-old pitcher Roger Clemens—has competed, his age is constantly noted as making his feats particularly remarkable.)

Not surprisingly, older faces are rare in movies, magazines, and television (save for public affairs programs).[40] Elders who are depicted in the popular entertainment media typically are presented either as victims[41] or as being quirky, resistant to change, mentally slow, physically frail, sexually neutered, forgetful, and/or cantankerous.[42] In brief, old people almost invariably are portrayed as being at best pathetic and at worst distasteful or even loathsome.[43] Moreover, these depictions leave hardly any room for exceptions; rather, generalizations—rising (or sinking) to the level of stereotypes[44]—sweep virtually all within their net.

A more benign, but really no less insidious, stereotypical image of the elderly entails what has been termed the *infantilization* of the old.[45] According to Arnold Arluke and Jack Levin, this imagery is seen in a number of contexts:

> [O]ld people are given the personality and moods of children. It is common, for example, in prescription drug ads to describe senility in terms normally associated with children. An ad for a tranquilizer "for the agitated geriatric" shows an elderly man angrily waving his fist. "TANTRUMS" is printed large across the page. Other tranquilizer ads use terms such as *nuisance, disruptive,* and *obstreperous* to describe the actions of elders. . . . Television shows and movies characterize the personality of older people as childlike whether it is "Mother Jefferson's" cantankerousness, the silliness of Johnny Carson's "Aunt Blabby," or the impulsiveness and recklessness of Ruth Gordon in the film *Harold and Maude.*[46]

It is easy to point out other examples of this phenomenon whereby the elderly are brought down to the level of children. Again, to quote Arluke and Levin:

> [O]ld people are encouraged to pursue the activities of children. In an article called "The Fun Life for Young and Old," a major city newspaper provided "a guide to August activities for senior citizens and children." Pictures were shown of a puppet show and a magic act. Even the "Kiddies Menu" of a popular Massachusetts ice cream parlor portrays an older man walking hand-in-hand with a young boy. As clearly stated on the face of the menu, "for all kids under 10 and over 65," the bill of fare consists of a "hot doggie," "kiddie burger," and "peanut butter and jelly sandwich."[47]

This process of infantilization, it has been argued, has several adverse consequences. According to Arluke and Levin, "The 'second childhood' stereotype tends to make young people [who have emerged into adulthood after years of being "second-class" citizens, i.e., minors] feel distant from their elders."[48] Moreover, this stereotype can generate fear of old age: "How many adults want to be thought of one day as a six-year-old who isn't toilet trained?"[49] As for old people themselves, Arluke and Levin say: "[T]he second-childhood stereotype creates a self-fulfilling prophecy."[50] They come to act like children and to engage in childlike activities—results that clearly are pernicious:

> First, such behavior lowers their social status. . . . Secondly, the perception of infantile behaviour may allow . . . [bad] things to be done to them that would otherwise not be considered: the prescription of psychoactive medi-

cations, [and] institutionalization. . . . Third, infantilization robs the "gray power" movement of adults who might otherwise work for political change and social betterment.[51]

The extent—or perhaps the thoughtless mundaneness—of American society's denigration of the elderly is highlighted by a study done by Dr. Erdman B. Palmore, a singularly prominent researcher in the field of gerontology. Dr. Palmore examined the role of humor—as expressed in jokes, cartoons, and greeting cards—as a means for conveying ideas about the elderly, and even here he found that negative notions prevailed. Five recurring themes, all negative in tone and/or substance, were identified, as recounted in a synopsis of his study:

1. *Physical ability.* Examples of physical decline included such jokes as the elderly couple who got married and spent their honeymoon just trying to get out of the car. Or the old man on bended knee who proposed to a young woman—when she rejects his proposal, he remarks: "Well, if you don't want to marry me, the least you can do is help me up."

2. *Mental ability.* There are many jokes about mental decline. For example, an old man remarks to his friend: "I'd like to live in the past, but I just can't remember any of it."

3. *Sexual ability.* Negative attitudes toward sexuality in old age are conveyed by such jokes as an elderly man staring at a pretty girl as she passes by; his wife witnesses the incident and remarks to a neighbor, "George has a wonderful memory for his age." And a definition of old age: "Where there's a will but no way."

4. *Longevity.* An often-told joke about longevity concerns an old man telling his doctor that if he had known that he was going to live so long, he would have taken better care of himself. Another is a doctor telling an old man that he's in good shape and should live to be 100; the old man replies, "But doc, I *am* 100."

5. *Age concealment.* Nearly all the jokes about age concealment concern women. For example, an elderly man remarks that his wife is a very thrifty lady as she had only 29 candles on her 40th birthday cake or [that] her cake was beautiful but her arithmetic was terrible.[52]

In another and much more important context we see that in the work world empirical studies, as well as hundreds of cases decided under the Age Discrimination in Employment Act of 1967, as amended (ADEA),[53] confirm that age-based discrimination is perpetrated against older men and women in a variety of ways.[54] In still another setting, but one also involving the generation of income, it has been reported that older authors have greater difficulty than do their younger counterparts in getting their works published:

> If you are 67 and have written your first book, you will have a harder time finding a publisher than you will, say, if you are 27. This is because agents and publishers are looking for authors with the potential, and time, for multiple books that can "build a brand," as one agent put it. On the other hand, if you are an older, published author with a track record of modest or declining sales, you may also have trouble because you are viewed as not having enough time left to turn around your career.[55]

Conclusion

Sophie Tucker, a famous entertainer of the vaudeville era, once said, "I've been rich and I've been poor. Rich is better." I would rework this to read, "I've been young and I've been old. Young is better." That is the message conveyed in countless ways in twenty-first-century America.[56] Yes, there are some positive images of aging. Yes, there is what might be termed *happy talk* about growing old—talk epitomized by the lines written by Robert Browning: "Grow old along with me! The best is yet to be."[57] But at a diffuse, pervasive level, ageism is the bias that infects us all.

3

Age Bias: Some General Propositions

I have lived some thirty years on this planet, and I have yet to hear the first
syllable of valuable or even earnest advice from my seniors. They have told
me nothing and probably cannot tell me anything, to the purpose.
—Henry David Thoreau, *Walden*

Socrates: I enjoy talking with the very aged. For to my thinking we have to
learn of them as it were from wayfarers who have preceded us on a road
on which we too, it may be, must sometime fare—what it is like. Is it
rough and hard-going or easy and pleasant to travel?
—Plato, *Republic*

Age Bias—An Inevitable Human Phenomenon?

What is it that causes people in the United States[1] generally to hold adverse
views—rising sometimes to the level of negative stereotypes and biases—regarding older people?[2] At first blush this question may appear inane because
the answer seemingly is so apparent: old age is a time when many of what are
seen as the positive aspects of life are on the wane. Physical vigor and health
typically decline; intellectual acuity may dissipate; the opportunities for form-
ing new relationships—sexual, romantic, platonic, or otherwise—usually diminish; the heady challenges of paths not yet chosen are for the most part
behind us; the gratifications generated by new knowledge, experiences, and
successes become elusive. Not surprisingly, the elderly who bear these dismal
traits of old age[3] evoke negative reactions: both for the young as well as the old
themselves, oldsters are messengers delivering unwelcome messages.

And yet—and admittedly this no doubt is a hard proposition to accept, it is
not necessarily the case that antipathies vis-à-vis older folks or the process of
growing old are the inevitable results of rational thinking. There have been,
after all, societies in which old age has been viewed more benignly than is the
case in the United States—societies in which old people have been accorded
respect and appreciation, rather than condescension, indifference, or even
worse, active dislike.[4] True, one could quibble as to the relevance of this obser-

vation by noting that many of these societies were (and for those that continue to survive today, still are) preindustrial—or what some would term *primitive*. Actually, however, there also have been more advanced societies in which old age or some variant thereof, such as parental status, has evoked respect and admiration. Moreover, such societies continue to exist today. For example, Chinese culture historically has accorded much honor to the elderly, and this apparently continues to be the case[5] (although veneration of the old now may be on the wane).[6] Likewise, respect for the elderly is at the core of Japanese culture[7] (although, again, the status of the old may be in decline),[8] as it is in other societies of the Far East.[9]

Thus, while aging itself is inevitable, distaste for the process or for the aged is not. It is useful, then, in trying to understand ageism and its consequences, to explore the forces that have generated and continue to nurture age bias in modern Western societies and, more particularly, in the United States. While this exploration may not in all respects reveal data that are seemingly directly applicable to the treatment of older participants in the American legal system, this endeavor nonetheless is integral to understanding the diffuse ageist bias that today permeates American culture and that thereby penetrates into the American legal system as well.[10]

First, however, it is necessary to highlight a couple of initial general propositions.

The Qualitatively Distinctive Nature of Age Bias

Some forces that motivate attitudes and conduct are deemed so pernicious that with rare exception they evoke unmitigated condemnation (at least for public consumption) by "right-thinking" people. Race, most pointedly, is a human characteristic[11] that in almost all instances is rejected as a relevant or acceptable basis for government decision making in the United States.[12] Even in the private realm, race for the most part is condemned (or at least we go through the ritual of condemning it) as an acceptable ground on which to base choices and to fashion decisions.[13] Gender is another facet of the human makeup that increasingly is being rejected as a lever for decision making by courts[14] and legislatures in contexts where, four or five decades ago (and even more recently, in some instances), it was commonly deemed acceptable.[15] In contrast, the age criterion generally is seen as being a less invidious and therefore a more acceptable basis for the allocations of rights, benefits, and responsibilities.

The proposition that age bias is of a different, less serious nature than the particularly odious vice of racism was convincingly articulated in a seminal study published in 1965 by the U.S. secretary of labor pursuant to the direction of Congress,[16] which had chosen during its consideration of Title VII of the Civil Rights Act of 1964[17] to defer pursuing statutory condemnation of age bias in the workplace. The Labor Department's report enunciated a rather benign perception of ageism (although this term was not actually used in the report):

> Discrimination in employment based on race, religion, color, or national origin is accompanied by and often has its origins in prejudices that originate outside the sphere of employment. There are no such prejudices in American life which apply to older persons and which would carry over so strongly into the sphere of employment.
>
> The process of aging is inescapable, affecting everyone who lives long enough. It is gradual, minimizing and obscuring differences among people. At all times there are people of all ages living in close association rather than in separate and distinctive social or economic environments. The element of intolerance, of such overriding importance in the case of attitudes toward other groups, assumes minimal importance in the case of older people and older workers.
>
> It is true that hiring officials are not immune to the brightness, vigor, and attraction of youth, nor always above exploiting these attributes for commercial advantage. But such choices involve preferences *for* one group, rather than antagonism *against* another.
>
> We have found no evidence of prejudice based on dislike or intolerance of the older worker. The issue of discrimination revolves around the nature of the work and its rewards, in relation to the ability or presumed ability of people at various ages, rather than around the people as such. This issue thus differs greatly from the primary one involved in discrimination on the basis of race, color, religion, or national origin, which is basically unrelated to ability to perform work.
>
> This is not to say that there is no intolerant prejudice against older persons as such. Determinations not to employ older workers can become deep-seated and even emotional in character. But were this the sole matter, the degree to which it exists would not warrant public concern.[18]

Judicial evaluations of age bias echo the foregoing relaxed view of age-based decision making. For one, the United States Supreme Court has noted with seeming approbation the secretary of labor's relatively benign assessment of age discrimination in the workplace.[19] More generally, in numerous constitutional rulings addressing equal protection challenges,[20] federal and state courts regularly and uncritically have rebuffed age discrimination claims arising not only in the workplace but in other settings as well.[21] Most significantly, the Supreme Court on several occasions has prescribed (or at least expressed approval of) a very easily satisfied minimum rationality test as the appropriate standard for scrutinizing age classifications under the United States Constitution,[22] rather than the far more rigorous standard used to address (and almost invariably to strike down) laws utilizing race distinctions.[23]

It was in the first of these Supreme Court decisions, *Massachusetts Board of Retirement v. Murgia*,[24] that the Court—in the course of upholding a mandatory retirement statute applied to state police officers at age 50—expressed two prime justifications for judicial deference. First, the Court reasoned that the histories of Draconian disadvantage and subjection to erroneous stereotyping that have exemplified the treatment of racial minorities are absent in the case of the elderly:

> While the treatment of the aged in this Nation has not been wholly free of discrimination, such persons, unlike, say, those who have been discriminated against on the basis of race or national origin, have not experienced a "history of purposeful unequal treatment" or been subjected to unique disabilities on the basis of stereotyped characteristics not truly indicative of their abilities.[25]

Although there actually is strong disagreement among historians as to the correct understanding of the treatment of the elderly in the American colonies and in the 100 or so years following the Revolution,[26] the Court had the matter pretty much right (despite its inattention to empirical data). Even the most vociferous critic of ageism is unable to point convincingly to a panoply of wrongs, injuries, and subjection to evil inflicted on the elderly that at all compares to the harm suffered by blacks since they were first brought to the New World in the 1600s.[27]

Second, the *Murgia* Court, in a statement that was simultaneously both cryptic and substantively provocative, pointed out a key distinction between the age characteristic and race: "[O]ld age does not define a 'discrete and insular group,' in need of 'extraordinary protection from the majoritarian political process.' Instead, it marks a stage that each of us will reach if we live out our normal span."[28] In other words, there is no need for special judicial concern because (although the Court did not explicitly spell this out) age-geared laws are enacted by legislators who either are themselves elderly or eventually will attain that status.[29] What is more, lawmakers—whether old or not—almost certainly have or have had caring relationships with people who *are* old (i.e., parents, aunts, uncles). These facts lead to the perception that those people who possess power in American society are not likely to exercise that power to hurt themselves today or their future selves tomorrow, nor are they likely to inflict harm on those with whom they have or have had positive emotional ties. Accordingly, so this reasoning goes, a law that singles out older people for differential treatment is very unlikely to be particularly noxious or harmful, and thus that law does not need the careful attention of life-tenured federal court judges.[30] Instead, the dynamics of human nature, operating in the political arena, will prevent inappropriate injury being done by young and middle-aged legislators to their parents, uncles and aunts, as well as their own future selves. What is more, common sense instructs that those legislators who already are old are hardly likely to support hurtful discrimination inflicted on themselves or their fellow oldsters.

In theory, the *Murgia* Court's cryptic assessment of legislators' psychology (as adumbrated by this author's latter-day interpretation) makes sense; in actuality, however, the Court's (imputed) assessment of human nature may have been unduly optimistic:

> One flaw lies in the Court's failing to take into account the psychology of youth, and even of middle age. The "non-old" do not expect to grow old. Of course they know that that fate lies ahead, as an intellectual matter. But as a factor which governs their actions today, it is a reality which is in some manner ignored or suppressed. Thus, to confidently rely upon the self-interest of the future old is to take a stance not quite fitting with the reality of the presently "non-old"; from their perspective, the old are in many ways "them," and not "us."
>
> Another defect in the Court's posture lies in its apparent analysis of how legislation comes to be. The underlying implicit assumption seems to be that a legislator makes a choice—either to hurt the old or not. But, in fact, as to any given piece of legislation there may be a variety of factors which complicate the computation. . . .
>
> Finally, there is the fact that legislation is selective. Even a legislator who appreciates in a directly felt way the fact that he will become old still may vote for a law forcing the retirement of police officers at age 50 or at age 60, given that he neither is, nor ever intends to be, a police officer himself.[31]

Criticisms notwithstanding, both the secretary of labor—who focused on the workplace—and the *Murgia* Supreme Court, which articulated a broader perspective (albeit one also emanating from an analysis of a workplace situation), were in good measure correct in their ultimate conclusions. Age bias indeed does appear to be a much more moderate form of bigotry (if even that) than is the prejudice that pits one racial group against another or that fuels hostility between religious factions. The depths of emotion, the excesses of rhetoric, the outrageousness of actions that accompany xenophobia, religious disputation, and racial divisions, all simply are absent when we look to the ways in which the young, middle-aged, and elderly interact in America.[32]

Moreover, there is another distinction between ageism and the more pernicious "-isms": while most people in our culture harbor some degree of antipathy toward old age per se, it seems fair to say that far fewer people entertain actively hostile feelings toward old women and men as individuals.[33] In this key respect, then, age bias again differs from racism, xenophobia, anti-Semitism, and other bigotries based on race, religion, color, and national origin. The neo-Nazi racist hates not only African Americans as a group and Jews as a group; he also hates individual African Americans and Jews. The typical ageist has the saving grace of being a much more benign character.

Another difference: age-motivated decisions are harder to discern than are those that are based on race, national origin, and sex.[34] After all, everyone has some modicum of age stored up and so, in terms of the age characteristic, the differences between people are not an either-or proposition; rather, everyone occupies some place on the age spectrum. Thus, a given decision or policy experienced adversely by an older person often may not easily be attributed to the grievant's age per se. Can one with confidence say that because Joe Smith is 60 rather than age 58, he was the victim of age bias rather than some other factor? After all, there is no reasonable way for an observer to readily determine, on the basis of observation alone, that someone is 60 rather than 58, or 62 rather than 65. In contrast, sex is a characteristic that almost always is apparent for any given individual: "Mary is a woman; Max is a man."[35] And while race may be a very problematic notion for anthropologists and geneticists,[36] casual racial identifications also are made more or less readily, if not necessarily accurately.[37] Race and gender, moreover, are—to use the jargon of equal protection case law—immutable. Age is not: the 16-year-old of today will be the 45-year-old of tomorrow and the 80-year-old of an even more distant future.

Still and all, ageism and racism are not so separate and distinct that no linkages make sense. There is a gap between the two, but not a chasm. Both generate stereotyped caricatures. Both entail generalizations. Both entail stigmatization.[38] Both involve ignorance on the part of the bigot. Both can and do inflict harm. Finally, and in any event, to conclude that ageism is less pernicious than racism or sexism is not to answer the question as to what animates ageism, however moderate (in comparative terms) it may be. And so exploration and reasoned analysis are still in order.

Context Matters

Age is a less malignant basis for making differentiations than is race, or gender, or color, or national origin, or religion. That does not mean, however, that any and all age-based distinctions are benign. Nor does it even mean that the significance and consequences of any and all age-based distinctions are equal.

Rather, the palatability of such distinctions varies with the contexts in which they are deployed. In some settings use of the age factor may be characterized as at most innocuous; in others, such use may be castigated as being meretricious.

For example, under the Age Discrimination in Employment Act of 1967, as amended (ADEA),[39] employers with 20 or more employees are prohibited from using age as a basis for making employment decisions.[40] Accordingly, it is illegal under this statute for an employer to refuse to promote a 65-year-old employee—let us call him Mr. Grayhead—because of that employee's age. Here, then, the political consensus, as reached and expressed in statutory form in 1967,[41] is that in the workplace age generally is an improper decision making criterion. The Act, however, does contain numerous exceptions and so age turns out to be an acceptable factor to take into account, after all, in those circumstances to which the exceptions apply.[42] Moreover, inasmuch as the statute in any event does not apply to employers with less than 20 employees, one must conclude that the political consensus at the time of the statute's drafting was that age was condoned as a tolerable decision-making criterion in smaller workplaces, of which there are millions.[43] And given that this numerosity requirement has never been changed, one must conclude that the consensus forged in 1967 still prevails today. In sum, in the workplace context age sometimes is and sometimes is not a legally permissible basis for employers' decisions.

Now suppose that our hypothetical Mr. Grayhead, who we will posit voluntarily left his job thanks to the impetus of a retirement incentive package made available to those 65 and older,[44] plans on moving from his apartment building. His 10 or so neighbors consider him to be a very good fellow tenant: quiet, cheerful, and willing to loan tools and food when needed. In brief, in the context of his little community his age has generated no negatives whatsoever insofar as his neighbors are concerned. But his popularity notwithstanding, Mr. Grayhead is leaving because he wants to stop paying non-tax-deductible rent, and so he plans on buying a condominium, which he intends to finance with a 30-year mortgage, the interest on which *will* be tax deductible. Some might wonder whether it would be permissible for a potential lender to take account of the actuarially established fact that the average 65-year-old white male has a future life expectancy of 15.9 years,[45] and so it is quite possible Mr. Grayhead will not live long enough to pay off in full his indebtedness. In brief, it arguably might not make economic sense to extend Mr. Grayhead a 30-year loan. In this particular context, then, the age factor obviously has different implications than it does in the workplace. As it happens, the federal Equal Credit Opportunity Act[46] comes into play here. Consistent with this statute, a lender may not refuse to make a loan to Mr. Grayhead because of his age, nor can it even deem his age a justification for charging him a higher rate of interest or for limiting him to a short-term loan.[47]

What if our 65-year-old newly retired Mr. Grayhead also has decided to pursue a new career as a medical doctor? To this end, he plans to seek admission to Health Care University. The typical annual cost of medical school matriculation far exceeds the tuition charged; the excess expense is largely paid for by taxpayer-funded governmental grants to, and contracts with, the schools, as well as government-guaranteed loans to students.[48] Would it be appropriate for the university to reject our aspiring doctor, the rationale being that by the time he will have completed four years of medical school plus another three or four years of residency, he likely will have little future work life remaining and so, to put the matter baldly, the taxpayers who will have supported Mr. Grayhead's education will receive inadequate return on their investment? Some individuals who would roundly deny that they are biased might answer in the affirmative in this particular situation. And indeed, at one time medical schools did set age caps—typically age 30 or so—for admission.[49] However, since the issuance in 1979 of regulations implementing the Age Discrimination Act of 1975, as amended,[50] which bans discrimination on the basis of age by recipients of federal financial assistance (subject to a number of exceptions), it would appear that such a restriction regarding admission is illegal insofar as schools that receive federal funds are concerned.[51]

Finally, suppose Mr. Grayhead plans on commuting by car from his condominium to Health Care University. He is required by a state statute applicable to those 65 and older to pass an annually administered driving test in order to retain his driver's license. In contrast, younger drivers' licenses are renewed automatically every four years.[52] The statute in question is grounded on empirical data showing (1) that older drivers as a group have more accidents per mile driven than does any other age group save those who are 16 to 24 years of age, and (2) that accident rates per mile driven rise steadily after age 70.[53] Given these facts, does the annual relicensure requirement unfairly discriminate against Mr. Grayhead? Again, some people (maybe most or even all) certainly would say no.

In sum, in each of the foregoing vignettes the matter of age was implicated in some way. Because of his age Mr. Grayhead was eligible for a retirement incentive package offered by his employer that was not available to younger workers. Despite his age, or perhaps because of it (or perhaps no one ever even thought about his age), Mr. Grayhead was a favorite of his fellow tenants. On the other hand, because of his age the financing of Mr. Graybeard's desired condominium could be seen as being problematic from a lender's perspective.

Because of his age, his admission to medical school was subject to question. And because of his age, Mr. Grayhead had to satisfy a driver's licensure requirement that was not imposed on younger folks.

In brief, while age is not a perfect proxy for concerns such as driver safety, or adequate return on tax dollars, or creditworthiness, or physical agility, or likeability, etc., the age factor is not invariably so far off the mark that its utilization by a decision maker always will elicit condemnation—or at least the same level of concern—no matter the setting. Rather, depending on the context and depending further on the nature of the use of the age criterion in that context, age may be an acceptable factor—indeed, even a beneficial one for the individual, for society at large, or for both—for making decisions and imposing obligations.

Conclusions

Age bias is manifested in a number of ways throughout American society. For the most part that bias produces negative consequences for older people. This bias, however, cannot blithely be equated with other 'isms'—racism, sexism, and so on. It is its own distinct phenomenon. The task now is to ascertain how this phenomenon manifests itself in the American legal system.

4

Age Bias and Its Multiple Sources

Iphis: Strong wrestler Eld, O how I loathe thy grasp,
Loathe them which seek to lengthen out life's span,
By meats and drinks and magic philtre-spells
To turn life's channel, that they may not die,
Who, when they are not but cumberers of the ground,
Should hence, and die, and make way for the *young*.
—Euripides, *Suppliants*

Somebody said old people should disassociate themselves and retreat to se-
rene meditation in the world. That was a beautiful theory for everybody
but the old people. If they would just disappear and vanish from sight, not
bother anybody. One of the real reasons for senility is that old people stop
doing things. They accept others' estimates of what they can do.
—Mary Herrick, educator, quoted in Bonnie Bluh, *The "Old" Speak Out*

Ageism as a Bias

In his classic study, *The Nature of Prejudice,* Gordon W. Allport articulated a
definition of prejudice in the context of exploring the causes of racism and
ethnocentrism:

> Ethnic prejudice is an antipathy based upon a faulty and inflexible generali-
> zation. It may be felt or expressed. It may be directed toward a group as a
> whole, or toward an individual because he is a member of that group.
>   The net effect of prejudice, thus defined, is to place the object of prejudice
> at some disadvantage not merited by his own conduct.[1]

Overall, a prejudice has three components: "a cognitive component (e.g., irra-
tionally based beliefs about a target group), an affective component (e.g., dislike), and a conative component (e.g., a behavioral predisposition to avoid the
target group)."[2] Given these factors, it is debatable whether ageism rises to the
level of a prejudice.[3]

Certainly, the degree of irrationality intrinsic to prejudices based on race,
national origin, and religion seems lacking in the case of the ageist: most
peoples' beliefs about older folks, while often exaggerated or misinformed,

have some degree of truth undergirding them. Moreover, while in American culture there is an aversion to old age as a state of being, much less often is dislike directed to old people per se. Rather, there is a distaste for the characteristics—declining health, loneliness, diminished intellectual acuity, and so on—that they are seen (rightly or wrongly) as exhibiting. Insofar as Allport's third factor—the element of avoidance—is concerned, this would not appear to be very much relevant to characterizing the relations of the young and the old. Many younger people are quite solicitous of the elderly; indeed, caregiving by family members is so common that a term has been devised, *sandwich generation,* to describe middle-aged people who provide financial, emotional, and other resources to their children on the one hand, and to their aged parents on the other.[4]

Still and all, it also is true that antipathy, condescension, and deprecation are directed toward the elderly. Consequently, while disavowal of the word *prejudice* as being too loaded a word may be in order, it seems appropriate at least to label ageism as a "bias": a skewing of attitudes and actions that typically (but not always) either works to the detriment of the subjects of those attitudes and actions or makes problematic "accurate" treatment of oldsters, that is, treatment that accords with objective, as opposed to subjective, reality. The task at hand is to determine how this bias has come to be harbored (in varying degrees of strength) by so many. Unfortunately, only one certain conclusion emerges from the forthcoming discussion: ageism has many likely sources.[5]

Ageism, History, and Cultural Conditioning

Most biases (and even more so, most prejudices) have long lives; they are passed on from generation to generation, although it seems fair to optimistically conjecture that biases, being less intensely held ideas, are more likely to be susceptible to withering away over time than would be the case for prejudices. Even so, biases must begin somewhere, at some time. Not surprisingly, however, both the genesis of ageism in America as a phenomenon, and the negative regard and even mistreatment accorded the elderly, are matters of considerable dispute.[6]

A dominant explanatory theme for a number of years has been modernization theory. This holds that the industrialization of Western societies in the eighteenth and nineteenth centuries caused a concurrent shift of the bulk of economic activity and populations from agrarian to urban settings. This in turn led to the economic disutility of the old, causing a concomitant loss of financial and intra-family power that produced major adverse changes in the ways in which the elderly came to be viewed and treated.[7] While modernization theory has been a potent force in the historical analyses of aging and the aged, in recent years it has come under serious attack. For example, Nancy Foner has argued that "the dramatic undermining of the authority of age in America [actually] came before urbanization, industrialization, and mass education had any effect."[8] Moreover, Foner writes, the depiction of the elderly as living in a preindustrial "Golden Age" is off the mark: "The situation of the elderly in preindustrial Europe and America . . . was no paradise on earth."[9] Perhaps the most salubrious means of finessing this debate is to conclude that industrialization, whether a first-order cause or a more removed one, no doubt has played a part in the changed economic roles and diminished social status of the elderly.[10]

The significance of industrialization per se aside, and critiques of modernization theory notwithstanding, there is general—albeit not unanimous—agreement that old age is a stage of life that has engendered different levels of respect, or disrespect, at different times in the United States.[11] In colonial days the elderly—at least those who were not destitute[12]—were objects of veneration, according to historian David Hackett Fischer.[13] Indeed, people actually endeavored to portray themselves as elderly, so Fischer claims:

> In a society where age conferred power, authority, and wealth, old people tried to make themselves seem even older than they actually were. Today when Americans report their ages to the census taker, they often subtract a few years. Even septuagenarians prefer to be sixty-nine. But in the seventeenth century, and increasingly in the eighteenth, people of advanced age made themselves a little older instead. Trends in clothing fashions were the same. In the eighteenth century men also tried to look older by powdering their hair and wearing clothes cut to imitate age. A clergyman in 1765 was advised not to wear his own hair "till age has made it venerable."[14]

Eventually, however, the elevated position of the elderly changed, according to Professor Fischer, who dates this reversal in fortune as occurring between 1770 and 1840:

> The idea of equality destroyed the hierarchy of age; the idea of liberty dissolved its communal base; the decline of deference diminished its authority; the growth of wealth stratification in America sapped its economic strength.[15]

Like Fischer, Professor W. Andrew Achenbaum also perceives a major change in cultural and societal views regarding the elderly, but he points to the period between 1865 and 1914 as constituting the time of "an important transition in the history of ideas about growing old."[16] Thomas Cole also has identified an adverse change in the status of elders in America: he has pursued

a historical and sociological analysis in concluding that the "origins of ageism
. . . lie *both* in the revolt against hierarchical authority [in mid-nineteenth
century America] *and* in the rise of Victorian morality."[17] He writes further:

> If old age in America had only suffered the usual misfortune of being iden-
> tified with an old order, the impact might have been short-lived. But old age
> came to symbolize not only the old world of patriarchy and hierarchical
> authority; it also represented an embarrassment to the new morality of self-
> control. The primary virtues of "civilized" morality—independence,
> health, success—required constant control over one's body and physical
> energies. The declining body in old age, a constant reminder of the limits of
> physical self-control, came to signify dependence, disease, failure, and sin.
> The devastating implications of ageism lay not in negative images alone but
> in the splitting apart of positive and negative aspects of aging, along with
> the belief that virtuous individuals could achieve one and escape the other.[18]

In contrast to the foregoing examinations of changing views over time regarding age in America, Professor Carole Haber puts forth a considerably
different analysis. Rather than delineating some particular era as marking a
change in the status of the old, she has identified victimization and denigration
of the elderly as being continuing phenomena throughout the course of American history.[19] (Actually, Professor Fischer did concede that certainly not all the
elderly were venerated.)[20]

Whatever the historical truth, once age bias came to the fore it was ready
and available to be transmitted from generation to generation through cultural
conditioning. George Eaton Simpson and J. Milton Yinger, two perceptive
students of how minority group biases become cemented into the culture of a
given society, have explained this conditioning process:

> An attitude toward a minority group can be seen, from one point of view,
> as simply one of the folkways, one of the learned ways of responding that
> are part of the standard cultural equipment. We are taught to be prejudiced
> against certain groups just as we are taught to dislike certain foods that
> people in other societies consider great delicacies. Individuals may be
> equipped with a number of culturally learned responses to minority groups
> that they are never called upon to use. These responses scarcely can be
> called functional, except in the general sense of representing the cohesive-
> ness of a culture group. They survive, however, as group-patterned ways of
> thinking, ready to influence one's response if an occasion arises. . . .
>
> Many, perhaps most, of the ways of behaving that are agreed upon by
> members of a society had their origin in an attempt to meet a specific need.
> The attempt was not necessarily rational or objectively valid, though it may
> have been, but somehow it came to be accepted as the appropriate way.

Individuals could not possibly bear the strain that would come from trying to decide, for each of the hundreds of actions they perform each day, what the best response might be. . . .

The things that are important about cultural norms . . . are their tendency to continue beyond the situation in which they appeared and their coercive power over individuals. . . .

Folkways change, of course, and today they doubtless change more rapidly than they did formerly; but in varying degrees they continue to control individual behavior and to furnish guides to thought and action. They may have outlived their original meaning, they may even bring pain and discomfort to those who follow them, they may seem absurd to the outsider; but they seldom die out abruptly. To contradict the folkways of one's group is to set oneself apart, to subject oneself to the charges of heresy and eccentricity with which the group tries to maintain its unity. It may be that each member of a group, as an individual, would gladly dispense with a given pattern of behavior, but none can take the first step.[21]

Biases and prejudices can persist, then, even when the circumstances or stimuli that first helped to generate them no longer exist, or at least have waned or changed. They assume lives of their own, divorced from the forces that initially prompted them. And so ageism survives today, whatever its initial impetus may have been. It is inculcated into us all in a myriad of ways: through negative attitudes thoughtlessly transmitted from parents to offspring; through children's fairy tales in which old women regularly pop up as evil witches; by means of negative depictions of oldsters in movies and on TV; through ageist jokes bandied about at social gatherings, in birthday cards, in cartoons, and by show business comedians looking for an easy mark to ridicule; and through elders' own expressions of self-doubt and self-dislike.[22] None of this is the product of malevolence; all of it has malevolent consequences.

In sum, while historical analyses may differ, it is indisputable that cultural conditioning is a powerful agent that re-creates in each generation persistent ageist bias. But of course this observation does not explain why that conditioning itself persists. Simpson and Yinger argue that bias may survive even when cut loose from its generative mooring, but in the case of ageism there actually are potent forces in the here and now that help to keep it alive.

Ageism, Productivity, Wealth, and Power

Productivity

One aspect of an economic rationale for explaining ageism highlights the matter of productivity. Perhaps the old in America engender disdain because ours is a culture that stresses productivity, and the elderly are seen as being unproductive.[23] In "primitive" and agrarian societies, an older man can be a contributor to the common good even if he no longer can hunt expertly, and an older woman still can be of economic value to her community and family even if she is unable to perform the strenuous work of harvesting crops.[24] In industrialized societies, the elderly are much less likely to be producers of desirable goods or services.[25] For the most part, they have left the ranks of the employed.[26] Even those oldsters who have not either voluntarily or more or less involuntarily retired[27] are seen as being deficient in terms of productivity.[28] Their skills often are deemed outmoded. Their roles as carriers and transmitters of tradition are devalued; even if the information they possess is seen as having some utility, that data usually can be equally or more effectively obtained in other ways—by and through books, the Internet, etc.

Worker Competence

Stereotypes regarding the competence of older workers obviously will be most relevant, and potentially most harmful, in instances involving employment discrimination claims. While such stereotypes ostensibly thus have a relatively narrow focus, the fact is that specific negative notions regarding older people may percolate through society and come to support generalized, diffuse negative perceptions. Thus, views regarding older workers are particularly relevant to explaining the ageism phenomenon.

Issues concerning the performance of older workers have generated a large body of literature.[29] For that matter, because both the federal Age Discrimination in Employment Act of 1967, as amended (ADEA),[30] and comparable state statutes prohibit age discrimination in the workplace, the courts also have had opportunities to address questions concerning older workers' competence in the context of thousands of lawsuits.[31] The data present a mixed picture.

It is true that physical strength on average declines with age: the typical 25-year-old is going to be stronger and more dexterous than the average 55-year-old. Moreover, "[o]lder workers are less 'healthy' than younger persons irrespective of how health is measured (e.g., by self-evaluations, by extent of disability, by functional limitations)."[32] But if "the question is whether the job performance of middle-aged and older workers suffers from these age-related health factors, the evidence is considerably less clear."[33] The studies vary both in results and in methodological adequacy.[34] One expert, reviewing these efforts, concluded that "the older worker has assets or experience and reliability which may compensate for the deficits in physical functioning."[35]

The data reveal that older workers have fewer workplace accidents than younger workers, but the severity of their accidents is greater than is the case for younger men and women.[36] Older workers tend to be absent from the job less frequently than their younger counterparts, but their absences—when they do occur—are for longer periods.[37]

The *deadwood* issue also is on the table when one considers the matter of worker competence. Are older workers less creative, less ambitious, or less dedicated to their jobs? Employee advocates reject the notion that older workers go stale on the job: lackluster employee performance, if it exists, flows from the repetitiveness of the tasks assigned the employee. Provide variety and the employee's performance will peak. In any event, age per se has no role in the deadwood problem, although it must be conceded that tenure on the job and age usually are correlated and so those with longer tenure typically will be those possessed of more years. Even so, a 40-year-old with 20 years in one station on the factory line is going to be just as stale as a 60-year-old with 20 years on that same production line; the only difference is that one started working at that job at age 20, the other at age 40.

Still, in this author's admittedly anecdotally based view, there is almost inevitably some decline in enthusiasm and ambition that correlates with long years in the workplace, even where aspects of the job change. When one is 30 and newly married, he wants to make a name for himself—as a lawyer, let us say—and so he is prepared to work very long hours to do so. (Indeed, he probably has little choice, given the general practices of the legal business today.) By the time he is 45, with three kids, his focus shifts. He likely feels less, perhaps no, need to prove his mettle to his peers in the legal world. He no longer looks to others to define his professional worth. Moreover, his interests have broadened: he has more desire to invest his energies and interests in his family, his community, cultural matters, golf, etc. Does that make him deadwood? The answer opens up the door to a variety of concerns: the nature of the particular workplace, the personality of the supervisor who is judging the value of her subordinates, the nature of the work product, and so on. In a workplace aimed at nothing more and nothing less than financial return, the young worker who can be exploited to the nth degree may be a more valuable commodity than the long-term, older employee, and here the appellation "deadwood" will be draped upon that latter's shoulders. A different workplace, with a more catholic culture, will preclude such a designation.

Wealth and Power

The Case for Resentment

Moving from the matter of productivity, there also are the very significant matters of wealth accumulation and control of wealth that come to the fore in searching for the sources of ageism.[38] Wealth—whether defined in terms of land, goods, or other assets—invariably is a source of power. He rules who possesses wealth and determines its disposition. In societies that support social or political systems that vest control over assets in an elder of the family or clan, social and familial control follows. But as the opportunities for the young to generate their own wealth and property have grown in entrepreneurial societies, the grip of the financially powerful elderly on their offspring and their communities has declined. Indeed, it is this expansion of access to the means of creating wealth that explains, according to modernization theory, the change in status experienced by the old in the nineteenth century. But even granting the vast expansion of opportunities in the nineteenth century and thereafter for wealth creation outside of the family context, the fact is that the elderly still control a tremendous amount of wealth in America. Thus, there is still plenty of occasion for resentment to be directed against those of advanced years who do continue to hold tightly to valuable assets and the power that goes with them.[39]

True, just a few decades ago there was a commonly held view that most old people in America were financially impoverished. That notion is almost certainly less prevalent today than it was 20 or 30 years ago, and deservedly so. Since the commencement of President Lyndon Johnson's War on Poverty in 1964, the lot of older folks has improved markedly in the United States. Medicare, Medicaid, increased Social Security benefits, and other governmental programs, along with a generally rising economy, have benefited the elderly in very considerable measure. Moreover, there was, and continues to be, privately generated wealth, and many older homeowners are well-off, with 15 percent of those ages 55–59 and 11 percent of those ages 60–64 having annual household incomes of $100,000 or more.[40]

Added to the wealth factor as an element in parsing the sources of ageism are other advantages held by older individuals. Older workers typically have longer tenure on the job, and so they possess greater protection from discharge than do their younger counterparts by virtue of seniority provisions in collective bargaining agreements negotiated in unionized industries. Workplace custom and practice, as well as civil service statutes, may provide the same protection in nonunion workplaces. In addition, older Americans have been quite successful in the last 40 years or so in winning major political victories, as evidenced by an array of statutes that range from proscribing discrimination in a number of contexts[41] to the creation and funding of governmental programs entailing expenditures of enormous sums of money.[42]

There are significant signs that these successes—both financial and political—have nurtured resentment on the part of the non-old.[43] This animus is expressed through a "greedy geezer" stereotype imposed on older Americans that depicts them as selfishly hogging a disproportionate share of scarce federal dollars.[44] Linked to this imagery is the allied notion that the elderly constitute a monolithic voting bloc. Their alleged self-serving voting affects—if not literally controls—politicians of all persuasions, thereby generating undue rewards for the old and, correlatively, neglect for, among others, politically powerless children.[45]

It is true that older people vote in much greater percentages than do younger adults, and so their political power thereby is enhanced.[46] And fodder for the perception of the elderly as excessively politically powerful is provided by the further fact that older individuals (particularly men) disproportionately occupy positions of political prominence.[47] Moreover, certain old-age interest organizations are seen by the public and politicians as possessing very considerable financial and political power, and this perception has to an important degree become a self-fulfilling prophecy.[48]

The Case for Debunking Wealth-Based Resentment

There is no question that a significant share of the federal budget is devoted to the elderly, particularly as a result of the Medicare program, which in federal fiscal year 2000 alone totaled $212 billion in expenditures.[49] Indeed, the alleged financial onerousness of these programs benefitting oldsters—now, and particularly in the future—is a constantly sounded refrain, with the common theme being that the elderly of today have it much better than will those who are young today when they reach the age of Medicare and Social Security eligibility years from now.[50] On the other hand, even if those dollars were not expended by the federal government, the needs of the elderly still would have to be addressed (unless Americans individually and collectively were to take the highly unlikely position that those in need should just have to suffer, and even die, for lack of financial resources).[51] Thus, the issue is not really so much one of undue amounts being spent; rather, the sticking point politically is where the money is to come from. Generally, we in the United States have expressed a clear preference for looking to government, rather than simply relying on the rough-and-ready mechanism of individual resources as the determinant of who gets how much. Thereby, some of the financial inequalities that exist between individuals are ameliorated: many (and in the case of Medicare, all) receive at least some financial support by means of governmentally operated programs.

Moreover, these programs serve another salutary social purpose (assuming that one perceives the foregoing minimal equalizing of unequals as a first salutary purpose): in a sense government is used as an impartial intermediary. It extracts money from taxpayers and then transfers to the elderly the funds through the Social Security and Medicare programs, rather than younger individuals being called upon to directly transfer resources to their parents. This system avoids the embarrassment for elders of having to ask their children for money for their financial and medical needs; they do not have to do so because they have statutorily based claims to that money. This system whereby government serves as an intermediary also helps to minimize the problems of stored-up resentment, alienation, etc., that may come to the fore when children are called upon to start acting, in a sense, as parents for their own parents.

Government programs aside, the notion that the elderly control a large portion of the financial resources in the United States is a valid one. Still, one should not leap to the conclusion that poverty no longer bears down upon oldsters. The older one gets, the more likely one is to wind up in grim financial straits:

> Household incomes fall as people age because most retire from the labor force and live on savings, pensions, and Social Security benefits. The median income of households headed by people aged 55 or older stood at $28,549 in 1997 below the median of $37,005 for all households. But incomes vary dramatically by age. The median household income of householders aged 55 to 59 was well above the national average at $45,985, while that of householders aged 75 or older was well below at $17,079.
>
> The proportion of households with . . . incomes [of $100,000 or more] declines with age to fewer than 3 percent among householders aged 75 or older. Among people aged 75 or older, nearly one in four has an income below $10,000.[52]

Conclusions

Certainly, the financially advantaged position of many older men and women can arouse resentment, which in turn can give rise to bias directed toward the elderly generally. It is very unclear whether the counter notion of the elderly as being mired in poverty is a view that can hurt or benefit those oldsters who participate in the legal system. Presumably, the elderly litigant may be the beneficiary of sympathy by virtue of being a member of a group that is seen as impoverished. On the other hand, some jurors may respond to elderly litigants by assuming that these oldsters are likely to be financially stressed and so they likely are recipients of government benefits. As a consequence, a given juror may resent the elderly litigant who is the beneficiary of governmental largesse that she herself does not receive, and that resentment may play itself out in the jury room. This would seem to be an unlikely eventuality, but there are insufficient data to draw any useful conclusions as to how perceptions regarding the impoverishment of the elderly may or may not affect participants in the legal process.

As for the matter of political power, the fact is that bloc voting is as old as the Republic, and so the joined efforts of a group of people who share common interests and who work together to achieve those interests are hardly un-American. In any event, the data reveal—worried politicians' perceptions of their constituencies notwithstanding—that the elderly do not typically vote as a bloc, nor are they so consumed with their own needs that they are oblivious to the interests and needs of others.[53]

Ignorance and Denial

Absent the intervening alternative of death, old age is inevitable. So any intelligent adult knows. And yet for most of those who are not yet old, the certainty of old age has a particularly elusive quality to it.[54] There typically is a psychological disjunction: a "disconnect" between one's depersonalized recognition of the abstract proposition that aging is inevitable and the personal "here-and-now" comprehension that old age is *my* inescapable fate (short of the alternative that is even harder for a young person to comprehend—his or her death at an early age).[55] Simone de Beauvoir, the noted French essayist and social critic, remarked upon this phenomenon of denial in *The Coming of Age:*

> Die early or grow old: there is no other alternative. And yet, as Goethe said, "Age takes hold of us by surprise." For himself each man is the sole, unique subject, and we are often astonished when the common fate becomes our own. . . . [W]e accept fortuitous accidents readily enough, making them part of our history, because they affect us as unique beings; but old age is the general fact, and when it seizes upon our own personal life we are dumbfounded.[56]

Thus most of us (whether 20 or 40 or 70) resist believing that *we* ever could be like the senile, wheelchair-bound nursing home residents glimpsed in periodic news media exposés of nursing home abuses. Nor can most of us, no matter what our age, even envision some day being like those more able, yet still diminished, elderly men or women driving in front of us at annoyingly slow speeds in no-passing zones.[57] And even the zestful gray-haired couple depicted in TV and magazine advertisements extolling the efficacy of Laxative X or the rejuvenating benefits of ocean cruises almost certainly are foreign to younger adults' expectations for themselves.

One can concede that there may be the rare young individuals who sincerely feel that they can comprehend, directly and with immediacy, their old age. But even if there are a few younger men or women who are so prescient, so well-informed, and so perceptive as to be able to envision their own future selves, the actual experience of *being* old is reserved only for those who *are* old. Malcolm Cowley, a noted literary critic, made this point in a book he wrote from the vantage point of having attained age 80: "To enter the country of age is a new experience, different from what you supposed it to be. Nobody, man or woman, knows the country until he has lived in it and has taken out his citizenship papers."[58] Similarly, Florida Scott-Maxwell, an analytical psychologist who at the age of 82 began a journal in which she recorded her feelings and thoughts, wrote the following: "*Old people* can seldom say 'we'; not those who live alone, and even those who live with their families are alone in their experience of age."[59] In brief, the immutable laws of physics and nature distance the non-old from the old; only the unvarying passage of time can bridge for each of us the gap between youth and old age.

Difficult as it is for the non-old to comprehend except in a very abstract way old age as their fate, and impossible though it is for the non-old to directly experience it, each of us is caught up in the same inexorable process of becoming old. The 15-year-old of today will be middle-aged 30 years from now and an oldster another 30 years after that. She will traverse, as did her parents and grandparents and those who went before them, the same progression from birth to death.[60] But a veil of ignorance makes the land of the old an alien one for those who have not yet crossed its borders. And so if one rejects for oneself the fate of old age (no matter how illogical that rejection is in terms of its conflicting with implacable fact), it is easy enough to reject as well those who are old. Likewise, if one can only know old age firsthand by being old, then those who are in the "country of age" are for the non-old foreign and alien, and rejection readily follows. Rejection of the "other" in turn gives rise to antipathy, and antipathy easily transmutes into negative age bias.

Decline, Dementia, and Death: A Fear-Generating Trio

Fear likely plays a significant role in explaining bias directed toward the elderly. Old age generally is accompanied by declines in physical well-being that are distressing both for those directly afflicted and for others who observe the process.[61] The incidence of certain types of intellectual and cognitive disorders, most specifically dementia, also increases with age. None of this is pleasant or enviable. Indeed, it is sad, anxiety-provoking, and even frightening. Understandably, "[t]he young do not want to be like the elderly because they want to avoid being treated like them or taking on their characteristics."[62]

One way to cope with that which we fear is to distance ourselves from the source of that fear. That distancing can be manifested literally, in terms of geographic separation; more commonly, it will take the form of emotional withdrawal from the source of the fear. By means of this process old people become residents of another country, so to speak; they are "them," not "us."

And thereby the job is almost done, for once separation, disconnection, and even segregation have been accomplished, disinterest, disdain, denigration, and resentment can follow in short order for those who are seen as decrepit and often burdensome in financial, psychological, or other terms.[63]

While there may be little one can do (or might want to do) in terms of making or enabling the young to recognize their own inevitable senescence, there *is* room for assessing and correcting erroneous impressions insofar as old age is seen as necessarily entailing only physical and intellectual decrepitude. Indeed, it is imperative to examine how strongly (if at all) the empirical data support the perceptions of decline—physical, intellectual, and psychological—because these perceptions help to generate the fear that in turn helps to produce ageist bias. Any reduction in erroneous impressions may provide a basis for mitigating the prevalence of such bias.

Physical Decline

A commonly held belief is that old people are in poor health. Indeed, in a survey of attitudes undertaken for the National Council on Aging (NCOA) in the early 1970s, it was reported that 51 percent of the general public deemed poor health to be a very serious problem for most people over age 65.[64]

The general perception that older people are physically declining—even decrepit—is a notion that can feed into stereotyping all older people as being physically impaired in significant ways. This mistaken impression may work serious mischief generally, as well as in legal settings in particular. For example, in a personal injury case a 75-year-old woman who seeks damages for loss of income as a result of an injury that precludes her from working likely will fare poorly, even if prior to the injury she was an active participant in the workforce.[65] The jury will assume, consciously or unconsciously, that her work-life likely would have shortly ended in any event due to age-related decline, and so the claimed adverse consequence of lost income inflicted upon her by the negligent defendant driver will be discounted. More generally, the images of physical decline and disability associated in the public mind with old age may well work to buttress broader ageist notions of the elderly as generally passive, mentally impaired, unproductive, and so on—notions that all can work to the detriment of believing the testimony of elderly witnesses or respecting the work potential of elderly plaintiffs or crediting the work product of older judges.

The truth is that the stereotype of physically impaired oldsters—like most stereotypes—is in some degree accurate, while at the same time also freighted with error.[66] Serious health problems *are* more common among the elderly than the young, and chronic health problems of a non-life-threatening nature, that is, hearing loss, vision impairment, arthritis, etc., do increase with advancing years.[67] Even so, it also is true that the majority of older men and women do not suffer from debilitating illnesses or disabling physical conditions:

> [M]ost older Americans are free of disabilities. Of those aged sixty-five to seventy-four in 1994, a full 89 percent report no disability whatsoever. While the proportion of elderly who are fully functioning and robust declines with advancing age, between the age of seventy-five to eight-four, 73 percent still report no disability, and even after age eighty-five, 40 percent of the population is fully functional.[68]

Not surprisingly, then, and in notable contrast to the perceptions of the general public, only 21 percent of those 65 and over who were surveyed in the NCOA study reported that poor health was a very serious problem for them personally.[69] More recent data are even more heartening: in 1996 only 17 percent of those ages 60 and above rated their health as poor. And as for the numbers of those who in 1996 rated their health as excellent or good, as contrasted with comparable data from 1976, the change was even more encouraging:

> The proportion of older Americans who rate their health as "excellent" has grown substantially since 1976. The share of people aged 50 to 59 who are in excellent health has grown from 23 to 30 percent. Among those aged 60 to 69, the rise has been from 18 to 23 percent. Only among people aged 70 or older has the share reporting excellent health not grown.
>
> The share of people in their sixties and seventies who report "good" health has also grown significantly. Consequently, the proportion of people aged 60 to 69 who say their health is good or excellent stood at a lofty 71 percent in 1996, up from just 50 percent in 1976. Among those aged 70 or older, the figure rose from 54 percent in 1976 to 63 percent in 1996.[70]

Granted, self-reporting may not be exactly on the mark—older people may be in worse, or better, health than their own assessments reveal. Indeed, there is some evidence to suggest that older people perceive themselves to be in better health than they actually are. But this is not a matter of deceit; rather, "the occasional dissonance between objective measures of health and people's perceptions . . . may reflect a remarkably successful adaptation to disability."[71]

On the other hand, it must be acknowledged that about 5 percent of those ages 65 and over are at any given point in time institutionalized in a long-term care facility. Some will stay there until they die, while others will be there only temporarily for transitional medical care—typically physical rehabilitation following an injury or a stroke.[72] But even as to those who are institutionalized, it is important to note that 81 percent are reported as experiencing no limitations on their activities of daily living, that is, bathing, dressing, using bathroom facilities, etc.[73]

Intellectual and Psychological Decline

Likely the most pervasive stereotype regarding older men and women is that they exhibit intellectual deficits—most particularly fading memories in the mildly affected, and severe dementia or senility in those most seriously afflicted. This imagery particularly can come into play when legal decision makers are called upon to assess the credibility of witnesses in courtroom disputes.[74] It is hardly surprising that hundreds—indeed almost certainly thousands—of jokes focus on the mental foibles of the old.[75] A middle-aged person's inability to remember some piece of data is half-jokingly dismissed as "a senior moment."[76] More ominously, most of us are increasingly fearful of the scourge of Alzheimer's disease, an affliction given heightened publicity by its most prominent recent victim, former President Ronald Reagan.

Regrettably, there typically is some degree of intellectual decline that accompanies the state of being old, particularly in the cases of those of advanced age, although this certainly is not universally so. It appears that some people experience a degree of short-term memory decline with advanced age,[77] although there are some data disputing this understanding.[78] There are other failings in memory function as well. For example, there is some age-associated deficit with regard to recalling sources of information. In this regard, in one experiment it was found that older subjects were less able than younger ones to identify words as having been words that they themselves had thought of or that they themselves had uttered.[79] They also performed less well in recalling whether certain spoken words were said by Speaker A or Speaker B.[80] Moreover, "some kinds of learning, especially those that require perceptual speed, physical coordination, and muscular strength, become more difficult and ultimately impossible in old age."[81]

On a related front, the incidence of dementia unquestionably increases with age—"from less than 1 percent of persons under age 65, to about 1 percent for those aged 65 to 74, 7 percent of those 75 to 84, and 25 percent of those aged 85 and older."[82] Actually, these figures may be too conservative; according to some experts, the prevalence of Alzheimer's disease—which is the main, but not the only, source of dementia—is much higher in the "old-old,"[83] that is, those 85 and over: "Because survival for a decade is common the prevalence increases from 3 percent at the age of 65 years to 47 percent after the age of 85 years."[84] And while some dementias are reversible, the possibility of effecting a reversal is quite slim (and certainly is nonexistent for the most prevalent dementias): "[t]he most common forms of dementia—those caused by

Alzheimer's and other degenerative diseases, such as Parkinson's, Huntington's, and Pick's—tend to be irreversible and progressive."[85]

This all is bad news, and it is very bad indeed.

The good news is that decline does not afflict all older men and women.
Certainly that is so, as the foregoing data confirm, for those 65–74 and even
for those 75–84. Declines in short-term memory can be offset to a significant
degree.[86] Moreover, "[r]esearch has demonstrated the remarkable and endur-
ing capacity of the aged brain to make new connections, absorb new data, and
thus acquire new skills."[87] And while there is some age-associated loss in the
ability to recall sources of information, there are in other instances no differences between the young and the old. Thus, in the earlier-noted study it was
found that "[t]here was no age deficit when subjects had to discriminate what
they [themselves] said from what they heard another person say . . . or when
they had to discriminate what they thought from what they heard another
person say."[88]

In brief, most older people—and particularly those in the earlier stages of
elderhood—retain their intellectual capacities.[89] More than that, there even is
some respectable support for the optimistic conclusion that older men and
women have the ability to expand their intellectual reach, as Paul B. Baltes, one
of the leading researchers on aging and intelligence, has pointed out:

> Certainly, there is decline in old age, especially at maximum limits of func-
> tioning in the basic mechanics of intelligence. However, for most normal
> elderly people there is also great reserve capacity and potential for new
> learning and growth. . . . If provided with cognitive enrichment and prac-
> tice, most elderly people up to age 75 or so are capable of remarkable gains
> and peaks of intellectual performance, including in those areas of function-
> ing such as memory where the typical expectation is one of early and regu-
> lar decline.[90]

Of course, in assessing the stereotypical views that prevail about intellectual
capacity, one must take care to note that a double standard typically is applied
in perceptions regarding memory lapses. A forgotten detail by a 40-year-old is
interpreted benignly, whereas the same lapse when experienced by a 70-year-
old is seen, rightly or wrongly, as indicative of intellectual decline.[91] Moreover,
there is another very important phenomenon of particular relevance: people
age at different rates and to different degrees.[92] Simply because John Smith and
Harry Jones are both 65, it does not follow that they are alike in terms of their
vascular, muscular, skeletal, endocrinological, and other attributes. John may
have the vascular system of a 55-year-old, the intellectual acuity of an 25-year-
old, and the muscles of an 80-year old, whereas Harry almost certainly will
have a different mix of physical and intellectual attributes. Thus, it is simply

misguided to group all the elderly together as a monolithic demographic entity for other than relatively simplistic purposes.[93] So Dr. Robert Butler, first director of the National Institute on Aging, has aptly observed:

> [T]here are greater differences in the rates of psychological, chronological, psychological and social aging within the person and from person to person. In fact, physiological indicators show a greater range from the mean in old age than in any other age group, and this is true of personality as well. Older people actually become more diverse rather than more similar with advancing years.[94]

Insofar as the social situations of older people are concerned, older men and women generally are perceived to be lonely and isolated. Unfortunately, this is often true. The friendships forged in the workplace wane following retirement. Friends and family members move away or die. Impaired mobility may narrow the opportunities for participating in activities where friends, acquaintances, and even strangers can provide emotional and intellectual stimulation and companionship. Still, the problems of loneliness and isolation are not as severe as younger people perceive them to be. While in the NCOA study earlier noted a full 60 percent of the general public perceived loneliness to be a very serious issue for most people over 65, only 12 percent of those 65 and over reported that loneliness actually was a very serious problem for them personally[95]—certainly not an insignificant figure, but still only one-fifth of that registered by the public at large.

It is true that depression is a significant medical problem for the elderly, but it also is true that this is a significant problem for younger individuals as well. Indeed, depression is the most common mental illness for all adults:[96] "During their lifetimes, approximately 15% of the population will experience at least one episode of depression."[97] Moreover, in terms of self-reporting, people between ages 65 and 74 are the happiest in America—albeit by a very slim margin![98]

Death

No doubt, old age and those who are old cause others distress because of what old age presages: death.[99] "The old," it has been suggested, "are avoided not only as helpless nuisances but as harbingers of mortality."[100] Inasmuch as in American culture death is not often deemed a desirable event,[101] that which reminds us of death likewise engenders negative response. (Why we fear death is an issue I leave for others to address.) Again, through a process of distancing ourselves from that which causes anxiety—the door is opened to antipathy vis-à-vis the messengers who trigger that anxiety, the old.[102]

Cognitive Processes

A common mechanism that people use, sometimes consciously but more often unconsciously, for structuring their worlds is generalization.[103] For example, I once heard a New Orleans jazz band perform. I did not like the music, and so I never go to jazz concerts, no matter whether the performers will be playing progressive jazz, modern jazz, Chicago jazz, or whatever. I have generalized from the particular, that is, New Orleans jazz, and placed all jazz music in a category labeled *ugly sounds*. In a similar vein, I once bit into a MacIntosh apple and I found it to be very sour. As a result, I have lumped all apples—and perhaps even all round apple-sized fruit, such as oranges, nectarines, etc.— together in a category labeled *bad to eat*.

Sorting out events, objects, and even people by means of generalizations and categories can be inefficient and even sometimes counterproductive: by generalizing from one sampling of jazz to all music involving jazz rhythms I have denied myself the possible pleasures of music that I might appreciate after all. By putting all red, round fruit into the same negatively identified category of distasteful food, I have denied myself the enjoyment I might possibly derive if only I were to try a Jonathan apple. But detriments notwithstanding, generalizing is—as cogently articulated by psychologist Eleanor Rosch—an essential survival mechanism: "Since no organism can cope with infinite diversity, one of the most basic functions of all organisms is the cutting up of the environment into classifications by which nonidentical stimuli can be treated as equivalent."[104]

In truth, even if I *were* to sample another jazz performance or to try a Jonathan apple picked by my neighbor from her backyard tree, I probably would not be able to find either experience pleasing because the generalizations that my brain has fashioned have developed into schemata or stereotypes:[105] knowledge structures that dictate both what external stimuli I perceive and how I interpret those stimuli. "[A]ctivation of a schema, such as a stereotype, can influence what aspects of . . . available information are attended to, how that information is interpreted as it is encoded, and hence what information will be available for later retrieval."[106]

Thus, let us imagine a mid-level supervisor employed by Company X who entertains the stereotype that older individuals are uncreative deadweight in the workplace. As a consequence, she typically fails (although not with conscious intent to do so) to take note of situations where older subordinates perform well; rather, she only mentally records instances of deficient performance. Moreover, insofar as she does take cognizance of those efforts of her subordinates that to an objective observer might appear innovative, she unconsciously and unintentionally interprets these efforts consistent with the stereotype that she entertains regarding older workers. Thus, she perceives their work products as trite and derivative. This powerful mediating force of stereotypes—shaping how we perceive the external world—has been cogently summarized by Professor Linda Hamilton Krieger:

> [S]tereotypes operate as "person prototypes," or "social schemas." As such, they function as implicit theories, biasing in predictable ways the perception, interpretation, encoding, retention, and recall of information about other people. These biases are *cognitive* rather than *motivational.* They operate absent intent to favor or disfavor members of a particular social group. And, perhaps most significant for present purposes, they bias a decisionmaker's judgment long before the "moment of decision," as a decisionmaker attends to relevant data and interprets, encodes, stores, and retrieves it from memory. These biases "sneak up on" the decisionmaker, distorting bit by bit the data upon which his decision is eventually based.[107]

Putting this all together in the case of ageism, we have an explanation revealing that age bias is not the intentional construct of malevolent individuals determined to devise negative depictions of old age. Rather, the very way in which human beings' brains work means that people are going to organize their worlds by means of generalizations and categories. Generalizations in turn generate stereotypes. "[S]tereotypes, like other categorical structures, are cognitive mechanisms that *all* people, not just 'prejudiced' ones, use to simplify the task of perceiving, processing, and retaining information about people in memory."[108] On the basis of isolated instances, then, we develop certain notions as to how old people look and act, and as to what they can do and should do, and then we unconsciously apply these notions—these schemas—to interpret and evaluate the looks, actions, condition, performance, capabilities, etc. of all old people with whom we come in contact. And as it so happens, in the case of elderly people the real world deployment of these nonvolitional processes is facilitated by the fact that age typically is a readily observable human characteristic.[109]

Were the stereotypes associated with old age perfectly accurate, they presumably would not be troubling. The problem is, however, that while stereotypical views of old age and old people are to some degree on the mark, they also are incorrect (a state of affairs probably characteristic of most, and perhaps all, stereotypes):

> Certainly few old people fit all the negative images. The millions of aged in this country show the same individual variations as everyone else. Some are sad; others are happy. Some have great wealth and power; others are destitute. Some are active; others are confined to nursing homes. Some are married and have many children and grandchildren living close by; others are completely alone. The tendency to stereotype old people is strong. Yet differences among old people are great.[110]

In any event, while cognition theory helps to explain the formation of stereotypes and the consequences of stereotyping, it does not explain why one person develops an initial cluster of ideas that come to be subsequently expressed in the form of one stereotype, whereas another person fashions a different generalization or stereotype from like facts. More concretely, why does White Male X—who once was threatened by a black kid on a bus—dislike all blacks and regard them as prone to crime and laziness, while White Male Y— who also had an unpleasant encounter with a black teenager—likes blacks and regards them as admirable? Or, bringing this discussion home to the matter of aging, why has Mr. Jones extracted from one negative childhood experience with an elderly relative the stereotype that all older people are cranky, obstinate, and slow-thinking, while Mr. Smith—despite having had a similar childhood encounter with a cranky oldster—entertains no particular generalized notions, positive or negative, regarding older people? The answer must be that cognitive processes, standing alone, are not sufficiently explanatory. Indeed, this proposition has been aptly voiced elsewhere:

> [S]ome readers of . . . [the] literature [regarding cognition] have mistakenly assumed that the cognitive approach argues that contemporary real-world instances of stereotyping and discrimination can be explained *solely* as due to biases in cognitive functioning. This is an inappropriate conclusion. Any particular form of stereotyping or prejudice, such as racism, is in all likelihood multiply determined by cognitive, motivational, and social learning processes, whose effects combine in a given social context to produce specific judgmental and behavioral manifestations. Therefore, any attempt to understand such phenomena as a product of one process is probably misguided.[111]

In sum, cognition theory affords very significant insights as to how bias— once having taken root in a given individual—can thrive. But it does not explain how bias—in this instance, ageism—comes to be in the first instance. For the answer to that mystery, we must turn back to the matters already discussed, history, cultural conditioning, resentment, etc., as well as to other matters that are the subject of the next two sections of this chapter.

Psychodynamic Theories

Prejudice as a Function of Group Identification

In his classic study of discrimination, *The Nature of Prejudice,* Gordon W. Allport maintained that "prejudice is basically a *trait of personality,*" and he elaborated on this perception in the following way: "When it [prejudice] takes root in a life it grows like a unit. The specific object of prejudice is more or less immaterial. What happens is that the whole inner life is affected; the hostility and fear are systematic [sic]." At the same time, however, Allport conceded that "it would be wrong to imply that deep-lying character-structure is the only factor that needs to be considered."[112] Allport suggested that one foundation of prejudice is a preference for one's own group: "[H]uman groups tend to stay apart. We need not ascribe this tendency to a gregarious instinct, to a 'consciousness of kind,' or to prejudice. The fact is adequately explained by the principles of ease, least effort, congeniality, and pride in one's own culture."[113]

From these foregoing seemingly prosaic factors—that is, it is easier to be around those who are like us, who speak like us, who have common experiences, etc.—something less salutary follows:

> Once this separatism exists, . . . the ground is laid for all sorts of psychological elaboration. People who stay separate have few channels of communication. They easily exaggerate the degree of difference between groups, and readily misunderstand the grounds for it. And, perhaps most important of all, the separateness may lead to genuine conflicts of interests, as well as to many imaginary conflicts.[114]

A consequence of the separation created between the "us's" and the "them's" is the development of group affinities and anti-group prejudices. "[A]ll groups (whether in-groups or reference groups [i.e., the group to which another group responds and reacts]) develop a way of living with characteristic codes and beliefs, standards and 'enemies' to suit their own adaptive needs."[115] Individuals within a given group are not necessarily unthinking automatons, of course, and in different societies there will be more or less psychological and cultural room for varying attitudes among individual members of a given society. Thus, in those societies where attitudinal conformity is not inculcated into its members as a social imperative, differing experiences and circumstances should play a role in how different people develop biases of differing strengths. Still, in Allport's view, group pressures play an enormous part in determining both how a given individual will react and what attitudes she will possess.

Thus, Allport identified (albeit not exclusively so) prejudice as the product of group affinities. From this foundation prejudice develops: "The group to which I belong is good; the groups to which others belong are not." But while the foregoing analysis certainly seems apt in analyzing racism and ethnic rivalries, its analogical force is problematic in the case of age bias. True, the old live in a different country, metaphorically speaking, than do the young. True, too, the old often appear different from the young in perceptible physical ways. It further is unfortunately the case that not inconsiderable numbers of older women and men (particularly those in their 80s and beyond) tend to have intellectual deficits. Moreover, they are prone to declines in social and psychological engagement that generally (but not invariably) separate them from more optimistic and intellectually engaged younger folks.[116] Still and all, the divides—psychological and sociological—between the old and the young simply do not approach, in depth or breadth, the typical geographic, cultural, economic, experiential, and/or physical differences that undergird racial, ethnic, and religious cleavages. And so, Allport's analysis, while certainly enlightening vis-à-vis its specifically identified concerns, that is, race and ethnic prejudice, seems to fall short in terms of persuasive explanatory force when age bias is the focus of inquiry.

Psychoanalytic Theory

Psychoanalytic theory holds that the human mind is divided into the conscious and the unconscious. The id operates at the unconscious level to deal with desires, wishes, and instinctual behaviors. The ego operates in the conscious realm of the mind; it imposes reason, logic, morality, and restraint on one's actions and thoughts, and thus acts as a control on the id.

Psychoanalytic theory suggests that racial and ethnic prejudices are born in the unconscious. In other words, racism is the expression of irrationality, rather than rational thought.

> [W]hen we say that racism is irrational, we mean that when people are asked to explain the basis of their racial antagonism they either express an instinctive, unexplained distaste at the thought of associating with the outgroup as equals or they cite reasons that are not based on established fact and are often contradicted by personal experience.[117]

Thus, a racist may insist with unswerving certainty that all blacks are lazy and untrustworthy—a view that does not square with reality. His beliefs are resistant to any empirical evidence of their falsity. Why? Because there is some psychological need that his bigotry satisfies.[118]

The application of such explication to ageism is a problematic proposition. Racism and ethnic hatred carry with them much greater degrees of animosity and inflexibility than is so in the case of persons who harbor negative views regarding older people. If there is a battle going on between the ageist's id and ego, it seems to be one of a muted nature. The element of irrational refusal to credit persuasive empirical data seems to be missing.

Another explanation for prejudice that has been afforded considerable currency entails the concept of the *authoritarian personality*. The idea here is that prejudice is one manifestation of a flawed personality type—a person who is very insecure, untrusting, rigid, uneducated, and repressed, and who views human relationships in terms of competition for power. In the seminal articulation of this analysis, *The Authoritarian Personality,* T. W. Adorno and his fellow authors saw prejudice as a pervasive *modus operandi* of the person exhibiting this personality type:

> The most crucial result of the present study . . . is the demonstration of close correspondence in the type of approach and outlook a subject is likely to have in a great variety of areas, ranging from the most intimate features of family and sex adjustment through relationships to other people in general, to religion and to social and political philosophy. Thus a basically hierarchical, authoritarian, exploitive parent-child relationship is apt to carry over into a power-oriented, exploitively dependent attitude toward one's sex partner and one's God and may well culminate in a political philosophy and social outlook which has no room for anything but a desperate clinging to what appears to be strong and a disdainful rejection of whatever is relegated to the bottom.[119]

Presumably, the authoritarian personality construct could offer insights with regard to the psychological makeup of the ageist man or woman. Perhaps there are some venomous individuals who really do have intense negative feelings regarding older people, and as to them the authoritarian personal paradigm may well apply.[120] But the paradigm fashioned by Adorno and his colleagues envisions a rigidity of attitude and a poverty of inner strength that just do not resonate in explaining most people who exhibit ageist attitudes. Perhaps the best one can conclude here is that there has been too little study of ageism at this point to venture any more certain conclusions as to Adorno's construct.[121]

Several other psychologically based theories—developed most fully in the context of analyzing racial prejudice—appear to afford potentially more fruitful rationales helping to explain the genesis of age bias. One powerful explanation for prejudice is the frustration-aggression hypothesis, which posits that an inevitable part of the human condition entails frustrations, both major and minor, that individuals confront in achieving their goals. These frustrations may be occasioned by other people; by circumstance, such as illness; by a lack of talent or innate ability; and so on. When an individual is frustrated in achieving a goal, negative impulses and feelings may result. Sometimes, however, there is simply no place to which, or person against whom, these negative feelings can be directed. For example, an illness that strikes one down affords no obvious target for the venting of hostility or frustration. On the other hand, sometimes an event or a person *can* be identified as the source of the frustration and disappointment. For example, "[o]ne person may be tied to another in an ambivalent relationship of both love and hostility, as is the child to the parent."[122] In this situation the "hostility may be stored up, or it may be directed toward oneself or toward some substitute target that is more accessible or less able to strike back."[123] Thus, "a 'free-floating,' undirected hostility may result from frustration when the actual frustrating agent cannot be attacked, and the social context often favors displacement of this hostility onto minority-group members."[124]

The aggression that frustrated individuals direct outward may generate, or have the potential to generate, guilt, for even the irrational bigot may be able to sense that what he is doing or thinking is arguably unfair. To ameliorate this real or potential guilt, the individual manages to convince himself that the object of his animus indeed and in fact deserves to be denigrated:

> In order to make themselves seem reasonable and moral, according to their own standards, those who have shown prejudice or discrimination toward a scapegoat look for justifications. They create or accept convincing reasons for hating or discriminating against members of the minority group. They discover and believe many kinds of evidence that "prove" that the members of that group thoroughly deserve the treatment given them. . . . Finally, to get rid of any sense of doubt and to give an absolute quality to their beliefs, prejudiced persons categorize all the individual members of the minority group by stereotypes, usually furnished by society, which help them to rationalize prejudice toward the whole group, despite the variations that characterize any human group.[125]

The frustration-aggression scenario affords a plausible explanation for age-based bias. It offers an analysis that particularly resonates in the instance of the adult child struggling to cope with a burdensome parent—an aged mother who is afflicted with a debilitating dementia, for example.[126] It makes sense, also, in the case of a relationship entailing an imbalance of power and/or wealth, where the senior is in control and the younger person is a resentful supplicant for some of the elder's largesse. And yet, in the final analysis, it is difficult to extract from these not rare, but also hardly universal, scenarios a rationale explaining the generalized negativism toward old age and old people that permeates American culture.

Prejudice also has been explained as being grounded on the need of the individual to enhance her self-esteem or to respond to a threat to that self-esteem: "In a culture that stresses the opportunities each person has for success but [which] prevents success, by its own definition, for a great many people, a shadowy image of success is created by the dominant group's placing itself categorically, above all members of groups perceived as inferior."[127] There may be something to this notion insofar as ageism is concerned.[128] Still, the relevance of this analysis to bias based on age does not seem to approach the aptness it has in the racial animus context. Denigration of the old resonates, but not emphatically so, as a mechanism (conscious or unconscious) to enhance younger folks' feelings of self-importance and heightened self-regard.

Perhaps some instances of age bias can be traced to family issues. An adult who has or had a troubled relationship with his or her parents may register dislike or other negative attitudes regarding those parents in particular or older people in general.[129]

Finally, still another psychological explanation focuses on the matter of self-concept: "[There is] a study which showed that those who accept negative attitudes toward old people tend toward self-derogation. . . . Psychologists use the term 'projection' here. If we feel negative about ourselves, we project it onto others. This might explain why prejudice against elders correlates with one's personal degree of anxiety about death."[130] This analysis takes us back to the fear-of-death syndrome discussed earlier: we disdain the elderly because they are messengers reminding us of our mortality. This rationale does ring true, but not so strongly that it can stand on its own as a dispositive explanation for the depth and breadth of ageism in American society.

Conclusions

There are several theories and analyses regarding cognition and psychodynamic processes that can be brought to bear in exploring the source or sources of age bias. Most of these were fashioned, however, in the course of seeking explanations for pernicious prejudices—racism, hatred based on national origin, and/or religious bias. Not surprisingly, then, the constructs that look to "-isms" other than ageism do not appear overly useful in assessing age bias. Others do have some relevance, but certainly none can confidently be deemed independently determinative.

Ageism and Biological Determinism

Biology as Destiny

The human brain, so cognition theory holds, is structured to operate in certain ways that have nothing to do with individual choice or will. One consequence of the nonvolitional processing of information is stereotyping, which in turn may develop into, or be associated with, various prejudices and biases. But perhaps one can go a step further. What of the notion that negative bias vis-à-vis the elderly (or at least an inclination of such nature) is itself inherent in the human makeup? In other words, the general aversion to old age that most of us possess (whether or not we readily admit to it) is the product of biological imperative.[131]

This argument brings to the fore the broader issue of evolutionary biology, also known as evolutionary psychology, behavioral biology, and/or sociobiology.[132] The operative proposition is that human attitudes and behaviors are genetically driven—a conception that has been a fertile referent for a variety of scholars, including in recent years members of the legal academy. More to the point, it is a very provocative—albeit ultimately probably unavailing—lever for inquiry regarding the genesis of ageism.

How might evolutionary biology possibly help to explain age bias as a mind-set built in over time into the modern human behavioral template? In the case of older women, almost certainly the lack of reproductive capability must be a key factor (if one subscribes to evolutionary biology as a valid explanatory discipline). "[O]urs is an androcentric culture," it has been observed, "in which women are valued and judged according to their reproductive capacity (or sexual attractiveness) and few are accustomed to thinking of post-menopausal women as having a function."[133] It is reasonable to posit that this androcentrism was even more dominant in preindustrial societies: postmenopausal women constituted (so the sociobiological argument would go) consumers of the community's resources who offered no offsetting benefit to the family, clan, or tribe in terms of enhancing their genetic legacies.[134] As for males, older men, while often still fertile (although typically decreasingly so as they aged),[135] were no longer able to effectively perform *their* physically demanding tasks, that is, hunting and defending the family or tribe from attack. The aged male thus also played at best a diminished role in his marginally viable community; instead, as a consumer of resources he too constituted a problematic factor in terms of enhancement of the survival of his community's gene pool.

Given the negative impacts of resource-depleting elders on the chances for survival of the current and future breeding young, younger members of the group were driven by an initially general genetically programmed survival instinct to respond in negative ways to superannuated males and females. By abandoning (or even killing)[136] their elders, younger adults preserved resources and thereby maximized both their own ability to breed successfully and the ability of their children to survive into breeding age. Ultimately, so the story goes, those who readily rejected oldsters prevailed in the struggle for genetic dominance over those whose survival instinct less imperatively directed the discarding of oldsters. This dominance of the "rejectionists" came to pass because more of their offspring over time survived than did those whose parents' attention and support were diverted to their own parents, aunts, uncles, and so on.

If the foregoing biologically grounded scenarios regarding older men and women ring true, one would have to ask, "Why, then, are women and men genetically programmed, or at least genetically permitted, to live beyond their peak reproductive years (in the case of women) and their prime fighting and hunting years (in the instance of men)?" What advantage for the human species is gained by people living into their 60s, 70s, 80s, and even beyond—which they in fact do?[137] Before suggesting an answer to this fundamental question, it is useful briefly to review the matter of aging as a biological phenomenon—a phenomenon whose commonality actually is of very recent vintage.[138]

The Causes of Aging

There are numerous theories as to why humans (and all living things, for that matter) age.[139] None yet has been proven to be fully on target. One way of organizing these theories is in terms of the level at which aging occurs. Aging is understood by some as organ-based, physiologically based, or genome-based; others have theorized in terms of "cellular-based, organ-system-based, population-based, and integrative theories."[140] Still other nomenclature denominates theories of aging as being causal, systematic, or evolutionary.[141] A different organizing regime identifies the various theories of aging as arising from "programmed and predetermined processes" or as arising from stochastic, that is, random, accidental processes.[142] At bottom, it would appear that all "[t]heories of aging can be divided into two broad groups: those that presume a preexisting master plan, and those based on random events."[143]

The notion of aging as being the product of programmed events is reflected in the suggestion that each of us has within his or her body some sort of a "biological clock based on a series of chemical events or physical changes in specific molecules."[144] Elucidations of such programming "include the theories that age changes are determined by switching on 'death' genes or by hormones secreted at a certain time by the hypothalamus or pituitary gland in the brain."[145] Another explanation that deems senescence to be a programmed process attributes aging to the progressive shortening of the ends of chromosomes, known as telomeres, each time chromosomes duplicate themselves.[146]

Insofar as random events are deemed to be the causative agents of aging, one postulated stochastic aging mechanism looks to free radicals, which are chemical compounds that are produced in the cells in a number of ways, including by means of exposure to oxygen, drugs, and radiation. These free radicals have toxic consequences that can cause cellular degradation and destruction.[147] Other stochastic explanations look to the accumulation of errors in important molecules such as DNA or to simple wear and tear.[148] "We age and die because the fitness benefits of maintaining a complex body against myriad insults diminish with age and finally approach zero. The intuitive view of aging—that 'things fall apart'—is the correct one."[149]

A very influential explanation for aging that merges the notions of programmed and stochastic events looks to what is termed *antagonistic pleiotropy*.[150] What this concept involves is the proposition that a given genetic endowment may confer advantage on younger individuals but may impose detriment on older people. For example, humans are genetically programmed to have a very strong predilection for sweet foods. At one stage of life this is a good thing because consumption of high levels of sugars produces quick accelerations of energy that in turn enhance the ability to successfully chase down fleeing prey, to fend off attackers, etc. Thus, the genetically driven desire for sugars helps to promote survival, thereby enabling the young, breeding population to produce offspring who will carry on the genetic legacy bequeathed to them by their parents and their parents' parents. The problem is that older, postreproductive individuals continue to be governed by the same strong desire for sweet foods. But for them high consumption of sugars leads—because of the aging body's decreasing ability to efficiently process sugars—to obesity, diabetes, and other detrimental health conditions associated both with heightened morbidity and even death. Thus, a genetic predisposition that is advantageous for the young is disadvantageous in later years.[151] "[S]enile decay . . . [is] simply a by-product of the accumulation in the gene pool of late-acting lethal and semi-lethal genes, which have been allowed to slip through the net of natural selection simply because they are late-acting."[152]

Even though no theory, or even group of theories, yet has won the day as being scientifically dispositive, the conclusion *is* warranted "that aging is a modifiable biological process under combined genetic and environmental control."[153] Moreover, whether aging is a stochastic process, a programmed one, or a combination of the two, there is almost certainly a genetic factor involved[154] such that it is not biologically mandated that humans will live only until their breeding capabilities (in the case of woman) or at least their prime capabilities (in the case of men) are exhausted. But equally important for an understanding of the aging process is recognition of the fact that environmental factors also play a role, as the foregoing quotation confirms.

Why People Survive into Old Age—The "Grandmother Theory"

We now can return to the inquiry as to how attitudes and conduct regarding old age result from postreproductive longevity. It earlier was postulated that older men and women have little or no genetic utility and, what is more, they represent a threat to the survival of the breeding young and their offspring because they consume needed resources. But there is a counterargument. Older individuals—although unable to bear children or to excel at food production or defense—nonetheless had value for their communities that apparently could exceed the cost of the resources they consumed.[155] The older male who passed on lore regarding the location of the spring that outlasted the worst drought, or who taught youngsters how to make effective blowguns and arrows while their fathers and older brothers were away on hunting expeditions, was a transmitter of knowledge and skills that, once acquired and perfected, would enhance the survival of the tribe. By virtue of his role he helped to increase the likelihood that his genes, part of the pool shared by his offspring and/or his interrelated tribe members, would persist through time. Likewise, the older woman who cared for a grandchild and thereby enabled the child's mother to leave the family campground or cave to gather seeds and edible plants improved the survival chances of that child and thereby she, too, increased the chances that her genetic legacy would be perpetuated.[156]

Given the positive roles that elders could play, after all, in helping to promote the survival of their descendants, the process of natural selection actually should have favored those who developed a genetic trait or mutation enabling them to survive beyond childbearing or child-siring years.[157] These longer-lived survivors would have provided support and protection for their grandchildren, who would share the same genetic trait, and thus would survive into their breeding years in greater numbers than those who lacked such support and protection.[158] Over time, those bearing the genetic markers for long life, as well as positive attitudes and behaviors regarding older men and women, such as altruism,[159] would achieve dominance over those not possessing these genetic traits.

The foregoing analysis holds up whether one subscribes to a theory of aging that looks to programmed events as explaining senescence, such as the cessation of a chromosome's ability to replicate itself, or one endorses a stochastic analysis of the aging process as being the product of random accidents and insults to chromosomes and cells. In other words, if Individual A had some random genetic mutation or trait that allowed his cells to replicate one or two more times than did the cells of Individual B, or that dictated slower cell decline than that which affected the cells of Individual B, he likely would live longer than B, even though both individuals' cells were programmed to replicate some finite number of times. Likewise, a person who bore a stochastically generated genetic trait or mutation enabling her DNA better to withstand wear and tear or free radical toxicity would be able to survive longer, on average, than someone lacking that trait or mutation. In either instance, his longer life—if protected and rewarded by the members of his clan—would help to advance the survival of his genetic heirs, who in turn both would live for longer periods and would as well be supportive of elders in their midst (at least as long as those elders did not unduly burden their tribe or clan).

Old age, then, actually affirmatively served—at least for a period of some years during which the older man or woman could function and contribute to the most basic function of a living organism: perpetuation of its genetic line.[160] Accordingly, no genetically promoted distaste for old age should have developed. Indeed, those who discarded still-functioning oldsters would have promoted their own genetic line's ultimate extinction because they would have been less able to bring to breeding age their offspring, given the lack of aid afforded by grandparents, great-aunts, and others.[161] Conversely, natural selection should have favored those who entertained and expressed positive social, cultural, and political responses to the elders in their midst.[162]

In sum, there is a sound argument to be made that the evolutionary process of natural selection should have led to behaviors in the past by the young favorable to the elderly. And those behaviors, the argument would continue, should persist today. Or, at the least, there is no necessary conclusion to be drawn that human evolutionary events explain negative age bias.

Of course, genes do not transmit beliefs or attitudes as such: I am a Democrat, and I hope my children are as well, but their political preferences are a product of acculturation, not genetics. Even so, there is a genetic component associated with a variety of behaviors and attitudes that humans exhibit.[163] For example, when we comment on how tenderly and lovingly a mother cares for her child, we are really noting the expression of a strong maternal instinct that the great majority of women across cultures and time exhibit—a behavior that is hardwired, so to speak, into the human species (and of course many others, as well.) Maternal love—expressed through emotions and through attitudes toward children—is no doubt a product of the genes. Fear, or at least suspicion, of the stranger, the "other," likewise appears to be a universal human trait; while we may call this a prejudice, manifested, for example, as racism or xenophobia, its universality strongly suggests that it is a genetically driven emotion or attitude that in turn generates observable behaviors. It has been noted, in the same vein, that the desire to adorn oneself with "ornamentation is universal among all modern human foragers."[164] The creation of, and positive responses to, music also are universal, as is the need to engage in some ordering of reality by construction of a mythology or religion that "seeks to explain the relation of the tribe to the rest of the world."[165] While we cannot with certitude attribute the impulses for ornamentation and religiosity and music to our genetic makeup, such attribution seems sensible and logical. Similarly, then, there is nothing remarkable in attributing attitudes toward the elderly to genetic prompting.

Still, attitudes and responses, whether to the "other," in general, or to the aged, in particular, cannot be the products of biology alone. If biology were all-controlling, we would expect a uniformity of treatment of the elderly throughout societies. Yet old age has been regarded differently in different cultures—including favorably in some (typically preindustrial) societies,[166] and this fact precludes the conclusion that age bias is the product solely of genetic determinism. Admittedly, it has been argued that "[c]ontrary to the common expectation that ageist attitudes [among children] differ cross-culturally, research suggests that children's negative attitudes toward older adults are universal."[167] Even so, at most this means that differing cultures' adults' responses to old people occur despite, rather than because of, a commonality of youngsters' reactions to the elderly.

Necessarily, then, social behaviors and attitudes have multiple sources—a perception cogently articulated by Barbara Myerhoff:

> [T]hose cross-cultural studies of aging that do exist make abundantly clear the cultural determinants of aging; if any generalizations can be made, they point to the great variety of styles and forms of aging in different cultural settings. Here one is struck by diversity rather than uniformity, by variation rather than universality. The studies that are available suggest that social scientists must be as diligent in including the role of cultural factors in aging as they are in including them in studies of childrearing and childhood. Not all anthropologists may agree, but in the opinion of many the data point toward the malleability of the human organism and the significant role of nonbiological factors; in other words, culture appears to explain more of the peculiarities and idiosyncrasies of aging than do the factors that are attributable to a "common humanity."[168]

In sum, even though biology very likely plays a role in the ageism equation, it is not a determinative one. To this end, Richard Dawkins, a leading voice in the field of evolutionary biology theory, has written the following: "[I]t is a fallacy—incidentally a very common one—to suppose that genetically inherited traits are by definition fixed and unmodifiable. Our genes may instruct us to be selfish, but we are not necessarily compelled to obey them all our lives."[169]

Nature *Plus* Nurture

If a sociobiological analysis does establish that age bias is not the product of genetic imperative, and indeed, that analysis can be used to support the case for humans positively valuing old age, how then does one explain modern-day negative age bias? The answer lies in the fact, of course, that there are forces other than the genes at work, as discussed in the preceding sections of this chapter. Cultural factors, in other words, can trump or at least mitigate genetically fashioned inclinations. After all, even in those societies that do accord the elderly high respect, eventually the time and resources needed to sustain oldsters will exceed the genetic or cultural payback.[170] At that point, the oldster's situation becomes exceedingly precarious. Indeed, in primitive societies it is not uncommon that the tribe will engage in some sort of death-hastening behavior toward the aged man or woman.[171] The tribe may even actively engage in killing the aged individual, or the mores of a given culture may instruct the elder that it is his duty to take his own life.[172]

As it happens, just as there are social and economic forces that explain the eventual downfall of the elderly in primitive societies, so are there such forces in advanced industrialized societies, such as the United States. We do not kill our elders, or demand of them (at least not explicitly so) that they kill themselves.[173] But we do demean them and even reject them once they offer no perceived economic or cultural value. Rejection on the job in the twentieth century most prominently took the form, until largely abolished by statute, of age-based mandatory retirement;[174] other forms of age-based workplace discrimination still persist.[175] Outside the workplace, the old may be subjected to condescension, expressions of distaste, and denigration.[176] They may be effectively removed from the community's presence by their consignment to segregated living situations, such as long-term care institutions,[177] board and care facilities,[178] and assisted living centers.[179] They may be assigned second-class legal status by virtue of being subjected to court-ordered guardianships.[180]

We call these manifestations of disrespect and rejection, and the negative perceptions animating them, "ageism."

Conclusions

Having an apt term to use, *ageism,* does not mean that one should or can simplistically analogize from general condemnation of like terms, such as racism, ethnocentrism, and sexism. Rather, ageism appears to be a distinct phenomenon quite unlike, in significant respects, the other "-isms." For one, the degree of animus involved in ageism is considerably less than that which one sees in the race, religion, and ethnic bias contexts. The distaste that is involved in the age context is more for the characteristic than it is for the bearer of that characteristic. In other words, we fear old age and in so doing we transpose negative attitudes onto those who bear the trait of old age. In contrast, the racist generally equally detests both the trait and those who possess it.

Second, the generating forces for ageism and the other "-isms," while in some instances similar, in others are not. An authoritarian personality, for example, may be inclined to be a racist; authoritarianism does not, however, seem to explain ageism. History is a useful window into understanding the present-day treatment of racial minorities in America; it offers less when it is ageism that we try to parse.

Third, and perhaps the most telling factor that sets age bias on its own bottom, rather than linking it closely with racism, is the fact that age is something we all possess. Unlike the white who will never be black, or the Latino who will never take on an Irish heritage, or the women whose sex is immutable, the 25-year-old of today will become (absent a premature death) the 75-year-old of a distant future. Thus, whatever urges there may be to define the old as "others," those urges likely are going to be tempered by the common fate that we all share. The universality of age accordingly makes age bias a unique matter.

There is a fourth important differentiating factor here, as well. That is the matter of affinity. As a white male I may well have no close relationships with Hispanics or blacks. As a Jew, I may have some, but comparatively limited, close relationships with Catholics and Muslims. But as a middle-aged man, I almost certainly will have had, or may still have, close relationships both with oldsters—my mother, who died at age 88; my father, who died at age 76; my father-in-law, a semiactive 87-year-old—as well as with young folks: my two sons and my daughter and my niece. Aggravating as some of these relationships were and are, and as stressful as they became in the case of my parents as they both descended into irreversible dementia, these people were and are objects of my love and concern. Such life experiences—ones that almost all adults share in some way or another—have to profoundly affect, for the better most of the time and sometimes perhaps for the worse, the ways in which we deal with, regard or disregard, respect or disrespect, ignore or heed, the elders and youngsters among us. Again, then, the play of the age factor is a quite different and distinct matter.

This all is not to deny that ageism exists, but rather to recognize its special nature—a recognition in part captured by a perspicacious student of the social and cultural aspects of aging, Professor Thomas Cole:

> The term *ageism* obviously derived its cultural resonance from contemporary movements for racial and sexual equality. Unfortunately, we still do not have the careful, critical scholarship that might justify or illuminate its analogies to racism and sexism. . . . They may be deeply flawed and misleading. At a minimum, however, we must be skeptical of the liberal assumption underlying these analogies—that age is irrelevant, that old people differ from young people only in their chronological age. . . . [T]raditional thought about the stages of life presupposed the opposite. In age, as in race and sex, the Scylla of prejudice is never far from the Charybdis of denial of human differences—differences that need to be acknowledged, respected, and cherished.[181]

Professor Cole's admonition is an important one: people *do* differ, and differences sometimes do make for meaningful and legitimate differentials in treatment. Yet, sensitivity such as that expressed by Professor Cole to the possible abuses of egalitarianism gone unchecked should not negate alertness to the perniciousness of uncabined bias: sometimes, ostensibly reasonable uses (conscious or otherwise) of the age factor may pass beyond the pales of accuracy, wisdom, and fairness. The task now at hand, then, is to assess how the age factor operates within the context of the American legal system for good or ill.

5

The Main Actors:
Plaintiffs, Defendants, and Witnesses

[T]o fulfill the meaning of age and to perform its duty one must be reconciled with old age and everything it brings with it. We must say yes to it. Without this yea, without submission to what nature demands of us, the worth and meaning of our days—whether we are old or young—are lost and we betray life.
—Hermann Hesse, *On Old Age*

O heavens, if you do love old men,
  if your sweet sway,
Allow obedience, if yourselves are
  old,
Make it your cause. Send down, and
  take my part.
—William Shakespeare, *The Tragedy of King Lear,* Act II, Scene 4

Courts in the American system of justice are passive institutions. Unlike legislators and members of the executive branches of government, judges do not—nor can they—seek out problems to resolve. Nor can they conscript litigants to bring lawsuits. Rather, the judiciary must wait for disputes to be brought to them, presented in ways that are compatible with the adjudicatory process. Moreover, judges have virtually no control over who chooses to initially pass through the courtroom doors as plaintiffs. (However, once the plaintiff *has* entered the courtroom, she comes within the court's authority and thence may be forced to depart, sometimes without even being able to reach the merits of her claim because of failures to satisfy technical,[1] jurisdictional,[2] and/or substantive grounds that give rise to various motions by the defendant.) As with plaintiffs, so too with defendants: courts have virtually no control over who is named—at least initially—as a defendant in a given case.

In sum, even though a dynamic 40-year-old Tom Cruise look-alike plaintiff might be the best advocate for the issue at hand, or even if a feisty 36-year-old Julia Roberts clone arguably would be the best person to defend the statute or contract under attack, the courts have no say as to selecting an exemplary, rather than a lackluster or even hateful, litigant. More to the point here, whether an adult plaintiff or defendant is old, young, or middle-aged, his or her chronological status generally is not a matter courts can control or even address.

There *are* caveats in the instance of minors. For example, a promise made by a minor is voidable because of the minor's imputed lack of capacity to enter into binding agreements;[3] likewise, a minor cannot validly consent (for legal purposes) to a sexual encounter.[4] But insofar as individuals who have reached the age of majority—which generally is age 18—are concerned, their ages are both irrelevant and beyond the ambit of legitimate judicial concern, absent some specific statutory focus on the matter of age. For example, the federal Age Discrimination in Employment Act of 1967, as amended (ADEA),[5] only protects persons over age 39,[6] and so for a court to have jurisdiction as to an ADEA claimant, the age of that individual is a relevant legal matter.

This irrelevance of age—at least as a formal matter—is both sensible and appropriate. After all, a breach of contract arising out of a moving company's tardy delivery of one's household goods is just that—that is, a breach of contract claim—whether the aggrieved party is 25, 45, or 80. A securities fraud prosecution is a securities fraud prosecution, whether the alleged wrongdoer is 40 or 60. Given the general irrelevance of age, it is hardly surprising that data are rare regarding the ages of parties engaged in contract disputes or tort actions or other private law litigation. In the same vein, the ages of prosecutors and defendants in criminal cases typically go unnoted.[7] And a like state of formal indifference exists with regard to the ages of nonparty witnesses.[8]

In actuality, however, neither the lack of data regarding litigants and witnesses, nor the age-neutral nature of most substantive legal claims, means that age plays no role in the courtroom. Quite the contrary. Sometimes the age of one or more of the parties will be substantively relevant. This already has been noted in the instance of an ADEA claimant. Similarly, a defendant in a criminal case may by statutory directive be subject to being charged with a more serious crime or being at risk of an enhanced penalty because his victim was over a certain age—let us say, age 60.[9] Or, as touched on earlier, the particular court in which a prosecution is pursued may be determined on the basis of the alleged perpetrator's being under a certain age and thus being entitled to treatment as a juvenile offender, rather than as an adult—again pursuant to a statutory mandate.[10] More often (and assuredly more subtly), age also almost certainly plays a role in the courtroom even absent formal directives set out in statutes. Plaintiffs and/or defendants can trigger differing responses by juries and judges by virtue of the ages of the litigants and/or the ages of the decision makers who are assessing and evaluating the litigating parties. Likewise, the age factor can be in play in terms of decision makers' responses to witnesses of varying ages. Lawyers and judges also may trigger varied responses based on their ages.

In this chapter, age is addressed as it relates to plaintiffs, defendants, respondents in guardianship proceedings, and witnesses who are called upon either to support or to debunk litigants' stories. Lawyers, and the relationship of lawyers to their clients, are the subjects of chapter 6.[11] In chapter 7 judges receive their due, and chapter 8 focuses on juries.

Data Regarding the Ages of Wards, Litigants, and Complainants

On rare occasion one can detect some clues—and sometimes one even can derive specific data—regarding the ages of one or more of the litigants in the courtroom. As earlier noted, such data are very sparse, however.

Guardianships

A well-grounded inference regarding the matter of age can be drawn in one prominent legal context involving the elderly: petitions for the appointment of guardians or conservators.[12] While it is true that guardians may be appointed by courts to handle the affairs of young people who are in need of court-supervised protection, most guardianships involve older people[13] who, it is claimed by the petitioners (typically family members),[14] are by reason of intellectual decline and/or physical frailty unable to attend to their own financial affairs, health needs, and/or activities of daily living. Thus, while we have no data regarding the specific ages of individuals as to whom guardianships are sought, it is safe to confidently conclude that most folks who wind up in this situation are elderly.

Age Discrimination in Employment Act Litigants

As already noted, the ADEA protects individuals ages 40 and older from discrimination in the workplace.[15] Thus, when one reads in the newspapers about a winning ADEA claim, one can conclude that the plaintiff necessarily was at least 40 years of age. Of course, most people in the United States live beyond age 40, so merely knowing that a plaintiff has sued under the ADEA tells one very little, after all: an ADEA plaintiff might be 41, 61, or 81.[16]

There is, however, a modicum of information available about such individuals by virtue of a survey undertaken by the author several years ago of all ADEA decisions that were published in 1996.[17] There were "325 decisions handed down in 1995 and 1996 that were published for the first time in 1996," and "[o]f these, 316 . . . [made] up the relevant data set—94 federal court of appeals decisions and 222 federal district court rulings."[18] In 73 of the federal appeals court cases, the ages of the plaintiffs were identified. Their median age was 54; the youngest was 40+ and the oldest was 68.[19] There were

131 age-identified plaintiffs in the 222 district court cases;[20] their median age was 55.[21]

> Of the 204 age-identified plaintiffs in the 1996 cases (that is, seventy-three plaintiffs whose cases wound up being addressed by appellate courts, plus 131 plaintiffs in the non-appealed district court rulings), ninety-three plaintiffs . . .—or 46.5%—fit within the fifty to fifty-nine age band. There were fifty-three plaintiffs between ages forty and forty-nine, i.e., 25.5%. And fifty-five plaintiffs, amounting to 27%, were between ages sixty and seventy. (There were three plaintiffs who were over age seventy).[22]

The data gleaned regarding defendants in this analysis were much sparser. In the 94 court of appeals decisions there were only three instances in which defendants' ages (or, more correctly, the ages of the defendant employers' employees who actually made the allegedly discriminatory decisions) were identified: their ages were 42, 46, and 60.[23] In the 222 district court rulings, again there were only three cases in which the ages of the decision makers were discernible. In one instance, the individual was 40; in another he was 60+; and in the third there were three decision makers, ages 44, 44, and 52.[24]

This information is not without utility, but of course it is very limited in scope. It reveals nothing about the comparative treatment of younger versus older ADEA plaintiffs. Thus, if one might hypothesize, let us say a higher success rate for plaintiffs who are between the ages of 40 and 49 than there is for plaintiffs between ages 50 and 59, that datum did not present itself, nor was it even examined, in this study. (However, there are so many variables apart from the age of the plaintiff in any given ADEA case that it would be virtually impossible to make any useful comparisons.)[25]

Criminal Cases—Victims

There is in the public consciousness a sense that older people are particularly likely to be the victims of crime. Thus, even without knowing the specific ages of such individuals, one might well assume that there currently are significant numbers of older men and women appearing as complainants in criminal courtrooms, and one further might assume that we are going to see dramatic increases in these numbers as the massive baby boom population continues to age. The incidence of victimization aside, there also is a general understanding that older people harbor a particularly acute fear of being victimized by criminals.

Insofar as the fear of crime is concerned, it turns out that there is a popular misconception operative here. On the basis of several studies, it appears reasonable to conclude that the elderly are no more fearful of being the victims of crime than are younger people.[26] Indeed, with respect to property crimes, one study determined that the elderly were the least fearful age group.[27]

With regard to the supposed heightened incidence of victimization, the data in fact do not support the popular conception, with one possible major exception, that is, instances of elder abuse. In fact, over the past 15 years or so there has been a decline in the crime victimization rates for the elderly insofar as violent crimes, personal theft, and household crime are concerned.[28] On a less salutary note, however, the data do reveal that when older people are victimized by violent crimes, they are more than twice as likely as younger victims to suffer serious injuries.[29] And when injured, almost half of the older victims require hospitalization for two or more days; in contrast, only one-fourth of younger victims need to be hospitalized.[30] Still, the bottom line—a heartening one, certainly—is that the age group least likely to be the victims of crime in America is that made up of men and women ages 65 and over.[31] For specific information, however, as to the actual ages of elderly crime victims, the data are nonexistent.

Elder Abuse

Notwithstanding the foregoing general data regarding the relatively low incidence of crime victimization of the elderly, there is one area where the statistics do go in the other direction. The number of reported acts of violence perpetrated against elderly men and women has been increasing steadily in recent years.[32]

Elder abuse entails a variety of types of wrongdoing inflicted on persons of advanced years. As discussed below, most states have enacted statutes making one or more forms of such abuse a crime. Typically, these statutes define who qualifies as an elderly person. It belabors the obvious, then, to note that in an elder abuse prosecution the victim can be identified by an observer as an elderly person. Data as to the specific ages of such individuals are lacking, however.

Criminal Cases—Defendants

With regard to the ages of those adults who are charged with and/or convicted of criminal activity, the data are mixed.[33] A common notion among some members of the public is that the rate of crimes perpetrated by the elderly has increased significantly in recent years. The actual statistics do not seem to bear out this perception, however—at least not to any significant extent:

> [A]fter being a nonissue for criminology for years, elder crime gained attention in the 1970s largely because of the marked increase of elders in U.S. society. The earliest studies predicted that elders would increasingly turn to crime and projected the emergence of yet another social problem. The topic

resurfaced in the late 1980s, when scholars questioned the validity of the earlier assessments. All the comprehensive studies [that ensued] . . . agree that elder crime, while on the increase, should not be characterized as a "geriatric crime wave." They also note that while elder crime had increased for some offense types, it had decreased for others. In particular, elder property crime was found to have increased, and within that category, larceny/theft, DWI, and other relatively minor city and ordinance violations. By the same token, elder crime was found to have decreased in the "victimless crime" categories, such as disorderly conduct, gambling, vagrancy, and public drunkenness.[34]

More recent data reviewed by Dr. Edith Elisabeth Flynn likewise establish that elderly individuals do not "significantly contribute to the nation's vexing crime problem."[35] More specifically, the "elder arrest rates for Index Crimes, violent crime, and property offenses remain very low."[36] Moreover, Dr. Flynn determined that elderly men and women have the lowest arrest rates of any age group in the United States. Her data, and her analysis of that data, also showed—in contrast to earlier studies—that there were steep declines for older individuals in the incidence of most property offense categories during the 1989–95 period. Thus, the commonly invoked caricature of the little old lady shoplifter is not borne out by the statistics.[37] Overall, moreover, somewhat more recent data show virtually no increase in arrest rates nationally for persons ages 60 and over.[38]

On the other hand, Dr. Flynn acknowledged that the incidence of violent crimes perpetrated by older individuals—most particularly, assaults and aggravated assaults—has increased in recent years.[39] Moreover, while the incidence nationally of murders, forcible rapes, and robberies declined in the period 1989–95, the declines for perpetrators between ages 55 and 59 and 60 to 64 were slightly less than the national declines.[40] And increases in the rates of crime committed by older people were noted in four categories: liquor law violations, offenses against family and children, drug abuse, and white-collar crime.[41] In addition, there are some data that show even more dramatic local increases in Florida—the state with the largest percentage of older individuals—than the national data reveal. More specifically, information gathered by the Florida Department of Law Enforcement covering a span of 18 years, 1980–98, revealed a significant increase over this time period in arrests in Florida of seniors for perpetrating violent offenses. The rate of forcible sex offenses by people ages 60 and over climbed 171 percent; there was a 168 percent increase in robberies committed by persons in this age group; and a 13 percent increase in aggravated assaults.[42] Again, data as to the specific ages of individual offenders are lacking.

Criminal Cases—Juvenile Offenders

Many statutes provide that juveniles—let us say, those under age 18—will be prosecuted in special courts, rather than in the courts in which adult alleged wrongdoers are tried.[43] Thus, one can infer with very good assurance that if John Smith is being tried in a juvenile court, he is under the statutorily prescribed age for being deemed an adult offender. This inference is not without ambiguity, however: one cannot know from the locus of the prosecution alone whether the youngster who is charged with being a juvenile offender is 16, 15, or any other sub-18 age.[44] Moreover, there often will be statutory or case-generated exceptions allowing for the prosecution of youngsters in adult courts in particularly egregious situations,[45] and so one cannot confidently conclude that every defendant in an adult courtroom is age 17 or older.

Future Legal Issues for an Aging America

General Factors Likely to Bring More Elderly Litigants into the Courts

Prognostication typically is a chancy enterprise. Even so, it seems only logical to predict that the imminent massive increase in the elderly population in the United States necessarily is going to be felt in the courts just by virtue of that increase. Over and above the growth in the numbers of older men and women, there are some other factors that further should generate an upsurge in the numbers of older litigants and nonparty witnesses. The older men and women of today and tomorrow are better educated than were the oldsters of the 1950s and 1960s and 1970s. They have more assets than their predecessors of 20 and 30 years ago. They are more likely to be involved in activities outside the home than those older men and women of past decades. Having reached adulthood in the 1960s and 1970s, which were times of political and legal activism by all sorts of claimants, ranging from blacks protesting segregated lunchrooms to neo-Nazis challenging bans on their claimed First Amendment rights of speech and assembly, the baby boomers are more accustomed to the notion of one's standing up for his or her rights. All these factors likely should lead these folks—in contrast to their predecessors of past decades—to assert significantly more tort, contract, and other civil legal claims, and to use the courts to combat perceived instances of social, economic, political, and other forms of injustice.

Legal Issues of Particular Relevance to the Elderly

Those who focus their legal practices on the needs of older clients have identified, albeit perhaps with a bias toward establishing elder law as a special legal discipline, a number of areas of civil (as opposed to criminal) law in which such needs are likely to be manifested. One effort was made in 1991. In a report entitled *Court-Related Needs of the Elderly and Persons with Disabilities,* the American Bar Association's Commission on Legal Problems of the Elderly, its Commission on the Mentally Disabled, and the National Judicial College identified several concerns that were thought likely to generate increasing caseloads for state courts: issues involving Medicaid, guardianship, discrimination, long-term care, protective services, mental commitment, health care decision making, and housing.[46] The National Academy of Elder Law Attorneys, Inc., identifies the legal needs served by elder law attorneys as including the following: "durable powers of attorney; estate planning and probate; financing long-term medical care; guardianship and conservatorship; health care decisions; health care quality issues; independent living options; trusts; Medicare, Medicaid, and other public benefits; elder abuse, neglect, and exploitation; and age discrimination."[47]

Discrimination

Discrimination against the elderly can arise in a variety of contexts. In some settings, age bias may be largely innocuous. In others, it can be of very serious import. In particular, age discrimination in the workplace is a continuing problem of significant dimension for workers and employers. In the 1990s hundreds of ADEA cases were decided annually by the federal courts.[48] And now an enormous growth in the numbers of older workers is just over the horizon. "[B]y 2005 over 56.7 million workers ages forty-five and older are expected to be in the labor force—an increase of 16.7 million over the numbers for comparably aged workers in 1994. This constitutes an overall increase of 41.7% in the numbers of men and women in this age grouping! Those aged fifty-five and over will increase from 15.5 million in 1994 to 22.1 million in 2005—a 36% increase."[49]

Given the fact that the prime years for falling victim to age discrimination in the workplace are the mid-50s,[50] and given further the foregoing numbers, it is only reasonable to expect that the number of ADEA claims will increase significantly.[51] Indeed, the percentage increase should considerably outstrip the overall percentage of older people, inasmuch as the percentage of such individuals in the workforce will be so much higher than the percentage of such individuals in the total population.[52]

Moreover, there is another statistic that further buttresses the prediction of a major increase in discrimination claims: this is the very significant increase in the numbers of women in high-level, high-salaried jobs. In the 1960s, 1970s, and 1980s relatively few women occupied such positions. As a result, even if a woman experienced age discrimination, there was little incentive or even ability for her to pursue legal recourse under the ADEA (which actually did not even go into effect until mid-1968.) The job or promotion she was denied typically was low-paying and thus not worth fighting for. What is more, there was a vicious circle here: even if she were of a mind to fight, she rarely had the financial wherewithal to pursue legal redress because she had been limited in her work life to low-paying jobs that precluded the accumulation of the significant assets needed to mount an effective legal assault against a well-funded employer. While women still are strikingly absent from the offices of the CEOs of major corporations,[53] they nonetheless have made major strides in recent years in moving into the management ranks of corporations and other institutions.[54] Thus, when a woman in the workforce today feels that her age has accounted for a job rejection or a demotion or a meager pay raise, she is much more likely to have both the incentive and the resources to not simply accept this affront and move on. Indeed, and consistent with the foregoing surmise, the earlier noted study of ADEA decisions published in 1996[55] revealed a striking 100 percent increase as between suits filed by women in 1996 and those filed in the earlier 18-year period running from 1968 through 1986.[56] Given the growing numbers of women in high-level jobs, and given the fact that these numbers should very significantly increase as women who have been in the workforce in recent decades seek to move into higher-ranking jobs in the coming years as they age into their 50s and 60s, we have a scenario further promising that the numbers of ADEA cases are bound to burgeon.

Guardianships and Elder Abuse

More and more older people no doubt will lead to more and more guardianship petitions, given—in particular—the rapidly expanding numbers of the old-old, that is, those 85 and older. This is the fastest growing age group in the United States; indeed, it is predicted that this group could make up nearly one-quarter of the elderly population by 2050, when there will be about 68 million individuals ages 65 and older in the United States.[57] It also is this population that is most likely to exhibit significant percentages of physical frailty and intellectual decline.[58]

A like prognosis of significant increase unfortunately is in order as to instances of elder abuse, which may in turn lead to growing numbers of prosecutions for violations of statutes making such abuse a crime. In brief, increased numbers of the elderly should lead, just in the normal course of things, to increased instances of physical, emotional, and financial mistreatment of older men and women.

Elder abuse can be manifested in a number of ways.[59] *Physical abuse* entails the intentional infliction of physical force on an elderly person. *Psychological* or *emotional abuse* arises when an elderly person is subjected to the infliction of mental distress by nonphysical means, including threats, intimidation, and verbal humiliation. *Neglect* by a caregiver occurs when someone who has the responsibility for seeing to the needs of an elderly person fails to provide the requisite care, albeit that failure need not necessarily arise out of an intent to do harm. *Self-neglect* arises from an elderly person's own failure to attend to the necessities of life: food, shelter, clothing, etc. *Financial exploitation* concerns various forms of theft, misappropriation, and wrongful use of an elderly person's property by another.

The actual incidence of elder abuse is a matter of some ambiguity.[60] A 1992 report by the American Association of Retired Persons (AARP) Public Policy Institute, looking to data that even then were already in some instances a few years old, detailed the following statistics:

> Recent studies have suggested that as many as 1 million to 2 million individuals may be victims of elder abuse each year. A 1990 congressional study estimated that the problem affects 1.5 million persons annually. The National Aging Resource Center on Elder Abuse (NARCEA) estimated that 2 million reportable cases of elder abuse occurred in 1988 in domestic settings. A study conducted in the metropolitan Boston area revealed that 32 per 1000 individuals age 65 and older residing in the community at large suffered from physical abuse, verbal aggression, and/or neglect. If a national survey yielded similar results, these findings could represent 700,000 to 1,000,000 victims per year *excluding* victims of financial abuse and self-neglect.[61]

Later data—derived from five community-based studies—suggest that the prevalence of elder abuse victimization ranges from 4 to 6 percent of the elderly American population.[62] "From an estimated 117,000 reports [of elder abuse], including self-neglect, in 1986, the total rose to more than 293,000 in 1996."[63] Of these 293,000 reported cases, "74,000 were substantiated cases of physical, emotional, financial abuse, and neglect (excluding self-neglect, which represents more than half the total)."[64]

A cautionary note is in order here, however. While the numbers of reported instances of elder abuse clearly have been rising, it is unclear whether the ostensible increase in recent years in instances of elder abuse reflects an actual percentage growth in the number of cases occurring. The rise in numbers may be due simply to better and more reporting than had existed in earlier years.[65]

As briefly pointed out in the foregoing statistical review, self-neglect cases—which not all experts agree even should be included within the definition of abuse—constitute the most common form of abuse. For example, in the foregoing AARP report it was noted that in Texas 56 percent of the abuse cases involved self-neglect, while only 20 percent involved caregiver neglect, 13 percent involved physical abuse, and 10 percent involved financial abuse.[66] In Wisconsin 46.6 percent of the cases concerned self-neglect, 16.3 percent involved physical abuse, 16 percent involved financial abuse, 13.6 percent concerned caregiver neglect, and 7.3 percent arose out of psychological abuse.[67]

Not surprisingly, there are several ways in which the phenomenon of elder abuse intersects with the legal system and with participants in that system.[68] Through their representational capacities, attorneys may come into contact with individuals whom they believe to be the victims of abuse.[69] While typically state mandatory reporting laws impose a legal obligation upon doctors, nurses, social workers, law enforcement officers, and/or clergy to report instances of suspected abuse,[70] attorneys generally are exempt from this obligation. Even so, in a jurisdiction that does not require reporting by an attorney, a lawyer should in dire instances report her suspicions to the appropriate authority—particularly when she obtains information from the alleged perpetrator (as opposed to the victim). Even if in so doing concern may arise as to a possible breach of attorney-client confidentiality, the Model Rules of Professional Conduct that most states have adopted[71] insulate the lawyer from charges of misconduct.[72] Moreover, state elder abuse laws further may provide immunity from civil or criminal liability for attorneys who in good faith report incidents of suspected or actual abuse.[73]

Reporting aside, an attorney may have occasion to extract an elderly person from the clutches, so to speak, of a friend or relative who is financially abusing her by drafting for the victim a power of attorney designating a trusted and honest person to control and administer her assets. Another ploy involves the victim's attorney seeking a court-ordered protective order barring the abuser from coming into contact with the victim. Thereby, the judiciary is brought into the picture. Other governmental intervention may occur through prosecution by law enforcement authorities of alleged abusers under state statutes making criminal various types of physical, emotional, and financial abuse. Here, too, judges take on a role in addressing the problem. So do jurors in those cases that are tried to juries.[74]

Asset Transfer and Reimbursement Issues

Other issues of particular concern to elderly individuals involve disputes regarding Medicare reimbursements, as well as proactive transfers of assets to enable declining men and women to become eligible for Medicaid reimbursement for nursing home expenses.[75] Indeed, when one reviews the major books written for lawyers concerning the practice of elder law, one finds that much of the substance of these volumes focuses on financial matters.[76]

Nursing Home Torts

The particular context in which one reasonably might expect to see a much larger percentage of older people than younger adults as tort victims is that involving long-term care facilities, that is, nursing homes. These are primarily—but not exclusively—populated by older individuals;[77] their population is projected to grow to about 4 million by 2018.[78] The occurrences of improper care in these institutions are not infrequent,[79] and so one might readily presume that a future expanding area of the law should be litigation arising out of torts inflicted upon nursing home residents. In fact, however, for more than a decade there have been articles written and conferences held that have more or less encouraged increased litigation,[80] to the ends both of redressing victims as well as creating pressure for nursing homes to correct their faults, and yet such litigation still is not common.

A key problem that likely deters more claims being made (assuming potential cases exist) derives from the fact that the main form of redress sought by tort plaintiffs is damages, and typically the plaintiff will be seeking damages based on past and future lost earnings resulting from the tort feasor negligence. Inasmuch as older people, and certainly older men and women who are confined to nursing homes, generally are nonparticipants in the workforce, the absence of this major damages element—which makes the handling of tort suits attractive to contingent fee attorneys who take a percentage of the award —strongly militates against such claims being pursued. Another problem for potential nursing home tort claimants stems from the fact that the likelihood of securing two other common elements of damages, that is, damages for future pain and suffering and for the cost of continuing medical and other care extending into the future, is diminished by virtue of the fact that elderly nursing home residents have abbreviated future life expectancies. The 25-year-old who is left a quadriplegic after an automobile accident can point to a future life expectancy, in terms of the statistical tables, of 40 or 50 years, all of which predictably will entail ongoing medical and supportive care. In contrast, the 85-year-old who is the victim of actionable negligence in the nursing home resulting in, let us hypothesize, a broken collarbone that will need regular medical attention because her osteoporosis makes it infeasible to reset the fragile bone, will be able to secure much less in monetary recovery because the statistical tables tell us that she is likely to die within the next few years. Again, then, both the potential plaintiff and her contingent fee attorney are going to have little financial justification for taking on what could be a costly lawsuit that at best will result in only a very limited recovery.[81]

Still another factor that likely accounts for a lack of legal activity is the fact that many people in nursing homes are totally isolated: their friends are dead, they have no family, and so they really have no one to take on an aggressive role in seeking private redress in the courts. Moreover, there is a fear factor operative here: the nursing home resident is enormously dependent upon her caretakers, and the pursuit of a legal claim may well constitute—or at least may be perceived by the resident as constituting—a prescription for engendering hostility on the part of the very people on whom the claimant so heavily relies. Consequently, she and/or her family, if she has one, may well be afraid to stir up trouble lest the consequences redound to the resident's detriment.

The American Legal System—The Big Picture

Even given the fact that there are legal issues that are of particular relevance to the elderly, the *large majority* of the work of the American legal system—both at the federal and state levels[82]—concerns issues other than those identified as being the special domain of the old. Thus, while there are going to be increases of older people participating as litigants, jurors, witnesses, etc., one must keep matters in perspective. Elderly litigants pursuing so-called elder law issues are not going to inundate the courts or swamp lawyers' offices!

Granted, insofar as ADEA claims, guardianship adjudications, elder abuse prosecutions, and the drafting of asset transfer devices are concerned, lawyers—and sometimes judges—will be critical figures in dealing with these matters. However, given the high costs associated with entry into the legal system, one might well expect to see a growing use of alternative institutions and of nonlawyers to deal with at least some of these age-correlated issues. Indeed, there already is movement in these directions. For example, the federal Equal Employment Opportunity Commission, which along with victims themselves enforces the ADEA, is emphasizing mediation of claims filed with it as an alternative to litigation.[83] What is more, there is good reason to conclude that many of the "legal" problems that most likely will arise for the older man or woman are not going to be the types of concerns that are needful of, or even appropriate for, resolution in a courtroom. Nor will they even need the attention of attorneys, as opposed to other trained problem-solvers, such as social workers and paralegals. Disputes about Medicaid eligibility and Medicare reimbursement, for example, rarely call for resolution by judges or juries; rather, they entail administrative issues that are amenable to being sorted out through administrative processes.

What, then, *are* the big issues generally for the courts?

Relational Issues

Marriage dissolution disputes constitute a major source of legal business for both lawyers and state court judges. Such disputes—which can involve property distribution matters, child custody, child support, and child visitation—certainly are most likely to arise between younger men and women.[84]

Legal clashes arising out of fractured contractual relations also generate an enormous number of legal claims at the state level and therefore a very large number of cases for state courts to address. But because many older people are no longer active in work or business, we would expect to see far fewer breach of contract claims per every 100,000 elders, let us say, than would be the case for the younger business people and professionals who are engaged in activities that often result in contracts, in the first instance, and disputes arising out of them, in the second.

Tort Actions

Personal injury cases make up a tremendous portion of the caseload of the state courts. Certainly older people can be, and are, involved in automobile accidents, slip-and-fall scenarios, etc., and so they do wind up as plaintiffs and/ or defendants in tort cases.[85] But there is no reason to conjecture that as a general matter older individuals currently are involved at a disproportionately higher rate than younger persons in the thousands upon thousands of tort cases annually filed, or that they will be in the future.

Estate Planning

Estate planning—particularly to the end of transferring assets so as to render the property holder eligible for Medicaid coverage of his or her nursing home expenses[86] is a fertile ground for activity by elder law attorneys[87] and absent changes in federal law it should continue to be so. There are other estate planning devices and issues that have particular relevance for older individuals, or at least become relevant as people start to contemplate the possibility of their dying at some relatively imminent date.[88] The fact is, however, that estate planning is a very broad field, and while the intricacies of Medicaid estate planning will largely be addressed in the context of dealing with elderly clients (and often their adult children, as well), a far greater range of estate planning issues are of concern for all adults. Thus, to identify estate planning as an area of particular focus for elder law attorneys and for elderly clients would be misleading.[89] Moreover, insofar as contests about wills and trusts wind up in the courts, it primarily is younger individuals who are the ones generating and pursuing claims, based on challenges to elderly decedents' allegedly ambiguous or otherwise flawed devises.

Criminal Matters

In the criminal setting we can expect to see more elderly victims testifying about their victimization, and we should expect to see more elderly defendants. These developments follow simply from the burgeoning numbers of elderly men and women. But it would seem safe to conclude, on the basis of what we know of the past several decades, that we are not going to see an unusual expansion either of elderly crime victims or elderly perpetrators that will exceed the percentage increase generally of aging baby boomers. The elderly do not appear to have a taste, if you will, for crime. Nor do they appear to have a heightened susceptibility to being on the wrong end of criminal acts. Still, there is one necessary caveat to these conclusions. That centers on the matter of elder abuse. Here, unfortunately, the trend in victimization already is an upward one (although much of the rise in absolute numbers in recent years may be a function primarily of better reporting, rather than being reflective of a surge in actual instances of abuse). Thus, the burgeoning numbers of oldsters in the 2010s and 2020s, when the baby boomers—those born between 1946 and 1964—will be in their mid-60s and 70s, do portend expanding numbers of instances of abuse.

Conclusions

More and more older people are going to be involved with lawyers and with the courts. In some instances these interactions will occur because of issues that particularly correlate with older age. More generally, however, older men and women will enter the legal system simply because there are going to be more and more of them. Thus, if older litigants today make up 5 percent, let us say, of plaintiffs and defendants in the federal and state courts,[90] at a time when elderly men and women make up 12 percent or so of the population, we reasonably should expect to see older folks making up 8 or 9 percent of the parties in court when the overall percentage of older Americans has grown.

But there is a critical point to be made here, lest once again the mere phenomenon of older faces comes to be used as a basis for unwarranted generalizations: while sometimes older people will be in the courts and in lawyers' offices in increasing numbers with issues that are more or less confined to older folks, they also will appear in these fora not because they are somehow different from younger adults but rather because they are the same! In other words, they have the same legal problems as will their more youthful counterparts. After all, a dispute with a neighbor about an allegedly encroaching fence is just that: a dispute with a neighbor. It does not matter whether the disputants are young, middle-aged, or old; the legal issues are the same. Likewise, the legal merits of a complaint about a defective refrigerator that brings the complainant into small claims court are unaffected by the ages of the buyer, the salesperson, and the men who delivered the appliance to the buyer's home.

In brief, one does not have to segregate and isolate older people as some different breed, so to speak, with special problems. More than that, one *should* not pursue the rhetoric of segregation and difference, for that tack simply feeds into ageist notions about the elderly as being unlike the rest of us in important, irreducible ways. To make the point bluntly, then: older people in the legal system are and will be simply people with legal issues that need addressing.[91]

To argue for the special nature of the older litigant, as some do, or to argue for the special nature of legal issues involving the elderly, *may* be to do an injustice, for those arguments can nurture stereotypes and biases based on supposed difference. And there is too much of that already. Let me stress the word *may* here, however. Elder law attorneys indeed are performing very important functions. They provide representation to people needful of attorneys' counsel. They offer expertise in areas of which too many attorneys are ignorant or with which they are insufficiently conversant. Even so, the carving out of a purportedly unique area of legal practice reinforces notions of difference and "otherness." And so great caution is in order when one argues for the special nature of older folks' legal problems and for the special legal skills needed to address these problems. Beyond the special problems and the special skills, there are simply people—people with more years than some of us, but still . . . people.

Older Witnesses

In 1986 Lois Haight Herrington, who at the time was the assistant attorney general for the United States Justice Department's Office of Justice Programs, testified before the House Select Committee on Aging. Asserting that the American criminal justice system was rife "with insensitivity towards the plight of older crime victims," she opined that police and judges frequently discounted the elderly as valuable witnesses because they failed to distinguish between such witnesses' physical infirmities and their still vital mental capacities.[92]

How Older Witnesses Are Perceived by Others

Assistant Attorney General Herrington's comments were unsupported by proffered empirical data, but actually there are a few useful studies regarding the perceived credibility of older witnesses.[93] Some of these in fact refute, at least in some measure, her view that older witnesses are regarded as less credible than their younger counterparts. For example, a more positive note than that articulated by Ms. Herrington was sounded by Professor A. Daniel Yarmey, a leading researcher regarding the correlation between age and perceived witness credibility:

> The contributions of witnesses in court depend very much upon their credibility. . . . [My] study found that the police, lawyers, the general public, probation officers, and the elderly themselves were supportive of "the elderly as witnesses in court." Officers of the court and the general public

generally felt that elderly witnesses are good, honest, and valuable. The fact that they were perceived as highly understandable by all subject groups strengthens their credibility as witnesses.[94]

In like vein, four researchers reported in 2003 on their study of 324 mock jurors who assessed the testimony of videotaped mock witnesses. Of the 83 witnesses, 33 were between ages 18 and 30, 26 ranged from 59 to 74, and the remaining 24 were ages 75 through 88. The mock jurors were asked to assess the credibility of the witness's testimony. To the surprise of the researchers, the mock jurors perceived no age-related differences:

> Participant jurors were not sensitive to age-related differences in testimony accuracy. The older seniors [those ranging from 75 through 88] were significantly less accurate than the young seniors and young adults but participant jurors rated witnesses of every age as equally credible.[95]

Four other researchers reported the results of an experiment that involved the viewing of a 50-minute videotape of a simulated drug trial by 114 middle-class, primarily white college students who were enrolled in an introductory psychology class. They were separated into groups of 10 to 15 individuals. The only variable in the tapes was the age of the prosecution's key eyewitness: in one tape the witness was an 8-year-old boy; in the second he was 21; and in the third he was 74. The researchers expected to find that the 21-year-old eyewitness would be rated the most positively. In fact, the results were exactly to the contrary: "the testimony of the child was rated as more accurate, confident, forceful, honest, and generally credible than when the identical testimony was given by the young adult. The elderly witness was viewed *more* positively than the young adult witness, but *less* positively than the child witness."[96] With regard to the willingness of the mock jurors to convict the mock defendant, the *ages* of the eyewitnesses did not have any effect. In other words, there was no indication of any discounting by the mock jurors of the testimony of children or oldsters, even insofar as the critical issue of conviction was concerned. On the other hand, there also was no discounting of the weight of the young adult's testimony—something that might have been expected given the considerably less positive rating accorded that testimony.[97]

Similar results were obtained when a different set of 102 student subjects were provided with a transcript of the trial, rather than a videotape. Again, only the age of the eyewitness was varied, and again the testimony of the elderly witness was viewed more positively than that of the young adult, but less positively than that of the child.[98] Again, the "subjects' ratings of the guilt or innocence of the defendant did not vary as a function of the age of the prosecution's key witness."[99]

Notwithstanding the foregoing studies' results, there are other data supporting the notion that older witnesses generally are regarded as being less reliable than younger individuals, as Assistant Attorney General Herrington asserted. Indeed, a third aspect of the just-discussed study bore that notion out. In this instance, 50 college students in the introductory psychology course responded to a questionnaire that asked them to rate four hypothetical witnesses—a 6-year-old, an 8-year-old, a 21-year-old, and a 74-year-old—in terms of four dimensions: witness accuracy, susceptibility to misleading or suggestive questions, honesty, and the weight they would accord the testimony of the witness. The students also were asked two questions: at what age would they deem a person to become capable of providing accurate and credible eyewitness testimony, and was there an age at which a person would be too old to be trusted as a witness? The mock elderly witness fared much less well on three of the four factors (and the mock child witnesses fared less well on all four): with the exception of the matter of honesty,[100] the hypothetical elderly eyewitness was rated lower than the young adult (but higher than the hypothetical children).[101] With regard to the question of at what age a person would be too old to render trustworthy testimony, the respondents estimated that would occur at 75.3 years.

A note—whether cautionary or merely one born of a need for precision—should be sounded here. The subjects in the foregoing experiments all were college students, and thus presumably were in their late teens or early 20s. Their youthfulness must be taken into account in assessing—and perhaps discounting—the weight to be accorded their responses.[102] On the other hand, in another study it was found that "elderly subjects themselves are even more likely than college students—as well as than [sic] lawyers, judges, and other randomly selected potential jurors—to hold a negative stereotype about elderly witnesses' ability to give accurate testimony."[103] Moreover, in still another study—this one entailing mock jurors evaluating the eyewitness testimony of younger and older individuals—the researchers endeavored mightily to construct a methodology that would foreclose the possibility of stereotyped thinking accounting for the responses of the subjects, who were once again college students. The students consistently rated the older witnesses lower than the younger ones in terms of description accuracy, confidence level, perceived competence, general accuracy, and credibility. The researchers insisted that the "young adults [in their study who] evaluate[d] the testimony provided by elderly eyewitnesses . . . [were] *not* biased by negative stereotypes of seniors' eyewitness capabilities."[104] Rather, the facts were that the older witnesses indeed were verifiably and objectively deficient in all the dimensions noted and that the subjects properly perceived the older individuals' inadequacies as witnesses.

How Older Witnesses Actually Perform

The foregoing studies dealt with the question of how elderly witnesses are perceived by others. There is a very considerable body of empirical data as to how elderly witnesses actually perform. While those data generally support the conclusion that elderly witnesses are less reliable than are their younger counterparts, the data certainly are not all of a piece on this score.[105]

Recall of Events and Recognition of Perpetrators

Witnesses—whether they are parties to the legal dispute or nonparty individuals who have knowledge of the events that gave rise to the litigation—often are called upon to testify as to what happened. In other words, they are asked to recall and recount the events in question.

There is a considerable body of studies addressing the correlation between older age and the accuracy of recall. These studies in the main—but not uniformly—establish that there is an age-related decline, such that older witnesses are less reliable than are younger adults. However, the import of this research must be tempered by the observation that none of these studies tested the accuracy of the memories of witnesses who were involved in real events, such as automobile accidents giving rise to injuries, which in turn gave rise to lawsuits. It would seem reasonable to conjecture that firsthand traumatic experiences, such as actually being struck by a moving vehicle, would have or at least could have consequences for recollection of the incident. In some instances, the trauma likely would lead to impaired or even no recollection of the accident, while in other instances the drama of the event might vividly impress upon the victim's memory the details with photographic clarity. Given such likelihoods, the studies that have been conducted, while useful, perhaps do not constitute an entirely adequate foundation on which to ground firm conclusions.

This cavil aside, one must credit the mixed, but ultimately mildly negative, conclusions rendered by Professor Yarmey. In summarizing one of his studies he reported that the elderly indeed are in some instances less reliable than younger witnesses:

> Accuracy of recall and eyewitness identification of a suspect, regardless of the age of the witness, are highly fallible. Although eyewitness identification is difficult this does not rule out the potential value of testimony. Eyewitness memory reports of elderly witnesses will contain more errors on the average than that of young adults, but this testimony still has to be considered by the courts. Young adults, on the average, are 7 to 20 per cent more accurate in their recall of crime-related events, and in their identification of a suspect. However, some elderly subjects are equally as accurate as young adults in recognizing a criminal suspect in a photo-lineup. The major differences between young and elderly adults in eyewitness memory

performance are the greater likelihood of older persons to make false alarms; less confidence in their memory; and an inferiority in verbal recall for crime-related incidents and for descriptions of the suspect.[106]

There are additional, and again mixed, data establishing some deficit insofar as the recall aspect of memory of older witnesses is concerned:

[E]lderly eyewitnesses' memory performance depends heavily on how their memory is assessed. In remembering details of a crime, they tend to recall less than younger witnesses but demonstrate little, if any, deficiency at recognizing details of the event. Older subjects' ability to identify a suspect's face also shows little impairment. They are more likely than younger adults to identify a bystander or novel stimulus as the culprit, but even this effect may be mitigated if they are provided with a rich, multi-perspective view of the suspect's face.[107]

The deficiencies of eyewitness testimony offered by older witnesses were identified in another study, in which three groups of individuals—one made up of 23 18–25-year-olds, another made up of 23 30–44-year-olds, and the third made up of 23 65–85-year-olds—were asked to view a videotaped mock crime and to then provide testimony, which was subjected to cross-examination, as to what they had seen. "The seniors were less accurate than the younger adults in response to both direct and cross-examination questioning."[108]

On a more positive note, Brian H. Bornstein has observed that "there is little evidence to suggest that eyewitness abilities deteriorate substantially with age."[109] "Older eyewitnesses," he writes, "are able to remember details of an event as well as younger witnesses if they are asked to recognize rather than freely recall them." Furthermore, while older witnesses "show a tendency to make more false identifications in face recognition . . . , this tendency may be a consequence of using impoverished and unrealistic target stimuli." In any event, this tendency "can be offset by providing more contextual cues at retrieval." Ultimately, according to Bornstein, "the only factor which has been reliably shown to affect elderly eyewitnesses more than young adults is post-event misinformation."[110]

Also in a positive vein, another researcher concluded that while eyewitness identification accuracy declines with age insofar as verbal reporting of observed events is concerned, there are no age differences seen in the recall of either details or main points.[111] And there is still more evidence that there are no age-related differences regarding eyewitnesses' reporting.[112] For example, it was found by a group of researchers that there was no difference between two subject groups—one made up of 40 individuals with a mean age of 69 and the other consisting of 40 adults with a mean age of 19.3—with regard to the recall of facts, where the video presentation of such facts involved the information being set forth in blocks of related data, rather than simply being put out in random fashion.[113]

In another study four researchers found very little difference between the performance on direct examination of "young adults," that is, those between ages 18 and 30, as eyewitnesses, and of "young" seniors—those between ages 59 and 74, but a significant difference between the performance of these two groups and "older seniors," that is, those ages 75 through 88. With regard to cross-examination, differences in the accuracy levels of the young adult group, on the one hand, and the two older groups on the other, were more pronounced. But overall, the testimonial accuracy of the young adults and the young seniors did not differ.[114]

Obviously, and in sum, the jury is out as to a definitive conclusion regarding the recall abilities of older witnesses; there are data both negative and positive.

Recall of Sources of Information

A number of experiments have been conducted to test the ability of older individuals to recall sources of information. The data support a less than solid conclusion that there is *some* age-related decline associated with source memory.

One study produced some negative findings, along with some positive ones. The researcher, Linda Chrosniak, found that younger adults performed better than older ones with regard to being able to accurately recall whether certain words were words that they themselves actually had uttered or were words that they only had thought. In addition, she found that the younger subjects performed better than their older counterparts in being able to recall whether it was Person A or Person B who had uttered the words in question. On a more positive note, however, "there was no age deficit when subjects had to discriminate [between] what they [themselves] said from what they heard another person say . . . or when they had to discriminate [between] what they [had] thought from what they [had] heard another person say."[115]

Two other researchers who investigated source memory concluded that there was a positive correlation between older age and deficient performance.[116] They had the subjects first move around an array of common objects, such as toothbrushes and spoons. They next had the subjects watch as the experimenter moved the objects. Finally, they had the subjects imagine moving the objects, without any physical movement actually occurring. The older subjects consistently made more errors than did their younger counterparts:

[E]lderly subjects had difficulty in remembering whether the source of an action was self or other, that is, whether they had performed an action themselves or whether they had watched someone else perform it. They had difficulty in distinguishing between external memory (actions that had been watched) and internal, self-generated ones (actions that had only been imagined). They also had difficulty in distinguishing between descriptions of actions that had never occurred and memories of ones that had occurred, and made more false-alarm errors than the young. The overall pattern of errors exhibited a marked bias toward claiming that actions had been watched when this was not the case.[117]

Another study comparing the performance of 40 men and women whose mean age was 69 with 40 subjects whose mean age was 19.3 also revealed an age-related decline in performance.[118]

Suggestibility

Another area of research has involved the question of whether witnesses are suggestible, for example, whether the accuracy of their recall of events or their recognition of parties involved in those events can be impaired by misleading postevent information received in the interval between witnessing the event and subsequently recalling it. For example, can the overhearing of another eyewitness's differing account of events, or the receipt from a biased police officer of misleading information in the course of an interrogation, alter the first witness's recollection of the events? Here, again, the studies yield mixed results.

Two researchers examined two groups of subjects—one of which was made up of individuals ages 24 to 45 and the other of which consisted of individuals ranging in age from 62 to 82. The two groups watched a video depicting a fight, a chase, and an ensuing abduction. Half of each group then was presented with a written version of the events that accurately recounted the details seen in the video, while the other half of each group received a written version that contained false data. The investigators determined that the elderly witnesses were much more easily misled by the postvideo error-filled written presentation than were their younger counterparts.[119] Moreover, the elderly misled witnesses "were often strongly convinced and highly confident that their mistaken recall of events was correct."[120] While the investigators noted the need to further explore the factors making older people vulnerable to false information, their bottom line conclusion was expressed in their admonition that the incidence of errors, compounded by the confidence of the witnesses that they were correctly reporting events, "should be taken into account when the credibility of elderly witnesses is being assessed in a legal context."[121]

On the other hand, two other investigators found that elderly witnesses were not more suggestible than young adults. In their study three groups—one made up of 52 children with a mean age of 8, another made up of 53 young adults with a mean age of 17, and the third made up of 42 adults with a mean age of 70—were shown a short video. Half of each group were then asked 17 questions about the video, 4 of which contained misleading information. (The other halves of the groups were the control groups.) Next, the subjects were asked 20 questions, and again 4 contained misleading information. The researchers then determined the number of these latter 4 questions as to which the subjects gave responses reflecting the postvideo misinformation that they had been given in the earlier 4 questions, as compared with the responses of the members of the control groups, who had not received any misleading information. The researchers "found that there was no significant difference between misinformed elderly and young adults in the amount of correct or misleading information recalled in response to critical questions."[122]

The foregoing conclusion was echoed by four researchers who conducted another study regarding the matter of suggestibility. They observed that "[d]espite research [by others] showing that aging is associated with some monitoring deficits . . . the effect of misleading suggestions was not greater [in their study] in older participants than in younger adults." Rather, they actually found that while there was no misinformation effect for older subjects, there was one for younger witnesses.[123] They also ventured some suggestions as to the age-related implications of these data for the legal system: "In evaluating the testimony of eyewitnesses, both jurors and law enforcement officials should attend to the possible influence of post-event information; but they do not need to be more concerned with its effect on older witnesses than with its effect on the adult population at large."[124]

Prospective Memory

Prospective memory is defined as "remembering to carry out future planned activities, such as remembering to keep an appointment or to deliver a message."[125] Katie Cherry and Denny LeCompte recently conducted a study of prospective memory and found that "the most conservative conclusion to be drawn is that for older adults of higher educational attainment and verbal intelligence, age may indeed have minimal effects on simple event-based prospective memory tasks."[126] On the other hand, lower ability older adults performed more poorly than did both younger adults and higher ability older adults.[127] In any event, it is unlikely that prospective memory would be involved in the testimony of a litigating party or of a nonparty witness.

Conclusions

Overall, the data are quite mixed as to whether older witnesses are less reliable than their younger adult counterparts.[128] While some studies indicate that ability declines with age, there are other data calling into question the notions that as to recall of events and sources, recognition of people, and suggestibility, the elderly do not perform as well as do young adults. In any event, one must recognize as a general matter that the testimony of elderly witnesses perhaps may be devalued because of unjustified bias: if one's stereotypical view of older people entails the expectation that an older witness likely will be inept,[129] that witness's hesitation in speaking and her stumbles in recollection then will be seen as confirmation of her lack of credibility.[130] Contrarily, similar hesitancy and stumbles by a young witness—a witness who is unaccompanied, so to speak, into the courtroom by a negative stereotype lurking in the shadows— may well not generate any doubts or second guessing as to that individual's lack of trustworthiness.[131]

An Agenda for Action

The empirical work engaged in by social scientists suggests that the capabilities of older witnesses are in some instances equal to those of younger individuals. On the other hand, in some instances younger witnesses perform better than do their older counterparts. The need for more research is clearly apparent.[132] To the extent that there are deficits that can be correlated with advanced age, there is an agenda for action that can respond to this state of affairs:

> [R]esearch is called for on additional techniques that can be used to opti-
> mize the recollections of elderly witnesses and to minimize pitfalls to which
> they are particularly susceptible, such as false positive identifications and
> the effect of misinformation. As such techniques are developed, elderly
> eyewitnesses should be able to demonstrate a high level of reliability and to
> make significant contributions to criminal investigations and trials.[133]

The prescription for more research aside, there already are available some mechanisms for enhancing the reliability and comfort of older witnesses. For example, the accuracy of courtroom identification testimony may be improved with increased lighting of the room. Identification of documents may be improved by transposing them into larger type. It is certainly worth exploring whether the format of questioning may in some instances be relevant to enhancing the accuracy of testimony. In this regard, there is a mode of interrogation pursued by police interrogators that is known as the *cognitive interview.*[134] Presumably, this methodology could be imported into the courtroom and deposition room settings.

The cognitive interview involves several facets: re-creation of the original context in which the event occurred, minimization of background stimuli, the asking of open-ended questions to the end of encouraging the witness's active participation, and encouragement of nonverbal responses.[135] This process has been found to elicit significantly more correct information than the standard interview technique.[136] However, it must be noted that the downside of the cognitive interview follows from the finding that, given the eliciting of more information, this technique appears to generate more errors than the standard interview, even while the accuracy rates (i.e., the proportion of correct responses) are equal for the two approaches.[137] Thus, cognitive interviewing, while a promising technique, requires further study.[138]

6

Lawyers and Clients

Lawyers are now the dominant profession in American society. Where once they were often distrusted and occasionally outlawed, professional attorneys now hold sway from courtroom to boardroom. They affect our destinies from before our birth to long after our death.
—Gerard W. Gawalt, *The New High Priests* (1984)

The more I see of lawyers, the more I despise them. They seem to be natural, born cowards, and on top of that they are God damned idiots.
—Mark Twain, letter to James R. Osgood, Jan. 25, 1876

A lawyer is a . . . public citizen having special responsibility for the quality of *justice.*
—American Bar Association, Preamble: A Lawyer's Responsibilities, *Model Rules of Professional Conduct* (1994)

Introduction

Attorneys are key actors in the American legal system. For good or ill, they advise, they draft documents both simple and complex, they negotiate, and they litigate. But notwithstanding their critical roles, the ramifications of age for what lawyers do and how they do it have gone unaddressed in significant respects.

Insofar as the career courses of lawyers are concerned, we have no hard data as to whether age affects attorneys' performance, or—if it does—how. We know a little about what happens to older attorneys in terms of the decline and termination of their careers, but this knowledge is garnered in the main from newspaper articles and word of mouth, rather than serious study. Correlatively, we know very little about how attorneys adjust (or fail to adjust) to retirement.

At a level of greater subjectivism, we know only a little about attorneys' attitudes and practices as triggered by the ages of the people with whom they come in contact in the course of their professional activities. Educated surmise, however, suggests that inasmuch as the general populace is ageist in varying degrees and in various ways, the same holds true for American lawyers.[1] A possible caveat may apply in the case of the small group of elder law specialists who work primarily or even exclusively with elderly clients.[2] Their career choices likely reflect, and the expertise and experience gained in pursuing those choices likely produce, perspectives different from—and hopefully more accurate than—those of the great run of lawyers who do not engage in this specialized area of practice.[3]

Insofar as the particular forum of the courtroom is concerned, there are some data regarding litigating attorneys' evaluations of the benefits and detriments of older and younger jurors.[4] These data, however, are so undisciplined as to at best rise to the level of no more than anecdote. The litigation context aside, there *is* one complex of issues involving the interaction of attorneys and older people that has received significant attention both from scholars and practitioners in recent years. These issues revolve around the question of client capacity, a concern that not infrequently arises when the client is an elderly man or woman who is seeking legal advice or—perhaps more commonly—when the older individual's family members are seeking direction as to matters involving their older parent, relative, or friend. Is the older man or woman capable of retaining an attorney? Is he or she capable of understanding the attorney's advice? Is she making responsible decisions regarding her finances, her health, and so on? Is the older person even the client, or is the client the older individual's adult child who has accompanied her to the lawyer's office (and who may even be paying the lawyer's bill)? These questions raise both practical and ethical concerns that not all attorneys even recognize, but even if these concerns are perceived they in any event are particularly difficult to resolve. Integral here are ethical standards—discussed below—by which attorneys are required to govern their conduct.[5]

The Demographics of the Legal Profession

Shakespeare's Dick the Butcher—the character who uttered the famous line "The first thing we do, let's kill all the lawyers"—of course would be stunned by a totally alien culture were he somehow to be transported to twenty-first century America.[6] More to the point here, he no doubt would be dismayed to find that not only have the lawyers not all been killed, but instead, they have proliferated enormously! Just in the last 40-plus years (not to even mention the previous 400 during which successive portrayers of Dick the Butcher have plied their thespian talents), their numbers have grown from about 250,000 attorneys in 1960 to 500,000 in 1980 to one million or so in 1999.[7]

Correlatively, as a result of the massive increases in law school matriculants that started in the 1960s and that have continued largely unabated each year since, the average age of attorneys fell very significantly during this period.

Between 1960 and 1980 it dropped from 46 in the former year to 39 in the latter.[8] But now, 20-plus years later, the age profile is going in the other direction: the large cohorts of men and women who entered the legal profession starting in the 1960s have been growing older and will continue to do so (absent the ultimate alternative), and so one readily can foresee the presence on the legal scene of larger and larger numbers of older lawyers in the next several decades, as well as a significantly increasing percentage of older lawyers in the total pool of attorneys.[9] Not surprisingly, and by way of example, it was recently reported that between 1991 and 2001 there was a 17 percent increase in the number of lawyers 45 years and older in California, so that as of the latter year 52 percent of the state's 174,000 attorneys fell into this age group. Breaking these numbers down, one finds that the percentage of California attorneys ages 45 through 54 increased in the 10-year period from 21 percent to 28 percent and the percentage of those 55 and older increased from 14 percent to 24 percent.[10] These trends will continue to generate bigger and bigger numbers for older lawyers, not only in California but nationally as well, as the green attorneys of the 1970s, 1980s, and 1990s become the gray-haired attorneys of the twenty-first century's teens, 2020s, and 2030s.

Lawyers and Their Career Paths

For the solo practitioner as well as lawyers in small firms—firms, let us say, with two to 10 or so attorneys—retirement is typically a matter of choice. In such settings there is unlikely to be any formal retirement policy forcing her unwilling departure; rather, when the aging lawyer is ready to throw in the towel, so to speak, she will be free to do so (provided she has the financial wherewithal to survive.) If she chooses to continue practicing, she likewise will be free to do so. But theoretical freedom aside, the fact is that as an attorney grows older, so do her long-standing clients—the ones with whom or which she forged relationships when she was an eager young lawyer working 80 hours a week to build up a successful practice. And so by the time our hypothetical solo or small firm attorney—an attorney whose practice typically will be made up of personal service types of activities like drafting wills and handling condominium closings, rather than mergers and acquisitions involving large corporations—turns 60 or 65, chances are quite good that her client base will have pretty much disappeared or at least dissipated. Long-term clients will have died or moved to other parts of the country, or simply will have no need for legal services. Potential new clients will go to younger attorneys who they know by reason of family or social connections.

As the aging lawyer's client base wanes, so too her professional activities will diminish in scope and in frequency. The end of her career, then, likely will come gradually and undramatically, rather than as the culmination of a frenzied rush to close a glut of client files: the (by-now) proverbial whimper rather than a bang, in other words.

In big firms older lawyers are likely to confront more abrupt changes in status. Many firms have formal age-triggered mandatory retirement policies.[11] Even for those that do not, few firms will tolerate the continuing support of aging attorneys with diminishing income-producing potential. In the "old days," so nostalgic recounting of elderly lawyers goes, a lawyer in a big firm stayed on even as his income-generating capacity declined and his work product diminished. A loyal, hard-working, productive attorney when he was in his 30s, 40s, and 50s, he was respected and retained in his later, less productive years—sometimes as a partner, sometimes in the honorific status of "of counsel." Today, however, the law firm world is more rapacious; the dominating factor in the large law firm world is the financial bottom line. A lawyer who does not produce a profit does not last.[12] The prevailing ethos appears to be "what have you done for us today and what will you do for us tomorrow?" Yesterday is irrelevant.

This emphasis on economics does not necessarily mandate condemnation. Partners in big firms generally are very handsomely rewarded financially; if they cannot generate income sufficient to cover their partnership draws and the expenses associated with their presence in the firm (office, secretary, etc.), their continuing presence is financially problematic. Given the costs of expensive offices, support personnel, and in-house libraries, as well as partnership income, there may be little choice in the view of the firm (or at least in the views of the younger firm heavyweights who do not want to reduce their own incomes so as to be able to distribute the extra dollars gained thereby to their older colleagues) but to allow financial pragmatism to win out over loyalty and deference based on past contributions.[13]

What makes this sketchy analysis of law firm economics pertinent here are the rapidly growing numbers of older attorneys. They make increasingly urgent the need of law firms to address their status. In those large firms that are facing an oversupply of older attorneys who are short of the retirement age and so cannot summarily be removed from the scene, one answer may be to lower the mandatory retirement age. Alternatively, one might conjecture that the firms' responses will be to reduce the numbers of young associates annually hired, and/or to elevate to the ranks of partners very few of those young lawyers who are hired as associates. Thereby, the older attorneys will be able to stay on rather than having to make room—both physically and financially—for younger lawyers. Such conjecture, however, is not realistic, because in actuality young lawyers are the lifeblood of big firms. They are the men and women who grind out long hours of work, which then can be billed to clients at high rates, with the resultant fees being used to fund the high incomes of the firm's partners. If fewer associates are hired, there will be fewer hours to be billed out. And if too few of the associates who are hired make partner, the key incentives, that is, money and status, for their staying on and tolerating the stress and deprivations imposed by grinding workloads will be weakened.[14] In the long run, then, both reductions in new hires and/or the unwillingness to elevate significant numbers of senior associates to partnership status will work to a firm's detriment.

Accordingly, as a pragmatic matter there is little flexibility at the young end of the big firm's employee complement for accommodating financial constraints. Rather, it is the long-tenured, and therefore older, highly paid partners who—unless they are "rainmakers," that is, attorneys with major income-generating clients—increasingly will find themselves marginalized, demoted, and forced into involuntary retirement.[15] In sum, then, older big firm attorneys can expect to be squeezed out, bought out, or "de-equitized" in their early 60s and even in their middle and late 50s.[16] And older attorneys seeking new positions are hardly likely to land partnerships with big firms, save for those lawyers who carry a heavy "book," that is, a retinue of financially lucrative clients that they can bring with them to the new firm.[17]

The changed demographic profiles that already are developing in law firms as a result of this scenario, with an emphasis on youth and a pronounced absence of older lawyers, have been graphically confirmed by Professor Marc Galanter:

> Increasingly, large-firm practice has become a younger person's game. A 1999 survey of 34 Chicago firms, ranging in size from 31 to 371 lawyers, found only 17.1% were over fifty years of age (compared to over 30% of the lawyer population of Illinois). In the 28 firms with more than 50 lawyers, 16.8% of the lawyers were over fifty; in the eight smaller firms, 21.9% of the lawyers were over fifty. This pattern is confirmed in a comprehensive picture of American law firms in 1995, derived from the American Bar Foundation's 1995 Lawyer Statistical Report. In firms of more than 50 lawyers, the median age of associates was thirty and the median age of partners was only forty-three. Only 13% of the partners in these firms were fifty-five or older and only 3% were over sixty-five. There is an inverse relationship between the size of firms and the presence of older partners. . . . "[A]lmost a quarter of partners in two-person firms are over fifty-five, but the percentage declines regularly with firm size, so that in firms of over 100 lawyers, just over an eighth are over fifty-five.[18]

Just what graying attorneys do with their time, once their lives as practicing lawyers end, is unclear. Given good luck or wisdom, or both, they may have saved enough and invested well enough to survive financially without any severe diminution in life style. (Maybe, in fact, the best places to undertake a study of big firm and even small firm lawyers are the golf courses of Florida, Arizona, and California.) But even for the financially secure retiree (and many may not be so lucky, after all, to fit this description), the likely loss of status, the undesired free time, and the possible flatness of lives devoid of work are negatives that financial comfort may not assuage.

Lawyers' Subjective Values and Feelings

Values

One of the most (perhaps *the* most) comprehensive studies of lawyers was undertaken some years ago by Professors John Heinz and Edward Laumann, who focused on members of the Chicago bar, 777 randomly selected members of whom were personally interviewed.[19] Of this total, 31.4 percent were under age 35; 28.2 percent were ages 35 to 45; and 31.3 percent were ages 46 to 64. The remainder, 9.1 per cent, were over age 65. The matter of age clearly was not a significant concern of the investigators, but there were some data developed that entailed the age factor.

In a chapter addressing the social values of attorneys, the authors sought to determine whether there was a correlation between the area of practice engaged in by a given individual and his or her value system.[20] In particular, they looked to two values—"economic liberalism" and "civil libertarianism." The researchers sought to measure the degree of correlation between an attorney's values, as manifested through his or her positions on these issue areas, and his or her area of practice. In so doing, they specifically addressed the variable of the respondents' ages because it is known, they asserted, that lawyers' positions on both economic and civil liberties issues vary significantly with age and income.[21] They wanted to see whether the values of the lawyers they surveyed "corresponded to the nature of their fields of practice even among the youngest lawyers, who will usually have practiced in the fields for the shortest periods of time, or whether the correspondence between field and values is greater among the older lawyers, who have usually been at it longer."[22] These data would afford insight as to whether (1) the correspondence between values and field of practice was a function of preconceived value positions that influenced the decision to enter a particular field, or (2) whether a lawyer's personal values might be attributable to adaptation to the field of law that he or she had pursued, or (3) whether the values/field of practice correlations were a function of both pre-entry notions and postentry adaptation.

Professors Heinz and Laumann identified four areas of practice—antitrust defense, securities, patents, and probate—as fields that are associated with conservative positions on the economic liberalism scale. They identified three other fields as being reflective of civil libertarian values: criminal defense, civil rights, and labor union work. They concluded that while younger attorneys both in the four conservative fields and the three liberal fields initially either were very close or relatively close in terms of their values to attorneys of the same age group who were employed in other fields of law, a divergence from the views of lawyers practicing in other fields increased steadily with age. Moreover, an internal divergence within both groups developed over time: "the older groups are consistently more conservative [than the younger groups] on both values scales."[23]

Several conclusions followed from the researchers' findings. For one, older attorneys, as just noted, were deemed to be more conservative in terms of their social values than younger attorneys. This conclusion was hardly surprising, given that older people in general regularly are found to be more conservative than younger people, according to Professors Laumann and Heinz.[24] Second, to the extent that there was a variance among attorneys as between "conservatives" and "liberals," this divergence was not a function of age. Rather, as Professors Heinz and Laumann explained, much of the variance was attributable to lawyers' early socialization experiences, that is, the values derived from their families, their prelaw experiences, etc. Third, to the extent that these early experiences did not explain value variances, "lawyers' positions on economic and civil libertarian issues appear[ed] to be determined in substantial measure by the kinds of law they practice[d] and by the kinds of client[s] they serve[d]."[25]

Lawyer's Feelings About What They Do

How lawyers feel about what they do is a matter of dispute. It has been correctly noted that "[b]oth the popular and the professional press have been full of stories about burnout, career abandonment, and general despair in the bar."[26] And yet, in a survey of Chicago attorneys 84 percent of the respondents reported either that they were very satisfied or satisfied with their jobs, only 5 percent stated that they were dissatisfied, and a minimal 1.6 percent reported that they were very dissatisfied.[27] The remainder—10 percent—were neutral on the issue.[28] These data are consistent with other research regarding job satisfaction generally: "most employed persons, in all professions and in all types of positions, are satisfied with their careers."[29] More to the point here, "[o]lder workers [not lawyers, specifically] consistently report greater job satisfaction than younger workers."[30]

While these Chicago data are interesting as a possible basis for gaining some insight into the mind set of older attorneys, closer analysis suggests that they are only minimally useful. Of the 675 practicing attorneys who were interviewed by the researchers, only 3 percent were over age 65, while another 27 percent were between the ages of 46 and 65. In other words, 70 percent of the respondents were age 45 and younger. Very few individuals—only 20 or so—were 65 or older and therefore what would generally be termed *elderly*. Moreover, even as to the 46 to 65 age group it is quite possible that the majority, or at least a significant minority, of those were at the lower end of that age distribution. Thus, any generalizations about older attorneys regarding the matter of job satisfaction must be ventured in very guarded fashion. While it can be gleaned from the Chicago study that none of the survey subjects who were 56 or older reported being dissatisfied with their jobs, "[n]o doubt this [figure] is, in at least in part, a self-selection effect," as the authors noted.[31] In other words, "[l]awyers who continue to practice to the age of fifty-six or beyond are likely to have been reasonably happy with their lot."[32]

The Treatment of Older Attorneys in the Courts

The Matter of Respect

In an extensive study of the District of Columbia federal courts, the survey teams inquired into the question of whether gender made a difference, or was perceived as making a difference, in interactions between and among court actors, that is, judges, attorneys, witnesses, etc.[33] The results established that the respondents believed that women attorneys were treated less well by judges than were male attorneys. For example, in focus group discussions women attorneys asserted that they were more likely to be subjected to interruptions by judges, or to be ignored by judges or other attorneys, than were male attorneys. And in a written survey of 2,700 male and female attorneys, these assertions were confirmed. Of the responding women lawyers, 25 percent "reported that they had 'often' or 'sometimes' observed judges in the courts of the D.C. Circuit cut off argument or examination by female counsel, while allowing male counsel more time and leeway."[34] In contrast, "[o]nly 4% of male respondents 'sometimes' or 'often' observed judges cutting off female counsel more than male counsel."[35]

An effort was made to determine whether the differing responses of male and female survey subjects were a function of age, rather than gender. The conclusion was in the negative: age was deemed to not be a significant element in the equation. Even when age did affect a respondent's answer, the age factor did not eliminate the effect of gender.[36] "[T]he differences between the responses of men and women . . . [could not] be explained by the fact that women attorney respondents are on the whole younger than the male attorney respondents."[37] In other words, age did "not account for the disparity between men and women attorneys' reports of differences in treatment."[38]

The Matter of Physical Appearance

There is almost universal agreement in the United States that perceptions of physical attractiveness and youthfulness are positively correlated.[39] There is no reason to think that older attorneys somehow are able to escape the onus of this consensus. While there apparently is nothing in the literature concerning the matter of attorneys' ages per se insofar as this factor affects their ability to persuade and to succeed, there *is* a body of data—mixed in its import—generally concerning physical attractiveness and its social significance.

One experiment was aimed at discerning the effect of physical attractiveness of communicators on their ability to effectuate opinion changes in their audiences. The findings established "quite strongly that communicator attractiveness enhances persuasion," but the other side of the coin was the fact that "there were no differences in subjects' ratings of source credibility, i.e., attractive and unattractive communicators were judged equally credible."[40]

Still, additional studies show that a person's physical attractiveness is associated by the observer with a number of positive attributes: "We assume that a physically attractive person has a more pleasant personality, is more successful in his occupation, has a better marriage, and is more intelligent, friendly, competent, and warm."[41] Accordingly, "the physically attractive attorney or witness will probably have an advantage in terms of being liked by jurors, ratings of competence, attributions of success and adjustment, and other positive attributions."[42] What might be assumed to be the in-court (as well as out-of-court) advantage of the physically attractive attorney is undercut, however, by further findings that "attractive sources also must possess expertise and provide supporting arguments in order to persuade an audience."[43] Moreover, there is a "wise old man" stereotype that can come into play in certain situations:[44] the older attorney may be seen as bringing to the legal arena an aura of expertise and wisdom that counterbalances the negatives generated by his wrinkles and bald pate.

Obviously, more study is needed before any definitive conclusions can be drawn.

Older Lawyers and Their Treatment of Fellow Lawyers

Considerable attention has been addressed in recent years to the questions of whether gender and/or race biases exist in the courts and, if so, how such biases are manifested, how severe they are, who the culprits are, etc.[45] Most of these studies have not touched on the age issue; this is understandable, given their avowed concerns with racism and sexism. However, in a couple of instances fleeting reference has been made to older lawyers being perceived by survey interviewees as lecherous.[46] There also is mention of observations made both

by younger male attorneys and by women attorneys of sexist comments being uttered and sexist attitudes being manifested by older lawyers: negative
comments concerning women lawyers' competence and assertions as to their
proper place being in the home.[47] These anecdotal references ought not to be
ignored, but they hardly support any global—or even narrow—generalization
that older lawyers are, as a group, properly to be denominated as either male
chauvinists or sexist bigots. Indeed, noting these references to older lawyers
probably accords such characterizations much more exposure than is de-
served. The only reason why mention is made is because so little data of any
kind are available about older attorneys' attitudes and conduct in relation to
other lawyers that any information is noteworthy just by virtue of its very
existence.

Lawyers and Their Competence as Professionals

The standard biased view of older men and women is that they are on the
decline, both physically and intellectually. There is some truth that undergirds
this image, in the sense that there is a statistical correlation between advancing
age and the increased likelihood of physical ills, as well as possible memory
impairment and dementia. Even so, most oldsters are intellectually and physically fit, and so—like many generalizations—the stereotype of decrepit oldsters reaches much too far.

Insofar as the performance capabilities of older attorneys are concerned,
there are to some degree competing images of older attorneys (aside from the
foregoing general stereotype that is applied to almost all older people, no
matter what they do). On the one hand, there is the caricature of the obfuscat-
ing, but sly, elderly lawyer who lives in the past, glorifies doctrine and values
of bygone days, and generally serves to stymie the forces of progress. By way
of example, one can conjure up the image of the over-the-hill William Jennings
Bryan, the lawyer representing the state of Tennessee in the famous *Scopes
"Monkey"* trial, which involved a state law barring the teaching of evolution
in the public schools.[48] That imagery is reinvigorated from time to time by
latter-day productions of the popular play based on the trial—*Inherit the
Wind*[49]—and by television airings of the movie of the same title. In like vein, in
law school classrooms across the country students regularly learn in their constitutional law classes of the "nine old men" who sat on the Supreme Court in
the 1930s and thwarted Franklin Delano Roosevelt and his New Deal Congress in their efforts to pull the country out of the Depression with innovative
legislation and policies that offended the hidebound, doctrinaire justices
whose outmoded economic and political values had been fashioned in the
laissez-faire era of the nineteenth century.[50]

The counterimage is that of the wise senior lawyer *qua* statesman: for example, Clark Clifford—a powerful Washington, D.C., presence in the 1970s, 1980s, and early 1990s (who ultimately fell from grace)[51]; Robert Strauss, a Washington heavyweight from the days of President Lyndon Johnson on through George H. W. Bush's presidency[52]; and Lloyd Cutler, a counselor to Democratic leaders, in particular Presidents Carter and Clinton.[53] It is invariably men of this ilk who are called upon at times of political gridlock or turmoil to right errant policies and to curb newly minted White Houses aides' inept efforts to force their bosses' political agendas down the throats of resistant senators and representatives.

Legal and Ethical Concerns

Attorneys are expected—indeed, required—to be professionally competent. Failure to provide competent representation can result in a lawyer being subjected to discipline by the regulatory body that governs attorneys in his or her state. This discipline may range from a mild slap on the wrist to the Draconian punishment of disbarment. Moreover, an attorney who fails to adequately represent a client, or who improperly takes advantage of a client, also may be subject to suit in the courts for malpractice and as a result he or she may be subject to the imposition of damages for the harm caused to the client. Some sense of the various strictures under which attorneys must operate is useful, then, as a means to gain a general appreciation of how missteps by lawyers can occur, and how they perhaps can be averted or at least mitigated. We then can turn to the case most of concern here: the potentially or actually impaired attorney who insists on continuing to practice past his intellectual prime.

The Model Code of Professional Responsibility was promulgated in 1969 by the American Bar Association (ABA). While the ABA has no law-making authority, the Code—which consists of various Canons, Ethical Considerations, and Disciplinary Rules—was adopted by a number of states either by means of statutory enactment or by promulgation of rules by state supreme courts. In 1983, however, the ABA replaced the Code with the Model Rules of Professional Conduct, which is a regulatory scheme consisting of both rules and comments regarding the rules. Most state legislatures or state court systems subsequently adopted these Model Rules as standards to govern attorney conduct,[54] and these rules thus have the force of law in their respective jurisdictions. Some states have adopted regulatory codes that rely in part on both the Model Code and the Model Rules.[55] California has rejected both and has formulated its own regulatory standards.[56]

Typically, a court-allied agency will serve as the enforcement body. In Illinois, for example, the relevant regulatory body is the Attorney Registration and Disciplinary Commission.[57]

The Model Code requires that "A Lawyer Should Represent a Client Competently."[58] There is little by way of exposition, however, as to just what this involves. The Disciplinary Rules that accompany the Code simply direct that an attorney should not handle a matter for which he or she lacks competence or is unprepared, nor should a lawyer neglect a client's case.[59] In a very similar vein, Rule 1.1 of the Model Rules reads, "A lawyer should provide competent representation to a client," and this rule further asserts, "Competent representation requires the legal knowledge, skill, thoroughness and preparation reasonably necessary for the representation."[60] While it is debatable whether this verbiage has much utility,[61] there are in any event Comments accompanying Rule 1.1 that do provide some general guidance, although at bottom the determination of whether an attorney performed competently in a given situation is going to very much be keyed to the particular facts.

Apart from the constraints and requirements imposed on lawyers by the Model Code and the Model Rules, lawyers also are subject to the inherent authority of judges to police the conduct of the attorneys who appear before them. A lawyer who acts inappropriately or ineptly in the courtroom can be criticized, chastised, removed, and/or held in contempt (which can involve a fine and/or incarceration) by the judge.[62] Sometimes there will be explicit regulatory or statutory language speaking to the matter of judicial control over the courtroom and those operating in it. For example, the Canons of Judicial Conduct of the State of Virginia provide as follows: "A judge should be patient, dignified, and courteous to litigants, jurors, witnesses, lawyers, and others with whom he deals in his official capacity, and should require similar conduct of lawyers, and his staff, court officials, and others subject to his direction and control."[63]

Occasionally, local governance codes directly address the matter of ageist conduct by attorneys. For example, Canon 3, Section B(6), of the 1990 Wyoming Code of Judicial Conduct speaks to this matter: "A judge shall require lawyers in proceedings before the judge to refrain from manifesting, by words or conduct, bias or prejudice based upon race, sex, religion, national origin, disability, age, sexual orientation or socioeconomic status, against parties, witnesses, counsel or others."[64] In like vein, the rules governing attorneys in Illinois bar discrimination on the bases of "disability, age, sexual orientation or socioeconomic status."[65]

The Impaired Attorney

Model Rule of Professional Conduct 1.16 specifically prohibits an attorney from undertaking to represent, or from continuing to represent, a client if the attorney's mental impairment materially impairs his or her ability to provide competent representation. Rules notwithstanding, there are going to be attorneys who choose to continue practicing even as their abilities to perform in a professionally competent manner become problematic. Most typically, the cause for this decline will be some sort of substance abuse,[66] but some of the adverse aspects of the aging process also can be a cause of impaired performance. How aging attorneys with declining abilities are dealt with is a little studied and seldom addressed matter, at least insofar as any published literature is concerned. Indeed, in a response issued in early 1998 by an American Bar Association official to an inquiry, it was noted that "[t]here were no ethics opinions located on the subject of what a lawyer should do when he suspects that another lawyer in his firm may have a disability due to illness, age or drug addiction that may affect the lawyer's ability to practice law."[67]

State rules governing attorneys are directly relevant here.[68] For example, the Illinois Supreme Court has created the Attorney Registration and Disciplinary Commission, which includes within its structure what is known as an inquiry board. This board can initiate action to remove from the practice of law an attorney who by reason of age-related (or other) disability is deemed unfit to practice:

> If the Inquiry Board has reason to believe that an attorney admitted to practice in . . . [Illinois] is incapacitated from continuing to practice law by reason of mental infirmity . . . , the . . . [head of the agency] shall file a petition with the Hearing Board [another component of the Commission] requesting a hearing to determine whether the attorney is incapacitated and should be transferred to disability inactive status pending the removal of the disability, or be permitted to continue to practice law [albeit] subject to conditions imposed by the court.[69]

If a final determination is made that the attorney indeed is disabled, either she will be transferred to inactive status and thereby will be barred from practicing law, or she will be permitted to continue practicing, but subject to conditions imposed by the court.[70]

Of course, before a regulatory body can take action, it must be made aware of the attorney's problematic status. In some instances the failing lawyer will simply retire, but in the case of the individual who denies, or is unaware of, his compromised competence, a voluntary departure from the ranks of practicing attorneys is hardly likely to occur. He certainly is very unlikely to bring to the attention of the state regulatory body his possible or actual incapacity. In such circumstance, that body unfortunately either is going to remain ignorant of the problem, or—more hopefully—is going to have to learn of it through some third party: a family member, a client, a judge before whom the attorney has appeared, fellow attorneys, or others.

No doubt the reporting of an attorney's possible incompetence is going to be an emotionally difficult step for a family member to take; it can be distressing as well for others who realize that the allegedly impaired lawyer's career is very dear to him. The result may be to temporize rather than to report the lawyer's possible ineptitude. While the family member or friend or even a client has no legal or formal ethical obligation to report his or her concern and so as a legal matter may shirk doing so, fellow attorneys face a more complicated situation: for them, ethical strictures may apply.

Actually, the problems occasioned for attorneys by their having to deal with an impaired lawyer come in three forms. First, there can be the question of determining what, if any, obligation exists for members of a law firm or lawyers in a corporate law department or other legal setting who have reason to believe that a colleague is mentally impaired and thus may not be able to perform in a manner consistent with the rules of professional conduct. Second, there is the issue of an attorney's duty, if any, to inform a local regulatory body and/or the client or prospective client when she knows that a colleague has— apparently because of an impairment—actually failed to represent a client in a manner consistent with the rules. And third, there is the matter of identifying the obligations, if any, of lawyers in a firm or other institutional setting when an impaired colleague leaves that setting but intends to continue practicing law.

The Lawyer's Obligation to Prevent Ethical Missteps by an Impaired Colleague

Rule 5.1(a) of the Model Rules requires that partners in a firm, as well as attorneys with comparable management authority in corporate legal departments and other settings, make "reasonable efforts" to establish internal policies and procedures aimed at achieving "reasonable assurance" that all the attorneys in the institution fulfill the Model Rules' requirements. In 2003 the American Bar Association's Standing Committee on Ethics and Professional Responsibility issued a formal opinion addressing the application of this language to the situation presented by an impaired attorney. The opinion sets forth the following admonitions:

> The firm's paramount obligation is to take steps to protect the interests of its clients. The first step may be to confront the impaired lawyer with the facts of his impairment and insist upon steps to assure that clients are represented appropriately notwithstanding the lawyer's impairment. Other steps may include forcefully urging the impaired lawyer to accept assistance to prevent future violations or limiting the ability of the impaired lawyer to handle legal matters or deal with clients. [Ultimately,] [i]f reasonable efforts have been made . . . , neither the partners in the firm nor the lawyer with direct supervisory authority are responsible for the impaired

lawyer's violations of the rules unless they knew of the conduct at a time when its consequences could have been avoided or mitigated and failed to take reasonable remedial action.[71]

The Situation Where a Violation of the Rules Already Has Occurred

The missteps of an impaired attorney may be subject to required disclosure by her firm or her supervising attorney. The Model Rules require that violations that raise a substantial question as to the alleged wrongdoer's honesty, trust-worthiness, or fitness as an attorney are subject to mandatory reporting.[72] Unfortunately, these standards really afford no guidance as to what constitutes a "substantial question," or how the lines separating honesty from dishonesty, or trustworthiness from lack of trustworthiness, are to be drawn. Moreover, there are caveats even when dishonesty can be discerned, according to the earlier-noted ABA formal opinion issued in 2003. For example, if the firm can avert further failings by means of close supervision of the impaired attorney, no reporting is required. (On the other hand, the opinion went on to assert that if "a lawyer's mental impairment renders the lawyer unable to represent clients competently, diligently, and otherwise as required by the Model Rules and he nevertheless continues to practice, partners in the firm or the supervisory lawyer must report . . . [the] violation.")[73] If the matter in which the ethical violation occurred is still pending, the firm cannot simply remove the impaired attorney and designate a new lawyer to handle the matter. The firm may have to discuss the issue with the client, according to the ABA formal opinion. Ultimately, even if the matter is no longer pending, the firm may have to take steps to mitigate any adverse consequences of the violation.

Obligations That Exist with Regard to an Impaired Attorney Who Has Left or Will Be Leaving the Firm

In 1998 the Pennsylvania Bar Association's Committee on Legal Ethics and Professional Responsibility addressed an inquiry that had been directed to it by a law firm seeking clarification as to its responsibility in the instance of an elderly attorney who was soon going to leave the firm, and who planned to maintain a solo practice despite his former partners advising him that his health problems—in particular his short-term memory loss—limited his ability to provide competent representation.[74] The firm wanted to know whether it could send a brief letter to the firm's clients—whom the retiring attorney planned on contacting—announcing the lawyer's impending retirement and asserting that in the judgment of the remaining partners it would not be in the best interests of existing clients or future ones that they be represented by the attorney in question.

The ethics committee responded in the negative. It interpreted the proposed letter as constituting a solicitation of clients by the firm, whereby the firm was effectively saying, "Stay with us." This contravened the ethical rule barring solicitation.[75] Moreover, the committee noted that there were opinions of other bar associations confirming that when a lawyer leaves a firm, the firm cannot communicate in any but neutral terms to clients about that departure. Thus, according to these opinions, a firm cannot offer subjective opinions as to the quality of service that the departing lawyer purportedly will provide, as opposed to the quality of service that it, that is, the firm, will provide.

The bottom line, then, in the view of the Pennsylvania Bar Committee was that the firm could not communicate with clients and potential clients regarding the departing partner. It could, however, contact the appropriate professional regulatory authority regarding the firm members' concerns that the attorney in question might commit unethical acts, albeit inadvertently. It would then be up to that authority to pursue the matter in its discretion.[76]

Two years later, the Philadelphia Bar Association's Professional Guidance Committee was asked to address a similar issue: how should a lawyer deal with the perceived age-related professional incompetence of another attorney? This matter arose when a two-lawyer firm dissolved after one of the two partners had several strokes that left him with a permanent reading disability and memory impairment. The disabled attorney's former partner learned that his former colleague intended to continue practicing without informing his clients of his disabilities. The healthy partner was told by the committee that there was no ethical requirement that he inform his former colleague's past or potential clients of the man's problems.[77] But the committee did not state that there was an ethical bar to the healthy lawyer's so doing—a position that *was* articulated in the Pennsylvania State Bar Association opinion.

In 2003 the American Bar Association's Standing Committee on Ethics and Professional Responsibility issued a formal opinion focusing on this problem, and this takes precedence (albeit not of any legally binding sort) over the earlier Pennsylvania and Philadelphia opinions in jurisdictions outside that state. The ABA opinion in some respects falls short, however, of providing clear-cut guidance. The committee wrote:

> While Rule 1.4 [of the Model Rules of Professional Conduct] requires the firm to advise existing clients of the facts surrounding the withdrawal to the extent disclosure is reasonably necessary for those clients to make an informed decision about the selection of counsel[,] . . . the firm must be careful to limit any statements made to ones for which there is a reasonable factual foundation.[78]

The problem with the foregoing formulation is that absent certainty on the firm's part that the departed lawyer indeed is intellectually impaired, it would seem that the requirement that the firm have a "reasonable factual founda-tion" for its communication would lead it to err in the direction of cautious silence.

The ABA opinion does unequivocally state that "[t]he firm has no obliga-tion . . . to inform former clients who already have shifted their relationship to the departed lawyer that it believes the . . . lawyer is impaired."[79] As for com-munications to the appropriate disciplinary authority, no such obligation ex-ists if the impairment has not resulted in a violation of the Model Rules. How-ever, as noted earlier, Rule 5.1 does impose an obligation to take reasonable steps to prevent violations of the Model Rules by impaired attorneys if the firm's management or a direct supervisor of the impaired attorney is aware of the risk of a violation arising from the impairment. Moreover, while no obliga-tion to report exists, the ABA opinion asserts that "[s]ubject to the prohibition against disclosure of information protected by Rule 1.6, . . . partners in the firm may voluntarily report to the appropriate authority its concern that the withdrawing lawyer will not be able to function without the ongoing supervi-sion and support the firm has been providing."[80]

Attorneys and Their Interactions with Older Clients, Witnesses, Etc.

The overarching issue in considering the relationship of attorneys to older clients is the tension between the ideal of client autonomy and the paternalistic (sometimes even manipulative) attitudes the attorney may bring to the table when dealing with an older client, particularly one as to whom the usual ste-reotypes regarding intellectual decline are applied. On the one hand, the attor-ney is regarded as the client's servant, if you will. Her duty is to represent the client in accordance with the client's wishes and to seek for the client the ends—damages, injunctive relief, the renewal of suspended benefits, the allo-cation of assets in accordance with a document drafted by the lawyer, etc.—that the client identifies as his desired goals.[81] In serving the client, the attorney is to act "with reasonable diligence and promptness"[82] and with undivided loyalty,[83] as long as she is not called upon to violate the law.[84]

On the other hand, there may be an inclination on the lawyer's part to substitute her own judgment for that of the client. This inclination typically is not born of sinister motives, but more likely is the product of solicitude for the client. The lawyer wants what she deems to be best for him and so she is tempted to substitute her own judgment as to the client's best interests for the client's own judgment because she perceives him as being unable—by reason of his age, physical frailty, and/or perhaps impaired intellectual acuity—to make the good decisions that she, the lawyer, *can* make.

Both concern for autonomy and paternalistic concern for the client's welfare will be in play in many lawyer-client relationships, but they will particularly come to the fore in those relationships that involve elderly clients.[85] The difficult pragmatic task for the attorney (as well as for the client, although the client is less likely to be aware of the subtleties involved in the relationship) is to make sure that neither of these concerns does violence to the other.

Much of the literature that addresses the roles of attorneys vis-à-vis older people starts with the perception of the elderly as raising special difficulties as to the lawyer's honoring the autonomy principle. In particular, extensive attention has been directed to the question of capacity.[86] Is the client capable of retaining an attorney? Is he or she capable of understanding the attorney's explanations and advice? Is the client capable of executing enforceable documents? Who, for that matter, is the client: is it the possibly disabled oldster, or the family member who brings the elderly mom or dad to the lawyer's office and who may even be paying the lawyer's bill?

Unfortunately, the emphasis in the legal literature on such questions can seriously mislead. The fact is that capacity generally is *not* an issue, no matter whether a client is old or young. Like the young, most older people are fully able to manage their affairs and to make decisions. These are the clients, however, one hardly ever reads about in the legal literature because these perfectly capable older individuals simply do not raise intellectually provocative (and therefore journal-worthy) capacity issues or concerns needful of special attention. Unfortunately, the intensive emphasis on the problems presented by older clients helps to create the impression that such problems are the norm. Thereby, the stereotype of the decrepit, inadequate, declining senior is strikingly, albeit unintentionally, reinforced. This is bad news, and it must be combated. The best way to do that is to keep in mind the normal functioning of most older women and men, even as one focuses on the particularized problems of those older individuals (and some younger ones, as well) as to whom questions concerning capacity and competency may arise.[87]

Lawyers and Stereotyped Approaches to Clients

As suggested earlier, there is no good reason to doubt that many attorneys harbor stereotypical views regarding the elderly.[88] Witness the comments of Seymour Wishman, a prominent criminal attorney, who wrote as follows in 1986: "Older people differ sharply from younger in many of their attitudes about such basic aspects of life as health, personal problems, and death. The old also tend to be more intolerant of political and social non-conformists than the young and more inclined toward favoring tougher law enforcement."[89] Particularly distinctive perspectives also were uttered by famed attorney Clarence Darrow, who offered the following advice regarding jury selection:

"Never take a German; they are bullheaded. Rarely take a Swede; they are stubborn. Always take an Irishman or a Jew; they are the easiest to move to emotional sympathy. Old men are generally more charitable and kindly disposed than young men; they have seen more of the world and understand it."[90]

One cannot know whether the two eminent attorneys just quoted would have understood their characterizations as embodying stereotypes. No matter, however. A number of insightful attorneys—most particularly those who focus their professional efforts on providing representation to older clients—have recognized the possibility of ageist bias on the part of lawyers. Writing in a journal directed to elder law attorneys, one such specialist cautioned against falling back on stereotypes in the context of representing someone whose capacity is in question:

> Just because a client is elderly or frail doesn't mean that he/she is mentally impaired. Attitudes toward the elderly can unconsciously obstruct communication with and perception of the client. It may result in a general perception that the elderly can't make their own decisions or explain their own problems. Also, it is just as easy to stereotype older people out of benevolence as out of prejudice.
>
> Begin with a presumption of capacity, recognize diversity in the older population, confront your attitudes toward the elderly, listen to the client, not just the family, understand the aging process and be patient.[91]

Still another very astute elder law expert, Peter Margulies, wrote in a similar vein: "It is easy to think of elderly clients as persons who are *not* citizens—whose wishes do not really count."[92] And an even more emphatic confirmation of the existence of biased perceptions entertained by lawyers was voiced in a thoughtful article by another attorney experienced in representing older men and women. Robert Rubinson identified "the idea of decrement"[93] as a pernicious notion infecting the attitudes of all of us, lawyers and nonlawyers, in dealing with the elderly,[94] and certainly as an idea that comes into play in the attorney-client relationship: "The influence of the idea of decrement highlights mental decline as the 'obvious' explanation for the behavior of an elderly client. Thus, lawyers often will assume that elderly clients have experienced declining competence, and attorneys often will seemingly—but mistakenly—find what they are looking for."[95]

It is hardly surprising, then, that "when counseling an elderly client, lawyers often assume that idiosyncratic decisions are the result of incompetence,"[96] when in fact these decisions may simply reflect the fact that the client is, by virtue of personality and choice, idiosyncratic. In other words, when she was 40 the client's nonconformity was applauded as an expression of her originality; now that she is 75 that same originality is seen as evidence of senility![97]

Adjusting to and for the Physical and Psychological Needs of the Older Client

General Concerns

Notwithstanding the foregoing insistence on avoiding the error of viewing older people generally as necessarily being compromised either physically, intellectually, or both, it is true, after all, that disabilities do tend to increase with age.[98] It has been noted, for example, that "retired people are roughly six times more likely to be hearing impaired than the population as a whole."[99] (However, cutting against this statistic, which seems to reinforce the stereotype of hard-of-hearing oldsters as constantly saying things like "What did you say?" is the further statistic that only one of five retired people is hearing impaired.)[100] Vision deficits also are common among the elderly: it has been reported (albeit without citation) that "[t]hree- quarters of older women and one-half of all older men experience moderate to severe vision difficulties."[101] And of course there are problems with intellectual acuity that, while rare among the young-old and the mid-old, do become more common among those at advanced ages, that is, people 85 and older.[102]

It follows that the attorney dealing with an elderly client should be sensitive to her client's possible (but not inevitable) frailties and accordingly should take steps to ameliorate their impact in her dealings with the client.[103] To this end, it has been urged by two elder law experts that "written materials and type used on exhibits [shown to older witnesses] . . . be plain and big," and that witnesses "should be given documents to read in a place without excessive glare."[104] The same authors, in addressing the needs of hearing-impaired older witnesses, admonish that "[w]hen talking . . . [the attorney] should establish eye contact before speaking; not stand in front of a light source . . . ; speak expressively (using gestures, facial expressions, and body movements); and use short and simple sentences."[105] Matters seemingly as prosaic as the shape and configuration of office furniture have elicited comment, as well:

> Office furniture can pose problems. The older or disabled person may be unable to arise from the deep, cushy waiting room couch. Chairs with arms to help lift oneself and straight chairs that are high enough for comfortable seating are easy answers. . . . Seating arrangements and lighting within the lawyer's office must be examined to ensure that the client can see the attorney's facial expressions and clearly hear what is said.[106]

Attorneys also must be cognizant of the psychological orientations and vulnerabilities of some elderly clients, litigants, and witnesses. (Unfortunately, but perhaps unavoidably, this focus brings to the fore the very stereotypes that militate against the fair portrayal—and sometimes the fair treatment, as well—

of older men and women in America.) It has been suggested that "[a]s people age, they tend to withdraw from social contacts and become restrained and introverted."[107] It further has been suggested that reticence about seeking legal assistance, in the first instance, and about disclosing private matters, in the second, are ways in which this introversion is expressed.[108] The attorney must deal with these issues, the same author advises, by providing support and encouragement to the reluctant, reticent client.[109]

Actually, whether this image of the introverted, reticent older client still holds true, or in any event is going to be on target 10 or 20 years from now, is debatable. For one, the elders of 2010 and beyond are generally going to have higher education levels than those of 1975, when the foregoing admonitions were written, and so they likely are going to feel more comfortable and confident in dealing with attorneys. Second, a general ethos of assertiveness and insistence on fairness that developed in the 1960s and 1970s and that continues today entails standing up for one's rights and even going to court if necessary to do so. People today, in brief, are much more willing to vigorously resist perceived mistreatment and unfairness. There are good reasons, then, for expecting that the conception of the passive, disengaged oldster reluctant to seek legal assistance is going to have much less force in the future.

A second psychological factor in the attorney-client relationship concerns the perception (albeit certainly a questionable one) that older people feel that they have no useful purpose to serve in society and thus lack self-esteem. In compensating for this situation, older clients supposedly tend—so it has been posited—to "strive to retain their participation and social status by taking an active role in affairs, particularly their own."[110] Assuming this perception is a correct one, the attorney should recognize the client's needs in this regard and indeed should work actively to encourage her client to be an active participant in the relationship, rather than the attorney taking on a paternalistic role.[111] (Of course, this should be the lawyer's posture vis-à-vis all clients—young, old, or otherwise.)

Howard Gelt, the proponent of the foregoing encouragement of client involvement, also focused on the matter of stability. He reasoned that "[o]ld people are more vulnerable to the effects of an unstable environment."[112] In this regard, he quoted the following analysis: "'Established patterns of activity and social relations serve a basic, psychologic function by helping the individual obtain a sense of his own identity and worth. Such matters are, so to speak, the prop which supports the self.'"[113] The importance of stability to the older man or woman has at least two consequences for the attorney who is advising the elderly client as to alternative ways of going about addressing the client's legal problem: "[First,] a less disruptive course might be preferable even though it is less productive in strictly economic terms. Second, . . . the need to involve clients in decision making is heightened when some significant change in their situation may occur as a result of their legal problems."[114]

The Question of Capacity

It is important to stress that older people in most essential respects are like the rest of us; they just happen to have more years to record on their résumés. Most of the legal problems that arise for older individuals are going to be the same as those that are of concern to their younger peers. The kid who continually crosses through his neighbor's backyard when he comes home from school is a trespasser, regardless of whether the victimized homeowner is 35 or 65. The purchaser who buys a defective refrigerator and cannot get satisfaction from the seller has a breach of warranty claim, no matter whether she is 40 or 70. In brief, the commonality of most substantive legal issues across age lines is an important proposition to iterate and reiterate, given the common pernicious temptation to identify the elderly as a breed apart.[115]

Still, it must be conceded that there are some legal issues that are likely to be of special concern to, and of relatively common incidence for, a more than negligible number of older men and women.[116] It is not the purpose of this enterprise to essay analysis of the substantive issues and legal doctrines that arise for lawyers and clients working on such matters (such as devices to achieve the transfers of funds in order to make older people eligible for Medicaid-supported nursing home care). These efforts have been undertaken elsewhere by a number of practicing attorneys, as well as by legal academicians.[117] But there are special problems of an ethical nature that confront attorneys who represent older clients and that require attention for at least two important reasons. First, the ways in which lawyers perceive the trenchancy of these ethical issues and the ways in which they go about addressing them cut across all, or at least most, areas of substantive law. The ethical issues are, in other words, of universal dimension in the legal system. Second, these issues are directly relevant to what are the foci of this book: the impact of age on the participants in the legal process and the age-related or even age-determined ways in which these participants react to each other.[118]

Issues Arising Out of the Question of Capacity. Capacity has been described as "the black hole of legal ethics."[119] An initial problem flows from the fact that there is no entirely satisfactory definition of capacity,[120] although a number have been suggested by different experts. The Uniform Guardianship and Protective Proceedings Act offers the following:

> "'Incapacitated person' means an individual who, for reasons other than age, is unable to receive and evaluate information or make or communicate

decisions to such an extent that the individual lacks the ability to meet essential requirements for physical health, safety, or self-care, even with appropriate technological assistance."[121]

Another formulation is that articulated in 1982 by the President's Commission for the Study of Ethical Problems in Medicine and Biomedical and Behavioral Research: "Decisionmaking capacity requires, to greater or lesser degree: (1) possession of a set of values and goals; (2) the ability to communicate and to understand information; and (3) the ability to reason and to deliberate about one's choices."[122] State laws embody other formulations. For example, in Florida the only factor that is considered is functional impairment: "An incapacitated person is defined as a person who has been judicially determined to lack the capacity to manage at least some of the property or to meet at least some of the essential health and safety requirements of such person. It is not tied to an underlying medical or psychiatric condition."[123]

Unfortunately, none of the definitions provides a road map taking the attorney from carefully devised formulations through the actual determination of whether a client or potential client has the requisite capacity for the task at hand, be that the retaining of the attorney in the first instance, the ability to articulate and to convey to her attorney her needs, or understanding a document drafted by the attorney. Compounding the difficulties for attorneys is the fact that by virtue of their lack of training they are ill-equipped to even essay the effort at ascertaining clients' competency. And the problem is further exacerbated by the fact that capacity may vary from issue to issue, as well as from time to time during a given day or week or month.[124]

And yet, if the attorney errs or shirks her task of taking account of the matter of capacity, she may wind up being party to the drafting and ratification of a document—a will or a trust agreement, let us say—that will not withstand later attack in the courts because the signatory was not competent. Moreover, the attorney even may find herself the subject of a lawsuit as a result of her failure to assess correctly the incapacity of her client, inasmuch as in a number of jurisdictions an attorney who negligently drafts a will can be held liable by the beneficiaries of the will.[125]

Even if the attorney might elude financial liability for her error, she still must deal with and comply with the ethical rules that govern attorneys' conduct in every state. In this regard, there are several possible sources of guidance for attorneys, depending upon the jurisdiction in which the lawyer practices: the Model Code of Professional Responsibility and the Model Rules of Professional Conduct, as well as the American College of Trust & Estate Counsel (ACTEC) Commentaries on the Model Rules of Professional Conduct.[126]

The dominant ethical guidepost today is afforded by the Model Rules, which have been adopted in 38 states and the District of Columbia. Rule 1.14 of the Model Rules directly addresses the disabled client:

(a) When a client's ability to make adequately considered decisions in connection with the representation is impaired, whether because of minority, mental disability or for some other reason, the lawyer shall, as far as reasonably possible, maintain a normal client-lawyer relationship with the client.

(b) When the lawyer reasonably believes that the client has diminished capacity, is at risk of substantial physical, financial or other harm unless action is taken and cannot adequately act in the client's own interest, the lawyer may take reasonably necessary protective action, including consulting with individuals or entities that have the ability to take action to protect the client and, in appropriate cases, seeking the appointment of a guardian ad litem, conservator or guardian.

(c) Information relating to the representation of a client with diminished capacity is protected by Rule 1.6. When taking protective action pursuant to paragraph (b), the lawyer is impliedly authorized under Rule 1.6 to reveal information about the client, but only to the extent reasonably necessary to protect the client's interests.[127]

As is obvious, no definition is provided by Rule 1.14 as to what constitutes incapacity. The Comments to the Rule provide very limited clarification. They acknowledge the complexities, but offer no solutions. Thus, the Comments note that "a client lacking legal competence often has the ability to understand, deliberate upon, and reach conclusions about matters affecting the client's own well-being."[128] Moreover, it is recognized that there are varying degrees of competence, such "that some persons of advanced age can be quite capable of handling routine financial matters while needing special legal protection concerning major transactions."[129]

Assessing Capacity. The Comments accompanying the Model Rules identify a number of factors that the lawyer should take into account in assessing the matter of client capacity:

[T]he lawyer should consider and balance such factors as: the client's ability to articulate reasoning leading to a decision, variability of state of mind and ability to appreciate consequences of a decision; and the consistency of a decision with the known long-term commitments and values of the client. In appropriate circumstances, the lawyer may seek guidance from an appropriate diagnostician.[130]

One approach to which some lawyers subscribe, wittingly or not, in both defining capacity and simultaneously determining whether a given individual possesses such capacity is what has been termed an *outcome test*.[131] This involves assessing whether the client's decision is a substantively correct one. The problem with this approach follows from its conflict with generally accepted current ideas supportive of client autonomy, inasmuch as it calls upon the lawyer to assume a paternalistic role that justifies him in supplanting his judgment for that of the client when he concludes that the client's decision is not, by the attorney's lights, a correct one. Rather than heeding the client's voice and choice, the attorney retains the discretion to override both.

The "status test" entails another approach; here, one "focuses on attributes that . . . [are] view[ed] as negating capacity—age, history of mental illness, or dependence on others."[132] Unfortunately, this approach also creates the risk that the decision maker's choice will be ignored, in this instance on the basis of criteria that may well not negate the correctness of the decision itself.

An approach that goes to the other extreme involves the proposition that mental illness and/or incapacity are social constructs that are used for political purposes of suppression and oppression. Consequently, according to proponents of this view, the notion of incapacity ought to be rejected in any and all circumstances, no matter how outlandish a client's wishes or decisions may be.[133] Application of this approach will be seen by some—indeed, many—as constituting an abdication of the attorney's role, inasmuch as it calls upon her to support decisions that may be hurtful to the client, to others, and/or to society at large.

Still another tack, and one that has been described as being closest to that adopted by the Model Rules,[134] is termed the *functional approach*:

> The approach emphasizes that capacity varies over time and with the decision involved. Rather than relying on supposedly objective testing instruments, the functional approach asks how people cope in their regular environment. For example, instead of asking a senior to name the date, and viewing her as dangerously disoriented if she cannot, the functional view asks whether the senior has a newspaper, magazine, or video source available if she wishes to know the answer to this question.[135]

Like every other proposal, the functional approach does not escape criticism. It focuses on the process of decision making, yet it has been argued that "[s]eparating substance from process in decisions about capacity is both wrong and impossible."[136]

Efforts have been made to formulate definitions that seek to overcome many, if not all, of the foregoing criticisms. One approach involves five steps in a lawyer's assessing the capacity or incapacity of a client or potential client. First, the attorney must obtain the individual's consent to being subjected to screening tests aimed at determining capacity.[137] Second, the attorney is to encourage the individual to undergo a physical examination, inasmuch as in some instances mental impairment is the consequence of correctable physical problems; third, the lawyer may ask the individual to answer a brief mental status questionnaire, of which there are several.[138] Fourth, the attorney should attempt to assess whether the individual has the capacity to understand and make decisions regarding the specific legal task at hand—be it the reviewing and signing of a will, the execution of a power of attorney, or whatever.[139] Finally, the attorney may see fit to seek advice from a medical or mental health expert,[140] although there can be confidentiality issues—and the attorney must be mindful of them—regarding what the attorney may disclose to that professional.

Still another commentator has identified six factors that are relevant in determining capacity: "(1) capability to articulate reasoning behind decision; (2) variability of state of mind; (3) appreciation of consequences of decision; (4) irreversibility of decision; (5) substantive fairness of transaction; and (6) consistency with lifetime commitments."[141]

Assuming the Role of De Facto Guardian. An attorney who deals with a client who is suffering from diminished intellectual capacity is in a very difficult situation if the client does not have a guardian or legal representative. In such circumstance the lawyer may wind up having to act as a de facto guardian—a situation acknowledged by a superseded Comment that formerly accompanied Rule 1.14 of the Model Rules of Professional Conduct.[142] Professor Jan Ellen Rein is one of the most cogent and constructive critics of this scenario. She has noted with particular concern the notion of the attorney acting as a de facto guardian, even while recognizing that there is some merit to the attorney taking on such a role. On the positive side, she has reasoned as follows: "[The de facto guardianship] permits an immediate response to prevent irreparable harm. It avoids the trauma and public humiliation associated with formal guardianship proceedings. It is less intrusive and does not directly pave the way to institutionalization. In a formal sense *de facto* guardianship is less permanent."[143] But the negatives outweigh the positives in Professor Rein's view:

> [T]he major objection is that there is no way to monitor what goes on within the attorney-client relationship [unlike the situation of a court-appointed guardian, who is required to report periodically to the court as to her actions and decisions]. . . . The fear that unmonitored attorneys acting as *de facto* guardians may abuse their trust is well founded. . . . An impaired or feeble client may lack the capacity or energy needed to discharge the lawyer.[144]

In February 2002, Model Rule 1.14 was modified by the House of Delegates of the American Bar Association, and the approval expressed for de facto guardianships was removed from the Comments. Even so, there is language in Comment [5], which accompanies the modified Rule 1.14, that seems to envision a role for the attorney tantamount to that of a guardian,[145] and thus the concerns expressed by Professor Rein (and others) remain valid ones.

Seeking Appointment of a Legal Representative. In the situation where the lawyer believes that a legal representative is needed, yet no such person exists, Model Rule of Professional Conduct 1.14(b) contemplates the attorney seeking the appointment of a guardian *ad litem,* conservator, or guardian.[146] Comment [7] accompanying Rule 1.14 further addresses the matter:

> If a legal representative has not been appointed, the lawyer should consider whether appointment of a guardian ad litem, conservator or guardian is necessary to protect the client's interests. Thus, if a client with diminished capacity has substantial property that should be sold for the client's benefit, effective completion of the transaction may require appointment of a legal representative. . . . In many circumstances, however, appointment of a legal representative may be more expensive or traumatic for the client than circumstances in fact require. Evaluation of such circumstances is a matter entrusted to the professional judgment of the lawyer.[147]

Both Rule 1.14 and Comments [5] and [7] call upon the attorney to make judgments regarding the client's interests, yet the determinations that are to be made are in fact very elusive ones at best, and the process of identifying what is good for the client certainly opens the door to a paternalism that can diminish the autonomy and thereby the personhood of oldsters. Moreover, the Comments further are flawed by virtue of their simply concluding that the evaluation of the various factors at stake becomes a matter of the exercise of professional judgment on the lawyer's part. The lawyer is given few helpful criteria to use and, more than that, the attorney very likely will have no training regarding the psychological detriment for the client that the just-quoted Comment [7] itself recognizes may flow from the appointment of a legal representative.[148]

Another problem involved with an attorney seeking the appointment of a legal representative, that is, a guardian or conservator, for an incapacitated client arises out of the fact that such appointment can only be made by a judge, and in order to persuade the judge to make such an appointment the attorney likely will have to disclose information about the client. Rule 1.14(c), quoted earlier, authorizes such disclosure, subject to protection of the client's interests. Comment [8] seeks to expand upon the matter of protection, even while acknowledging that in fact the "lawyer's position in such cases is an unavoidably difficult one."[149]

Withdrawal from Representation. For the attorney who finds the role of de facto guardian unacceptable (for whatever reason) and who further is unwilling to take on the task of seeking appointment of a guardian for the client, Rule 1.16 of the Model Rules of Professional Conduct (1994) offers another option—withdrawal from representation of the client:

> [E]xcept as stated in paragraph (c), a lawyer may withdraw from representing a client if withdrawal can be accomplished without material adverse effect on the interests of the client, or if: . . .

> (2) a client insists upon pursuing an objective that the lawyer considers repugnant or imprudent; . . .

> (5) the representation will result in an unreasonable financial burden on the lawyer or has been rendered unreasonably difficult by the client; or

> (6) other good cause for withdrawal exists.

The problem with the withdrawal option lies in the very facts giving rise to this possibility. The incapacitated client who is incapable of understanding the attorney, or who is unwilling to take the attorney's advice to heart because of the confusion and even paranoia that sometimes accompany dementia, is the very client who needs representation but is unlikely to have the ability to seek out another attorney. Thus, the lawyer, if she abides by the Rule's requirement that withdrawal not have a material adverse effect on the client, is unlikely to actually be able to withdraw. On the other hand, if one reads Rule 1.16 as allowing withdrawal even if the client's interests *are* adversely affected, one is left with a situation involving a client bereft of the counsel he or she needs.

Conclusions

Given the complexities for attorneys who are involved in representing, or considering taking on the representation of, persons with intellectual deficits, it is no wonder that there is a very large and thoughtful body of literature exploring the issues. There is also no surprise in finding that there are numerous alternative approaches discussed in these articles, without any sure answers emerging.[150]

Identifying Who the Client Is

Former Surgeon General Dr. Everett Koop, movie star Clint Eastwood, Senator Robert Byrd, news anchor Dan Rather, TV newsman Mike Wallace, and a host of other folks who by virtue of their years qualified in 2004 as elderly hardly fit the stereotyped image of dependent or diffident oldsters. And yet there are older people who do find that confronting the needs and sometimes difficulties of day-to-day life leads them to reliance upon their family members—particularly their adult children. Not uncommonly, then, an attorney who has been called upon to provide service to an older woman or man will find that her potential new client is accompanied, when first they meet, by an adult son or daughter (who may or may not be paying the lawyer's fee). Often, in fact, the initial contact with the attorney will have been made at the insistence of the adult child, who wants his mother, let us say, to get her affairs in order. His accompanying her to the attorney's office likewise may be at his own insistence, but it may also be that he is there at his parent's behest: she feels more comfortable with her son present and indeed she chooses to defer to him regarding decisions that the attorney requests be made concerning such matters as the allocation of assets by means of a will or trust, the sale of the elderly parent's house, and so on. Who, then, is the client: the oldster, or her adult offspring, or both?[151]

The need to resolve this question becomes exacerbated when the influential 45-year-old son is urging (or even instructing) his mother to authorize the lawyer to draft a will that divvies up her assets in a way that will benefit the son's children, to the detriment of mom's daughter and the daughter's children. The lawyer knows that the proposed one-sided document will no doubt cause a rupture in relations between the mother and her daughter, should the latter learn of it while her mother is still alive. Who, then, should the lawyer serve: the son who obviously strongly influences his mother, or the compliant mother who does not seem to realize the implications of the proposed will?

The problem obviously is a difficult one to resolve, as lawyers who practice in the field of elder law readily will acknowledge.[152] As an ethical matter, however, the lawyer must avoid being caught up in a conflict of interest,[153] and so he must determine who the client is. Let us hypothesize that the attorney concludes that it is the fragile mother who is the client. The lawyer then must go on to flesh out for her the potential conflicts that can arise by virtue of the son's participation in the lawyer's consultations with the client. Here, again, the situation is rife with complexity:

> Attorneys disagree on the proper course of action. Some may try first to exclude the family member and speak to the client alone. Others may explain the ethical problems in the presence of the family member and have the client sign a waiver of conflict of interest; others may see the "family unit" as the client, while others may refuse to conduct the [initial] interview with the family member present. The Model Rules offer some guidance, but limited practical application in dealing with this kind of situation.[154]

No good answer is apparent. For example, with regard to an effort to speak with the client outside the presence of the controlling son, this may well be easier said than done: "Many older persons are suspicious about or intimidated by consulting an attorney in the first place. If the attorney excludes a person upon whom the client is emotionally or physically dependent, the attorney-client relationship may be put under immediate strain."[155]

Difficulties notwithstanding, the attorney must be clear as to who the client is, and the client must be apprised of the implications of admitting into the relationship a third party. Whether she can appreciate these implications, and whether—even if she can—she has the fortitude to stand up to her son are of course real concerns that are necessarily going to undermine the relevance and utility of discussions in the abstract about identifying the client.

How Older Clients Assess Attorneys

Still another issue that arises in examining the role of age in the attorney-client relationship concerns the views of older clients vis-à-vis lawyers. Information is sorely lacking. However, an unpublished study conducted in the 1980s, sought to ascertain, inter alia, older individuals' attitudes regarding lawyers.[156] The researchers surveyed, by way of questionnaires, men and women who were age 65 and older and who were contacted through four senior citizens community centers in Albuquerque, New Mexico. They received 196 responses from 80 men and 110 women, as well as 6 individuals who did not report their gender.

One of the questions addressed to the survey subjects was the following: "What kinds of things keep you from seeking a lawyer when you might otherwise think you need to see one?" The subjects were provided five specific choices by way of responses, as well as a sixth catch-all "other" response. Lack of trust in lawyers was identified by a not inconsiderable 17 percent of the respondents, and the perception of not being treated with respect by lawyers was selected by 4 percent. On the other hand, 42 percent responded that there was nothing that prevented them from seeing an attorney. The costliness of lawyers elicited a 52 percent response, and the perception that the respondent's problem did not warrant seeing an attorney generated a 25 percent selection rate. Six percent selected the "other" response.

An Agenda for the Present and the Future

As is commonly the case in this multi-chapter effort to plumb the depth and breadth of ageism in the legal system, information is in short supply. We need to know much more, and so there is much work to be done:

(1) We need to know about the lives of lawyers: their career paths, how their careers draw to a close, and what happens to them thereafter.

(2) We need to find out how older lawyers are treated by judges, fellow attorneys, and court personnel.[157]

(3) We need information about the attitudes and beliefs of attorneys, both those who regularly provide representation to elderly clients and those for whom such representation may occur only sporadically. We must try to understand if, and the extent to which, attorneys are swayed by misconceptions, biases, and stereotypes in their dealings with older individuals.

(4) We need to know more about how older attorneys perform, and how regulatory mechanisms work in those instances where questions arise regarding performance.

(5) Information also is needed about the attitudes and beliefs of law students—the lawyers of the future—so that efforts can be mounted in the most obvious setting, that is, the classroom, to ensure that they know truth from fiction and accurate depiction from stereotype, and so that they have some ability to detect their own biases and understand how these biases may influence the ways in which they will deal with future clients.

(6) We need to know how attorneys in practice actually cope with the problem of determining the capacities of their clients, and how attorneys deal with the ambiguities involved in deciding who actually is the client.

Research aside, we do know enough already to justifiably conclude that action—apart from the initiation of intensive research efforts—should not be delayed. A major educational effort is in order and it should be pursued *now,* with refinements added as more data are gathered and more insights obtained. After all, there are operative today misconceptions and biases of which lawyers and law students need to be disabused. There are clients today who need wise and informed representation. And there are lawyers practicing their profession right now who need help. We do not have time to stand by as the first cohorts of 1960s law graduates—people who typically graduated from law school at age 25—enter their 60s in the early years of the twenty-first century. And we need not and should not wait for the massive annual cohorts of baby boomers to start entering their 60s in 2006, with millions more to follow each year, even as their predecessors move on into their 70s, 80s, and 90s in ensuing decades.

The efforts to educate, elucidate, improve, and reform can take a variety of forms, including videos, manuals, continuing legal education seminars, and classroom instruction.[158] These efforts can and should address a variety of matters, including the subtle insidiousness of ageism; the aging process and its effects (or lack thereof) on the capacities (and incapacities) of older individuals; data regarding the potential weaknesses of older witnesses and what steps can be taken to avert and/or ameliorate these weaknesses;[159] mechanisms and methods for enhancing the comfort and confidence of older clients, thereby improving the attorney-client relationship; and training in recognizing, and trying to resolve, the difficult ethical issues raised by the Model Rules of Professional Conduct and other ethical guidelines.

Very simply, better lawyering is dependent on better information, as aptly put by Professor Linda Smith:

> The attorney who represents elderly clients should be knowledgeable about aging and about the actual differences between young and old individuals. This knowledge will help the attorney avoid prejudice against the elderly. It should also, perhaps more importantly, allow the attorney to accommodate for actual differences so as to respect his/her client's individuality and promote his autonomy.[160]

In like vein, it has been observed that "[a] lawyer's understanding (or ignorance) of the aging process, dementia, disability, long-term care, and family relationships informs the way in which ethical dilemmas are conceived and resolved."[161]

There is some reason for optimism that such educational endeavors can succeed.[162] In this regard, analogical insight is afforded by studies supporting the conclusion that while psychologists, as well as both students and practitioners in nursing and medicine, view working with the elderly in a negative light,[163] other studies concerning medical and nursing students suggest that training and exposure can significantly improve attitudes regarding older people[164] and that these changes can be long-lasting.[165]

7

Judges

The judiciary is the nation's premier geriatric profession.
—Judge Richard A. Posner, *Aging and Old Age* (1995)

What of our jurists, our augurs, our philosophers?
Old they may be, but how much they remember!
—Cicero, *On Old Age*

At twenty, stooping round about,
I thought the world a miserable place,
Truth a trick, faith a doubt,
Little beauty, less grace.
Now at sixty what I see,
Although the world is worse by far
Stops my heart in ecstasy,
God, the wonders that there are!
—Archibald MacLeish, *With Age, Wisdom*

Juries occupy a very special place in the American psyche: they are seen by many as constituting the core of what an ideal system of citizen-based justice should embody. In fact, however, most disputes actually are resolved long before lawsuits are ever filed, let alone actually litigated.[1] And of those rare grievances that ultimately get to a courtroom and survive various technical motions, very few in any event are resolved by juries; rather, the vast majority are addressed in bench trials, that is, trials conducted by a judge without a jury.[2]

In either scenario—jury or bench trial—it is the judge who is master of the courtroom. In jury cases she controls the empaneling of the jurors. She educates the jury members as to what their duties are. She is the arbiter of what the jurors hear. At the close of the trial she instructs the jury members as to the legal precepts that are to guide their deliberations in the privacy of the jury room. Even after the jurors have finished their work, the judge retains the authority to reject jury verdicts under some circumstances if she concludes that the jurors went too far astray.[3] In conducting bench trials, the judge has even more determinative control. She not only presides over the trial proceedings; she also decides the parties' fates.

Clearly, any analysis of the impact of age in the American legal system must address a number of issues concerning judges—these 18,000+ enormously important participants in the legal system.[4] How well do older judges perform? Does age play a role in their value systems? Does the age of the judge influence how she or he responds to litigants, witnesses, and attorneys? Do the ages of the litigants, witnesses, and attorneys affect how judges respond to them?

How Well Do Older Judges Perform?

Typically, and consistent with the generally negative notions regarding older people that pervade American society,[5] there is a perception—or at least a suspicion—that older judges are less likely than their younger counterparts to be mentally alert and intellectually astute. Moreover, there is a tendency—in part borne out by historical experience—to assume that older judges are out of touch with current social, political, and economic values. In this latter regard, the premier example of course is that of the elderly Supreme Court justices who in the 1930s made up a majority that appeared to oppose key New Deal legislation[6]—an opposition generally attributed to these justices' commitments to outmoded economic and political values forged in the nineteenth century.[7]

Does the age of a judge in fact matter (without regard to the ages of the litigants, attorneys, or other parties in a given proceeding) as to how he or she performs the job of judging? The very asking of the question reveals a critical problem: inasmuch as judges are reactive actors, responding to argumentation made by lawyers, to testimony offered by witnesses, to questions asked by jurors, and so on, it is very difficult to assess judicial performance in isolation. And so, if the age of the individual who prompts a given judicial response matters for the way in which that response is fashioned (and apparently it sometimes does), it is a flawed exercise to address the judge's performance in isolation without taking into account the ages of the litigants, witnesses, attorneys, etc. Even so, the task is not impossible, although the data are sparse.[8]

Analyzing judicial decision making pure and simple, irrespective of the ages of any party to whom a judge might be responding, Judge Richard A. Posner, who sits on the Court of Appeals for the Seventh Circuit (on which he served as chief judge for seven years), ventured a cautious conclusion. "[T]here is an age-related decline in judicial performance, but . . . it does not set in until a relatively very advanced age."[9] He further narrowed his position by asserting that of the four elements that in his view make for outstanding judicial quality– "analytic power," "legal learning," "general culture," and "the ability to write graceful and powerful English"—only the first is "likely to decline with age."[10] Judge Posner used what is by his own admission a flawed gauge to assess the quality of judicial performance: the average number of judicial citations by other judges to a given judge's opinions. He reviewed published majority opinions of federal court of appeals judges who had been appointed between 1955 and 1984 and who were still on the bench in 1993. His conclusion was that age played very little role as to the quality of judicial performance, at least insofar as citations were the measure of quality.[11] Looking to the somewhat different matter of productivity, Russell Smyth and Mita Bhattacharya analyzed the work of the Federal Court of Australia, which is an intermediate appellate court that primarily adjudicates civil matters. Based on their study of judicial citations, they concluded—in an article published in 2003—that judicial productivity peaks when judges are in their late 60s or early 70s.[12] Somewhat by way of contrast, Smyth and Bhattacharya earlier had reported that the productivity of judges sitting on Australia's highest court peaked at age 63 or 64.[13] In explaining the difference between their findings regarding the judges of the two courts, the analysts suggested that "[t]o the extent that intellectual deterioration is responsible for a decline in productivity with aging, the earlier peak in productivity in the High Court might reflect the fact that most of the legal issues to be resolved in the High Court are more complex and intellectually more demanding than those in the Federal Court."[14]

While both Judge Posner's endeavor and the studies of the Australian researchers afford some useful information, the fact is that at most they look to a very narrow group: appellate court judges. Most judges sit on trial courts, not appellate courts, and most of these trial court judges only occasionally, if ever, write opinions. Rather, they typically are engaged in making oral rulings from the bench on lawyers' various motions, objections, and requests. Thus, analyzing judicial performance on the basis of written work product at best offers only minimally pertinent information regarding the work and abilities of the great majority of judges in America.

One might also try to rate judges in terms of the rectitude of their rulings. The task, however, of defining what is the "right" result typically will be a particularly unproductive one, as well as a venture so malleable and so susceptible to subjective evaluations that it would be valueless at best and abusive at the worst.[15] Most likely, any conclusion would reflect in good measure no more than the biases of the observers, inasmuch as there rarely is any absolute benchmark of correctness external to a ruling by which to evaluate the decision.[16] Matters such as demeanor in the courtroom, treatment of witnesses, and expressions of respect or disrespect for attorneys may be relevant factors to consider in determining whether there is an age effect that is operative in the context of judicial performance, but these factors, too, can be difficult to assess objectively.[17]

In sum, rating judicial performance is an exceedingly dicey enterprise. Assessing how a particular factor, such as age, affects that performance makes the effort an even more difficult enterprise.

Data Regarding Judges' Ages and Their Responses to Issues and Parties

In some instances the age factor is injected into judicial proceedings by virtue of statutory directive. For example, some criminal offenses are defined in terms of the age of the perpetrator or the victim or both: that is, statutes defining unlawful sexual acts can turn on the ages of the persons involved.[18] A battery may be designated as "aggravated" if the perpetrator knew that the victim was age 60 or older.[19] In the civil context a considerable number of state statutes have focused on age as a criterion to consider in guardianship proceedings, although statutory language to this effect is less common than it was 20 or 30 years ago.[20]

When a legislature or other authoritative body has spoken, judicial acquiescence must follow unless there is some overriding basis, such as a conflicting constitutional provision or a factual distinction, that justifies or even compels taking a different tack. Accordingly, if a statutory directive is in play that entails age, reliance by the judge upon that particular age factor cannot be seen as indicative of ageist bias on the judge's part. If there are no express statutory directives, questions concerning possible bias do come to the fore if age appears to be a part of the judge's decision making repertoire. Judicial attitudes can be revealed both by what judges say and by what they do. Of course, there is much room for subjective interpretation: gauging a judge's attitude toward an issue or a person is a problematic enterprise, and the effort may tell us more about the person assessing the judge than about the judge herself. One must approach with some caution, then, the results of studies concerning bias in the courts, of which there have been a number in recent years.[21] Moreover, insofar as the particular matter of age bias is concerned, at best these studies only offer some hints as to what might exist, inasmuch as they have focused on race, gender, and/or ethnicity issues and not directly on the matter of age.

In any event, one finds that racial, ethnic, and gender bias on the part of judges has been reported by some of those surveyed. For example, in a study of the federal courts of the First Circuit[22], "[a]pproximately one-third (33.8%) of female [court] employees . . . reported gender bias by judges who were not their supervisors," and, "[o]ver twenty percent (22.9%) of the female respondents and 11.1% of male [employee] respondents reported gender bias by judges who were their supervisors."[23] With regard to attorneys practicing in the First Circuit federal courts, of those who reported a negative experience with a judge, 21.9 percent attributed that experience to gender bias.[24] Very few, however, attributed their negative experience to racial or ethnic bias. As for other court users, that is, litigants, witnesses, relatives of litigants, courtroom observers, members of the press, paralegals, messengers, and victims, "[t]he two most frequently reported experiences, reported by over 30% of the respondents, were *opinions or views were not taken seriously,* and *treated in a rude manner* [31.3%]."[25] With regard to the first category, 15.9 percent of the respondents reported that the mistreatment occurred at the hands of a judge; as for the second category, 11.4 percent of the respondents reported rude treatment by a judge.[26] More aggressive, albeit less impressively documented, instances of racism on the part of judges in other courts also have been recorded.[27]

What the studies establish is that judicial bias—even bias based on those factors, that is, race, gender, and ethnicity, which command the broadest degree of general societal condemnation—exists or is perceived to exist by people entering the court system in the roles of employees, attorneys, and other users of the system. It does not take much of a logical leap to reasonably conjecture that ageism likely also is manifested by judges. Indeed, given the only negligible social opprobrium engendered by age-based and age-biased comments and conduct, it is reasonable to conjecture that instances of victimization likely are more common than is the case when gender or race or ethnicity are involved. Still, at best one can only so surmise; the data at this point have not been gathered or, for that matter, even sought out.

The Relation between Age and Judicial Resolution of Substantive Issues

Sheldon Goldman, a dominant figure in studies of the American court system, has examined the performance of judges on the federal courts of appeals and has found statistically significant correlations between judges' ages and their treatment of a number of issues: "Older judges simply tended to be more conservative on the criminal procedures, civil liberties, labor, injured persons, political liberalism, economic liberalism, and activism dimensions [that he constructed for a study of 2,115 nonunanimous decisions rendered from fiscal year 1965 through fiscal year 1971]."[28] On the other hand, "[t]here were no . . . statistically significant correlations with the private economic and the government fiscal categories [of his issue-defined matrix]."[29]

Goldman sought through regression analysis to determine the importance that a number of variables had in accounting for variations from the mean. The variables were political party, age, religion, prior candidacy for political office, prior judicial experience, years of service on the court of appeals, and prosecutorial experience. He found that age was the single most important variable for decisions concerning civil liberties claims. Age also was important in explaining the variance from the mean in cases involving criminal procedures, personal injuries, and political liberalism. In fact, "[a]mong the seven background variables tested for association with [judicial] voting behavior, [political] party [affiliation] and age emerged as the most important," and thus Goldman concluded that, "party and age seemed to have some limited importance in explaining the variance in judicial behavior."[30]

In another study of federal court judges, the researchers undertook to examine how litigants fared in the federal courts in trying to establish the necessary (and difficult to prove) element of intent in cases arising under the Fourteenth Amendment's Equal Protection Clause.[31] The investigators endeavored to determine whether the personal characteristics of a judge might play a role in the outcomes of district court cases. They concluded that "older judges . . . treat intent cases more favorably than . . . [do other] judges."[32]

Still another study also confirmed some relationship between judges' ages and the nature of their performance (as opposed to the rectitude of their decisions). Involving the work product of five California trial court judges who ranged in age from 34 to 51, the data revealed that the judges' verbal and nonverbal behaviors—some of which were praiseworthy and some not—were related to their ages:

> [F]or this sample of 34 trials and for this sample of five judges, older as compared to younger judges tended to be rated in the normal condition as relatively warmer, more open-minded, more dominant, more dogmatic, and wiser, but less honest, more hostile, and more anxious in delivering the jury instructions.
>
> Interestingly, although raters tended to perceive older judges as warmer, more open- minded, more dominant, more competent, more dogmatic, and wiser than younger judges in the content-present conditions . . . , older judges were rated as substantially less professional, less open-minded, less competent, less dogmatic, less wise, more hostile, and more anxious than younger judges in the purely nonverbal (content-absent) conditions. . . .
>
> This pattern of results suggests that while older judges may appear to jurors as "judicially competent," they may be perceived as substantially less judicially competent, compared to younger judges, in the purely nonverbal channels.[33]

There is only a little more by way of available information or observation: one student of the judicial process—writing in the context of a very impressive article—observed that "[t]he strength of an individual's [i.e., judge's] moral sense of what is right or wrong is largely determined by the individual's *age,* education, experiences, religion, cultural background, and emotions."[34] This assertion, however, was only supported by one citation.

Anecdotal Data Regarding Judicial Attitudes

At the anecdotal level, the following explication of a Los Angeles trial court judge's views vis-à-vis jurors suggests that there is much work to be done (if one engages in the reasonable assumption that this judge was not unique), both in assessing the nature and significance of judicial attitudes and in addressing the matter of stereotyping:

> Mental age is more important than chronological age.
>
> Physical faculties, memory, and attentiveness tend to diminish with age.
>
> Older jurors generally are more tolerant of human frailty and more sympathetic to the injured than younger jurors. However, they tend to be conservative as to damages. They tend to have more respect for authority and more prejudices than younger jurors. They are inclined to be prejudiced against single persons and the young (except young children), and to identify with other elderly persons.
>
> Among the elderly, those who have led successful (success can be in terms other than money), full lives are open-minded. Those with a narrow background and who are set in their ways are conservative and less sympathetic than others.
>
> Young jurors tend to be tough-minded and unsympathetic to pain and suffering, yet more generous when satisfied as to the existence of real disability. They are optimistic about rehabilitation. They are inclined to be prejudiced against wealthy people, authority figures, and executives. Ordinarily, they are not very influential.
>
> The young tend to be rash, unforgiving, and impulsive. It is not unusual for them to have difficulty in refraining until the end of the case from forming an opinion.[35]

Some further unsubstantiated generalizations were put forth at just about the same time by a Texas state court judge:

> Age often can be a critical factor in accepting or rejecting a juror. Young people, though they sometimes are inclined to see things in black and white, tend to have had less time to acquire fixed ideas. They are, accordingly, more susceptible to [the] presentation of new ideas and information in court than their elders. In personal injury cases, young people, believing, in all probability, that they are immortal, may not identify with the injured party. The very old may envy the younger plaintiff receiving a large settlement. Both groups are thus potential defense jurors in personal injury cases. The ideal plaintiff's juror is probably a middle-aged individual who carefully and cautiously takes his or her seat, sits stiffly without leaning back, and then rises very gingerly—sure signs of a chronic bad back.[36]

Another judge, while ostensibly ascribing ageist attitudes to lawyers, seemed to reveal his own stereotypical thinking by virtue of the following observations:

Lawyers would prefer to keep "little old ladies of either sex" off of their juries, according to Gordon Gray, judge of the criminal district court of Tarrant County, Texas. "There was a little old lady on one of my juries who, when polled, said she really hadn't decided guilt or innocence but just wanted to go along with whatever the other jury members wanted," Gray said. "And there was the little old lady on another jury—the jury reported that it had voted eight, three, and one. Eight for guilty and three for innocent and one for the little old lady. So I asked her what was her vote. 'Me? I voted undecided,' she said."[37]

Age-Correlated Responses to Litigants

Juries convict; judges sentence. In a study published in 2000, Darrell Steffensmeier and Mark Motivans examined statewide data from Pennsylvania for the years 1990–94 to determine whether older offenders received more lenient treatment in terms of sentencing than did their younger counterparts and whether such treatment, if it existed, was manifested as to both male and female offenders.[38] Their data base consisted of 175,000 cases, over 8,000 of which involved defendants ages 50 and older. The researchers found that older age did make a difference for both men and women (although less so for the latter):[39]

On average, the probability of defendants in their 60s being incarcerated is about 25% less than defendants in the 21–29-year-old group; and, if incarcerated, the older defendants received incarceration sentences on average 8 months shorter. The differences are even larger for defendants in their 70s—they were about 30% less likely to be incarcerated than 21–29-year-olds and received prison terms about 13 months shorter.[40]

(Steffensmeier and Motivans also found that offenders ages 18–20 were the beneficiaries of more lenient sentencing than were their counterparts ages 21–49, but they did not focus their attention on this group.)[41]

In seeking to explain why, in the first instance, older offenders were treated more leniently than younger ones and why, in the second instance, the differential in treatment was more pronounced for older men than for older women, Steffensmeier and Motivans offered several suggestions.[42] With regard to the general matter of leniency for older offenders, they reasoned that there were differing societal, and therefore judicial, expectations concerning older and younger offenders in terms of their posing threats to society:

Aging tends to soften attributions such as danger, unconventionality, and commitment to "street life" that contribute to harsher sentencing of younger defendants. The decline in physical prowess and pugnacity with advanced age leads to the expectation that older persons are less aggressive and less able to use force in threatening or harming others.[43]

The recidivism factor also played a role: "Judges (and other court officials) may . . . perceive older offenders as less likely to recidivate"; in addition, "[t]he behavior of older offenders is more likely to be seen as idiosyncratic—that is, explained away as the result of forces outside of their control (e.g., extreme environmental circumstances, problems with health associated with advanced age)."[44] There also was the possibility that "older offenders, from experience, may be more able to convince the judge of a more lenient sentence by showing remorse or reform."[45] Still other factors that Steffensmeier and Motivans conjectured might have played a role in the judges' sentencing decisions were the physical and psychological stress imposed on older individuals by imprisonment; the greater impact of lost years on older men and women than on younger persons;[46] and the financial costs imposed on the prison system by individuals who likely would need special attention, diets, and health care.[47]

As for the male-female disparity, Steffensmeier and Motivans reasoned that younger males were regarded as much more dangerous than older males, but the difference in propensity for violence as between younger and older females was much less. Accordingly, the sentencing leniency attributable to the age factor played a more significant role for older men than it did for older women.

A 1981 study also revealed that judges showed more leniency toward younger defendants and those over age 60 than they did toward middle-aged offenders.[48] A 1993 study, however, failed to find an independent relationship between the age of the defendant and the magnitude of his or her sentence.[49] Even so, in this later study, which entailed the review of three magistrates who presided in 52 trials over a 20-week period in the Johnson County, Iowa, Magistrate Court, the investigator, Peter David Blanck, found that "judges' expectations for guilt [were] . . . stronger for older defendants, while judges' expectations for a finding of not guilty tend[ed] to be more prevalent for younger defendants."[50] He further noted that "no other defendant background variables related to judges' expectations for trial outcomes."[51]

Another study that was conducted in 1980 reviewed the work of 121 Florida County Court judges who presided over nontraffic criminal cases.[52] The 97 judges who responded sat on courts in all sorts of counties—rural, suburban, and urban. They ranged in age from 29 to 70, with 1–34 years of experience on the bench. The researchers, Gary Feinberg and Dinesh Khosla, reported the responses of the judges to a number of statements and questions. First, the judges were asked to react to the assertion that the elderly are not accorded enough respect in our society. Fifty-seven percent agreed, 22 percent disagreed, and 21 percent were neutral. There was no correlation between the judges' ages and their answers. On the basis of these responses, as well as those made to two other statements,[53] the researchers rated the judges in terms of their level of sympathy toward the elderly. Fifty-five percent of the judges were rated affirmatively, 22 percent were deemed "distinctly unsympathetic," and 20 percent were considered neutral. Again, the ages of the judges were not considered relevant to their positions, nor was their length of judicial experience.[54]

Asked whether elderly misdemeanants should be accorded special consideration, 38 percent of the judges responded in the affirmative. Neither older nor more experienced judges were more receptive than their younger and/or less experienced colleagues. However, judges who had agreed that the elderly had paid their dues and ought to be looked after by society were "significantly more likely to believe in according special consideration to elderly misdemeanants."[55] With regard to the sanctions imposed on elderly shoplifters, there were some differences that did correlate with the age of the judge:

> Young judges . . . are twice as likely as older ones to require community service work (57 percent to 26 percent). Similarly, they are more inclined than older judges to use counseling (20 percent to 12 percent). Older judges use probation and economic sanctions more frequently. Incarceration is likely to be used about equally by either age group, whereas pretrial intervention is much more common with young judges.[56]

In terms of more general conclusions, Feinberg and Khosla suggested that there was no agreement as to any single sanction being appropriate for elderly perpetrators of minor crimes, but there was an observable rejection by judges—those both young and old, experienced and inexperienced—of "the more clearly rehabilitative sanctions of counseling and pretrial intervention in favor of the somewhat more retributive sanctions of fines and probation."[57]

There also is "evidence that judges may be more lenient in sentencing physically attractive criminal defendants."[58] Inasmuch as in American culture there is some correlation between perceived physical attractiveness and age,[59] these studies have relevance here.

Apart from their uttering explicit statements of a biased nature—something that presumably intelligent and discreet judges are usually astute enough to avoid doing and, in any event, something that typically will elude public attention unless the utterance is repeated in a written opinion by the judge in question—judges may indicate their biases through nonverbal cues: smiles, looks of disbelief, etc. One of the leading researchers on judicial conduct, Peter David Blanck, has focused on bias that is revealed subtly by nonverbal means. As earlier discussed, Blanck, Rosenthal, and Cordell studied five California trial court judges ranging in age from 34 to 51. The researchers constructed an empirical design for assessing the incidence and impact of nonverbal judicial behavior, and they then videotaped the judges as they delivered final jury instructions in 34 trials to 331 jurors, who ranged in age from 19 to 81, with the average age being 42. The researchers employed 80 individuals to rate the videotapes and audiotapes of the judges in terms of different verbal and nonverbal dimensions, which were denominated as "content-present," meaning involving normal speech cues, and "content-absent," which entailed tone of voice. Blank and his coauthors found that what they termed the background characteristics of the jurors related to, and perhaps influenced, judges' expectations for trial outcomes: "This sample of judges showed a tendency to expect that the verdict *should be* guilty on count 1 in trials with more educated jurors, and a tendency to expect that the verdict *should be* guilty on count 2 with relatively younger jurors."[60]

Conclusions

Judges react to plaintiffs, defendants, witnesses, and even jurors. Anyone who has litigated knows that judges react, as well, to attorneys. Jurors in turn take cues and guidance from judges. So do lawyers. While the data are sparse, there is no reason to believe that judges are different from other human beings. And so it is reasonable to conclude that the age factor is at play in all this. But is the age factor such that it adulterates the legitimacy of the judicial process? In other words, does intrusion of age into the scenario negatively and unduly distort the directions judges give and the decisions they are called upon to make?

The easy scenario to resolve entails blatant prejudice. A judge who avers that all criminal defendants under age 24 are recidivists and thus should without exception receive the longest sentences possible arguably thereby would be utilizing an unconstitutional irrebuttable presumption.[61] She also likely would be transgressing statutes and/or ethical guidelines governing judicial performance, discussed below. Likewise, a judge who demonstrates irrefutable partiality in employment discrimination cases—civil rather than criminal—for plaintiffs who are over age 60 likewise does violence to her proper role as an arbiter, again in violation of judicial ethical strictures.

While the foregoing situations lend themselves to easy evaluation, life typically is much more complicated. Age bias, in particular, is diffuse and thus difficult to detect. Moreover, and in any event, perhaps the truth is that age concerns, reflective as they are of general views held by the public, are appropriate elements in the constellation of permissible judicial poses, attitudes, statements, and rulings. Certainly from the perspective of those who are benefited, age bias is a judicial trait to be encouraged rather than deplored. For example, judicial leniency toward older criminal offenders no doubt is applauded by defendants and defense attorneys. A judge who has a cynical view of corporate decision making and thus generally is reluctant to grant defendants' motions for summary judgment in cases arising under the federal Age Discrimination in Employment Act of 1967, as amended (ADEA),[62] because the grant of such motions deprives plaintiffs of their opportunity to go to trial on their claims, is both a boon to plaintiffs as well as a counterweight to what arguably is a federal judiciary unduly oriented in favor of defendants.[63]

In sum, one readily can condemn the racist judge. The ageist judge—assuming, albeit without documentation, that she exists—poses a more problematic case. Ultimately, one has to take a leap of faith, so to speak. On balance, that leap is best made in the direction of limiting to the extent feasible the role of ageist bias—no matter which way that bias cuts—in the judicial enterprise. If some oldsters in ADEA cases presided over by sympathetic judges thereby lose a litigation edge, that is the necessary price to be paid in the course of protecting other older ADEA plaintiffs who are on the wrong side of judges' negative biases against older workers. If some older offenders were to receive longer sentences than they otherwise would under an age-biased sentencing regime because their judges were to be barred or dissuaded from exercising the age-influenced lenity that the studies indicate now prevails, that is the price to be paid for insulating other offenders from conversely receiving undeserved severe sentences imposed by judges with age biases that lead to detrimental consequences for age-defined offenders.

Let me hasten to stress that the present-day beneficiaries of positive age bias would not be converted into some sort of sacrificial lambs by this stance. If the offense and background of an offender who happens to be young warrant a stiff sentence, so be it. If the crime and situation of an offender who happens to be older warrant leniency, fine. The point here is that age per se should not be used as the rationale for that sentence.[64] Rather, the judge should rule based on the age-independent facts of the case and not on the basis of age in isolation.[65] Admittedly, age may strongly correlate with the age-independent facts. For example, statistical data support the view—noted earlier—that older men convicted of crimes (other than sex crimes) have a lower recidivism rate and are less prone to violence than men in their teens and 20s. Thus, one might say that reliance by a sentencing judge on the criterion of "low recidivism potential" is nothing more than the use of a proxy for age. Still, by focusing on the recidivism data and not on age per se, one helps to sanitize the process and thereby to avert misuses of age in other sentencing situations. In sum, the fact that a decision-making criterion correlates with age does not condemn use of that criterion.

So how to get from here to there? Arguably one way to deal with age bias in the courts is to focus on the composition of the judiciary—the 18,000+ men and women who sit as judges throughout the country. Another useful effort is to focus on ethical and statutory constraints on bias in the courtroom. Finally, there is the matter of education, because the best offense for combating age bias is knowledge.

Controlling the Demographics and Quality of the Judiciary

State Court Judges and Mandatory Retirement

Notwithstanding the lack of decent objective evidence, numerous states have utilized negative assumptions about older judges in adopting constitutional provisions or enacting statutes that bar judicial service beyond some specified age, the result being both to force the retirement of elderly judges and to bar the election or appointment to the judiciary of individuals past the statutorily set age.[66] These statutes generated several legal challenges in the 1970s and 1980s, but the large majority of state and lower federal courts that addressed these laws upheld them, both in cases involving claims of elected state court judges and in those brought by individuals who held office by virtue of appointment by a governor or some other appointing agency.[67] Several of the cases[68] involved unavailing invocation of the ADEA, which bans discrimination in the workplace as to individuals over age 39, subject to a number of exceptions.[69] A large number involved unsuccessful reliance upon the Fourteenth Amendment's Equal Protection Clause.[70]

Any possibility of a change in the pro-retirement posture of the lower courts was laid to rest by the U.S. Supreme Court in *Gregory v. Ashcroft*,[71] in which the Court addressed a mandatory retirement provision contained in the Missouri constitution that required judges to retire at age 70. The judges in *Gregory* who sought relief initially had been appointed by the governor; subsequently, each won a retention election. Insofar as the ADEA was concerned, the Court rested its ruling on technical grounds: absent a "plain statement"[72] by Congress that it had actually addressed and resolved the issue of whether the federal Act should supplant state authority, the Court would not conclude that in enacting the ADEA Congress had intended to intrude upon the state's prerogative, as expressed in its constitution, to regulate who could exercise government authority. No such plain statement making the ADEA applicable to age restrictions vis-à-vis judges was seen, and so the Court rejected the plaintiffs' challenge.

The *Gregory* Court also rejected the grievants' equal protection claim. In so doing it turned from the federalism concerns regarding federal-state relations that animated its ADEA discussion and focused on the substantive merits of a mandatory retirement requirement for judges. Confirming that minimum rationality analysis is appropriate for age classifications—a position articulated in previous rulings addressing mandatory retirement laws that had been applied to public employees other than judges[73]—the Court deemed the plaintiffs' constitutional argument wanting. In so doing, it approvingly quoted from an earlier state court ruling, *O'Neil v. Baine*,[74] in which the Missouri Supreme Court had upheld a state law imposing a mandatory retirement age of 70 on magistrate and probate judges:

> "The statute draws a line at a certain age which attempts to uphold the high competency for judicial posts and which fulfills a societal demand for the highest caliber of judges in the system"; "the statute . . . draws a legitimate line to avoid the tedious and often perplexing decisions to determine which judges after a certain age are physically and mentally qualified and those who are not"; "mandatory retirement increases the opportunity for qualified persons . . . to share in the judiciary and permits an orderly attrition through retirement"; "such a mandatory retirement provision also assures predictability and ease in establishing and administering judges' pension plans. . . ." Any one of these explanations is sufficient to rebut the claim that "the varying treatment of different groups or persons . . . is so unrelated to the achievement of any combination of legitimate purposes that we can only conclude that the [people's] actions were irrational." [*Vance v.*] *Bradley,* . . . 440 U.S. [93,] at 97 [(1979)].[75]

The *Gregory* Court then went on to state in its own words a number of additional reasons why it deemed the mandatory retirement requirement rational and therefore constitutional:

> The people of Missouri have a legitimate, indeed compelling, interest in maintaining a judiciary fully capable of performing the demanding tasks that judges must perform. It is an unfortunate fact of life that physical and mental capacity sometimes diminish with age. . . . The people may therefore wish to replace some older judges. Voluntary retirement will not always be sufficient. Nor may impeachment—with its public humiliation and elaborate procedural machinery—serve acceptably the goal of a fully functioning judiciary. . . .
>
> The election process may also be inadequate. Whereas the electorate would be expected to discover if their governor or state legislator were not performing adequately and vote that official out of office, the same may not be true of judges. Most voters never observe state judges in action, nor read judicial opinions. State judges also serve longer terms than other public officials, making them—deliberately—less dependent on the will of the people. . . . The people of Missouri rationally could conclude that retention elections—in which state judges run unopposed at relatively long inter-

vals—do not serve as an adequate check on judges whose performance is deficient. Mandatory retirement is a reasonable response to this dilemma.

This is also a rational explanation for the fact that state judges are subject to a mandatory retirement provision, while other state officials—whose performance is subject to greater public scrutiny, and who are subject to more standard elections—are not.[76]

There is no question that minimum rationality analysis such as that used in *Gregory* affords great latitude to lawmakers. Indeed, the Supreme Court's case law demonstrates that this standard of judicial scrutiny is so deferential that it will allow a law to be upheld if any conceivable rational basis for it can be conjured up.[77] And there likewise is no question that expedience, ease, and convenience—factors accorded independent dispositive weight by the *Gregory* Court in the just-quoted passage—are understandably desirable, as well as rational, goals for government to embrace. Nonetheless, mandatory retirement at the same time does violence to a basic notion of fairness by its imposing a burden on older men and women irrespective of their individual merits and abilities to perform. In fact, the *Gregory* Court itself acknowledged that age 70 (or any other age, for that matter) is no marker or predictor of intellectual or physical decline: "It is far from true that all judges suffer significant deterioration in performance at age 70. It is probably not true that most do. It may not be true at all."[78] The bottom line, however, in terms of constitutional analysis is that it is too late in the day to mount a successful challenge to the application of the minimum rationality test to age classifications, including the use of age as a basis for imposing mandatory retirement.[79] That battle first was lost in 1976, when the Supreme Court upheld a law requiring the retirement of Massachusetts state troopers at age 50 in *Massachusetts Board of Retirement v. Murgia*.[80] And later rulings—including *Gregory*—have confirmed the continuing vitality of *Murgia*.[81]

The Special Case of Life-Tenured Judges

Because federal judges are guaranteed life tenure by Article III of the United States Constitution,[82] the experience of the federal judiciary—populated as it is and has been by older individuals—affords the best test case for assessing whether age is negatively correlated with judicial performance. The federal experience also provides a useful model of an alternative to age-based mandatory retirement, which as just discussed is the practice commonly used to remove from the bench state court judges, who are either elected or appointed to fixed terms and do not have life tenure.

Looking to the limited record we have of the debates at the convention at which the United States Constitution was drafted,[83] it would appear that while the members were insistent upon life tenure for federal judges, the possibility that aged judges might remain on the job past their prime was not an issue of concern. It is possible that the Founding Fathers were not troubled about the prospect of superannuated judges because long life was uncommon and so the overpopulating of the federal courts[84] by such individuals was an unlikely specter. After all, in 1790 only 2 percent of the American populace was over age 64;[85] the median age at the time was only 16.[86] Actually, however, this rationale must be assessed with some caution. While the life expectancy of the average newborn was relatively short, it does not follow that old age was unknown to the drafters of the Constitution. Indeed, at the Convention itself, one of the leading figures was the elderly Benjamin Franklin, a man held in almost universally high esteem by his contemporaries.

To gain an accurate demographic portrait of the populace at the time of the Constitution's drafters, who of course would not have entertained the notion that any but adult white men would or could hold judicial office, one would have to look to the life expectancy of an average adult white male American— a person whose very existence on the scene established that he had survived the standard childhood illnesses and dangers of the time. The data suggest that if a male survived to age 20, he had a reasonably good chance of living to age 60 or even 70.[87] Still, the numbers of oldsters were sufficiently small—given the comparatively low percentages of those surviving to old age (as compared to today), and given further both the high birth rate as well as the constant infusion of youthful immigrants into the country—that old age was a phenomenon that likely did not loom large on the intellectual horizons of the drafters.

In *Federalist* Paper No. 78 Alexander Hamilton addressed the role of the proposed life-tenured federal judiciary.[88] He made no mention of any concern that life tenure could have adverse consequences. Rather, Hamilton extolled life tenure on several grounds, of varying significance. First, he invoked recent history and practice in pointing out that the guarantee of holding office during good behavior was "conformable to the most approved of the state constitutions,"[89] including the constitution of the state of New York, the populace of which was the intended audience for his tract. Second, and much more importantly, life tenure assured judicial independence—a value particularly prized in light of the attacks made on state court judges in earlier times in the colonies by the Crown.[90] Hamilton wrote as follows:

> The complete independence of the courts of justice is peculiarly essential in a limited constitution. By a limited constitution I understand one which contains certain specified exceptions to the legislative authority; such for instance as that it shall pass no bills of attainder, no *ex post facto* laws, and the like. Limitations of this kind can be preserved in practice no other way than through the medium of the courts of justice; whose duty it must be to declare all acts contrary to the manifest tenor of the constitution void.

Without all, all the reservations of particular rights or privileges would amount to nothing.[91]

Hamilton also invoked the matters of expertise and economic *realpolitik:*

> [A] voluminous code of laws is one of the inconveniences necessarily con-
> nected with the advantages of a free government. To avoid an arbitrary
> discretion in the courts, it is indispensable that they should be bound down
> by strict rules and precedents. . . . [I]t will readily be conceived . . . that the
> records of those precedents must unavoidably swell to a very considerable
> bulk, and must demand long and laborious study to acquire a competent
> knowledge of them. Hence it is that there can be but few men in the society,
> who will have sufficient skill in the laws to qualify them for the station of
> judges. . . . [T]he government can have no great option between fit charac-
> ters; and . . . a temporary duration in office, which would naturally discour-
> age such characters from quitting a lucrative line of practice to accept a seat
> on the bench, would have a tendency to throw the administration of justice
> into hands less able, and less well qualified to conduct it with utility and
> dignity.[92]

Again, no mention was made of the possibility of incompetent aged jurists.

Dealing with Older Federal Court Judges

One means for regulating the makeup of the federal judiciary in terms of age
would be to impose, by practice or by statute, a minimum or a maximum age
for appointment to the bench. Nothing in the Constitution precludes such a
requirement, be it age 25, 40, or 60. And, in fact, during the administrations of
Presidents Ronald Reagan and George H. W. Bush, age apparently was an
operative, albeit not publicly asserted, factor in the selection process, the goal
being to staff the federal court with relatively young appointees. The aim,
however, was not the benign one of broadening the age profile of the federal
courts. Rather, the idea seemed to be that by placing young, conservative
judges on the bench, the federal judiciary could be captured by these conservatives for decades to come inasmuch as they would typically serve for many
more years into the future than would older appointees.[93]

Apart from the apparent efforts of the Reagan and first Bush administrations to staff the federal courts with younger individuals, there also at one time
was an informal policy utilized by the American Bar Association and heeded
by both Republican and Democratic administrations to deny appointment to
the federal bench to individuals over age 63 or so.[94] In 1980, however, both the
Senate and the House adopted resolutions expressing the sense of the two
chambers that "the Standing Committee on Federal Judiciary of the American
Bar Association . . . [which at the time issued recommendations as to federal

court nominees] and the Attorney General take all measures necessary to end discrimination against potential lifetime federal judges who do not qualify solely as a result of age barriers."[95] These resolutions did not have the force of law, however. And as the preceding discussion reveals, certainly in the ensuing twelve years of Republican presidents there was no demographic tilt toward hither-to disfavored older appointees.

At the other end of the career continuum, which starts with joining the judiciary, is the matter of who departs from it. Given the Constitution's guarantee of life tenure, a federal court judge cannot be forced to retire. Congress, however, has devised incentives that make both retirement and semiretirement attractive to these women and men, and a considerable number do annually avail themselves of these incentives. For one, a judge who becomes permanently disabled and has served in office for ten or more continuous years may retire and continue to receive a salary for the rest of her life equal to that of sitting judges.[96] If the judge served for less than ten years, she will receive half salary for the remainder of her life.[97] Alternatively, by statute federal court judges, including Supreme Court justices, may (and do) leave active service by opting for what is known as senior status.[98] Such election is available in accordance with what is known as the "rule of eighty": to be eligible for senior status the jurist must have a combination of age and years on the bench that totals at least eighty. The average age of such judges as of 2000 was 67.9 years.[99]

Senior status entails a number of features. The senior status justice or judge receives a full salary, even though she enjoys a reduced workload in terms of numbers of cases handled. Such judges also are not burdened by presiding over criminal matters. Finally, a senior justice or judge must annually be certified either by the chief justice of the Supreme Court, in the instance of a Supreme Court justice, or by the chief judge of the circuit, in the instance of a circuit or district court judge. This certification entails several factors, all directed to assuring that the justice or judge in question performed work in the preceding calendar year that equaled the amount of work an average judge in active service would perform in three months.[100] While this certification process does not directly entail confirmation of the mental or physical competency of a life-tenured federal jurist, in fact the matter of competency is implicated inasmuch as a judge who is mentally or physically incapacitated presumably will not be able to satisfy the three-month work requirement necessary for certification.

In the instance of a federal judge who does not elect to retire or take senior status, but who is not able to perform the job, there are statutory provisions facilitating that judge's essentially being shunted aside from work assignments. For this to occur, certain procedures are prescribed. A certificate of disability must be signed by a majority of the members of the judicial council of the judge's circuit in the case of a circuit or district judge. This certificate then is presented to the president, who must make a finding that the judge is "unable to discharge efficiently all the duties of his office by reason of permanent mental or physical disability and that the appointment of an additional judge is necessary for the efficient dispatch of business." Assuming all the foregoing occurs and that an additional judge indeed is appointed, the disabled judge is to "be treated as junior in commission to the other judges of the circuit, district, or court."[101]

There are further provisions allowing for complaints to be made by "[a]ny person alleging that a judge or magistrate suffers from mental or physical disability."[102] Such a complaint can trigger an investigation, which in turn can result in a report calling upon a judicial council to certify the disability of the judge and/or requesting the judge to voluntarily retire.[103]

Restoring Older Judges to the Courts, While Still Assuring Quality Performance

What particularly damns mandatory retirement—the practice commonly used at the state level to remove older judges from the bench—is the fact that both at the federal level and even in states that impose this burden on older men and women who seek to serve as judges, there are many elderly individuals who do continue to serve and who, from all appearances, do so admirably. At the federal level, senior judges carry heavy caseloads and they thereby provide essential service to a severely understaffed federal judicial system.[104] At the state level, it turns out that there are elderly former judges who regularly are called back by state supreme courts to serve on special status on the lower state courts from which they earlier had been removed or as to which they had been barred from seeking reelection by virtue of their ages.[105]

The work product of these older judges proves that age is not a barrier to competent (and even better) performance. Moreover, one can surmise that if judges who are not competent to serve can be culled out by not being certified, at the federal level, or by not being called back into service at the state level, it follows that there are mechanisms at work that can be, and are, used to assess who is and who is not able to perform the job. It follows, therefore, that an unrefined policy of forcing judges out at 65 or 70 or 75, no matter their ability to perform well, is not really a necessary device for averting bad judging.

But what of the Supreme Court's *Gregory* ruling? The fact is that notwithstanding the green light afforded to the states by the *Gregory* Court to bar judges from the bench on the basis of age, that invitation can be rejected by those states that do not choose to pursue such an option.[106] *Gregory,* after all, does not require mandatory retirement; rather, the Court simply held that the practice is permissible under both the United States Constitution and the ADEA.

For those who may subscribe to the supposition that decline accompanies age, there are other, more finely tuned alternatives to mandatory retirement statutes. One could, for example, utilize a judicial fitness panel that would review periodically the competence of judges over a certain age and would certify those deemed fit to serve. Absent certification, a given judge would be automatically retired. Indeed, as already discussed, there is somewhat of an analogue for this approach afforded by the federal judicial system. At least in this way one would have individualized treatment, rather than the blunderbuss approach embodied in mandatory retirement requirements that oust everyone at the designated age, individual ability notwithstanding. Or one could place more faith in the democratic system than the *Gregory* Court did; in other words, one could rely upon the voters to oust those state court judges who cannot perform.

Would one have to suffer some incompetence? Not likely. Might age diversity on the bench be diminished?[107] Quite unlikely. Younger men and women still would be appointed or elected. Moreover, diversity could be enhanced at the state level insofar as older judges—now absent from the bench save when called back for special duty—once more would be working in the courtrooms.

Would we retain valuable judges? Yes. Would a larger, positive symbolic purpose be served? Yes. Each time an ageist policy is utilized, it increases or at least reinforces popular misconceptions about the abilities of older folks. Eliminate the policy, and one eliminates one piece of the diffuse structure that conveys the message that older men and women are decrepit, incompetent, and in decline.

Ethical and Statutory Constraints on Judicial Bias

Admonitions

Canon 3, Section (5) of the Model Code of Judicial Conduct, promulgated in 1990 by the American Bar Association (ABA), speaks to judicial impartiality generally and to the matter of age bias specifically:

> A judge shall perform judicial duties without bias or prejudice. A judge shall not, in the performance of judicial duties, by words or conduct manifest bias or prejudice, including but not limited to bias or prejudice based upon race, sex, religion, national origin, disability, age, sexual orientation or socioeconomic status, and shall not permit staff, court officials and others subject to the judge's direction and control to do so.

Almost every state has enacted statutory provisions, or through its courts has adopted court rules, that stem either from the Model Code of Judicial

Conduct promulgated by the ABA in 1972 or from the ABA's revised 1990 Model Code.[108] In Illinois, for example, the Illinois Supreme Court in March 2001 amended both the rules governing judges[109] and those governing attorneys.[110] Prior to the amendments, these rules banned discrimination on the bases of race, sex, religion, and national origin; the amendments added to the list "disability, age, sexual orientation or socioeconomic status."

In contrast, at the federal level the Code of Conduct for United States Judges[111]—which initially was adopted by the federal Judicial Conference on April 5, 1973 (under a slightly different appellation)—is much less satisfactory in terms of its dealing (or failing to deal) with age bias. The Code, which has been revised on a number of occasions, does not erect an enforceable set of statutory rules; it only sets forth aspirational goals.[112] Canon 2 of the Code admonishes federal judges to "not hold membership in any organization that practices invidious discrimination on the basis of race, sex, religion, or national origin."[113] No mention is made of age. More potentially useful in dealing with age bias is Canon 2's directive that "[a] judge should . . . act at all times in a manner that promotes public confidence in the integrity and impartiality of the judiciary."[114] However, the Commentary to this provision is notable for failing to expressly mention age:

> The duty under Canon 2 to act in a manner that promotes public confidence in the integrity and impartiality of the judiciary applies to all the judge's activities, including the discharge of the judge's adjudicative and administrative responsibility. For example, the duty to be respectful of others includes the responsibility to avoid comment or behavior that can reasonably be interpreted as manifesting prejudice or bias towards another on the basis of personal characteristics like race, sex, religion, or national origin.[115]

The most that can be said insofar as the matter of age bias is concerned is that this Commentary is written broadly enough in the last quoted sentence— which makes clear that the list of personal characteristics set forth therein is not exclusive—to hold open the possibility of bringing ageist comments and behavior within its purview, even though the matter of age bias is not directly addressed.

Enforcement

Pursuant to various state statutes a judge may on her own motion disqualify herself from hearing a case. Additionally, a party may move for a judge to recuse, or remove, herself,[116] and the judge then will have to determine whether to grant the motion.[117] At the federal level, 28 U.S.C. § 144 authorizes a party to any proceeding in a trial court to move for the recusal of the judge based on the judge's alleged "personal bias or prejudice either against . . . [the moving party] or in favor of any adverse party." According to one court, the moving party must establish that "the facts [are] such, their truth being assumed, as would 'convince a reasonable [person] that bias exists.'"[118] Another federal statute, 28 U.S.C. § 455(a), calls for a federal court judge to disqualify herself "in any proceeding in which . . . [the judge's] impartiality might reasonably be questioned." Self-disqualification also is called for by 28 U.S.C. § 455(b)(1) when, *inter alia,* the judge "has a personal bias or prejudice concerning a party."

With regard to § 455(a), "[t]he standard for determining whether a judge is required *sua sponte* to recuse [herself] from sitting on a case . . . is whether 'a reasonable objective person, knowing all of the circumstances, would have questioned the judge's impartiality.'"[119] As for § 455(b)(1), the same standard used with regard to § 144 applies,[120] that is, for a judge to be disqualified there must be a situation where a reasonably objective person, knowing all the circumstances, would question the judge's impartiality. Under both statutes (including both subsections of § 455) the disqualifying bias must be personal, that is, directed against a specific party in court, and typically—but not always—it must be derived from an extrajudicial source.[121] Thus, recusal or disqualification of a judge who is biased generally against persons over age 65, let us say, will have to arise out of that bias being directed against a particular plaintiff in a case over which the judge is presiding. General ageist antipathy—just floating out there in the air, so to speak—will not suffice.

As for the "extrajudicial source" requirement, which applies—according to the case law—to both § 144 and § 455(a) and (b), it evades easy definition. It was addressed, although not completely clarified, by the Supreme Court in *Liteky v. United States.*[122] In speaking to the phrase "bias or prejudice" that is set forth both in §§ 144 and 455(b)(1), the Court emphasized that "[n]ot *all* unfavorable disposition towards an individual (or his case) is properly described by those terms."[123] The Court then continued: "The words connote a favorable or unfavorable disposition or opinion that is somehow *wrongful* or *inappropriate,* either because it is undeserved, or because it rests upon knowledge that the subject ought not to possess . . . or because it is excessive in degree."[124]

The *Liteky* Court went on to stress that the bases for recusal or disqualification are not confined just to extrajudicial sources:

> It is wrong in theory, though it may not be too far off the mark as a practical matter, to suggest, as many opinions have, that "extrajudicial source" is the *only* basis for establishing disqualifying bias or prejudice. It is the only *common* basis, but not the exclusive one, since it is not the *exclusive* reason a predisposition can be wrongful or inappropriate. A fa-

vorable or unfavorable predisposition can also serve to be characterized as "bias" or "prejudice" because, even though it springs from the facts adduced or the events occurring at trial, it is so extreme as to display clear inability to render fair judgment. (This explains what some courts have called the "pervasive bias" exception to the "extrajudicial source" doctrine.)[125]

In addressing some specific scenarios, the *Liteky* Court offered examples of what would and what would not establish bias:

[J]udicial rulings alone almost never constitute a valid basis for a bias or partiality motion. . . . Second, opinions formed by the judge on the basis of facts introduced or events occurring in the course of the current proceedings, or of prior proceedings, do not constitute a basis for a bias or partiality motion unless they display a deep-seated favoritism or antagonism that would make fair judgment impossible. Thus, judicial remarks during the course of a trial that are critical or disapproving of, or even hostile to, counsel, the parties, or their cases, ordinarily do not support a bias or partiality challenge. They *may* do so if they reveal an opinion that derives from an extrajudicial source; and they *will* do so if they reveal such a high degree of favoritism or antagonism as to make fair judgment impossible. . . . *Not* establishing bias or partiality, however, are expressions of impatience, dissatisfaction, annoyance, and even anger, that are within the bounds of what imperfect men and women, even after having been confirmed as federal judges, sometimes display.[126]

A judge's general negative attitudes regarding older people would appear to qualify, in theory, as bias that fits within the contours of the *extrajudicial source* doctrine. But it is very unlikely that a given instance of such bias would rise to a level warranting recusal, either on the judge's own motion or on motion of a party. After all, no judge is, nor is he expected to be, a *tabula rasa*. Like every human he has opinions, attitudes, likes, and dislikes.[127] Obviously, then, "a judge is not prevented from sitting because he comes into every case with a background of general personal experience and beliefs."[128] Moreover, age bias hardly ever is going to match the depth, virulence, or venality characteristic of racism and of hostility based on national origin, and so the milder nature of ageism may preclude this "-ism" from satisfying the *Liteky* Court's insistence that condemnable extrajudicial bias entails "a favorable or unfavorable disposition or opinion that is somehow *wrongful* or *inappropriate* . . . or excessive in degree."[129]

Even if a judge, rather than harboring a generalized level of ageist bias, were to express an ageist bias toward a particular party in the course of a judicial proceeding, disqualification only would be justified, according to one court, if the judge "displayed deep-seated and unequivocal antagonism that would render fair judgment impossible."[130] Or, as another court put it, "the judge [would have to evince] . . . a deep-seated antagonism as opposed to a judgment formed on the basis of information he is entitled to consider."[131]

In sum, then, ageism is as a general matter unlikely to rise to a level sufficient to support litigants' motions to recuse. In any event, and abstract assertions aside, the fact is that one necessarily would have to look at the particular judicial comments, rulings, etc., in any given case in order to determine whether the requisite level and kind of bias existed. Analogies afforded by the existing case law are not helpful. There are very few cases dealing with judicial disqualification based on one of the classic "-isms": bias based on race, national origin, religion, and—more recently—gender.[132] They offer no particular instruction. There are no cases dealing with age bias. There is some dictum that is of analogical relevance, but it is of such a general nature that it offers little useful guidance.[133]

Moving from the issues of recusal and disqualification, it is relevant to note that there are evidentiary standards, constitutionally or otherwise grounded, which establish that it can be reversible error for a judge to communicate favoritism or overt preference toward a litigant or witness in a given trial. Of course, denominating a comment or ruling as going over the line is a very difficult enterprise. On the one hand, judicial "[r]emarks and comments made . . . in the context of court proceedings ordinarily will not be considered indicative of improper bias or prejudice unless they go so far as to show that the judge has closed his or her mind about a case."[134] On the other hand, "remarks made in court by a judge that will be taken as manifesting improper prejudice are those such as racial or religious epithets indicating that a judge does not possess an appropriate judicial temperament and might be swayed by irrational factors."[135] These generalities read sensibly, but their application to any given specific utterance or set of utterances necessarily will very much turn on tone, nuance, and context—factors very difficult to quantify.

Conclusions

No doubt during the past two hundred years there have been rare instances when elderly judges unfit for further service have remained on the federal bench, including the Supreme Court.[136] One must conclude that sometimes age and performance have meshed in unfortunate ways. However, isolated instances that are conveniently consistent with negative stereotypes should not be allowed to override fair analysis. Unwarranted concentration on the rare senile or otherwise compromised elderly judge leads to undeserved discrediting of the unexceptionable—sometimes even brilliant—performance of numerous other competent elderly judges. Moreover, such undue focus on the errant oldster further creates the risk of obscuring the fact that youth is no guarantor of judicial competency: lack of intelligence, honesty, and/or commitment to doing a good job are failings that young and middle-aged judges can—and no doubt in some instances do—possess.[137]

In any event, there are affirmative arguments to be made in praise of aged judges. With age comes experience—an asset to be valued. Also, older judges bring to the bench a longer view that enables them to put into useful perspective ideas that may turn out upon reflection to be no more than passing fads.[138] Moreover, when older judges do make a break with the past, as they did, for example, in the historic 1954 Supreme Court decision in *Brown v. Board of Education*[139] rejecting on constitutional grounds the legitimacy of racially segregated public schools, they may be able by virtue of their age and experience to bestow on such rulings a political legitimacy that younger judges would not be able to provide.[140]

Insofar as there is a reasonable basis for concern as to the purported lack of competence of older judges (and it may well be that such concern is primarily an expression of ageist stereotypes), there are means whereby those who cannot perform can be dealt with, short of the unrefined use of age-based mandatory retirement statutes that sweep out the able along with the possibly impaired.

Finally, it must be stressed that ageist bias—whether entertained by young, middle-aged, or older judges—has no proper place in the courtroom. An elderly judge has no more warrant for favoring or disfavoring people appearing before her because of their ages than does a young judge.

An Agenda for Action

The Development of Empirical Data

A number of studies of racial, ethnic, and gender bias in the justice system have been conducted in the past decade. A particular focus of such studies has been the ways in which women attorneys, litigants, etc., are treated by judges. A comparable effort is in order vis-à-vis the judiciary insofar as the age factor is concerned.

Judicial Education

While studies of judicial behavior are needed, we already know enough to act. Education offers the best route to follow, the aim being to educate judges out of their ageist biases by offering information regarding issues such as the nature of the aging process; the significance of age for such matters as witness reliability,[141] sentencing,[142] and recidivism; and the availability and use of practices and devices—such as enhanced courtroom lighting and exhibits printed in large type[143]—to enhance optimal performance by participants in the legal process. The forms that these educational efforts may take are obvious: training videos and manuals, structured seminars and conferences, lectures offered by way of distance learning methodologies, and more.[144]

Mandates as to Judicial Performance

Every state should adopt a code of judicial conduct that, *inter alia,* prohibits expressions of age-based bias. In similar vein, the federal Code of Conduct for United States Judges should be amended to specifically condemn age bias on the part of federal judges.

Abolition of Mandatory Retirement

Age-based mandatory retirement imposed on judges—a common practice in many states—is unwarranted and unnecessary. It is unwarranted because the practice reinforces stereotypes of incompetence and intellectual decline that commonly are attached to the elderly. It is unnecessary because there are more nuanced means for assuring the continuing competence of judges—be they 45-year-old substance abusers or 80-year-old victims of Alzheimer's disease. The practice should be abolished.

8

Juries

I consider [trial by jury] as the only anchor ever yet imagined by man,
by which a government can be held to the principles of its constitution.
—Thomas Jefferson, letter to Thomas Paine (1789)

A jury reflects the attitudes and mores of the community from which it is
drawn. It lives only for the day and does justice according to its lights.
The group of 12 who are drawn to hear a case, makes the decision and
melts away. . . . It is the one governmental agency that has no ambition.
It is as human as the people who make it up. It is sometimes the victim of
passions. But it also takes the sharp edges off a law and uses conscience to
ameliorate a hardship. Since it is of and from the community, it gives the
law an acceptance which verdicts of judges could not do.
—Supreme Court Justice William O. Douglas, *We, The Judges*

The Cultural and Political Significance of Juries

Disagreements and arguments are unfortunately, but apparently inevitably,
aspects of the human condition. Most occasion little note. They generally are
transitory in duration and of only minor substance. While some quarrels are
more weighty, in most instances the antagonists are able to achieve some sort
of closure short of recourse to external dispute-resolution mechanisms. Still,
some arguments do generate greater heat, and they resist ready resolution.
These are the disagreements that wind up being referred to mediators or arbi-
trators or that give rise to lawsuits. In the latter instance, however, few of these
suits ever actually see the light of a courtroom; instead, most potential litigation matters are settled before trial. Even for those cases that do go forward,
only a small percentage actually are resolved by juries; rather, bench trials, that
is, trials conducted by a judge alone, are standard both in criminal and civil
cases.[1]

Despite this winnowing process, the incidence of jury trials in the United
States is in absolute numbers not inconsiderable.[2] And in any event, numbers
aside, juries play a significant symbolic role for the American public: they are
generally seen as bulwarks—albeit imperfect ones—of fairness and justice.[3]
Indeed, jury trials occupy to some degree a mythic role in American culture.

Trials ("combat") between lawyers, fought out in the courtroom ("arena"), with each attorney ("combatant") vying for the jury's favor, are the stuff of movies and TV programs and best-selling novels.[4] Not surprisingly, the political and social values served by juries in America typically have been described in stirring laudatory terms, such as the following:

> Juries advance democracy at many levels. They are the one arena where average citizens can participate directly in government, where they can have a direct impact on events and ultimately the state of their lives. And despite some administrative burdens associated with juries, the frustrations of some jurors and the occasional unsound jury verdict, the consensus among judges, lawyers, and jurors themselves is that the system works extremely well.
>
> Jurors, representative members of the community, are randomly chosen to sit in judgment of others, deliberate carefully, render competent and just verdicts, and then fade anonymously back into the community. Their decisions reflect community values that judges may lack, and therefore their verdicts may differ from judges' opinions.[5]

In sum, juries serve a powerful totemic role in the American legal system, and they function as important real-life components of this system.[6]

Jurors' Ages and the Quality of Juror Performance

The data regarding the competence of jurors to do a good job (whatever that may be) are very sparse. This is not surprising. How, after all, could one determine whether a given juror is or is not up to the task, when the job is one that is performed in secret, the qualifications for it are resistant to definition, and the fulfillment of a juror's role is so tied to the peculiar facts of the case before her?

There are a number of empirical studies that address in nonjury contexts issues of memory and information retention, as these are affected by age.[7] There is one such study that examined jurors' performance. The subjects were 124 individuals who were divided into two groups—one made up of younger adults (ages 19–35) and the other of older adults (ages 55–75)—and asked to take on the roles of mock jurors.[8] They viewed a two-hour video of a complex civil trial, and they then were tested for free recall, recognition memory, source identification, and the accuracy of their verdicts.

All of the subjects were allowed to take notes.[9] The element that was manipulated was the point in time when the jurors received jury instructions as to how to do their job. Some subjects were instructed before viewing the video as to the legal concepts involved in the case, such as the issues of liability and compensatory damages. Others did not receive instructions until after viewing the video and thus were dealt with in the way juries throughout the United States customarily are.[10] Later, the jurors were asked to provide written accounts of what took place during the trial. The researcher found that both groups benefited from note taking. He also determined that both younger and older adults provided more cohesive and detailed accounts in those instances where they received instructions before the trial on the merits and the presentation of evidence regarding compensation.

There were *some* age-correlated differences, however. For one, the researcher found that generally note-takers were "more evidence oriented; that is, their accounts . . . [had] a higher proportion of probative information," and "[t]he preinstruction intervention also . . . [had] a positive effect, but only for older jurors."[11] More specifically, the older jurors who received instruction before hearing the evidence "produce[d] a higher proportion of probative statements and a lower proportion of merely evaluative statements."[12] In sum, "preinstruction helps older adults construct accounts that are relatively more evidence based."[13]

There were other age-correlated findings as well. The subjects were presented with a series of written statements and asked to indicate whether they had heard any of these statements during the trial. Here, the researcher was testing for source, or recognition, memory. Of the 48 statements, 12 presented pro-plaintiff facts; 12 involved pro-defense facts; 12 entailed neutral facts; four were pro-plaintiff *lures;* and six were pro-defense *lures.*[14] The results showed no difference between younger and older adults insofar as the correct identification of the number of statements made at trial was concerned. However, with regard to statements involving neutral facts, the researcher found that "[p]re-instruction appears to be associated with positive effects that are stronger in older adults"; in fact, "[p]reinstruction totally eliminates the age differences for neutral facts."[15] Finally, and with regard to the matter of the verdicts rendered for the four mock plaintiffs, each of whom suffered a different degree of harm, "[o]lder jurors . . . more clearly distinguished between the most and least severely injured plaintiff when pre-instructed."[16]

In sum, the data supported the conclusion that providing instructions before trial to jurors regarding the legal concepts involved in the trial they were about to sit through was of more benefit to older jurors than younger ones: "Overall, . . . when there are effects of preinstruction, they are found primarily for older adults rather than younger adults. Significant [positive] interactions between age and timing of instructions . . . [were] found for the probative and evaluative variables for free recall, for the neutral facts variable for source memory, and for the verdict quality variable."[17]

The Age Factor in Juror Responses to Litigants and Legal Issues

Academicians' General Views

Most academic researchers contend that demographic factors, including age, play very little role, or even no role, in jurors' decision making. The following assertions are illustrative of this position:

> Overwhelming scientific evidence indicates that such factors as race, age, gender, occupation, and so on fail to relate in any meaningful way with jury verdicts—and, indeed, often *increase* the error rate during voir dire. Attorneys should keep this primary psychological rule uppermost in their minds when selecting juries: *Those variables that are most observable are least predictive of verdicts and jury behavior.*[18]

While not taking as hard and fast a position, jury expert Rita Simon, after reviewing the literature regarding the anecdotally grounded views of practitioners regarding juries, debunked this body of experience-based opinion and in so doing discounted the significance of jurors' personal characteristics, such as their ages:

> [T]he lore about how different types of people will react to the issues presented to them in criminal and civil cases is enormously more developed than are the facts needed to substantiate the lore. It is readily apparent from a perusal of legal cookbooks that date as far back as 75 and 100 years that lawyers, traditionally, have enjoyed playing amateur psychologist. Some of the most colorful members of the bar have written and spoken at great length about their intuitive or learned ability to challenge those jurors who are likely to cause their client trouble, and to retain those who will be sympathetic and understanding of their clients' plight. They have worked out prescriptions that would fit almost every type of juror: the fat, the lean, the tall, the short, the smart, the dumb, the rich, the poor, the male, the female, the educated, and the ignorant. . . .
>
> The irony of all this is that these beliefs have so little basis in fact. The evidence as manifested by empirical studies shows that there is some relationship between verdicts and the jurors' personal and social characteristics, and that the relationship is in the expected direction; *but* the relationship is not strong. It is not nearly strong or consistent enough to merit as much attention and effort as the practice of challenging and selecting jurors has received from the bar.[19]

Another of the leading students of juries in America, Shari Seidman Diamond, took a like position in an article that she wrote with two other experts:

[B]ackground characteristics [including age] show only a modest association with verdict preferences, a pattern that demonstrates the weakness
of relying solely on these indicators in exercising peremptory challenges
during jury selection. The failure of these measures [i.e., age, gender, race,
politics, education, income, etc.] as strong predictors emphasizes the fact
that focusing on demographic characteristics neglects the substantial variation in response within categories, for example, among college-educated
jurors or among women. . . . An alternative approach to predicting verdict
preferences, and one that also turns out to be more informative, directs
attention to the attitudes and beliefs that jurors bring to the case rather
than to their background characteristics.[20]

Notwithstanding their downgrading the significance of demographic factors, both Diamond and Simon did concede in the foregoing excerpts that these
factors do play somewhat of a role in the juror decision-making process. So,
too, does Professor Michael Saks; he has observed that juror differences "appear to make a significant difference in some contexts."[21]

These basically amount to situations where the evidence is highly ambiguous. Jurors then look to their assumptions and biases in order to fill the
informational gap. This finding is what [Harry] Kalven and [Hans] Zeisel
[in *The American Jury* (1966)] referred to as the "liberation hypothesis"—
close, ambiguous cases liberated jurors from the discipline of evidence.
Thus, in particularly close cases, juror differences are likely to increase in
importance. Some cases are characteristically beset with ambiguous evidence, such as rape where consent is the defense.[22]

Another student of jury decision making, Phoebe Ellsworth, also has expressed
a position crediting the role of jurors' personal characteristics:

Most of the published writing on the effects of individual differences on
jurors' verdicts consists either of overoptimistic claims that various personality or background variables are reliable indicators of a proprosecution or
prodefense juror, or of gloomy criticisms of these claims, typically ending
with the equally simplistic claim that the evidence determines the verdict
and that individual differences do not. A review of the relevant research
indicates that the usual hoary or trendy stereotypes are not very useful
(race, class, gender, occupation, and nationality on the hoary side; power
speech, color preferences, locus of control, and dress on the trendy side;
authoritarianism somewhere between). But we also know that juries are
rarely unanimous on the first ballot, and thus, because the evidence presented is the same for all the jurors, individual differences must make a
difference. The evidence presented is the same, but the evidence perceived
by the jurors is not.[23]

Studies of Age-Based Differentials in Responses to Issues and Litigants

Given the actual as well as symbolic importance of the jury, it is hardly surprising that there is a very considerable body of literature[24] regarding the decision-making dynamics of juries and jurors.[25] What *is* surprising is that the literature is sparse with regard to the questions of whether and how the ages of jurors, as well as other trial participants, play roles in juror decision making.[26] After all, it would seem reasonable to assume, given the physiological reality that each of us is possessed of age, that our reactions to others in part correlate—consciously or subconsciously and from time to time—with our own ages, the ages of those to whom we react, or both. If this is so, age-associated consequences presumably can ensue inside the jury room. In this regard, the following observation is particularly on point here:

> Overall, there is clear indication that the characteristics of the litigants in any case will affect the jurors' verdict. As the most fundamental type of bias, stereotypes are particularly dangerous. Juror selection strategy must identify them in juror thinking at an early point in our trial preparation. We must learn how stereotypes are going to affect the verdict. Will they determine Psychological Anchors, which are the issues on which jurors decide the case? Will they affect witness credibility? Will they play a significant role in causal attributions? Very likely the answer will be yes to all the above.[27]

Little well-documented data address the intersection of jurors' ages with those of litigants and witnesses. The commonly accepted mythology that holds sway among members of the bar is that federal court juries are unduly sympathetic to plaintiffs in cases arising under the federal Age Discrimination in Employment Act of 1967, as amended (ADEA).[28] The unverified explanations for this alleged undue favoritism are twofold: jurors in age discrimination cases, so it is speculated, have themselves suffered wrongs at the hands of superiors in the workplace, and the age profile of federal court jurors generally skews toward the upper age ranges, that is, the 50s and 60s. The consequence of these two factors—so it is conjectured—is that they identify with aggrieved plaintiffs, who typically also are in their 50s and 60s.[29] Surmise aside, there is some empirical evidence—although it is sparse—that does confirm the accuracy of the perception of jurors being particularly sympathetic to plaintiffs in age discrimination in employment cases.[30]

Outside the employment setting, there is a report of a telephone study of 1,000 individuals who were read a test scenario describing an accident that involved a driver named Jim and that posited his suffering certain specified injuries. The researchers sought to determine whether the ages of the survey

subjects and the victim intersected in some way with respect to the ultimate
matter of ascribing blame. Jim's age was varied for different call recipients. The
researchers found no connection between Jim's age and the age of each respondent insofar as the answers elicited from the respondents were concerned.
(Obviously, this scenario did not address responses based on actual visual
exposure of the putative plaintiff to the respondent, nor did it involve consideration of the age factor in terms of witness credibility.)[31]

Apart from age per se, the physical appearance of litigants may well be a
factor also playing a role—at least at the margins—in the jury room. In this
regard, the following observations are relevant:

> So, what impresses people first about others? Whatever causes that ini-
> tial gut response to fire off, and at the primary threshold that is in a pretty
> basic arena left over from our outdoorsy ancestors. Not quite at the flight-
> or-flight level, but along very similar lines, is a pattern-recognition program
> we've all got which essentially answers by observation the unspoken ques-
> tion, "How much is this person like me or not like me?" Be sure to draw a
> distinction between "like me" meaning "sits, stands, or sounds like me"
> and the more cognitive "believes, thinks, or understands like me." It is the
> first version that we all use to begin building our impressions, long before
> the latter distinctions ever get any voice.[32]

There are a number of studies concerning juror responsiveness to defendants based on the defendant's physical attractiveness or the lack thereof.[33]
Such studies with only rare exception ignore the age factor, however.[34] But
given the fact that in American culture attractive physical appearance is
strongly correlated with youthfulness,[35] one can look to these studies as offering some useful clues vis-à-vis the age factor's significance for the evaluation by
jurors and judges of older witnesses' and litigants' testimony. What the studies
reveal is that physically attractive people elicit more positive responses in terms
of persuasiveness and intelligence than do unattractive individuals.[36]

Apart from the possible age-influenced reaction of a young juror to an
elderly witness or of an older juror to a young witness, there is the more general
proposition to consider that people of different ages may well differ in some
respects (although this certainly is not an undisputed notion)[37] as to their attitudes and values—not *because* of their ages per se, but rather because of interests and experiences that correlate with age.[38] In support of this proposition,
the Supreme Court of California observed as follows in *People v. Wheeler:*[39]

> [I]n our heterogeneous society jurors will inevitably belong to diverse and
> often overlapping groups defined by race, religion, ethnic or national ori-
> gin, sex, age, education, occupation, economic condition, place of resi-

dence, and political affiliation; . . . it is unrealistic to expect jurors to be devoid of opinions, preconceptions, even deep-rooted biases derived from their life experiences in such groups.

This is not an unfamiliar theme:

Interest-group theorists and legal "realists" agree with Justice Scalia's assertion [in *Powers v. Ohio*, 499 U.S. 400, 424 (1991) (Scalia, J., dissenting)] that "all groups tend to have particular sympathies and hostilities—most notably, sympathies towards their own group members." In fact, scientific research suggests that a juror's background is likely to influence the way she perceives and evaluates information. Jurors tend to "mold information into a plausible 'story' or 'schema' based on their prior experiences" [B. Michael Dann, *"Learning Lessons" and "Speaking Rights": Creating Educated and Democratic Juries*, 68 Indiana Law Journal 1229, 1242 (1993) (citations omitted)]. These stories are "usually derived from personal experience and 'common sense'" [Irwin A. Horowitz and Thomas Willging, The Psychology of Law: Integrations and Applications 210 (1984)]. Therefore, while no societal group possesses a single, uniform perspective, each juror possesses an "interpretive bias" based on her own personal background and experience.[40]

Important, albeit dated, empirical support for the existence of age-associated attitudinal differences was developed by Professor Jon M. Van Dyke more than 20 years ago; he recounted survey data showing notable age group differences among jurors regarding the credibility of police witnesses, the fairness of judges, and other issues.[41] He also reported on some other data regarding age-correlated attitudinal differentiations:

The young . . . differ with their elders on the proper approach to the questions of drugs, other victimless crimes, abortions, and the general question of how tough society should be on persons who violate the general norms. Typical is a 1972 Gallup poll on the death penalty, which reported that among persons 18–24 48 percent favored the death penalty and 44 percent opposed it; among persons over 50, 60 percent favored the death penalty and only 27 percent opposed it.[42]

In like vein, researchers who conducted a later study of attitudes concerning police reported that "[a]ge and ethnicity are both important variables effecting [*sic*] attitude structures."[43]

Starkly contrasting age-correlated views concerning the Social Security system (which admittedly is rarely addressed directly in litigation involving jury determinations) were revealed by a study—albeit not one focused on jurors or even mock jurors—that was conducted in the late 1990s:

Fully 82% of those age 50 and older say making Social Security financially sound should be the No. 1 priority for Clinton and Congress this
year. Younger Americans place education first. . . .

When asked how they would use any budget surplus, . . . [a] plurality of
those age 50 and older would fix Social Security (46%) compared to just a
quarter of those under 50 (25%). Those under 50 would spend the money
on today's domestic programs (42%) compared to 16% of older Americans who would do so.

Reflecting these different priorities, Americans also split along generational lines on the role they expect Social Security to play in their own lives.
Among working Americans 55 and older, half say Social Security will provide for most of their living expenses when they retire. But barely one in ten
(12%) workers under 55 feel the same way.[44]

Another more recent study, directed to determining attitudes regarding
claimants under the Americans with Disabilities Act,[45] provides further information regarding age-correlated viewpoints. This enterprise involved 507 jury
pool members. The investigator, Dan Gallipeau, reported that "[j]urors over
age 45 held attitudes significantly more pro-plaintiff than those under age
45."[46] One question Gallipeau asked was whether the survey subjects thought
that employers discriminated in their hiring practices against disabled appli-
cants. The results differed dramatically for younger and older respondents:

Over 45	Disagree	14%
	Neutral	17%
	Agree	69%
Under 45	Disagree	55%
	Neutral	25%
	Agree	20%

Gallipeau also asked whether the jury pool members thought that employers
discriminated against the disabled with regard to promotion decisions; again,
the age-correlated differentials in responses were striking:

Over 45	Disagree	20%
	Neutral	31%
	Agree	49%
Under 45	Disagree	60%
	Neutral	24%
	Agree	16%[47]

Other age-correlated differentials were even more stark. Gallipeau asked
whether employers were willing to pay for special equipment needed by em-

ployees with disabilities so that they could perform their jobs. All of the respondents over age 45 stated that companies indeed did not want to incur this expense. In total contrast, of those respondents under age 45 none took the position that employers were unwilling to incur such costs, 56 percent rejected the notion that they were unwilling, and 44 percent were neutral on the matter.[48] The respondents also were asked their view as to whether "companies will do anything they can to not pay for special equipment that an employee with a disability needs to do the job." The responses were as follows:

Over 45
Disagree   30%
Neutral   24%
Agree   46%

Under 45
Disagree   62%
Neutral   30%
Agree   8%

In still another study the investigators determined that "[i]n rape cases, older people were more likely to convict," whereas "[f]or murder cases . . . older people were less likely to convict."[49] More generally, the investigators concluded that of four variables—sex, race, age, and education—"age was the best predictor of verdicts for murder cases; age and education (in opposing directions) for rape cases; and sex for robbery cases."[50]

Practitioners' Views

At a perhaps more pedestrian level, there is a body of literature made up of guides written by practicing attorneys who, on the basis of their experiences, offer conclusions as to the various aspects of the litigation process. A leading student of the jury, Rita Simon, reviewed this literature and derived a "set of maxims that are representative of the rules of thumb lawyers are urged to follow."[51] Three of these relate to the age issue:

1. A young juror is more likely to return a verdict favorable to the plaintiff than to the defendant.
2. An older juror is more likely to be sympathetic to the plaintiff than to the defendant in civil, personal injury cases.
3. A juror whose age closely approximates the age of the client, lawyer, or witness, is more likely to give a favorable verdict.[52]

A judge who in his earlier years had been a trial attorney recounted a survey of "experienced trial lawyers" who were asked to rate a number of juror factors in terms of relative rank and importance; age was ranked as "important."[53] A still-practicing trial attorney maintained that the ages of jurors can be significant with regard to how those jurors react to certain defendants and certain crimes.[54] And Mark Hansen quoted a civil litigator in 2002 as expressing the opinion that in products liability cases young jurors are more sympathetic to plaintiffs than are older jurors: "'If you were the plaintiff,' he says, 'you probably wouldn't want some 70-year-old guy who comes from an era when people did a lot of things for themselves—things that are now considered dangerous—hearing your case about a defective product.'"[55] Hansen quoted another attorney as saying that "Gen Xers, as a rule, tend to hold technology companies in higher regard than baby boomers do" and that "baby boomers are generally thought to be more sympathetic to the plaintiff in medical malpractice cases than Gen Xers are."[56] Trial consultants, that is, those who possess, or claim to possess, expertise in sizing up potential jurors, appear to be split as to the significance of the age factor.[57]

Ultimately, no firm consensus can be attributed to legal practitioners as a group, the foregoing comments notwithstanding. Indeed, despite the just-quoted commentators, some practitioners caution against assuming that age is at all a useful indicator of jurors' likely decisions.[58]

Juror Perceptions of Their Experiences

The chief concerns of this chapter thus far have been the ways in which jurors perform and/or are perceived to perform. A different slant—one little explored but nonetheless deserving of note—entails the question of how jurors themselves assess the process.

In this regard, Professor Nancy Marder conducted a study of 26 criminal juries. She addressed four issues in seeking to determine whether juror diversity in terms of gender, race, and age made a difference concerning (1) the level of hostility generated in the course of juror deliberations, (2) the level of juror satisfaction with the process, (3) the degree of thoroughness of deliberations that the jurors ascribed to their experiences, and (4) the question of whether diversity rendered the jury unable, or triggered an expectation in jurors that they would be unable, to reach a verdict. Most of the jurors who responded to Marder's questionnaire were young (15 percent were 18–24 years old; 22 percent were 25–34) or middle-aged (20 percent were 35–44; 26 percent were 45–54). Only 14 percent were between 55 and 64, and 3 percent were 65 or older.

While Marder interpreted her research data as supporting the conclusions that as to factors (1), (2), and (3) gender diversity played a positive role, age diversity was seen as having an effect—a positive one—only with regard to factor (2). "As the jury became more age diverse, the jurors became more satisfied with their experience as jurors, and they estimated that other jurors would be more satisfied with the verdict."[59]

Conclusions

There are two views as to the significance of demographic factors and demographically correlated attitudes. One is based on anecdotal observations, derived from the actual handling of litigation, by legal practitioners. For them, age matters. The other view is that of the research-grounded academicians; for them, age is a much less significant—although not completely irrelevant—factor. To the question, then, whether it makes a difference for a young juror's decision making if a claimant is elderly or young, one could expect quite different answers depending upon whether the respondent is a practitioner relying upon anecdotal information or a scholar conversant with presumably well monitored and well devised empirical studies. The same, of course, would hold for the question of whether it makes a difference for an older juror if a plaintiff or defendant is young or old.

One is tempted to accord the most credence to the academics; they claim to ground their assessments on incontrovertible scientific evidence. On the other hand, those who are in the legal trenches, so to speak, cannot simply be ignored just because of their supposed lack of academic sophistication. To take such a position would be to give the unwarranted back of the hand to a factor enormously important in the law, that is, real-life experience. The simple solution to these conflicting views entails accepting the reality that there is ambiguity here. From there, one proceeds to the conclusion that given such ambiguity it is best to err on the cautious side, which is to conclude that the age factor indeed is of some relevance in the jury room. But that seemingly temperate conclusion actually invites very weighty questions of normative dimension.

Should we care whether age matters? If we should, should we deem the involvement of age in jury decision making as a positive, a negative, or neither? If the infusion of age into the decision-making equation is seen as either a plus or a minus, what should we do? Discussion of these issues, which call for the rendering of value judgments rather than empirically grounded solutions, is reserved for later exposition.

Jurors' Ages and Their Responses to Judges and Attorneys

Neither anecdotes nor empirical studies are very informative when one looks at whether the age of the juror has any significance in terms of how she or he reacts to an older and/or a younger judge or to an older or a younger attorney. Indeed, these questions seldom have been addressed, even though judges and attorneys play essential roles in the American justice scheme.

Not surprisingly, data suggest that judges play a very influential role for jurors.[60] But some recent survey data, though quite undifferentiated in terms of specifics, suggest a different picture—one that is particularly relevant in terms of the concern here for the significance of age. In a study (not limited to jurors) of generational attitudes toward judges, the investigator found a correlation, significant at the .10 level, between age—at both ends of the age spectrum—and lack of confidence in the individuals occupying judicial roles: "Only 9.2% of 18– to 30-year-olds and 9.2% of citizens 60 years of age and older held local judges to be 'above average quality,' while over 20% of individuals in other age groups gave local judges high marks. . . . [T]his difference is probably a function of familiarity with the courts and with local judges—a life-experience difference."[61]

Jurors also react to attorneys (as do nonjurors).[62] One attitudinal lever may be generalized political or social views regarding the legal profession. With regard to correlations between the age factor and public attitudes regarding lawyers, Robert G. Boatright developed data revealing a skewing regarding younger individuals, but not older ones, in terms of their perceptions of lawyers as being too powerful in American society: "When we asked our surveyees whether they thought attorneys have too much power, younger citizens were much more inclined to answer affirmatively than any other age group; 44.6% of 18– to 30-year-olds felt this was true; in no other age group was the percentage in agreement greater than 40%."[63]

Apart from trying to assess the role of age per se in the judge/juror/lawyer scenario, it also is useful to take a somewhat different, but related, tack. As discussed earlier, physical appearance matters. This is so not only in terms of jurors' reactions to litigants but also with regard to the reactions that other participants in the legal process elicit. In this regard, two lawyers and a psychologist recently made the following observations as to the role that the appearance of attorneys plays:

> Physical appearance . . . influences jurors. Physically attractive individuals are generally, but not always, more persuasive than unattractive ones, the research shows. The conclusions of one 1984 study of attorney persuasiveness in the courtroom indicated that because humans want to identify with attractive people, we tend to agree more with what they have to say. People tend to perceive attractiveness in similarity. So, as the jury pool becomes more diverse, it's more important to have attorneys with whom the jury can identify.[64]

To the extent, then, that older individuals, or younger ones, are perceived as physically attractive or not, age may indirectly insert itself into courtroom dynamics. And inasmuch as older individuals generally are seen as less attractive, there may well be negative consequences for juror determinations when jurors are confronted with older attorneys and judges.

The Ultimate Normative Judgment

Age is an operative factor in the jury room. But is it a factor that adulterates (or enhances) truth-seeking and, ultimately, justice? Are verdicts in criminal cases and/or in civil cases affected in meaningful ways by the juror's age and/or the interaction of the juror's age with the age of another of the participants in the trial process (the litigant, the judge, a witness, and/or an attorney)? If the answer to any of these questions is an affirmative one, whether for all situations or even only some, then arguably there is cause for some sort of action to cleanse the process of ageist bias—whether that bias works to the favor or the disadvantage of those who come to court seeking the fair administration of justice.

No clear answers emerge. It belabors the obvious to observe that jurors do not approach a case as mindless automatons, devoid of values, opinions, inclinations, and even biases. No such people exist. What is more, we not only expect, but we also want these values, etc., to be brought to bear in the jury room: Jurors, after all, are expected to represent their community and its values. Actual problems only emerge when a juror's biases or inclinations are allowed to intrude in response to a factor that we deem inappropriate for consideration in deciding issues of innocence and guilt, as well as in choosing kinds and levels of remedies. Race, for example, is a human characteristic that we would like to exclude from the jury room as a fulcrum for jurors' decisions. Justice based on the color of a litigant's skin (whether the juror views that factor as favorable or unfavorable) is justice compromised and even denied in significant respects.[65] But race, in truth, is a special case. The age factor obviously is different. As discussed in chapter 3, it is much more innocuous in terms of a historical record of abuse, in terms of its invocation as a basis for denying political power, in its role as a trigger for deprivation and mistreatment, and so on.

So what do we do? Do we deem age a sufficiently low-profile factor to let its use and influence go by the boards? Or do we instead condemn it as a perverting element in the jury's decision-making enterprise? Or, conversely, do we praise its role in the jury room as appropriately reflecting society's acceptable values? For my part, I think there are enough data establishing that age can have an adverse impact, generally, on optimal decision making to give pause. (By optimal decision making I mean a process that focuses directly on issues of guilt, responsibility, and liability, with matters extraneous to these bedrock issues for the most part being excluded.)[66] But I think there is enough uncertainty as to consequences that we ought to accept age, for the most part, as a factor that, if not to be encouraged as an exclusive basis for decision making, is at least a tolerable part of the equation. The task is to inject refinements into the system, rather than to revamp it.

An Agenda for Action

Voir Dire

Effective voir dire by the judge and/or the attorneys in a given case may be a useful way of flushing out excessive or inappropriate age bias. Voir dire, which involves questioning prospective jurors as to their knowledge of the case, their biases, possible prejudgments, etc., is conducted in some jurisdictions by the attorneys for the litigants and in some by both the attorneys and the judge. In the federal courts, typically only the judge conducts voir dire.[67] In any of these scenarios, the aim is to discern inappropriate biases so that the juror possessed of such bias can be dismissed for cause[68] or on the basis of a peremptory challenge exercised by the attorney opposed to that person being seated.[69]

The voir dire process, however, hardly is a foolproof device for ferreting out individuals who should not sit as jurors. For one, "the power of the judge in the courtroom, which is conveyed in both direct and subtle ways to jurors, may incline . . . [the prospective juror] to give socially desirable responses, among which is the denial of . . . prejudice."[70] In other words, the prospective juror will try to provide the politically correct answer, even if that answer may not accurately reflect her real views. Moreover, the observation further has been offered that "[t]he influence of class and status is only partially minimized when lawyers participate in the *voir dire*."[71]

Another problem flows from the format in which voir dire is conducted. It has been suggested that individualized questioning of prospective jurors out of the presence of other prospects is more effective than voir dire conducted in a group setting. In the latter situation, the questioner's asking whether any member of the group is prejudiced requires the individual who is biased to so identify himself before a group of strangers. As a practical matter, few people are likely to put themselves on the spot as being possessed of a socially inappropriate viewpoint.[72]

Another problem, albeit a soluble one, arises in the particular context of age bias, which is an inherently ambiguous matter. In some settings doubts or negative attitudes regarding elders may be without merit. For example, the Age Discrimination in Employment Act of 1967, establishes as a statutory imperative that bias directed toward older workers, manifested by adverse workplace decisions, is improper. On the other hand, age-based views in other contexts sometimes are warranted. For example, those who believe that age matters in the case of older drivers because elderly men and women are seen as being more dangerous than middle-aged drivers, and who thus favor more stringent relicensure requirements for older folks, are correct interpreters of the facts.[73] Thus, questions that would be aimed at detecting the improper bias of a prospective juror necessarily would have to be carefully framed to focus solely on that matter of bias, lest the prospective juror's empirically supported assessments and attitudes regarding the elderly (or the young) be confused with inappropriate ageist prejudice.

Still, while perfection in any part of the legal process is unattainable, the flaws of the voir dire process certainly are not so damning that they provide a legitimate excuse for not using the voir dire opportunity to try to cleanse the courtroom of bias.

Jury Instructions

An additional sensible locus of attention is jury instructions. There are a couple of issues here.

For one, it may be worth considering the use of pretrial instructions, given the earlier described study showing that older jurors who receive such direction arrive at more accurate conclusions. The task for lawyers of identifying the relevant legal concepts in advance of trial is hardly novel: in the federal courts attorneys are required to develop extensive pretrial documentation of just this nature.[74]

Timing aside, if the judge has reason to believe that the age factor may play an inappropriate role in jury deliberations, a cautionary posttrial instruction delivered by the judge on her own initiative would be in order. Moreover, either the plaintiff, the defendant, or both should be able to secure the judge's giving such an instruction upon a reasonable showing of possible risk to the trial's fair outcome. Of course, it certainly is debatable as to how much value an instruction concerning the avoidance of age bias would have. To the extent that general response patterns are age-correlated, it would seem to be exceedingly difficult for a judge to instruct jurors with any useful specificity as to how to overcome their ingrained, often unconscious, attitudes. Relatedly, given the nature of these attitudes, it may be fruitless and/or even misplaced to ask jurors to somehow shed their age-tinged attitudes and (often unconscious) thought processes, while still retaining the integrity of their value systems and general response patterns.

In sum, a cautionary jury instruction may be useful as a matter of form to enable attorneys and judges to feel comfortable as to the procedural adequacy of the trial. It may not in substance be adequate or effective.

Jury Composition

If one cannot evict ageism from the jury room, perhaps a practical means for tempering the ill consequences of ageist bias is to ensure that *all* biases are admitted into the room, to the end of at least mitigating their respective impacts by their canceling each other out. In this regard, John Guinther, a leading student of jury performance, made the following observation: "[O]ne conclusion . . . does suggest itself from the research on jury selection, namely, that *the more heterogeneous the jury's composition, the greater the likelihood of rich and unbiased performance,* largely and apparently due to the great variety of life-experiences and points-of-view that will come into play from such a body when the time for deliberation arrives."[75] However, rather than acknowledging that jurors may entertain differing age-correlated values and attitudes, and thus ruling in ways to ensure that juries are not age-skewed, the courts in fact have turned a blind eye to the matter of jury composition, as discussed below.

Jury Profiles in Terms of Age

The creation of a jury is a three-step matter. First there is the compilation of a list of potential jurors.[76] The individuals included on such lists constitute the jury pool. Second, from time to time those individuals whose names are on the list will be summoned for jury service. Those who respond constitute the jury venire. And third, it is from this group that individual jury members—those who sit on what is correctly termed the *petit jury*—are selected.

For a variety of reasons, younger adults generally are disproportionately absent from both civil juries and criminal grand and petit juries: their percentages on juries do not reflect their percentages in the general population.[77] There are several explanations for this phenomenon. For one, a few state statutes set minimum ages for jury selection.[78] These typically have withstood challenge.[79] Sometimes individuals of less than a certain age were excluded in the past (and possibly currently, as well) simply by practice, despite statutory silence on the issue.[80] Today, there are age-neutral factors that may result in the absence of individuals at the lower end of the age spectrum.[81] Most significantly, the use of voter lists for the preparation of jury pools leads to the underrepresentation of the young, inasmuch as the percentage of registered young voters is considerably less than young men's and women's actual share of the voting age population.[82] The use of such lists has withstood constitutionally based attack.[83] Age-based peremptory challenges directed to young jurors likewise have been held to be constitutionally acceptable.[84]

The situation regarding older jurors is more complex. For example, in an extensive study published in 1991 that reviewed eight state courts and eight federal courts, the percentage of federal court jurors ages 60 and over ranged from 13 percent in Boston and 14 percent in Denver to 21 percent in Bismarck, North Dakota, and 25 percent in Phoenix.[85] At the state court level, the percentages ranged from 12 percent in Boston to 23 percent in Montgomery, Alabama.[86] At the far end of the age spectrum, that is, those individuals 70 and over, there also were varied percentages, ranging from just 1 percent up to 8 percent.[87] The absence of older individuals is in part explicable by statutes,[88] court rules,[89] and/or common practice, all of which allow elderly men and women to voluntarily excuse themselves.[90] Such exemptions from jury service have been upheld in the face of legal challenge.[91] Older jurors also wind up being excluded by virtue of age-based peremptory challenges, and these, too, have withstood legal attack.[92] There also have been statutes barring older people from serving on juries, and while direct attacks on such laws have been rare, these statutes were upheld by several courts when challenged.[93] (However, in some of these same, as well as other, jurisdictions, there are statements by the courts—albeit in cases not directly addressing exclusionary statutes—which suggest that such laws would not survive if attacked today.)[94]

The Fair Cross-Section Principle

Almost all of the more recent case law flows from challenges to the composition of juries, rather than to the per se exclusion of age-identified individuals. The basic constitutional principle under the Sixth Amendment, which applies to federal and state juries,[95] is that the composition both of the pool and the venire in criminal cases must reflect a "fair cross-section of the community."[96] The fair cross-section principle also has been seen as a goal that may be vindicated pursuant to the Supreme Court's inherent supervisory authority over the lower federal courts.[97] This principle, whose very rubric is largely self-explanatory, has been explained by the Supreme Court:

> The purpose of a jury is to guard against the exercise of arbitrary power—to make available the commonsense judgment of the community as a hedge against the over-zealous or mistaken prosecutor and in preference to the professional or perhaps over-conditioned or biased response of a judge. . . . This prophylactic vehicle is not provided if the jury pool is made up of only special segments of the populace or if large, distinctive groups are excluded from the pool. Community participation in the administration of the criminal law, moreover, is not only consistent with our democratic heritage but is also critical to public confidence in the fairness of our criminal justice system. Restricting jury service to only special groups or excluding identifiable segments playing major roles in the community cannot be squared with the constitutional concept of jury trial.[98]

While the constitutionally grounded fair cross-section principle requires that both in the construction of the jury pool and in the selection of those who make up the jury venire governmental authorities must act so as to compile groups that fairly represent the community at large, the Constitution does not require that the jury members who are actually seated reflect demographically the community at large.[99] So the Supreme Court has established: "[Although] the Sixth Amendment guarantees that the petit jury will be selected from a *pool* of names representing a cross-section of the community, we have never held that the Sixth Amendment requires that 'petit juries *actually chosen* must mirror the community and reflect the various distinctive groups in the population.'"[100] Still, even if the petit jury need not be demographically representative, the requirement that the venire be made up of a fair cross-section of the populace should increase the likelihood that the petit jury also will be so constituted, or that it at least will come closer to that ideal than would otherwise be the case.

While Sixth Amendment claims are limited in that they may be raised only by criminal defendants, the defendant who makes such a claim need not be a member of the excluded group.[101] Accordingly, if a 65-year-old is excluded because of her age from a criminal jury venire, she will have no Sixth Amendment claim to make, but the defendant will.[102] (The excluded potential juror could, however, make an equal protection argument, as discussed below, and so could the defendant.)[103] According to the leading ruling, *Duren v. Missouri*,[104] in order to establish a Sixth Amendment fair cross-section claim the aggrieved defendant must satisfy several requirements: "[T]he defendant must show (1) that the group alleged to be excluded is a 'distinctive' group in the community; (2) that the representation of this group is not fair and reasonable in relation to the number of such persons in the community; and (3) that this under-representation is due to systematic exclusion of the group in the jury-selection process."[105] As the foregoing quotation establishes, distinctiveness— or cognizability–is key. The following is a representative, and often quoted, definition of this notion:

A group to be "cognizable" . . . must have a definite composition. That is, there must be some factor which defines and limits the group. A cognizable group is not one whose membership shifts from day to day or whose members can be arbitrarily selected. Secondly, the group must have cohesion. There must be a common thread which runs through the group, a basic similarity in attitudes or ideas or experience which is present in members of the group and which cannot be adequately represented if the group is excluded from the jury selection process. Finally, there must be a possibility that exclusion of the group will result in partiality or bias on the part of juries hearing cases in which group members are involved. That is, the group must have a community of interest which cannot be adequately protected by the rest of the populace.[106]

Insofar as an individual who is excluded from a jury pool or venire is concerned, he or she can challenge that exclusion under the Fourteenth Amendment's Equal Protection Clause,[107] which applies to federal and state petit and grand juries, both civil[108] and criminal.[109] Her claim would be that she has a constitutionally protected right to not be excluded from jury service on the basis of "state-sponsored group stereotypes rooted in, and reflective of, historical prejudice."[110] In other words, she must establish that a recognizable, distinct group of which she is a member has been singled out for different, adverse treatment; in addition, the equal protection claimant must show substantial underrepresentation of that group.[111]

While there are a few cases in which it has been held or at least stated that no age-defined group whatsoever is distinctive or cognizable,[112] the largest body of decisions—made up of rulings involving both the Sixth Amendment and the Equal Protection Clause—is focused on particular age groupings: for example "young people," or persons between ages 18 and 25. The claims for cognizability in these cases have been almost uniformly rejected.[113] Typical rhetoric was set forth by the Court of Appeals for the First Circuit in *King v. United States,* where the criminal defendant argued that the petit and grand juries failed to reflect a cross-section of the community because they comprised persons selected from a list devoid of individuals who were exempted under state law, that is, individuals under age 25 and over age 70:

> The difference in viewpoint between ages 21 and 25 would not seem to us of any great significance. Nor would there seem to be any substantial effect upon the composition of a jury as a result of eliminating persons over 70 as might be competent to stand duty. We regard it as highly speculative whether the decisional outlook of such excluded persons would be different than that of persons a mere few years older or a few years younger.[114]

Apart from *King,* only a few other courts have touched on the cognizability of age-defined groups at the higher end of the age spectrum; in so doing they, like the *King* court, have rejected the cognizability argument.[115] In only one ruling did a federal appellate court—relying on the inherent supervisory authority of federal circuit courts over federal district courts—rule that older adults constitute a cognizable group.[116] By far most of the case law involves only younger individuals.[117]

Given that in almost all instances defendants' arguments have foundered on the issue of the cognizability of the group whose members were not seated on the jury, there are few cases in which courts have had the occasion to go on to address the *Duren* Court's insistence that for a Sixth Amendment claim to be established there must have been systematic exclusion of an age-defined group. On those relatively rare occasions when this issue has been broached, the courts have rejected arguments that the challenged selection processes entailed the systematic exclusion of age-defined groups.[118] As for the third *Duren* requirement, that is, the matter of underrepresentation, there is even less case law in the age context because defendants so often have failed at the first step of the *Duren* formula, that is, establishment of the distinctiveness of the age-defined group at issue.

Assessing the Likelihood and Advisability of "Reform"

If one views juries as insufficiently composed of age-representative individuals, one presumably would urge that the courts revise their hitherto unreceptive posture vis-à-vis constitutional claims arising out of the exclusion from juries of individuals fitting within age-identified groups. For now, however, this effort would be tantamount to tilting at windmills. It isn't going to happen, and that is so for a variety of reasons.

For one, there is really very little pressure from any source, that is, the public, the bar, politicians, and so on—to bring about any change. Moreover, there are no judicial precedents giving rise to gnawing doubts about the accuracy of earlier decisions. Nor is there any impetus from the Supreme Court to revamp jury selection procedures.

In addition, the difficulties of devising a solution are considerable. It is easy enough to assert that all age-correlated viewpoints should be represented; the problem lies in figuring out how to accomplish that ostensibly laudable goal. Line drawing is the key sticking point here. How do we define identifiable age groups, in order that we can ensure their representation in the jury process?

Perhaps we could use age bands: for example, groupings of people 40–49, 50–59, and so on. But this tack would be problematic in practice. For one, there is nothing to suggest that a 59-year-old in one age band is any different than a 60-year-old in the next age band. Secondly, and conversely, one cannot be confident that there are no differences between the 50-year-old, who is at the young end of a 50–59 age band, and the 59-year-old at the other end. One commentator has suggested use of the age lines drawn by the U.S. Constitution for voting (age 18) and holding federal elected office (age 25 for representative, 30 for senator, and 35 for president and vice president).[119] But these parameters offer little in the way of enhancing jury "representativeness." The lines used in the advertising and media worlds, where adults to be targeted for marketing campaigns often are identified as those individuals between 18 and 49 or so, are no better.[120] In sum, no good answer emerges.

There is another problem here—one of a philosophical nature. For more than 20 years, those who have styled themselves—or have been styled by others—as being advocates for an ageism-free society have deplored the use of age as a basis for formal and informal decision making. Rather, the correct course, it has been vigorously maintained, is to judge people on their own merits and abilities: discard the flawed use of generalization—"people over 55 are such-and-such," or "people over 65 can't do X," and so on. There thus is something anomalous, if not even perverse, about the notion of importing age as a factor that *must* be taken into account in the jury selection process. The whole point of the civil rights effort has been to eliminate age from the public and private consciousness; here, a demand for age-based assignments of jurors would go exactly contrary to that ethos.[121]

Still, there are some things that can and should be done, all to the end of endeavoring to construct jury pools and ultimately juries that are inclusive of all age groups.

- Bases for creating jury pools other than voting registration lists should be used, inasmuch as such lists do not sufficiently bring young people into the fold.
- Voir dire should be used to exclude those unduly influenced by age concerns.
- Jury instructions can be utilized to try to avert misuses of the age factor.
- Statutes and policies should be discarded that unreflectively allow persons who have attained a certain age, let us say, 65 or 70, to excuse themselves. Granted, the notion that oldsters should be relieved of jury duty responsibilities is based on beneficence: "These folks have done enough for the common good," or "Jury service can be a rigorous task and so we ought to give older men and women a break." But there also is an element of covert condescension here: "Old folks are not up to the task." Age should not be equated with inability, and only demonstrated inability to serve should be an acceptable basis for excusal.

Structural and Technological Changes

For years, students of jury performance have urged various reforms. Many of these promise improvement regardless of the juror's age. Some have more particular relevance to older jurors.

One practice that is endorsed increasingly is jury note-taking. This is a practice that, according to its advocates, enhances juror decision making.[122] Written or taped jury instructions that the jurors can take with them into the jury room for continuing reference also have been promoted as being advantageous for the process.[123] And pretrial instructions, discussed earlier, also are worth considering, although great care would have to be taken—were this innovation to be adopted—to avoid influencing jurors.

With respect to the particular needs and performance of older jurors, a number of barriers impeding older individuals' physical access to the courts may exist that can be readily rectified, such as the lack of adequate accessible parking,[124] the existence of adequate public transportation to bring people to and from the courts, and appropriate sound amplification equipment, etc.[125] Other accommodations to facilitate service by older jurors should be devised;

these could include increased lighting in jury rooms and the removal of physical impediments, such as stairs, to access to jury boxes and courtrooms.[126]

Conclusions

Juries serve a very important symbolic role in American society. They are critically significant components of the American legal system. While it would be absurd to expect jurors to leave their values and experiences outside the jury room, and indeed it would not even be desirable for them to do so, it does not follow that the age factor is innocuous as it plays out in jurors' decision-making efforts. Indeed, it is not.

Granted, ageism does not rise to the level of perniciousness that characterizes racism and prejudice based on a disliked individual's national origin. Nonetheless, jurors' age bias has consequences—consequences that may be benign or adverse, depending on one's perspective. So long as we cannot ensure that all manifestations of age bias—ranging from expressions of unshakable prejudice to iterations of mild preference—will have their day in the jury room, it is best to seek to mitigate the effects of this bias, whether those effects are benign or malignant.

9

A Time for Action

Old age will only be respected if it fights for itself, maintains its own rights, avoids dependence on anyone, and asserts control over its own to the last breath. I approve of the young man who has something of the old in him, and likewise of the old who has something of the young; if a man follows that principle, he may grow old in body, *but never in spirit.*
—Cicero, Cato Maior de Senectute (44 B.C.E.)

We only grow in one direction: older. And because of a surge in births in the United States in the twenty or so years following the end of World War II, there are today an unparalleled number of Americans who are doing just that—growing older into their 50s and thence, in the near future, their 60s and later on their 70s and beyond. This demographic tidal wave is implacable and irresistible.

And yet it has been little noted, even though it is so quickly apparent upon reflection, that the American legal system is going to be caught up in this phenomenon. It is going to be both affected by, and will itself affect, the middle-aged and elderly litigants, judges, jurors, lawyers, and witnesses who increasingly will animate and operate within this system that governs—both directly and by indirection—virtually everything we do.

The first task for us is to recognize that there is inevitably going to be this intersection of an aging America with the pervasive system of laws, regulations, and enforcement mechanisms that governs our conduct and our relationships. The second task is to identify what steps—whether they be minor adjustments, major revisions, or measures in between—are going to be needed to enable the legal system to work better. Better both for its own purposes of meting out justice and for the particular sake of the aging individuals operating within that system.

A number of proposals have been set forth here, including the following:

- Research and study to identify and to better understand a variety of aspects of the legal system's collision with an aging America
- Education of judges, lawyers, and law students to disabuse them of their biases, or at least to make them aware that those biases are operative

- Improved techniques for enhancing the performance of older witnesses and older jurors
- Abolition of mandatory retirement requirements imposed upon judges
- Amendment of judicial codes of conduct to condemn age bias by judges
- Accommodation of aging individuals' physical needs in the courtroom
- Greater attention to the needs of aging attorneys

And so the task now is to begin to act.

Notes

Chapter 1. Demographics, Destiny, and the American Legal System

The epigraphs are from the following sources: "The Love Song of J. Alfred Prufrock" (1915), in *T. S. Eliot, Collected Poems, 1909–1962*; "Borge's Chord," by Howard Reich, *Chicago Tribune*, July 28, 1996, Sec. 7, p. 6; http:/www.wiseoldsayings.com/humorous1.html.

1. Alan Pifer and Lydia Bronte, eds., *Our Aging Society* 3 (1986).

2. In 1999 the five states with the largest populations of people 65 and older were Florida (18.1 percent), Pennsylvania (15.8 percent), Rhode Island (15.6 percent), West Virginia (15.1 percent), and Iowa (14.9 percent). The states with the smallest percentages were Alaska (5.6 percent), Utah (8.7 percent), Georgia (9.8 percent), Colorado (10.1 percent), and Texas (10.1 percent). The states with the largest percentage increases between 1990 and 1999 were Nevada (61 percent), Alaska (55 percent), Arizona (31 percent), Hawaii (30 percent), and Colorado, Utah, and New Mexico (tied at 23 percent). As of 1999 about 50 percent of persons 65 and older lived in the suburbs, 27 percent lived in central cities, and 23 percent lived in metropolitan areas. Administration on Aging, U.S. Department of Health and Human Services, *A Profile of Older Americans:(2000)*. These data were derived from the U.S. Bureau of the Census, Population Estimates Program, Population Division.

3. U.S. Bureau of the Census, *Projections of the Total Resident Population by 5-Year Age Groups, and Sex with Special Age Categories, Middle Series, 2001 to 2005* (Jan. 13, 2003).

4. Ibid. The number of youngsters through age 17 was projected to be 60 million.

5. U.S. Bureau of the Census, *Projections of the Total Resident Population by 5-Year Age Groups, and Sex with Special Age Categories: Middle Series, 2025–2045* (Jan. 13, 2003).

6. U.S. Senate Special Committee on Aging, American Association of Retired Persons, Federal Council on the Aging, and U.S. Administration on Aging, *Aging America—Trends and Projections 1991 Edition* xix (n.d. 1991). What makes this future demographic equilibrium so notable is the fact that as recently as 1995 28 percent of Americans were 19 and younger, while less than half that percentage—12.8 percent—were elders!

7. According to a United Nations issuance released in June 2002, 10 percent of the world at that time was 60 or older; by 2050 20 percent will be. The largest concentrations of the elderly (in percentage terms) are in the developed countries: 20 percent of Europeans in 2000 were 60 or older, whereas only 5 percent of Africans were. Division for Social and Policy Development, United Nations, *The Aging of the World's Population* (June 11, 2002), http://www.un.org.esa/socdev/ageing/agewpop.htm. But even in some less-developed non-Western countries the numbers already are, or soon will be, enormous. For example, "in China . . . the population aged 65 and over will increase from 6.4 percent (71 million people) [in 1993] to about 20 percent (270 million people) in 2050" and "India, which has the second largest elderly population [after China] should experience [an] even greater proportionate increase." S. Jay Olshansky, Bruce A. Carnes, and Christine K.

Cassell, *The Aging of the Human Species,* 268 Sci. Am. 46, at 48 (Apr. 1993). Other figures are even more daunting: It has been reported that by 2045 China will have 400 million people age 60 and over—25 percent of the populace. John Leicester, "China Population Hurtles Toward Old Age; Pension, Retiree Facilities Pushed as Crisis Nears," *Chicago Tribune,* March 19, 2000, Business, p. 7. By 2030 one-third of the population of Germany will be 60 and over. Arthur Kreuzer and Ulrike Grasberger, *Elders and the Criminal Justice System in Germany,* in *Elders, Crime, and the Criminal Justice System* 273, at 273 (Max B. Rothman, Burton D. Dunlop, and Pamela Entzel, eds. 2000).

8. See, e.g., Steven M. Albert and Maria G. Cattell, *Old Age in Global Perspective* 36–37 (1994).

9. See, e.g., an interview with Dr. Harold Hodgkinson, director of the Center for Demographic Policy at the Institute for Educational Leadership, in Washington, D.C., as reported in the *New York Times:*

Nobody in 1980 assumed that the number of adults going to college would be so high today. Of the 15 million students in college, almost half of them are adults with kids and jobs. . . .

. . . A lot of people are beginning to come back to higher education for a capstone experience in their 40's, 50's, and 60's. Not for a better job, but for a vindication of their life. . . .

Older students have different needs. A whole lot of 30- and 40-year-olds have been out of education a long time. They may have a lot of innate smarts, but they don't remember the quadratic equation. So a lot of remedial education is to get 40-year-olds [and assumedly 65-year-olds, as well] to remember how to write a good theme, and that is fine.

Karen Arenson, "Reading Statistical Tea Leaves," *New York Times,* Aug. 5, 2001, Education Life, Sec. 4A, p. 14.

While in 1998 only 0.5 percent of Americans ages 55 and older were enrolled as full-time students, this percentage should increase as more and more baby boomers move into their 50s and 60s. Sharon Yntema, ed., *Americans 55 & Older* 61 (1999). In terms of part-time college students, 225,000 men and women ages 55 and over were enrolled in 1996; they constituted 1.5 percent of total college enrollees and 3.7 percent of the part-time students. Id. at 63. As for adult education, 28 percent of men and women ages 55–64 and 15 percent of those 65 and over were participants in such classes in 1995. Id. at 65.

10. Health care in the United States in fact is rationed through financing schemes, such as Medicaid and Medicare, that dictate the types of care that will be funded and the duration of such funded care. We also rely upon the private marketplace to effectively ration care: wealthy people have access to more and better care than do those who, while not poor and therefore eligible for Medicaid, are financially stressed.

There is an extensive body of literature regarding health care rationing. See, e.g., Robert H. Binstock and Stephen G. Post, eds., *Too Old for Health Care?* (1991); Daniel Callahan, *Setting Limits* (1987); Howard Eglit, *Health Care Allocation for the Elderly: Age Discrimination by Another Name?* 26 Houston L. Rev. 813 (1989); John F. Kilner, *Who Lives? Who Dies?* (1990). These publications constitute only a small sampling of the literature.

11. Senior citizen housing complexes and so-called retirement communities are proliferating. See, e.g., Andrew Jacobs, "Still Working Boomers 'Retire' to Resorts," *New York Times,* Aug. 26, 2001, pp. 1, 27. Typically, these types of housing entail restrictions (a)

requiring that the residents (or at least one member of a married couple) be no less than 55 years of age, and/or (b) barring children. Both case law, see, e.g., Taylor v. Rancho Santa Barbara, 206 F.3d 932 (9th Cir. 2000); Maldini v. Ambro, 36 N.Y.2d 481, 330 N.E.2d 403, 369 N.Y.S.2d 385 (1973), *cert. denied,* 423 U.S. 993 (1975); Taxpayers Assn. of Weymouth Township, Inc. v. Weymouth Township, 71 N.J. 249, 364 A.2d 1016 (1976), *cert. denied,* 430 U.S. 977 (1977); White Egret Condominium v. Franklin, 379 So.2d 346 (Fla. 1979), and a federal statute—the Federal Fair Housing Act, as amended, 42 U.S.C. § 3607—do not regard these factors as constituting illegal discrimination. See generally Howard Eglit, 2 *Age Discrimination* ch. 13 (1981 and annual supps.). As to data regarding nursing homes, board and care facilities, and assisted living facilities, see chapter 4.

Apart from formally organized retirement communities, there are also a burgeoning number of what have been termed *naturally occurring retirement communities*—communities in which a significant number of older people are aging in place and in tandem. See Alan Feuer, "High-Rise Colony of Workers Evolves for Their Retirement," *New York Times,* Aug. 5, 2002, pp. A1, A15.

12. It has been noted:

Mobility is critical to the physical, social, and psychological well-being of the elderly. Physical health depends upon access to medical facilities and other social services. The ability to maintain an active social life in old age depends upon accessibility to family and friends as well as recreational and cultural activities. Key ingredients of psychological health which are enhanced by mobility are freedom from isolation and the ability to choose one's range of activities.

Martin Wachs, *Transportation for the Elderly* 1 (1979); see also Diana K. Harris, ed., *Sociology of Aging* 379–387 (2d ed. 1991).

13. One also should be cognizant of the millions of formal documents that frame the relationships between private parties: contracts for the delivery of goods, deeds, trust agreements, wills, and so on. While negotiated and written in nongovernmental contexts, these documents utilize language that is drafted to conform to statutory and judicially devised standards; moreover, they are executed and followed in explicit or implicit contemplation of ultimate enforcement through the legal system if otherwise insoluble disputes or questions arise. In brief, the legal system looms in the background of every such written instrument and so both the art of drafting legal documents and the act of providing legal advice are performed "in the shadow of the court." Carrie Menkel-Meadow, *The Trouble With the Adversary System in A Post-Modern Multicultural World,* 38 Wm. & Mary L. Rev. 5, 7 (1996); see also Robert Mnookin and Lewis Kornhauser, *Bargaining in the Shadow of Law: The Case of Divorce,* 88 Yale L. J. 950 (1979).

Documents aside, there are hundreds of millions of daily interactions between people that are premised, albeit not consciously so, on the existence of a backdrop of legal rules and standards that, if worse comes to worst, are available to be invoked in the context of the legal system by grievants. For example, I do not think twice about driving down a two-lane street with no median strip and with another car coming toward me; I assume that the oncoming car will not cross the lane into mine. While my willingness to trust that stranger in the other car is in part based on his presumed desire for self-preservation, it also is partly grounded on the fact that there is a law—which I certainly could not cite by formal nomenclature nor even directly quote—making it unlawful to cross median lines into other folks' lanes. That law forms a backdrop governing the conduct of both the other driver and me, and thus is a part of the legal system that embraces and regulates all of us, whether or not we consciously take note of it.

14. It is tricky to define who the elderly are and what old age is. Increasingly, those conversant with gerontology and geriatric dialogue speak of the "young-old" and the "old-old." See Bernice L. Neugarten and Gunhild Hagestad, *Age and the Life Course*, in *Handbook of Aging and the Social Sciences* 35, at 46 (Robert H. Binstock and Ethel Shanas, eds. 1976):

> Still another division [among older people] seems to be appearing, that between the young-old and the old-old. . . . The young-old, drawn mainly from those aged 55–75, is a group who are relatively healthy and vigorous, relatively comfortable in economic terms, and relatively free from the traditional responsibilities of both work and parenthood.

It has been observed that while in past decades age 65 was often seen as the critical trigger in the United States for elderhood, that benchmark is losing its significance:

> The societal view has been that . . . [old age] starts at sixty-five when most people retire from the labor force. But in the United States today, most people retire before that age. . . . At the same time, with continued good health some persons are staying at work full-time or part-time until their eighties. So age sixty-five and the event of retirement are no longer clear markers between middle age and old age.
>
> Alternatively, old age is often said to begin when a person requires special health care because of frailty or chronic disease, or when health creates a major limitation on the activities of everyday life. Yet half of all persons who are now seventy-five to eighty-four report no such health limitations. Even in the very oldest group, those above eighty-five, more than one-third report no limitations due to health; about one-third report some limitations, and one-third are unable to carry out everyday activities. Thus, health status is also becoming a poor age marker.

Bernice L. Neugarten and Dail A. Neugarten, *Changing Meanings of Age in the Aging Society*, in *Our Aging Society* 33, at 35–36 (Alan Pifer and Lydia Bronte, eds. 1986).

"The World Health Organization classifies persons . . . between 60 and 75 as elderly[,] [those] between 76 and 90 . . . as old, and those over 90 . . . as very old." Alexander P. Spence, *Biology of Human Aging* 8 (1989). Another increasingly common set of delineations identifies those persons ages 65 to 74 as the "young-old," those 75 to 84 as "old," and persons 85 and over as the "old-old." See Cynthia M. Taenber, U.S. Department of Commerce, Special Studies P23-178, *Sixty-Five Plus in America* 1–2 (1992).

For a survey of definitions of old age across cultures, see Nancy Foner, *Ages in Conflict* 7–27 (1984).

15. Age Discrimination in Employment Act of 1967, as amended, 29 U.S.C. §§ 621–634 (extends protection to persons upon attainment of age 40).

16. Equal Credit Opportunity Act, 15 U.S.C. §§ 1691–1691f.

17. Two influential early scholarly works were authored by pioneers in the law and aging field, Professor George Alexander and Professor John Regan. See George J. Alexander and Travis H. D. Lewin, *The Aged and the Need for Surrogate Management* (1972) and John Regan, *Protective Services for the Elderly: Commitment, Guardianship, and Alternatives*, 13 Wm. & Mary L. Rev. 569 (1972). See also Peter M. Housman, *Protective Services for the Elderly: The Limits of Parens Patriae*, 40 Mo. L. Rev. 215 (1975). There were useful congressional reports and studies as well. See, e.g., Select Committee on Aging, U.S. House of Representatives, *Surrogate Decisionmaking for Adults: Model Stan-*

dards to Ensure Quality Guardianship and Representative Payeeship Services, Comm.
Pub. No. 100-705, 100th Cong., 2d Sess. (1989); Special Committee on Aging, U.S. Sen-
ate, *Protective Services for the Elderly—A Working Paper,* 95th Cong., 1st Sess. (1977); see
also American Bar Association Commission on the Mentally Disabled and American Bar
Association Commission on Legal Problems of the Elderly, *Guardianship—An Agenda for
Reform,* 13 Mentally & Physically Disabled Rptr. 271 (1989).

18. Between 1980 and 1992 "every state in the nation made some revisions in its
guardianship law, and a significant number of these were major reforms." Penelope A.
Hommel, *Guardianship Reform in the 1980s: A Decade of Substantive and Procedural
Change,* in *Older Adults' Decision-Making and the Law* 225, at 228 (Michael Smyer, K.
Warner Schaie, and Marshall B. Kapp, eds. 1996).

Guardianship is a system that operates at the state (as opposed to the federal) level. As
to one analyst's focus on a particular state system, see Alison Patrucco Barnes, *Florida
Guardianship and the Elderly: The Paradoxical Right to Unwanted Assistance,* 40 U. Fla.
L. Rev. 949 (1988); as to state systems generally, see Lauren Barritt List and Saidy
Barinaga-Burch, *National Study of Guardianship Systems: Summary of Findings and Rec-
ommendations,* 29 Clearinghouse Rev. 643 (1995); Erica F. Wood, *State Guardianship
Legislation: Directions of Reform,* 29 Clearinghouse Rev. 654 (1995).

As typically is the case, the reforms have generated criticism and calls for reform of the
reforms. See, e.g., Lawrence A. Frolik, *Guardianship Reform: When the Best is the Enemy
of the Good,* 9 Stanford L. & Policy Rev. 347 (1998).

19. See, e.g., Mary Adelaide Mendelson, *Tender Loving Greed* (paperback ed. 1974);
Special Committee on Aging, U.S. Senate, *Nursing Home Care: The Unfinished Agenda,* S.
Rpt. 99-160, 99th Cong., 2d Sess. (1986); Special Committee on Aging, Subcommittee on
Long-Term Care, U.S. Senate, *Nursing Home Care in the United States: Failure in Public
Policy,* S. Rpt. No. 93-1420, 93d Cong., 2d Sess. (1974); Clair Townsend, *Old Age—The
Last Segregation* (1971); U.S. General Accounting Office, Report to the Special Committee
on Aging, U.S. Senate, *California Nursing Homes—Care Problems Persist Despite Federal
and State Oversight,* GAO/HEHS-98-202 (July 1998); Bruce C. Vladeck, *Unloving Care*
(1980).

20. In 1987 the Omnibus Reconciliation Act of 1987 was enacted; it included broad
legislative provisions aimed at ensuring quality care and protecting patients' rights. Omnibus Reconciliation Act of 1987, Pub. L. No. 100-203, 101 Stat. 1330-175, 1330-179,
1330-182 (1987) (codified at 42 U.S.C. §§ 1395i-3(a)-(h), 1396r(a)-(h) (1994)). As to
federal regulatory efforts generally, see David A. Bohm, *Striving for Quality Care in
America's Nursing Homes: Tracing the History of Nursing Homes and Noting the Effect
of Recent Federal Government Initiatives to Ensure Quality Care in the Nursing Home
Setting,* 4 DePaul J. of Health Care 316, 331–354 (2001).

21. The most prominent of these were Medicare, 42 U.S.C. § 1395 *et seq.,* and programs created by the Older Americans Act, 42 U.S.C. § 3001 *et seq.*

22. The work of the American Bar Association's Commission on Legal Problems of the
Elderly, based in Washington, D.C., the Center for Social Gerontology, based in Ann Arbor, Michigan, and Legal Counsel for the Elderly, based in Washington, D.C., confirm that
outstanding talent has been brought to bear by the private sector to advocate in law-related
contexts for the rights and interests of older men and women. In fact, one study that
touched on some of the issues addressed more extensively in this book was issued in 1991
by the ABA Commission. See American Bar Association Commission on Legal Problems of

the Elderly and American Bar Association Commission on the Mentally Disabled, *Court-Related Needs of the Elderly and Persons with Disabilities* (1991).

A number of law schools operate clinics that provide free or low-cost legal services to older clients. See Sally Balch Hume, ed., *Elderlaw Directory of Seminars, Courses, and Clinics in U.S. Law Schools* (1993). In the last few years there also has been an aggressive effort on the part of the National Academy of Elder Law Attorneys, Inc., based in Tucson, to promote elder law as a discrete area of legal practice.

23. The executive director of the National Academy of Elder Law Attorneys, Inc. (NAELA), the largest association of such attorneys, has defined elder law as "a specialty [area] of law that caters to the needs of older clients and those with disabilities." Laury L. Adsit, *Elder Promoting Law*, IX NAELA News 3 (Nov./Dec. 1997). Ms. Adsit continued: "It encompasses areas such as probate and estate planning, Medicaid, Medicare, Social Security, disability planning, long-term care, housing options, powers of attorney, etc."

24. The term *baby boomer* applies to the 70 million-plus Americans born between 1946 and 1964. As to how age 65 has come to have such symbolic and actual significance in American society as the marker for movement into elder status, see Howard Eglit, *Of Age and the Constitution*, 57 Chi.-Kent L. Rev. 859, at 859–860 n. 3 (1981); Arnold M. Rose, *The Subculture of the Aging: A Topic for Sociological Research*, in *Middle Age and Aging* 29, at 32 (Bernice L. Neugarten, ed. 1968); see also chapter 2.

25. See, e.g., Mark E. Doremus, *Wisconsin's ElderLinks Initiative: Using Technology to Provide Legal Services to Older Persons*, 32 Wake Forest L. Rev. 545 (1997).

26. See Eglit, *Of Age and the Constitution*, note 24 supra.

27. See, e.g., Howard Eglit, *The Age Discrimination in Employment Act at Thirty: Where It's Been, Where It Is Today, Where It's Going*, 31 U. of Richmond L. Rev. 579, at 656 and 656 n. 200 (1997).

28. See chapter 8.

29. In the past decade or so, a number of studies were undertaken regarding possible racial, ethnic, and/or gender bias in the courts, but the age issue was not, and continues to not be, examined. See, e.g., *Report of the First Circuit Gender, Race and Ethnic Bias Task Forces*, 9 Boston U. Public Interest L. J. 173 (2000), and a number of other reports listed therein at 184 n. 1.

30. As to these perceptions and attitudes, see chapter 2.

31. See, e.g., Becca R. Levy, *Mind Matters: Cognitive and Physical Effects of Aging Self-Stereotypes*, 58B J. of Gerontology P203, at P204 (2003) ("As an indication of the continuity between aging stereotypes and aging self-stereotypes, elders express attitudes toward their own group that are as negative as those expressed by the young toward the old"); Thomas H. Hess, Corinne Auman, Stanley J. Colcombe, and Tamara A. Rahhal, *The Impact of Stereotype Threat on Age Differences in Memory Performance*, 58B J. of Gerontology P3 (2003); Jack Levin and William C. Levin, *Ageism: Prejudice and Discrimination Against the Elderly* 100 (1980); Becca R. Levy and Mahzarin R. Banaji, *Implicit Ageism*, in *Ageism* 49, at 55, 66–67 (Todd D. Nelson, ed. 2002). It is hardly surprising that if one has been inculcated from one's earliest days with negative notions regarding old age and old people, one is going to have a mighty struggle to avoid self-loathing when one becomes old. See generally Gordon W. Allport, *The Nature of Prejudice* 150–153 (paperback ed. 1994). Allport wrote as follows:

> We . . . [apply] the term self-hate to one's sense of shame for possessing the despised
> qualities of one's group—whether these qualities be real or imaginary. We . . . [ap-

ply] it also to repugnance for other members of one's group because they "possess" these qualities. Id. at 152.

Judge Richard A. Posner, in addressing the matter of employment discrimination, has taken a different view of the likelihood of one who is himself old disliking others who possess the same characteristic. He has made the argument (while wearing a different hat than that of judge) that inasmuch as it is older individuals who hold positions of authority in businesses and other employment settings, it is unlikely that, in making employment decisions vis-à-vis older subordinates, they "harbor either serious misconceptions about the vocational capacities of the old . . . or a generalized antipathy toward old people." Richard A. Posner, *Aging and Old Age* 320 (1995). Judge Posner offered no empirical support for this proposition.

32. Brian H. Bornstein, *Memory Processes in Elderly Witnesses: What We Know and What We Don't Know,* 13 Behavioral Sciences & the Law 337, 339 (1995). (It is true that this differential in assessments regarding the competency of older witnesses perhaps may be an accurate evaluation by those best equipped to assess the abilities of older people.)

33. Erdman B. Palmore, *Ageism: Negative and Positive* 20 (1990), citing Mark Werick and Guy J. Manaster, *Age and the Perception of Age and Attractiveness,* 24 Gerontologist 408, at 409 (1984).

34. See Levy, *Mind Matters: Cognitive and Physical Effects of Aging Self-Stereotypes,* note 31 supra, at P206; Susan Krauss Whitbourne and Joel R. Sneed, *The Paradox of Well-Being, Identity Processes, and Stereotype Threat: Ageism and Its Potential Relationships to the Self in Later Life,* in *Ageism* 247, at 265–266 (Todd D. Nelson, ed. 2002); Levy and Banaji, *Implicit Ageism,* note 31 supra, at 59–62; see also chapter 2.

35. I also concede that it sometimes can work to some individuals' advantage. See chapter 7 regarding lenient criminal sentences imposed on older offenders.

36. This task is circumscribed in one important respect by my excluding from my effort attention to prisons and the "graying" of the American prison population. Thus, I note but do not address a considerable body of literature dealing with the phenomenon of aging prisoners. See, e.g., Evelyn S. Newman, Donald J. Newman, and Mindy L. Gewirtz, eds., *Elderly Criminals* (1984); William E. Adams, Jr., *The Incarceration of Older Criminals: Balancing Safety, Cost, and Humanitarian Concerns,* 19 Nova L. Rev. 465 (1994); Nadine Curran, *Blue Hairs in the Bighouse: The Rise in the Elderly Inmate Population, Its Effect on the Overcrowding Dilemma and Solutions to Correct It,* 26 New Eng. J. on Crim. & Civil Confinement 225 (2000); John J. Kerbs, *The Older Prisoner: Social, Psychological and Medical Considerations,* in *Elders, Crime, and the Criminal Justice System* 207 (Max B. Rothman, Burton D. Dunlop, and Pamela Entzel, eds. 2000); Victoria Kidman, *The Elderly Offender: A New Wrinkle in the Criminal Justice System,* 14 J. of Contemporary Law 131 (1988); James L. Knapp and Kenneth B. Elder, *Assessing Prison Personnel's Knowledge of the Aging Process,* 4 J. of the Okla. Crim. Justice Research Consortium (Aug. 1997/1998); David Shichor, *An Exploratory Study of Elderly Probationers,* 32 International J. of Offender Therapy and Comparative Criminology 163 (1988). I justify the exclusion of issues involving prisons and prisoners on the basis of the facts that penological theories, correctional institutions, and methodologies for dealing with prisoners and postprison releasees are distinct matters separate and apart from the issues addressed in this book.

Chapter 2. Age and Ambivalence

The epigraphs are from the following sources: Richard A. Posner, *Aging and Old Age* 204 (1995); Robert A. Butler, *Why Survive? Being Old in America* 11 (1975).

1. Howard Eglit, 1 *Age Discrimination* 1-2–1-3 (2d ed. 1994 and annual supps.) (footnotes omitted).

2. Id. at 1-9–1-10; see also Howard P. Chudacoff, *How Old Are You?* 184–185 (1989): First, age grading [the assignment of roles and expectations to people based on their ages] has resulted from the urge for rationalization. A modern, industrial society needs an orderly, calculable means of organization, a way of making all forms of activity sensible, uniform, predictable. . . .

Second, age grading has provided the organizing principle for social control. Family and community sanctions no longer suffice in a world of large-scale industrial production and heterogeneous cities. Proponents and administrators of institutions, such as schools and social welfare systems, have needed standards to guide the establishment and operation of those institutions. . . . [A]ge has filled that need.

Third, age has replaced more informal mechanisms for determining access to certain positions. In previous eras, people succeeded to certain ranks when they were "ready"—that is, had mastered a skill or acquired the requisite physical strength or biological capacities (such as childbearing)—or when a position became vacant through death or other forms of removal. The complexities of modern life require more regular systems; though competition survives, age norms and rules of seniority often prevail.

Finally, age has functioned as a method of integrating the multiple roles and responsibilities individuals assume in modern society.

3. See Hammond v. Marx, 406 F. Supp. 853 (D. Me. 1975) (exclusion of 3-year-old from kindergarten).

4. See Purdie v. University of Utah, 584 P.2d 831 (Utah 1978).

5. See, e.g., Mo. Ann. Stat. §§ 565.180–184 (abuse of person age 60 and over is a crime).

6. See, e.g., 21 U.S.C. § 859(a) (penalty doubled for persons over age of 18 who distribute narcotics to persons under age 21); Ariz. Rev. Stat. Ann. § 13-702.D.12 (increase in sentence if victim is 65 or older); Nev. Rev. Stat. Ann. § 193.167 (additional penalty if victim is 65 or older). See generally William E. Adams and Rebecca C. Morgan, *Representing the Client Who is Older in the Law Office and in the Courtroom,* 2 Elder L. J. 1, at 34 n. 170 (1994).

7. Established in 1965 under Title XVIII of the Social Security Act, 42 U.S.C. § 1395 *et seq.,* Medicare covers certain medical and health care costs for eligible individuals over age 64. (The program also covers certain disabled persons who are under age 65.)

8. See, e.g., 753 Ill. Comp. Stat. Ann. § 5/2-1007.1 (where party is 70 or older and has substantial interest in case); see generally Adams and Morgan, *Representing the Client Who is Older,* note 6 supra, at 37 n. 184.

9. See, e.g., State *ex rel.* Oleson v. Graunke, 119 Neb. 440, 229 N.W. 329 (1930); see generally Wayne F. Foster, Annotation, *Validity, Construction, and Application of Age Requirements for Licensing of Motor Vehicle Operators,* 86 A.L.R.3d 475 (1978).

10. The president must be at least 35. U.S. Const., Art. II, § 1. So, too, must the vice president. U.S. Const., amend. XII (vice president must meet the same qualifications as

president). Senators must be at least 30. U.S. Const., Art. I, § 3. Representatives must be at least 25. U.S. Const., Art. I, § 2.

11. See generally Howard Eglit, 4 *Age Discrimination* § 21.04 (1981 and 1992 supp.).

12. See, e.g., Eglit, 1 *Age Discrimination,* note 1 supra, at 1-4–1-5.

13. See, e.g., Ashley Montague, *Don't Be Adultish!* Psychology Today 46, 49 (1977): Most older people have a way of acting as if they were older. They're playing a role. This role of the aged has not only been imposed by others upon them, but is self-imposed. They think, "I'm this age, so I have to behave this way." They feel they must say, "Oh well, when you're my age . . ." or "When I was your age . . ." That sort of thing, to emphasize the fact that they're older. The perception of a difference between the old and the young comes not only from the young but from the older person who, by his behavior, accepts the definition of being old.

14. See, e.g., Bernice L. Neugarten, Joan W. Moore, and John C. Lowe, *Age Norms, Age Constraints, and Adult Socialization,* in *Middle Age and Aging* 22 (Bernice L. Neugarten, ed. 1968).

15. See Simone de Beauvoir, *The Coming of Age* 46 (1972):
If old people show the same desires, the same feelings, and the same requirements as the young, the world looks upon them with disgust: in them love and jealousy seem revolting or absurd, sexuality repulsive and violence ludicrous. They are required to be a standing example of all the virtues. Above all, they are called on to display serenity; the world asserts that they possess it, and this assertion allows the world to ignore their unhappiness. The purified image of themselves that society offers the aged is that of the white-hearted and venerable sage, rich in experience, planing high above the common state of mankind; if they vary from this then they fall below it; the counterpart of the first image is that of the old fool in his dotage, a laughing-stock for his children. In any case, either by their virtue or by their degradation, they stand outside humanity.

In contrast to de Beauvoir's grim analysis, Dr. Bernice Neugarten, one of the pioneers in elevating gerontology to a respected academic discipline, expressed a much more optimistic view in the 1980s regarding what she perceived as the increasing options for older men and women to be free of age-correlated restrictive societal expectations:
There are . . . [growing] changes in the traditional rhythm of the life cycle: increasing numbers of men and women who marry, divorce, then remarry; increasing numbers who rear children in two-parent, then one-parent, then two-parent households; some men who, in May-December marriages, create second families when they are middle-aged. There are increasing numbers of women, but also of men, who enter, exit and reenter our educational institutions, who enter and reenter the labor force; who change jobs at various points, and who undertake second and third careers. All this adds up to what some observers are calling the fluid life cycle, one marked by an increasing number of role transitions, by the proliferation of timetables and by the lack of synchrony among age-related roles.

The society is becoming accustomed to the 70-year-old student, the 30-year-old college president, the 22-year-old mayor, the 35-year-old grandmother, the 50-year-old retiree, the 65-year-old father of a preschooler, and even the 85-year-old mother caring for her 65-year-old son. Age norms and age expectations, then, are diminishing in importance as regulators of behavior.

Bernice L. Neugarten, *Policy for the 1980s: Age or Need Entitlement?* in *Age or Need?*

Public Policies for Older People 21 (Bernice L. Neugarten, ed. 1982). With regard to the phenomenon of older fathers, of which Dr. Neugarten made mention, see Thomas Vinciguerra, "Old Fires, New Sparks: Call Them Start-Over Dads," *New York Times,* Dec. 12, 1996, Living Arts, pp. B1–B2.

16. See Diana K. Harris, *Sociology of Aging* 60 (2d ed. 1991).

17. This notion was highlighted by the comments of a 68-year-old lady attending an AARP conference in Chicago in 2003 who was interviewed for an article about the conference:

> "The thing I can't stand about aging," said [Elizabeth] Marrs—who really does look like Rue McClanahan [of TV's *Golden Girls* fame] and who announced earlier that she has been married seven times—"is being this age but not feeling old. I want to do everything, but people tell me I can't do certain things at my age. Well, yes I can."
>
> Still, Marrs said, "It's not the same as it was. I'm flamboyant, but I feel like I have to slink into a bar or restaurant now because of my age."

Emily Nunn, "One for the ages," *Chicago Tribune,* Sept. 10, 2003, Tempo, pp. 1, 4, at p. 4. But see Diana K. Harris and William E. Cole, *Sociology of Aging* 55 (1980) (data support the conclusion that few social norms apply specifically to older people; rather, "[m]ost norms apply to all age groups").

18. See, e.g., Lynn C. Lancaster and David Stillman, *When Generations Collide* 298 (2002):

> Many members of the older generations would rather collect an unemployment check than be managed by someone younger. They loathe the thought of reporting to someone the age of their son or daughter, especially since they can't exactly give their boss a time-out.

See also Ron Zemke, Claire Raines, and Bob Filipczak, *Generations at Work* 217–218 (2000).

19. See Darrell Steffensmeier and Mark Motivans, *Older Men and Older Women in the Arms of Criminal Law: Offending Patterns and Sentencing Outcomes,* 55B Journals of Gerontology: Social Sciences §141 (2000). As to statutory prescriptions for taking age into account in sentencing, see chapter 7.

20. See, e.g., *Re* T, 81 Misc.2d 535, 365 N.Y.S.2d 709 (1975); *Re* Adoption of Ann, 461 S.W.2d 338 (Mo. 1970); *Re* Adoption of Shields, 4 Wis.2d 219, 89 N.W.2d 827 (1958).

21. A particular striking example of this was the setting of age 65 as the age of eligibility in the Social Security Act of 1935. The casual way in which this occurred was described by Wilbur Cohen, one of the chief staff aides involved in the drafting of the Act, who wrote as follows:

> The simple fact is that at no time in 1934 did the staff or members of the Committee on Economic Security deem feasible any other age than 65 as the eligible age for the receipt of old age insurance benefits. There is, therefore, very little material available to analyze the economic, social, gerontological, or other reasons for the selection of this particular age. The Committee made no detailed studies of alternative ways or of any proposal for voluntary retirement or of any flexible retirement program in relation to the disability of any individual.
>
> It was understood that a reduction in the age below 65 would substantially increase costs, and, therefore, might impair the possibility of . . . acceptance of the plan by Congress. A higher retirement age, of say 68 or 70, was never considered

because of the belief that public and congressional opposition would develop
against such a provision in view of the widespread unemployment that existed.
Wilbur Cohen, *Retirement Policies Under Social Security* 17–18 (1957) (footnotes omitted); see also Irma R. Withers, *Some Irrational Beliefs About Retirement in the United
States,* 1 Indus. Gerontology 23, at 24 (Winter 1974 New Series).

22. See generally Matilda White Riley, Marilyn Johnson, and Anne Foner, 3 *Aging and
Society* 397–456 (1972).

23. The legal scenario in the modern-day United States has been described as follows:
Every state has at least some protections for those who have not yet reached the age
of majority. Children generally are not held responsible for their contracts or their
torts. States set minimum ages for drinking, driving, gambling, smoking, purchasing
pornographic material, voting, marrying, and serving on juries. The United States
government will not draft people under age eighteen into the armed forces. . . .

The Supreme Court's consideration of the constitutional rights of children also
reflects the sentiment that the law should accommodate their inexperience. The
Court has recognized that children have constitutional rights but that these rights
may be qualified to reflect their particular vulnerabilities.

Nicole A. Saharsky, Note, *Consistency as a Constitutional Value: A Comparative Look at
Age in Abortion and Death Penalty Jurisprudence,* 85 Minn. L. Rev. 1119, at 1121–1122
(2001) (footnotes omitted).

24. See generally Georges Minois, *History of Old Age* 6 (1989); William H. Harlan,
Social Status of the Aged in Three Indian Villages, in *Middle Age and Aging* 469 (Bernice
Neugarten, ed. 1968); see also Edward O. Wilson, *Sociobiology—The New Synthesis* 553
(25th anniversary ed. 2000).

25. Leo Simmons, *The Role of the Aged in Primitive Society* 79 (1945). Ultimately, even
in these societies the elderly—if they lived long enough—reached a stage that usually entailed loss of prestige, honor, and often even life:

The Omaha Indians . . . continued to defer to their elders well beyond the onset of
physical weakness. Bodily infirmities did not deter such aged leaders from playing
an active role in society; their status was based on their knowledge and experience.
In contrast, the Shilluk usually labeled their king overaged at an early stage of his
existence. Unable to meet the sexual demands of his many wives, he was considered
to have outlived his usefulness and was put to death by the tribal chieftains. Other
groups equated disease with individuals' inability to provide for their own basic
necessities. Once the aged became a burden to others, they lost their value to society.
Like the sickly Hottentots left in a deserted hut, or the decrepit Lapps bludgeoned to
death, these aged individuals were literally eliminated from playing any part in their
societies.

Carole Haber, *Beyond Sixty-Five* 2 (paperback ed. 1983); see also Leo W. Simmons, *Aging
in Preindustrial Societies,* in *Handbook of Social Gerontology* 87 (Clark Tibbits, ed.
1960).

Historian David Hackett Fischer has written in a similar vein:

There was another stage of life beyond that of "elder." That final period was called
by many different names; it was the stage of the "overaged," or the "sleeping period," or the age of the "already dead," or the "age grade of the dying." Those few
persons who were so unfortunate as to reach it were sometimes treated with great

brutality. Even as most primitive societies honored their elders, many societies (though not all) showed little mercy toward senility or decrepitude. When the old were no longer able to contribute to the common welfare, and no longer able to look after themselves, they were often destroyed. A minority of primitive tribes killed their aged members outright, sometimes in horrible ways, and with the active collaboration of the victim. The people of Samoa, for example, buried their elders alive, and the victim even helped to organize the elaborate ceremony. Those bizarre rites were uncommon; more typical were tribes which disposed of the aged by abandonment or deliberate neglect. Some encouraged suicide among the aged; in eleven of seventeen tribes for which evidence is available, suicide was a "frequent" or "customary" practice in the last stage of life. In any case, senecide was widely practiced. David Hackett Fischer, *Growing Old in America* 9–10 (expanded paperback ed. 1978).

26. See generally Carole S. Slotterback and David A. Saarnio, *Attitudes Toward Older Adults as Reported by Young Adults: Variation Based on Attitudinal Task and Attribute Categories,* 11 Psychology & Aging 563 (1996) (while attitudes toward the elderly are relatively more negative than they are with regard to young and middle-aged adults, there is not a uniform manifestation of negativity except with regard to elders' physical appearance; rather, the expression of negative attitudes will vary with the way in which information is elicited from those being queried and depending upon which personal characteristics are the subject of inquiry).

With regard to the status of the elderly in the United States in colonial and postrevolutionary times, there is disagreement among students of aging and history as to the nature of elders' standing. See chapter 3.

27. See Erdman B. Palmore, *Ageism: Negative and Positive* 29 (1990) (ageism has produced some positive images of old people).

28. U.S. Department of Health and Human Services, Health Care Financing Administration, *2001 HCFA Statistics* 22, Table 26 (n.d.).

29. 42 U.S.C. § 1395 *et seq.* The Medicare program also provides coverage for certain disabled persons under age 65, but the large majority of beneficiaries are elderly women and men.

30. In the author's view, elderhood does not even begin until 65, at the earliest. (Of course, the defining of "old" turns out to be a very problematic endeavor. See chapter 1.) However, from the perspective of young Americans, the state of old age no doubt is seen as starting much sooner. In their view, presumably, it is old folks who run the executive branch of the federal government, given (as of August, 2003) a 57-year-old president, a 62-year-old vice president, and a 61-year-old attorney general. And further tipping the balance in the executive branch were 66-year-old Secretary of State Colin Powell, 71-year-old Secretary of Defense Donald Rumsfeld, 64-year-old Treasury Secretary John Snow, 70-year-old Education Secretary Rodney Paige, 61-year-old Secretary of Health and Human Services Tommy Thompson, and 72-year-old Transportation Secretary Norman Mineta.

As for the federal legislative branch, as of November 2002—just before the elections held on November 5, more than half of the senators were age 60 or older, and 14 were age 70 and above. R. W. Apple, Jr., "Political Issue for the Ages," *New York Times,* Nov. 3. 2002, A1, A18, at A1. Senator Jesse Helms (Rep., N.C.) was 81, Senator Robert Byrd (Dem., W. Va.) was 85, and Senator Strom Thurmond (Rep., S.C.) was 99.

On the Supreme Court, as of February 26, 2004, all but one justice was 64 or older: Justice Stevens (83), Chief Justice Rehnquist (79), Justice O'Connor (73), Justice Ginsburg

(70), Justice Scalia (67), Justice Kennedy (67), Justice Breyer (65), and Justice Souter (64). Justice Thomas was 55. With regard to the average age, year by year, of Supreme Court justices from 1789 through 1998, see David N. Atkinson, *Leaving the Bench*, 188–192 (1999).

31. A little more than 40 years ago an investigator asked 141 American male workers, most of them under age 60, which years they deemed to be the worst for themselves (as opposed to for others), and they responded as follows:

Age Groups	Percentage
Up to 20 years old	4.3 percent
20–35 years	2.5 percent
36–45 years	4.3 percent
46–60 years	8.6 percent
60 and up	80.3 percent

H. Meltzer, *Age Differences in Status and Happiness of Workers*, 17 Geriatrics 831, at 833 (Dec. 1962). Likewise, a 1975 national survey of over 4,000 American individuals ages 18 and over found that 69 percent of the respondents considered the teens, 20s, and 30s as "the best years of a person's life;" only 2 percent of the public felt that way about the 60s and less than 0.5 percent so regarded the 70s. As for those respondents who were 65 or older, 46 percent viewed the teens, 20s, and 30s as the best years, while 8 percent identified the 60s and 70s. Louis Harris and Associates, *The Myth and Reality of Aging in America*, 2 (1976).

Thomas Cole, a noted student of the cultural history of aging, cogently captured this situation with the following astute, but at the same time dispiriting, observations:

In the last twenty years, we have witnessed [in the United States] an important social movement aimed at eliminating age discrimination and at generating new positive images of old age. But this recent attack on ageism—as valuable as it is—has yet to confront the de-meaning of aging rooted in modern culture's relentless hostility toward decay and dependency. In the late twentieth century, later life floats in a cultural limbo. Old age remains a season in search of its purposes.

Thomas R. Cole, *The Journey of Life* xxvi (paperback ed. 1993).

32. Robert N. Butler, *Why Survive? Being Old in America* 6–7 (1975).

33. The term *ageism* denotes a bias that relies on age-based perceptions and distinctions that utilize stereotypes to categorize and classify people on the basis of a particular trait, age, rather than on the basis of their individual merits and defects. While Dr. Butler confined the term to prejudice directed toward the old, it is important to note that age-based bias actually can be brought to bear against individuals who range across the age continuum. The 5-year-old, the 35-year-old, and the 70-year-old all can be the targets of stereotypical thinking whereby the criterion of age is utilized as a basis for making assumptions and generalizations that are devoid of, or at best are only partially based on, empirical grounding. See generally Georgia M. Barrow and Patricia A. Smith, *Aging, Ageism, and Society* 8 (1979).

34. See generally Frank Nuessel, *The Language of Ageism*, 22 Gerontologist 243 (1982). In a related vein, 20 or so years ago 50 college students between the ages of 18 and 35 were asked to list the first four words that came to mind upon seeing the word *aged*. (There is no reason to think that, 20 years later, a like survey would yield different re-

sponses.) Their responses were divided by the researchers into three categories—physical, social, and psychological. (The most frequent response was *old,* but the authors excluded this as being synonymous with *aged.*) With regard to the word *physical,* the students responded as follows (in descending order of frequency):

wrinkled/wrinkles
white/gray hair
slow/feeble/tired
dead/dependent
helpless/dependent
crippled/decrepit/disabled
rest home/convalescent hospital
sickly/illness
over-the-hill
false teeth, glasses
thin, overweight
wizened
looking bad
somewhat deformed
paunchy stomach
stooped shoulders
bent over with cane
heart attacks
resuscitator calls
rocking chair
soft featured
survivor

Barrow and Smith, *Aging, Ageism, and Society,* note 33 supra, at 74.

The responses in the "social category," again set out in decreasing order of frequency, were as follows:

grandparents, parents
alienated/forgotten
poor/poverty/in need
experienced
fixed income/high expenses
useless/nothing to do
quiet/stable
respect/dignified
left out
alone
isolated
trapped
teachers
senior citizen
retired
mobile home park
bleak

Id. at 74–75. The "psychological" category included the following, in decreasing order of frequency:

nice/kind/friendly
senile
lonely, lost
wise/wisdom
love
intolerance
anxiety, confused
unaccepting/prejudiced
sad/sorry
hopeless/desperation
content, calm
knowledge
interesting
set in their ways
developed personality
mean, grouchy
hate
frightening
don't want it

Id. at 75.

35. Stereotypes are so prevalent and so embedded in our culture that they often are used in the media without any obvious first, let alone second, thought. Here is one example, from an article about consumer advocate Ralph Nader that appeared in the *New York Times* a few years ago:

As the new year opens, Ralph Nader, consumer advocate and scourge of business, is well into the fourth decade of his crusade. By now, the press has nearly run out of biblical metaphors. David versus Goliath. Avenging Angel. Saint Ralph. And, more recently, Lazarus back from the dead.

Methuselah may be next. Mr. Nader, a bald spot spreading at the back of his head, will be 62 years old in February, an age when many people retire and activists of a certain age have long since decamped to Wall Street or married Ted Turner.
. . .
But if Methuselah is beating the physical decay associated with aging, some might say he is displaying a classic behavioral symptom of the old-timer: a refusal to bend to changing times. The tendency manifests itself in a variety of ways, from turning on his old allies in the Government and the press to refusing to abandon his type-writer for a computer. And while his admirers view his stubbornness as a principled stand against compromise, his detractors say it weakens his influence just when it is needed most to defend the consumer cause.

Anthony Ramirez, "Consumer Crusader Feels a Chill in Washington / Nader Remains Un-bent by Winds of Change," *New York Times,* Dec. 31, 1995, Sec. 3, pp. 1, 10, at p. 1.

Notice how the author buttressed the commonly held notion that older men are (ought to be?) not working: "62 years old . . . , an age when many people retire." Note also how the author first recounted, without cavil, the "classic behavioral symptom of the old-timer," i.e., a "refusal to bend to changing times." And notice that the author used, without a pause, what could well be read as a pejorative, ageist term, *old-timer*. Note further how the author made no effort to venture that perhaps Ralph Nader was just being his typical stubborn self. Rather, Nader was described as acting like other members of the group to which he belongs: his fellow "old-timers." (The best the author offered by way of nonstereotypical thinking was his reporting that Nader's admirers [obviously a biased group?] saw Nader as being principled.)

36. Carole A. Barbato and Jerry D. Feezel, *The Language of Aging in Different Age Groups,* 27 Gerontologist 527, at 527 (1987).

37. See Georgia M. Barrow, *Aging, the Individual, and Society* 35–38 (5th ed. 1992).

38. Slotterback and Saarnio, *Attitudes Toward Older Adults Reported by Young Adults,* note 26 supra, at 567–568.

39. See, e.g., Peter N. Stearns, *Old Age in European Society: The Case of France* (1976), quoted in Harris, *Sociology of Aging,* note 16 supra, at 72. Arguably, the Senior PGA Tour, for which a golfer must be at least 50 to compete, cuts against this analysis, but few players over 60 actually participate. In any event, the seniors' golf tour is unique; there is no seniors' baseball league or seniors' football or basketball leagues.

40. See generally Amy J. C. Cuddy and Susan T. Fiske, *Doddering but Dear: Process, Content, and Function in Stereotyping of Older Persons,* in *Ageism* 3, at 3 (Todd D. Nelson, ed. 2002); Barbara Whitaker, "In Hollywood No One Gets A Casting Call for This Role," *New York Times,* March 12, 2000, Art and Living, p. 8; Peter M. Nichols, "Some Keep Shining, but Most Just Fade to Gray," *New York Times,* Feb. 23, 1997, Art and Living, pp. 15, 23. Nichols wrote as follows:

"Our senior performers have all but disappeared from television, and they're prac-tically invisible in feature films," says Richard Masur, 48, president of the Screen Actors Guild and a younger older actor with dozens of credits in films and televi-sion. "And I'm not talking about people over 65," he says. "I'm talking about 50." If you're a woman, make that 40.

That state of affairs may seem surprising in an aging population whose dominant segment, the baby boom generation, is already turning 50. Nevertheless, Mr. Masur says, Hollywood feels as free as ever to pursue a young audience that tends to be satisfied with formulaic movies and characters.

Id. at p. 15.

41. "When older Americans are featured, it is usually in the context of programs deal-ing with the 'plight' of the elderly." Linda S. Whitton, *Ageism: Paternalism and Prejudice,* 46 DePaul L. Rev. 453, at 464 (1997), citing Betty Friedan, *The Fountain of Age* 39–41 (1993).

42. A number of lawsuits have been filed over the years under the Age Discrimination in Employment Act of 1967, as amended, 29 U.S.C. §§ 621–634 (ADEA), by TV person-alities claiming—albeit not always successfully—to be victims of age discrimination at the hands of employers who allegedly have deemed these individuals to be underperforming and/or too old to either attract or retain younger viewers. See, e.g., Ryther v. KARE 11, 108 F.3d 832 (8th Cir.), *cert. denied,* 521 U.S. 1119 (1997); Izquierdo Prieto v. Agustin Mercado Rosa, 894 F.2d 467 (1st Cir. 1990); Carlson v. WPLG/TV-10, 70 FEP Cas. (BNA) 1596 (S.D. Fla. 1996); Sheahan v. CBS Inc., 1994 U.S. Dist. LEXIS 2623 (S.D.N.Y. 1994); Combes v. Griffin Television, Inc., 421 F. Supp. 841 (W.D. Okla. 1976). Age bias in the media is nothing new. See Richard H. Davis, *Television and the Aging Audience* 63–70 (1980); Select Committee on Aging, U.S. House of Representatives, *Televised Advertising*

and the Elderly, Comm. Pub. No. 95-128, 95th Cong., 2d Sess. (1978); Select Committee on Aging, U.S. House of Representatives, *Age Stereotyping and Television* 95–109, Comm. Pub. No. 95-109, 95th Cong., 1st Sess. (1977); Gerald Astor, "The Elderly as Television's Forgotten Men and Women," *New York Times,* Aug. 4, 1974, p. D15; Bill O'Hallaren, "Nobody (in TV) Loves You When You're Old and Gray," *New York Times,* July 24, 1977, p. D21.

In a study of children's television cartoon programs it was found that (1) old age is not a dominant theme, but (2) when older people are presented or referred to, typically the presentation or reference is a negative one. James M. Bishop and Daniel R. Krause, *Depictions of Aging and Old Age on Saturday Morning Television,* 24 Gerontologist 91 (1984).

In a related vein, there recently have been reports of age bias directed against television screen writers: the gist of these reports is that anyone over 40 essentially is deemed to be over the hill and thus unemployable. See Robin Pogrebin, *At 40, They're Finished, Television Writers Say,* at www.SalaryExpert.com (Jan. 30, 2001); see also Pat Maio, "High noon for older writers," 42 *AARP Bulletin* 17 (June 2001).

43. It must be noted, however, that there is significant dispute as to whether the general absence of older people and the negative depiction of older people when they do appear have significant consequences for viewers' attitudes regarding aging and old people. Compare George Gerbner, Larry Gross, Nancy Signorielli, and Michael Morgan, *Aging with television: Images in television drama and conceptions of social reality,* 30 J. of Communication 30, at 37–47 (1980) (negative effect exists) with Patricia M. Passuth and Fay Lomax Cook, *Effects of Television Viewing on Knowledge and Attitudes About Older Adults: A Critical Reexamination,* 25 Gerontologist 69 (1985) (little or no effect). Professors Passuth and Cook conclude: "[The] underrepresentation [of older people] does not appear to result in more negative attitudes for any age group of heavy viewers or in less knowledge for any group of heavy viewers except young adults." Id. at 76.

44. Stereotyping has been explained as follows:
Stereotyping is the most fundamental category of bias. A stereotype is an attitude set. Psychologists noted many years ago the tendency among people to form overall impressions of other people, or objects, on the basis of a relatively small number of traits. Thus, jurors often have attitude sets in place which they use to form overall impressions in this way. Usually, these impressions are negative. Stereotyped attitude sets, for example, may involve the attribution of negative traits to people simply because they are members of a certain group.
Donald E. Vinson, *Jury Trials: The Psychology of Winning Strategy* 86–87 (1986).

45. Arnold Arluke and Jack Levin, *Another Stereotype: Old Age as a Second Childhood,* Aging 7–11, at 8 (Aug./Sept. 1994).

46. Id. at 8–9.

47. Id. at 9–10. Another example is afforded by a play review published in the *New York Times.* The play, entitled *Everett Beekin,* and written by Richard Greenberg, followed an American family as it progressed over time from poverty to affluence. The reviewer concluded his review with a line from the play: "'Old people are like little children,' Nell reassuringly says to Celia, who has been talking about recent, uncomfortable revelations from their addled mother. 'They stir up everything they hear and present it as the truth.'"

Ben Brantley, "To Survive, Ma, Never Look Back," *New York Times,* Nov. 15, 2001, p. E5; see also Friedan, *The Fountain of Age,* note 41 supra, at 56–57.

48. Arluke and Levin, *Another Stereotype,* note 45 supra, at 10.

49. Ibid.

50. Ibid. See also Robert Rubinson, *Constructions of Client Competence and Theories of Practice,* 31 Ariz. St. L. J. 120, at 140 (1999) ("Claude Steele's work on a process he calls 'stereotype vulnerability' demonstrates that victims of stereotypes have a tendency to perform in accordance with the expectations generated by the stereotypes," citing Claude M. Steele and Joshua Aronson, *Stereotype Threat and the Intellectual Test Performance of African Americans,* 69 J. Personality & Soc. Psych. 797, at 808 [1995]).

51. Arluke and Levin, *Another Stereotype,* note 145 supra, at 10.

52. Harris, *Sociology of Aging,* note 16 supra, at 6–7, summarizing Erdman B. Palmore, *Attitudes Toward Aging as Shown by Humor: A Review,* in *Humor and Aging* 101–119 (Lucille Nahemow, Kathleen A. McClusky-Fawcett, and Paul E. McGhee, eds. 1986); see also Erdman B. Palmore, *Attitudes Toward Aging as Shown by Humor,* 12 Gerontologist 181–186 (1971).

53. 29 U.S.C. §§ 621–634.

54. See Howard Eglit, *The Age Discrimination in Employment Act at Thirty: Where It's Been, Where It Is Today, Where It's Going,* 31 University of Richmond L. Rev. 579, at 669–672 (1997).

55. Fred Brock, "For Older Authors, a Steeper Hill," *New York Times,* Nov. 5, 2000, Business, p. 11.

56. It should be pointed out, however, that there is what has been termed *the paradox of well-being,* the high level of life satisfaction among the old, "despite the fact that they are confronted on a daily basis with fear and devaluation from others within society." Susan K. Whitburne and Joel R. Sneed, *The paradox of well-being, identity processes, and stereotype threat: Ageism and its potential relationship to the self in later life,* in *Ageism* 247, at 247 (Todd D. Nelson, ed. 2002); but see Meltzer, *Age Differences in Status and Happiness of Workers,* note 31 supra; Louis Harris and Associates, *The Myth and Reality of Aging in America,* note 31 supra, at 2.

57. Robert Browning, *Rabbi Ben-Ezra* (1864), in *The Oxford Book of Aging* 306 (Thomas R. Cole and Mary G. Winkler, ed. 1994).

Chapter 3. Age Bias: Some General Propositions

The epigraphs are from the following sources: Henry David Thoreau, *Walden* 9 (J. Shanley, ed. 1971); Plato, *The Republic, Book I,* in *Plato: The Collected Dialogues* 578 (Edith Hamilton and Huntington Cairns, eds., 1966).

1. The phrasing of this sentence is not meant to suggest that negative attitudes regarding old age and the aged are peculiar to the United States. That certainly is not the case. The intent here is to focus on that society most accessible to this author in terms of experience and research resources.

2. The manner in which this question is posed obviously rests on the assumption that age bias is a reality. This assumption has not gone unchallenged, however. There is a body of literature suggesting that even if negative attitudes regarding old people do or did exist, they are on the wane or have disappeared entirely, and thus ageism at the least is diminishing and may even be extinct. See David R. Austin, *Attitudes Toward Old Age: A Hierarchical Study,* 25 Gerontologist 431 (1985); Clark Tibbits, *Can we invalidate negative stereotypes in aging?* 19 Gerontologist 10 (1979); David Schonfield, *Who is Stereotyping whom*

and why? 22 Gerontologist 267 (1982). The evidence contradicting this position seems too persuasive to reject, however. See, e.g., chapter 2.

3. Tragically, the enumerated physical traits of old age are not exclusively reserved for those who have accumulated many years of living. There are a very small number of children who age prematurely and thus are old physiologically, albeit not chronologically. Progeria is a rare genetic condition characterized by accelerated aging. The classic type is the Hutchinson-Gilford Progeria Syndrome; the other type is known as Werner Syndrome. The former affects children, who typically die at around age 12. The incidence of this syndrome is about 1 in 4 million. The general characteristics include small size, baldness, a pinched nose, a small face and jaw relative to head size, and wrinkled skin. Werner Syndrome appears after puberty, with the full range of symptoms appearing at ages 20 to 30.

4. Study of the history of the treatment of old people and of attitudes regarding old age is of relatively recent vintage. Particularly prominent is the work of Georges Minois, who wrote as follows by way of a brief crosscultural review of the status of old people:

Anthropologists remark . . . frequently on the importance of the privileges enjoyed by old people in present-day traditional societies. Georges Condominas noted concerning South-East Asia:

This privilege of old age can be found at every level. The old man, surrounded by affection, is entitled to a huge number of privileges. It is regarded as normal for him to make use of what strength is left to him to obtain all sorts of satisfactions. . . . If the old man is thus surrounded by considerations, it is not on account of the duty to protect a weaker creature but because happiness imbues and favours the entourage of a man thus privileged. Attaining a great age is considered a happiness and a cause of rejoicing, especially if the old man has many descendants; he has then reached the height of felicity. He cannot be put aside, as happens with us, and be sent off to an old people's home, he stays among his own people because he is the living proof of the group's success.

[Citing Georges Condominas, *Aines anciens et ancetres en Asie du Sud-Est*, 37 Communications 63 (1983).] For his part, Louis-Vincent Thomas observed in black Africa how the old enjoyed considerable prestige among the 22 ethnic peoples he was able to study.

Experience, availability, eloquence, wisdom, knowledge, these all justify the idyllic picture black Africans have of old people, in spite of the reality of old people who can be senile, egoistical, tyrannical or cantankerous, just as they are everywhere in the world. This is because a purely oral society needs its old people, the symbols of its continuity, both in their role as the group's memory and as the prerequisite of its reproduction. So, in order to make their power more bearable and also to enhance one's own value by esteeming them, the group does not hesitate to idealize them. Since nothing can be done without old people, they might as well be attributed every quality—and their somnolence taken for meditative contemplation.

[Citing Louis-Vincent Thomas, *La vieillesse en Afrique Noire*, 37 Communications 85 (1983).]

Georges Minois, *History of Old Age* 6–7 (1989); see also Nancy Foner, *Ages in Conflict* 29–66 (1984).

184 / Notes to Page 15

Women usually count for little in terms of prestige and power in "primitive" societies, and so they typically do not gain a degree of status equal to that of men by growing old. See chapter 4. Sometimes, however, women do gain prestige and power with advancing age. See, e.g., Foner, *Ages in Conflict,* at 67–92.

5. It has been noted:

Filial piety [i.e., respect and devotion to parents] has been a paramount value in China for centuries and has welded the generations together. . . . After the Communist revolution, Marxists at first stressed equality of the generations and tried to reduce the power of parents by abolishing their control over children's marriages. However, filial piety is so deeply embedded in Confucian norms that it remains a strong theme in Chinese life that results in an almost automatic sense of obligation to care for one's frail parents.

Gordon F. Streib, *Traditional Cultural Patterns: China and the United States,* in *Sociology of Aging* 87 (Diana K. Harris, ed., 2d ed. 1991); see generally Sik Hung Ng, *Will Families Support Their Elders? Answers From Across Cultures,* in *Ageism* 295 (Todd D. Nelson, ed. 2002). (Of course, respect and solicitude for one's own parents do not necessarily translate into like responses to other old people.)

6. See, e.g., Philip Olson, *The Elderly in the People's Republic of China,* in *The Cultural Context of Aging* 143 (Jay Sokolovsky, ed. 1990); see also *Researchers Say Educated U.S. Kids Respect Their Elders,* Univ. of Kansas Office of University Relations, http://www.ur.ku.edu/News/96N/MayNews/May14/elders.html. (2002) (reporting that the commonly held view that Chinese youths revere the old, whereas American youths do not, may be wrong, according to a University of Kansas researcher who surveyed youths in Hong Kong and California and concluded that "'the young Chinese viewed the elderly as conservative, unproductive, inactive, lonely, pessimistic, and sad'").

7. See generally Erdman B. Palmore and Daisaku Maeda, *The Honorable Elders,* in *Sociology of Aging* 105 (Diana K. Harris, ed., 2d ed. 1991). "[R]espect for elders is [even] one of the basic dimensions built into the Japanese language," which involves three basic forms of speech, one of which is "the honorific form . . . used in speaking to or referring to someone who is older or otherwise socially superior to the speaker."

8. It has been argued that while in modern Japan "the Japanese elderly enjoy comparatively high prestige," they "are currently neither more powerful nor more secure than their American age-mates." Christie W. Kiefer, *The Elderly in Modern Japan: Elite Victims, or Plural Players?* in *The Cultural Context of Aging* 181, at 186 (Jay Sokolovsky, ed. 1990).

9. Not surprisingly, given its historical linkages to China and Japan, Korean society has been exemplified by a pronounced respect for the elderly. However, a recent survey conducted by UNICEF revealed that the status of the elderly has declined considerably among the young. See Mark Magnier, "Confucian Respect for Elders is Withering Away," *Herald Tribune,* Nov. 23, 2001, http:/www.iht.com/articles/39811.html; see also Nicholas D. Kristof, "Hanoi Journal: Bean Paste vs. Miniskirts: Generation Gap Grows," *New York Times,* May 5, 1999, p. A4 (re elders in Korea).

10. Granted, some of the stereotypes regarding the elderly may not seem to be directly relevant to the issue of age in the context of the American legal system. For example, events in the courtroom and relationships between attorneys and clients outside the courtroom are not likely to implicate the commonly accepted notion of older people as being asexual—a notion entailing some degree of truth, but also a considerable degree of error:

Sexual activity *does* tend to decrease in old age. However, there are tremendous individual differences in this intimate aspect of life. We know . . . that these differences are determined in part by cultural norms, by health or illness, and by the availability of sexual or romantic partners. When it comes to sexual activity, as in so many other aspects of aging, chronological age itself is not the critical factor. In men, the decline in testosterone with age is highly variable and linked only loosely with sexual performance. . . .

For older women, . . . regularity of sexual activity depends primarily on the availability of an appropriate partner.

John W. Rowe and Robert L. Kahn, *Breaking Down the Myths of Aging,* in *Aging in America* 119, at 136 (Olivia Smith, ed. 2000); see also Diana K. Harris, *Sociology of Aging* 152–167 (2d ed. 1992); Margot Tallmer, ed., *Questions and Answers About Sex in Later Life* 1–2 (1995).

Even so, the generally negative congeries of notions associated with old age, of which this perception regarding sexuality is one, contributes to the overall negative perception of old age.

11. I use the word *race* and describe it as a human characteristic for convenience's sake, to make a point. The fact is that the concept of race as a physiological reality is dubious.

The basic tenet of racist thinking is that physical differences such as skin color or nose shape are intrinsically and unalterably tied to meaningful differentials in basic intelligence or "civilization." Yet, in spite of periodic assertions of such a linkage by white supremacy groups and pseudoscientists, no scientific support for this assumed linkage exists.

Indeed, there is no distinctive reality called "race" that can be determined by objective scientific procedures. The social, medical, and physical sciences have demonstrated this fact.

Joe R. Feagin and Clairece Booker Feagin, *Racial and Ethnic Relations* 8 (1996); see also Natalie Angier, "Do Races Differ? Not Really, Genes Show," *New York Times,* Aug. 22, 2000, Science Times, pp. 1, 6; Ian F. Haney Lopez, *The Social Construction of Race: Some Observations on Illusion, Fabrication, and Choice,* 29 Harv. Civ. Rts.–Civ. Lib. L. Rev. 1 (1994); David L. Wheeler, "A Growing Number of Scientists Reject the Concept of Race," *Chronicle of Higher Education* A8 (Feb. 17, 1995).

Notwithstanding the concept of race being devoid of a legitimate biological basis, it exists as a socially constructed reality. For good or ill, groups define themselves, and are defined by nonmembers of the group, in terms of this construct. See Feagin and Feagin, *Racial and Ethnic Relations* supra, at 8.

12. A strict scrutiny test is used by the courts to assess race-based laws and government policies that are challenged under the Due Process Clause of the Fifth Amendment or under the Equal Protection Clause of the Fourteenth Amendment. See, e.g., Adarand Contractors, Inc. v. Pena, 515 U.S. 200 (1995); Loving v. Virginia, 388 U.S. 1 (1967). Very, very few laws and policies have survived such scrutiny; for the very rare instance of a policy being upheld in light of strict scrutiny analysis, see Grutter v. Bollinger, 539 U.S. 306 (2003), which involved a state law school's efforts to achieve student body diversity.

13. See, e.g., Title VII of the Civil Rights Act of 1964, 42 U.S.C. § 2000e–2000e-17, which bans discrimination in employment on the bases of race, color, religion, national origin, and sex. Even Title VII, however, does not establish a blanket rejection of race in the workplace. Only employers with 15 or more employees for 20 or more weeks in the current or preceding calendar year are covered by the statute. 42 U.S.C. § 2000e(b).

Thereby, small employers get a statutory "pass" insofar as their racist practices are concerned. On the other hand, while Title VII affords a *bona fide occupational qualification* (BFOQ) affirmative defense to employers in instances of their utilization of the sex, national origin, and religion factors, thereby allowing employers to engage in practices that would otherwise be illegal, no such defense is available insofar as race is concerned. 42 U.S.C. § 2000e-2(e).

14. See, e.g., United States v. Virginia, 518 U.S. 515 (1996); Mississippi Univ. for Women v. Hogan, 458 U.S. 718 (1982).

15. See, e.g., Title VII of the Civil Rights Act of 1964, 42 U.S.C. §§ 2000e–2000e-17 (banning discrimination on the basis of sex in employment); Title IX of the Education Amendments of 1972, as amended, 20 U.S.C. §§ 1681–1688 (banning discrimination on the basis of sex in federally assisted education programs).

16. Civil Rights Act of 1964, Pub. L. No. 88-352, § 715, 78 Stat. 287, 316.

17. 42 U.S.C. §§ 2000e–2000e-17.

18. *The Older American Worker—Age Discrimination in Employment, Report of the Secretary of Labor to the Congress Under Section 715 of the Civil Rights Act of 1964* 5–6 (June 1965).

19. See Hazen Paper Co. v. Biggins, 507 U.S. 604, at 610–611 (1993); EEOC v. Wyoming, 460 U.S. 226, at 231 (1983).

20. The Equal Protection Clause of the Fourteenth Amendment, § 1, provides that "no State . . . [shall] deny to any person within its jurisdiction the equal protection of the laws."

21. See Howard Eglit, 3 *Age Discrimination* 10-4–10-6 (2d ed. 1994 and annual supps). However, there are some rare departures from this pattern. For example, the Louisiana constitution has been interpreted by the Louisiana Supreme Court as mandating rigorous judicial scrutiny of age classifications. Pierce v. Lafourche Parish Council, 762 So.2d 608 (La. 2000).

22. See, e.g., Kimel v. Florida Board of Regents, 528 U.S. 62 (2000); Gregory v. Ashcroft, 501 U.S. 452 (1991); City of Cleburne v. Cleburne Living Center, Inc., 473 U.S. 432 (1985); Vance v. Bradley, 440 U.S. 93 (1979); Massachusetts Board of Retirement v. Murgia, 427 U.S. 307 (1976).

In *Murgia* the Court rejected the argument that an age-based mandatory retirement requirement imposed by state law upon state police at age 50 warranted more than minimum rationality scrutiny under the Equal Protection Clause of the Fourteenth Amendment. See notes 24–30 and accompanying text infra. In *Vance* the Court again applied minimum rationality scrutiny in upholding a federal mandatory retirement statute directed to foreign service officers. The *Gregory* Court endorsed the minimum rationality test's application to a mandatory retirement age imposed by a state constitutional provision upon state court judges. See chapter 7. *Kimel* also concerned an employment dispute, although its primary focus and the basis for disposition of the case was the Eleventh Amendment. In *Cleburne*, which did not concern an employment issue, the Supreme Court approvingly quoted from *Murgia*, characterizing it as an apt model of minimum rationality analysis. 473 U.S. at 441–442.

23. See generally Howard Eglit, *Of Age and the Constitution*, 57 Chi.-Kent L. Rev. 859 (1981).

24. 427 U.S. 307 (1976).

25. Id. at 313–314.

26. See chapter 4.

27. On the other hand, it is clear that the elderly have not gone unscathed in terms of social opprobrium and devaluation. See chapter 2.

28. 427 U.S. at 313–314, quoting United States v. Carolene Prods. Co., 304 U.S. 144, 152–153 n. 4 (1938).

29. See chapter 2.

30. Federal court judges appointed pursuant to Article III of the U.S. Constitution enjoy life tenure. Thus, they are immune from political pressures and so are more able—as a pragmatic matter—than are elected state court judges to extend legal protection to individuals and groups who engender dislike but, by virtue of their limited numbers, are unable to ward off discriminatory legislation adopted through the majoritarian political processes that operate at the federal level and in each state.

31. Eglit, *Of Age and the Constitution,* note 23 supra, at 890–891. (As to the inability of the young to comprehend their own inevitable senescence, see chapter 4.)

32. See generally Amy J. C. Cuddy and Susan T. Fiske, *Doddering but Dear: Process, Content, and Function in Stereotyping of Older Persons,* in *Ageism* 3, at 10 (Todd D. Nelson, ed. 2002).

33. This is not to say that antipathy regarding the elderly is nonexistent. Quite the contrary. See chapter 2.

34.

One dilemma in combating ageism is that many older people attribute age-related discrimination to other causes. For instance, many older people of ethnic minority backgrounds cite their ethnicity, before their age, as a probable cause of discrimination. Women are likely to attribute discriminatory behavior to sexism before ageism . . . , and white males who have experienced ageism in the job market often attribute the discrimination to outdated skills. . . . Additionally, "elderly" is a relative term. . . . This leaves few people willing to identify themselves as victims of ageism, which is possibly why it often goes unchecked in the American society. . . . Because few people recognize ageism when confronted with it, and no one agency is responsible for keeping statistics on this form of discrimination, there is no reliable information regarding the frequency or prevalence of ageism.

Amie M. Ragan and Anne M. Bowen, *Improving Attitudes Regarding the Elderly Population: The Effects of Information and Reinforcement for Change,* 41 Gerontologist 511, at 511 (2001).

While age bias can be difficult to pin down, there actually are several reasons to question the foregoing comments, not the least of which is that the authors' assertions really do not gibe with this writer's perceptions of the work world. Older men who are discharged consistently ascribe their job losses to age discrimination, not lack of skills. (After all, it is only human nature to blame others, rather than to attribute to one's own self a deficiency, such as declining performance.) Women workers likewise generally are sensitized to the age issue. As for the purported lack of a single agency to maintain data on instances of ageism, the fact is that no agency maintains complete data on any "-ism." But the U.S. Equal Employment Opportunity Commission does maintain data regarding administrative charges made under the Age Discrimination in Employment Act of 1967, as amended, 29 U.S.C. §§ 621–634, as to alleged age discrimination in the workplace, so some data indeed do exist.

35. I recognize that I am oversimplifying a little bit. There are hermaphrodites and transvestites, as well as people who have undergone sex change operations. In the great

majority of instances, however, the choices regarding sexual identification are two: man or woman. And in the great majority of instances, one's sex is obvious to observers. Moreover, at the genetic level, transvestites and those who have undergone sex change operations typically will be identifiable as either male or female, even if such identification is inconsistent with the way they appear to the world. (Admittedly, gender—as opposed to "sex"—can be a much more subtle proposition, with gradations rather than stark either-or contrasts.) For an interesting recounting of the feelings and experiences of a man who underwent a sex change operation to become a woman, see Deirdre McCloskey, *Crossing: A Memoir* (2000).

36. See note 11 supra.

37. There is increasing formal recognition of persons of mixed racial composition. Indeed, in conducting the 2000 census the U.S. Census Bureau introduced a category for such people to check off in identifying themselves. For good or ill, however, lay observers very much tend in the United States to identify people as either black, white, or Asian.

38. See generally Charles R. Lawrence III, *The Id, The Ego, and Equal Protection: Reckoning with Unconscious Racism,* 39 Stanford L. Rev. 317, at 349 *et seq.* (1987).

39. 29 U.S.C. §§ 621–634.

40. 29 U.S.C. § 630(b).

41. The ADEA was signed into law on December 15, 1967. Pub. L. No. 90-202, 81 Stat. 602 (1967). Its effective date was delayed, however, for six months, until June 12, 1968. Pub. L. No. 202, § 15, 81 Stat. 606–607 (1967).

42. See generally Eglit, 1 *Age Discrimination,* note 21 supra, at chapter 5.

43. According to the Equal Employment Opportunity Commission, reporting in 1998, there were at that time 542,000 employers in the United States with at least 20 employees. Equal Employment Opportunity Commission, *Waiver of Rights and Claims Under the Age Discrimination in Employment Act (ADEA),* 63 Fed. Reg. 30631, 30627 (June 6, 1998). As for the number of smaller employers, i.e., those with fewer than 20 employees, there were approximately 4,323,000 establishments of this size in 1998. U.S. Bureau of the Census, *Statistics About Business Size,* http:/www.census.gov/epcd/www/smallbus.html (2002).

44. Pursuant to section 4(f) of the ADEA, 29 U.S.C. § 623(f)(2)(B)(ii), it is legal to offer an employee a voluntary retirement incentive plan so as to encourage her departure, and it further is legal to condition eligibility for such retirement plan on the employee's having attained a certain minimum age, let us say 55 or 60. See, e.g., Karlen v. City Colleges of Chicago, 837 F.2d 314, 318 (7th Cir.), *cert. denied,* 486 U.S. 1044 (1988); Mason v. Lister, 562 F.2d 343 (5th Cir. 1977); Wehrly v. American Motor Sales Corp., 678 F. Supp. 1366 (N.D. Ind. 1988).

45. Russell Wright has explained:

Life expectancy is an average. A life expectancy of 70 years at birth means that 50 percent of the people born that year will live to be 70. A life expectancy of 15 years at age 70 means that 50 percent of the people turning 70 that year will live to be 85, i.e., another 15 years.

Russell O. Wright, *Life and Death in the United States* 12 (1997).

46. 15 U.S.C. §§ 1691–1691f.

47. See generally Howard Eglit, 1 *Age Discrimination* chapter 12 (1982 and annual supps.). Should Mr. Grayhead die before the loan is paid off, the lender will be able to recover the amount due from Mr. Grayhead's estate. Should the estate not have sufficient

funds to pay off the loan, the lender should be able to secure a lien on the property, and then recover the amount due from the proceeds obtained from the sale of the property. In sum, then, the lender is not forced by the Equal Credit Opportunity Act to make financially nonsensical loans to older borrowers; recourse will exist to make the lender whole.

48. For example, in a 1998 article in the *Minnesota Daily,* it was reported that at the University of Minnesota Medical School students' tuition payments constituted only 4 percent of the school's annual $280 million budget. Federal grants and subsidies, endowment, faculty contributions, and state funds made up the remainder. http:/www.daily.umn. edu/daily/1998/10/26/news/cost/ (1998).

49. See U.S. Commission on Civil Rights, *The Age Discrimination Study* 76 (1977).

50. 42 U.S.C. §§ 6101–6107 (ADA). See generally Symposium, *National Conference on Constitutional and Legal Issues Relating to Age Discrimination and the Age Discrimination Act,* 57 Chi.-Kent L. Rev. 805–1116 (1981).

51. That was the position asserted by the federal agency originally charged with enforcement of the Act—the now-defunct U.S. Department of Health, Education, and Welfare. See 44 Fed. Reg. 33774 (June 12, 1979). (Enforcement authority for the Act now resides in the U.S. Department of Health and Human Services.)

A like issue can arise in the employment context when an employer does not want to pay for advanced training for an older employee because the employer feels that its investment in the worker will not generate a sufficient return, given the relatively few remaining years that the employee likely will remain on the payroll. See Esberg v. Union Oil Co., 47 P.3d 1069, 28 Cal.4th 262 (2002), where the employer prevailed by virtue of the California Supreme Court's concluding that the state antidiscrimination statute upon which the plaintiff relied did not cover employee benefits, which the proposed employer-subsidized graduate degree program was deemed to constitute. *Esberg* notwithstanding, the "inadequate return on investment" justification would not pass muster under the federal Age Discrimination in Employment Act of 1967, as amended, 29 U.S.C. §§ 621–634 (ADEA): discrimination on the basis of age as to any conditions or privileges of employment is illegal. See Coates v. National Cash Register Co., 433 F. Supp. 655 (W.D. Va. 1977); see generally Eglit, 1 *Age Discrimination,* note 21 supra, at § 4.02.

52. A few states have enacted statutes setting special or additional licensure restrictions for the elderly. See generally Vasiliki L. Tripodis, Note, *Licensing Policies for Older Drivers: Balancing Public Safety with Individual Mobility,* 38 Boston College L. Rev. 1051, 1059 (1997). As to the powerful significance for the elderly of retaining one's license to drive, see Susan A. Eisenhandler, *The Asphalt Identikit: Old Age and the Driver's License,* in *Growing Old in America* 107 (Beth B. Hess and Elizabeth W. Markson, eds., 4th ed., 1991); David V. Lampman, II, Comment, *Fun, Fun, Fun, 'Til Sonny (or the Government) Takes the T-Bird Away: Elder Americans and the Privilege to be Independent,* 12 Albany L. J. of Science & Technology 863, at 871–872 (2002).

53. The published data establish these propositions as fact, rather than mere conjecture. See generally David T. Levy, Joy S. Vernick, and Kim A. Howard, *Relationship Between Driver's License Renewal Policies and Fatal Crashes Involving Drivers 70 Years or Older,* 274 J. Am. Medical Assn. 1026, at 1026 (Oct. 4, 1995); see also Lampman, Comment, *Fun, Fun, Fun,* note 52, supra; Robert W. Stock, "Balancing the Needs and Risks of Older Drivers," *New York Times,* July 13, 1995, p. B5. "Once in a crash, older adults are more likely to incur a disabling injury or die than are younger drivers." Cynthia Owsley, Gerald McGwin, Michael Sloane, Jennifer Wells, Beth T. Stalvey, and Scott Gauthreaux,

Impact of Cataract Surgery on Motor Vehicle Crash Involvement by Older Adults, 288 J. of American Medical Assn. 841, at 841 (2002).

Chapter 4. Age Bias and Its Multiple Sources

The epigraphs are from the following sources: Euripides, *Suppliants* 1008–1113, in *Euripides: Plays, Vol. 1,* at 230 (A. S. Way, translator, 1956); Mary Herrick, quoted in Bonnie Bluh, *The "Old" Speak Out* 31 (1979).

1. Gordon W. Allport, *The Nature of Prejudice* 9 (paperback ed. 1994).

2. John F. Dovidio and Samuel L. Gaertner, *Prejudice, Discrimination, and Racism: Historical Trends and Contemporary Approaches,* in *Prejudice, Discrimination, and Racism* 1, at 3 (John F. Dovidio and Samuel L. Gaertner, eds. 1986).

3. Working through the complexities and nuances of ageism is an exceedingly difficult task, as perceptively documented by Mary E. Kite and Lisa Smith Wagner, *Attitudes Toward Older Adults,* in *Ageism* 129 (Todd D. Nelson, ed. 2002). In this regard, they make the following observations:

> [Our] chapter is about attitudes toward older adults. In many cases, this implies "other" older adults ("not me; not us"). But because "the aged" is a group that we will all likely join, it is, at a minimum, about attitudes toward a current or future in-group. And because there are visible markers that indicate age and we do not live in a completely age-segregated society, it is also about attitudes toward a group with which most of us have had some interactions throughout our lives. Given that we are aging as we speak (or as we type or read), it is also about attitudes toward the aging process in general and our own aging process in particular. These complexities make studying and understanding ageism a challenge.

Id. at 153.

4. See, e.g., Dorothy A. Miller, *The "Sandwich" Generation: Adult Children of the Aging,* 26 Social Work 419 (1981); Bernice L. Neugarten, *The Middle Generation,* in *Aging Parents* 258 (Pauline K. Ragan, ed. 1979); Olivia J. Smith, ed., *Aging in America* 83–110 (2000).

5. See David L. Hamilton and Tina K. Trolier, *Stereotypes and Stereotyping: An Overview of the Cognitive Approach,* in *Prejudice, Discrimination, and Racism* 127, at 153 (John F. Dovidio and Samuel L. Gaertner, eds. 1986).

6. See generally David Hackett Fischer, *Growing Old in America* (expanded ed. 1978); Lawrence Stone, *Walking Over Grandma,* New York Review of Books 10 (May 12, 1977); David Hackett Fischer and Lawrence Stone, *Growing Old: An Exchange,* New York Review of Books 47 (Sept. 15, 1977); Daniel Scott Smith, *Old Age and the "Great Transformation": A New England Case Study,* in *Aging and the Elderly: Humanistic Perspectives in Gerontology* 285 (Stuart F. Spicker, Kathleen M. Woodward, and David D. Van Tassel, eds. 1978); John Demos, *Old Age in Early New England,* in *Aging, Death, and the Completion of Being* 115 (David D. Van Tassel, ed. 1979); W. Andrew Achenbaum, *Old Age in the New Land,* (1978); Carole Haber, *Beyond Sixty-Five* chapters 1, 12 (paperback ed. 1983). One eminent student of aging issues has observed as follows: "Although historians have spilled a good deal of ink debating the power and status of old age in early America, we do not yet have enough empirical data—especially outside of New England—to justify strong generalizations." Thomas R. Cole, *The Journey of Life* 48 n. 1 (paperback ed. 1993); see also Erdman B. Palmore, *Ageism: Negative and Positive* 60–64 (1990).

7. A leading proponent of modernization theory wrote as follows:

In all historical societies before the Industrial Revolution, almost without exception, the aging enjoyed a favorable position. Their economic security and their social status were assured by their role and place in the extended family. The extended family was often an economic unit of production, frequently a household unit, and always a cohesive unit of social relations and of reciprocal services between the generations. But the balance of prerogatives of property, power, and decision making belonged to the aging. This Golden Age of living for older persons was disturbed and undermined by the Industrial Revolution. . . . In all countries of Western culture, this older patriarchal type of family structure and kinship relationship was profoundly altered by industrialization and urbanization. . . .

. . . [T]he general effect of industrialization is to break up the extended family into independent nuclear units with the extended family no longer a closely knit unit but rather a network. . . .

Urbanization not only weakened family relations and undermined the extended family as an economic unit but also made it more difficult for children to support their needy aged parents. More and more, the parents lost the economic independence guaranteed by ownership of a farm or a shop. An increasing number of employees could be dismissed or retired at will by the employer with no further obligation of support.

Ernest W. Burgess, *Western Experience in Aging as Viewed by an American,* in *Social Welfare of the Aging* 349, at 350–351 (Jerome Kaplan and Gordon J. Aldridge, eds. 1962); see generally Nancy Foner, *Ages in Conflict* 194–196 (1984).

8. Foner, *Ages in Conflict,* note 8 supra at 196.

9. Ibid.

10. See Palmore, *Ageism: Negative and Positive,* note 6 supra, at 60.

11. This focus on the United States certainly is in no way intended to suggest that American culture is unique. The Old Testament, Greece, Rome, the Middle Ages, and so on are all part of the American heritage. Thus, a comprehensive effort to explore the historical roots of attitudes regarding old age would have to extend back thousands of years. Such efforts indeed have been essayed. See, e.g., Cole, *The Journey of Life,* note 6 supra; Georges Minois, *History of Old Age* (1989). The effort here is a more modest one, premised on the proposition that one can gain some useful insights about the American experience—and more particularly the American legal system's treatment of older men and women—without having to travel so far back in time.

12. See note 20 and accompanying text infra.

13. Professor Fischer writes:

In early America the old were few in number, but their authority was very great.

. . .

In an era when few people survived to old age, and even fewer expected to do so, the young were trained to treat the survivors with a special form of honor called "veneration"—a feeling of religious awe, or reverence. . . .

In a world where literacy was limited, elders were keepers of their culture, and agents of its communication from one generation to the next. In an economy which was slow to change, the practical experience of the old remained continuously relevant to the young. In a tradition-bound society, which looked backward for its social models, elders were living representatives of the past, armed with ancient precedents and cloaked in the authority of ancestral ways. Regular recourse was made to the memory of the "oldest inhabitant," to the judgment of "ancient men," to the experience of "reverent women."

Most important, old people in early America were also believed to be "closer to God."

Regard for age was not a voluntary act. Where it was not freely forthcoming, it was forced. In an agrarian society, old people controlled the land, and were slow to surrender it to their children.

Fischer, *Growing Old in America,* note 6 supra, at 220–222 (footnotes omitted).

14. Id. at 223 (footnote omitted). Professor Fischer's analysis has generated strong dispute. For example, it has been asserted: "Perukes made of grey hair were considered the best and cost the most in mid-eighteenth century England . . . but little other evidence supports Fischer's claim that insignia of age were actually preferred." David Lowenthal, The Past is a Foreign Country 129 (1999). Professor Fischer also wrote:

The Puritan image of Christ was very different from the Christ of our modern devotional painting. He was not a muscular young hippie with a handsome Haight-Ashbury beard, but the Christ who appears in the Book of Revelation, with hair "white like wool, as white as snow." And their idea of an angel was a man in his seventies. When a white-haired septuagenarian suddenly appeared in the New England town of Hadley, some of the inhabitants mistook him for a heavenly messenger.

Id. at 35 (footnotes omitted).

15. Fischer, note 6 supra, at 225.

16. Achenbaum, *Old Age in the New Land,* note 6 supra, at 39; see also Linda S. Whitton, *Ageism: Paternalism and Prejudice,* 46 DePaul L. Rev. 453, at 461–462 (1997).

17. Cole, *The Journey of Life,* note 6 supra, at 90.

18. Id. at 90–91.

19. Professor Haber writes:

In America . . . certain types of persons have always been characterized as overaged and outdated. Even in colonial times, those elderly individuals who lacked family, wealth, or occupation composed a powerless group. They passed from town to town, were boarded out with neighbors, or spent their final years as almshouse residents. Weakness and poverty defined the distinctiveness of their final years. Retaining few ties integrating them into society, they were inevitably seen as superannuated.

Such an evaluation did not pertain only to the most poverty-stricken and debilitated persons. In some cases, even pillars of colonial society experienced feelings of uselessness as their final days approached. Cotton Mather, for example, repeatedly noted the discontent of his elderly father and searched for the proper activity to occupy his aging mind. No longer consulted on matters of great importance, Increase Mather felt himself segregated by reason of his age and infirmities. In the more than two decades he spent preparing for death, the elder Mather expressed numerous complaints about his assumed decrepit condition. As an old man, he believed he was shown little respect or veneration.

Mather was not alone in his feelings. Throughout American history, old people have voiced similar complaints; in contrast to their status in middle age, senescence seemed a time of uselessness.

Haber, *Beyond Sixty-Five,* note 6 supra, at 2–3.

20. Professor Fischer writes:

The aged poor suffered severely. Old slaves with callous masters were left to look after themselves. Widows without property were sometimes abandoned by their own children, and driven out of town by neighbors mindful of the poor-tax. Old people who violated the moral laws of the society were treated as social outcasts.

And none were venerated all of the time. Running beneath the surface of respect was an undercurrent of resentment which rose to the surface from time to time.

Fischer, *Growing Old in America,* note 6 supra, at 223.

21. George Eaton Simpson and J. Milton Yinger, *Racial and Cultural Minorities* 91–92 (1985).

22. See chapter 2.

23. It is true that youngsters are also unproductive in an economic sense. But they are seen as having productive potential when they mature, whereas the elderly promise no such future.

24. See notes 155–156 and accompanying text infra.

25. See generally Haber, *Beyond Sixty-Five,* note 6 supra, at 29–34.

26. The following table sets forth the data regarding the percentages of older Americans in the workforce at the end of 2000:

Age	Percent
55–59	68.8
60–64	47.1
65–69	24.4
70–74	13.5
75 and older	5.3

William J. Wiatrowski, *Changing retirement ages; ups and downs,* 124 Monthly Labor Rev. 3, at 8 (Apr. 2001). These numbers reflect what has been a steady decline in workforce participation by older men:

In 1950, almost half (46 percent) of all men 65+ were in the labor force. . . . This figure had dropped to 33 percent by 1960 and to 27 percent by 1970. By 1980, only 17 percent of older men were in the labor force. . . . The decrease in male labor force participation extends even to men in their 50s. By 1989, the labor force participation rate among men 55 to 59 had dropped to 79.5 percent from almost 92 percent in 1960.

U.S. Senate Special Committee on Aging, American Association of Retired Persons, Federal Council on the Aging, and U.S. Administration on Aging, *Aging America, Trends and Projections, 1991 Edition* 94 (1991); see also Howard Eglit, *The Age Discrimination in Employment Act at Thirty: Where It's Been, Where It Is Today, Where It's Going,* 31 U. of Richmond L. Rev. 579, at 665–666 (1997).

The data regarding older women reveal a different picture:

In 1950, 9.7 percent of women 65+ were in the labor force, but in 1989, their participation fell to 8.4 percent. Over the same period, [however,] women in the 55 to 64 age group joined the work force in growing numbers. In 1950, only 27 percent of women in this age category were in the labor force, but by 1970, their participation had risen to 43 percent. The labor force participation for these women . . . [was] relatively constant since then, and by 1989, it was 45 percent.

Aging America, Trends and Projections, 1991 Edition supra, at 94. While these data regarding women arguably should offset any perception that older individuals are not contributing economically, it remains the fact that generally men continue to occupy the most prominent positions in the work world, and thus the absence of older men from the workforce is going to be more noticeable than is the presence of older women.

27. While age-based mandatory retirement generally is illegal under the Age Discrimination in Employment Act of 1967, as amended, 29 U.S.C. §§ 621–634 (ADEA), insofar as employers with 20 or more employees are concerned, see Howard Eglit, 1 *Age Discrimination* § 4.10 (2d ed. 1994 and annual supps.), there are subtle (and not so subtle) ways whereby employers can make known their wishes for employees to depart the workplace. In this regard, it should be noted that under the ADEA it is legal to offer an employee a voluntary retirement incentive plan so as to encourage her departure. See chapter 3. Thus, "as a general matter, the mere query to an employee by an employer as to his or her interest in early retirement would not constitute evidence of discrimination." Eglit, 1 *Age Discrimination*, at 4–35, citing Wingfield v. United Technologies Corp., 678 F. Supp. 973, 981 (D. Conn. 1988). Nor will the actual offer of an early retirement program support an inference of discrimination. Colgan v. Fisher Scientific Co., 935 F.2d 1407, 1422 (3d Cir.), *cert. denied*, 502 U.S. 941 (1991). "[E]ven an employer's urging an employee to retire would not necessarily in and of itself establish discriminatory intent." Eglit, 1 *Age Discrimination*, at 4–35, citing Young v. General Foods Corp., 840 F.2d 825, 831 (11th Cir. 1988), *cert. denied*, 488 U.S. 1004 (1989).

28. Watson Wyatt Worldwide, a global consulting firm headquartered in Bethesda, Maryland, conducted a survey in 1997 that elicited responses from 773 chief executive officers and more than 1,000 other highly placed corporate executives throughout the world. The aim of the survey was ascertainment of the respondents' views as to the peak years of productivity of employees. In a summary of the study published by AARP (formerly the American Association of Retired Persons), the following data were reported:

Latin American executives set the age of top performance at almost 43, slightly older than their counterparts in the Asian/Pacific region, who said 42, and in Europe, who said just over 41. But it is in the US where executives show the most confidence that employees will continue improving their performance with added years. They put the age of maximum performance at almost 48. However, Americans said the length of sustained performance was shorter than did executives from most other countries participating in the survey.

This survey provided little opportunity to explore what factors influenced executives' perception that performance declines with age. No reliable study supports their conclusions. Nor was it possible to explore how demographics, national retirement practices, youth unemployment, and pension questions, among other issues, influenced the perceptions.

A Global View of Age and Productivity, 3 Global Aging Report 3, at 3 (May/June 1998).

29. See, e.g., AARP, *Valuing Older Workers* (n.d.); Michael E. Borus, Herbert S. Parnes, Steven H. Sandell, and Bert Seidman, eds., *The Older Worker* (1988); Irving Bluestone, Rhonda J. V. Montgomery, and John D. Owen, eds., *The Aging of the American Work Force* (1990); Howard Eglit, *Of Age and the Constitution,* 57 Chi.-Kent L. Rev. 859, at 886–887 and 886–887 nn. 141–143 (1981); Robert McCann and Howard Giles, *Ageism in the Workplace: A Communication Perspective,* in Ageism 163 (Todd D. Nelson, ed. 2002); National Commission for Employment Policy, *Older Workers: Prospects, Problems and Policies,* 9th Annual Report (1985); Sara E. Rix, ed., *Older Workers: How Do*

They Measure Up? (Public Policy Institute, American Association of Retired Persons 1994).

30. 29 U.S.C. §§ 621–634.

31. See generally Eglit, 1–3 *Age Discrimination,* note 27 supra.

32. Parnes and Sandell, *Introduction and Overview,* in *The Older Worker* 1, note 29 supra, at 11.

33. Ibid.

34. Ibid.

35. Berkowitz, *Functioning Ability and Job Performance as Workers Age,* in *The Older Worker* 87, note 29 supra, at 111; see also McCann and Giles, *Ageism in the Workplace: A Communication Perspective,* note 29 supra, at 172.

36. Berkowitz, *Functioning Ability and Job Performance as Workers Age,* at 111.

37. Ibid.

38. A Marxist analysis would define prejudice as a mechanism devised to justify economic exploitation. Thus, race prejudice "is a social attitude propagated among the public by an exploiting class for the purpose of stigmatizing some group as inferior so that the exploitation of either the group itself or its resources both may be justified." Oliver C. Cox, *Caste, Class, and Race* 393 (1948). Thus, by way of analysis, as a political/economic matter ageism also could be explained as a device to rationalize the exploitation of older people. For example, one could reason that society (or, more accurately, those in a position of power) promotes an ageist notion, that is, older people are mentally incompetent to manage their affairs, as a means to justify the imposition of guardianships by means of which control over their assets is taken from them and reposed in the hands of their guardians. (As to ethical issues regarding lawyers' participation in guardianship matters, see chapter 6.)

One need not impose a Marxist overlay to bring to bear a cynical view of abuses of the guardianship process. (See chapter 1 regarding guardianship system reforms adopted over the past 20 or so years.) Simple human greed, without any political seasoning, can explain abuses whereby older people are consigned through guardianship proceedings into second-class status. More generally, the press of the Marxism analogy is undercut by the fact that the economic exploitation of racial minorities and of women that one sees in the American past, and even today, does not seem to be equaled in the case of older individuals. Thus, the Marxist explanation—if it is to be credited at all in some settings—does not seem to work very convincingly in analyzing the phenomenon of ageism.

39. See, e.g., Gordon D. Jensen and Fredricka B. Oakley, *Ageism Across Cultures and in Perspective of Sociobiologic and Psychodynamic Theories,* 15 International J. of Aging & Development 17, at 24 (1982–1983). Of course, there also is the possibility of gratitude, occasioned by transfers of wealth from the elderly to their adult offspring, both during the lifetimes of the old and upon their demise. In fact, there are data showing that in great degree wealth flows in one direction, from the elderly to their offspring, rather than vice versa. See Natalie Angier, "Weighing the Grandma Factor," *New York Times,* Nov. 5, 2002, Science Times, pp. D1, D4, at D4.

40. Sharon Yntema, ed., *Americans 55 & Older* 126 (1999); see also Howard Eglit, *Health Care Allocation for the Elderly: Age Discrimination by Another Name?* 26 Houston L Rev. 813, at 829–830 (1989).

41. See, e.g., Age Discrimination Act of 1975, as amended, 42 U.S.C. § 6101 *et seq.;*

Age Discrimination in Employment Act of 1967, as amended, 29 U.S.C. §§ 621–634; Equal Credit Opportunity Act, 15 U.S.C. §§ 1691–1691f.

42. See National Academy on Aging, *Old Age in the 21st Century: A Report to the Assistant Secretary for Aging, U.S. Department of Health and Human Services* 3 (1994): "Today, federal expenditures on aging are well over 30% of the [federal] budget." See also U.S. General Accounting Office, An *Aging Society—Meeting the Needs of the Elderly While Responding to Rising Federal Costs* (Sept. 1986), at 14:

> In 1960, less than 15 percent of the federal budget went to programs for the elderly. In fiscal year 1985, that proportion had nearly doubled, to 28 percent. As a percentage of the gross national product (GNP), expenditures on the elderly also have been rising. In 1970, pension and health care financing programs consumed 6.1 percent of GNP; by 1986, 9.6 percent, an increase of over one-half.

43. See Eglit, *Health Care Allocation for the Elderly: Age Discrimination by Another Name?* note 40 supra, at 823–832.

> For example, a prominent financial columnist for the leading Chicago newspaper wrote in 1987: "I have nothing against the over-65 gang. Indeed, I hope to make it there myself one day. But it seems to me that this group has become too politically potent and developed too much of an 'entitlement' attitude for the country's own good." Within the past few years the elderly were portrayed in one magazine article as "taking America to the cleaners," and the author of another recent article asserted: "Simply put, in economic terms we are consuming our children. . . . [T]he real cause of the problem [is]: The old are getting richer at the expense of the young." Still another popular journal writer reviewed what he perceived to be a growing number of restrictive laws imposed on young people in such contexts as access to contraceptives and alcohol and concluded that the demographics have "produced a significantly older population, making the youthful minority more susceptible to discrimination." In a related vein, the largest advocacy group for seniors—the American Association of Retired Persons (AARP)—has garnered popular media depiction as a narrow, self-serving organization driven by parochial needs and economic greed.

Id. at 825 (footnotes omitted); see also Phillip Longman, *Born to Pay* (1987).

44. See Harris Meyer, *Senior Bashing,* Hospitals & Health Networks 29 (Dec. 5, 1996). Meyer wrote as follows:

> [Gerontologist] Ken Dychtwald has become a leading voice among a growing group of politicians, policy wonks and journalists who harshly criticize America's elderly as greedy geezers. In often strident terms, they charge that seniors receive an unfair share of federal spending through entitlement programs—mainly Medicare, Medicaid, and Social Security—at the expense of children and working families. Heavyweights in this camp include both Republican and Democratic politicians like [former New Hampshire senator] Warren Rudman and [former Nebraska senator] Bob Kerry, businessmen like Pete Peterson, economists like Lester Thurow, and reporters and editorial writers at major news organizations.

Id. at 29.

45. Professor Samuel Preston, a noted demographer, maintained that "in the family, in politics and in industry the growing number of older people and the declining number of children have worked to the advantage of the group that is increasing in size," with the result being that "[s]ince the early 1960's the well-being of the elderly has improved greatly

whereas that of the young has deteriorated." Samuel Preston, *Children and the Elderly in the U.S.,* 251 Sci. Am. 44, at 44 (Dec. 1984); see also Rose C. Gibson, *Children: Treasured Resource or Forgotten Minority?* in *Our Aging Society* 161 (Alan Pifer and Lydia Bronte, eds. 1986).

46. See, e.g., Yntema, ed., *Americans 55 & Older,* note 40 supra, at 43.

47. See Robert B. Hudson and Robert H. Binstock, *Political Systems and Aging,* in *Handbook of Aging and the Social Sciences* 369, at 380 (Robert H. Binstock and Ethel Shanas, eds. 1976); see also chapter 2.

48. See, e.g., Robert H. Binstock, *Aging, Politics, and Public Policy,* in *Growing Old in America* 325, at 334–335 (Beth B. Hess and Elizabeth W. Markson, eds., 4th ed. 1991).

49. U.S. Department of Health and Human Services, Health Care Financing Administration, *2001 HCFA Statistics* 22, Table 26 (n.d.)

50. Professor Richard Kaplan has explained:

A prevailing myth among current *workers,* rather than current retirees, is that the Social Security program is so doomed to insolvency that the program will not be there for them at all. . . .

The idea that Social Security will disappear is a particularly pernicious canard, because it demoralizes younger workers whose current taxes are needed to fund the program. It is also patently untrue. Regardless of whether one can fully receive one's contributions to Social Security, the program will continue to provide retirement benefits for future generations of retirees. Those retirement benefits may not be as generous as those received by the current generation of retirees, and the qualifying retirement age may be delayed, but Social Security will certainly continue to pay benefits when people retire.

Richard L. Kaplan, *Top Ten Myths of Social Security,* 3 Elder L. J. 191, at 198–199 (Fall 1995).

51. Actually, the majority of states have enacted filial responsibility statutes imposing parental support obligations upon adult offspring and providing for enforcement mechanisms when those offspring fail to satisfy their obligations. In practice, these statutes are rarely invoked, however. See generally Seymour Moskowitz, *Adult Children and Indigent Parents: Intergenerational Responsibilities in International Perspective,* 86 Marquette L. Rev. 402 (2002).

52. Yntema, ed., *Americans 55 & Older,* note 40 supra, at 126. The financial plight of minority group elders is particularly serious.

White householders aged 55 to 59 had a median household income of $48,625 in 1997, far greater than the median $29,120 median for blacks, and $29,174 median for Hispanics. . . .

Hispanic householders aged 75 or older have the lowest household incomes, just $11,105 in 1997. The income of black households in the age group is not much greater, at $12,101. White householders aged 75 or older had a median householder income of $17,410 in 1997.

Id. at 129. Minority women are especially disadvantaged:

Older women are much more likely to be poor than older men—13 percent of women aged 55 or older are poor versus just 7 percent of men. But older women and men are less likely to be poor than the average female (15 percent) or male (12 percent). Black and Hispanic women are much more likely to be poor than their male counterparts. Among blacks aged 75 or older, 31 percent of women and 26

[percent] of men are poor. Among Hispanics aged 75 or older, 33 percent of women and 22 percent of men are poor.
Id. at 180.

53. See Binstock, *Aging, Politics, and Public Policy,* note 48 supra, at 331; Diana K. Harris, *Sociology of Aging* 290 (2d ed. 1991); Bruce Jacobs, *Aging and Politics,* in *Handbook of Aging and the Social Sciences* 349, at 351, 357 (Robert H. Binstock and Linda K. George, eds. 1990); but see Richard A. Posner, *Aging and Old Age* 150 (1995).

54. There is likely to be a personal recognition of one's inexorable attainment of old age by those who, by virtue of their accumulation of years, are shortly to enter the ranks of the old. And yet, typically there is a tendency as one grows older to change one's perception of when critical chronological demarcations come into play: for the 25-year-old 40 is the start of middle age. But for the 40-year-old 50 is, and it is age 60 for the 50-year-old. Bernard Baruch, a noted public figure of the mid-twentieth century, once said, "To me, old age is always fifteen years older than I am." *The Oxford Dictionary of Modern Quotations* 20 (Tony Augarde, ed. 1991).

Empirical support for this phenomenon is found in a study done in 1954 of 1,032 persons who ranged in age from under 20 (79 of the individuals) to over 80 (19 of the individuals). They were asked to identify themselves as either young, middle-aged, or old; the results were as follows:

> Under age 30, the respondents all classified themselves as young. From age 30 to 60, increasingly larger numbers classified themselves as middle-aged. Starting at age 60, a small proportion described themselves as old, but even at ages past 80, when 53 per cent of the group called themselves old, 11 per cent continued describing themselves as young. Self-classification, they concluded, is a function of the self-concept, an important reference factor in the process being the "acceptance of, and stereotyping of, the cultural attitudes toward aging."

Leonard Z. Breen, *The Aging Individual,* in *Handbook of Social Gerontology* 145, at 155 (Clark Tibbitts, ed. 1974).

I make no effort to identify the age at which one moves into the ranks of the old. As noted in chapter 1, however, it has become increasingly common—at least among gerontologists—to speak of the young-old and the old-old. Even if one does not subscribe to these appellations, it still is important to recognize that chronological age may not correlate with physiological or intellectual age. One can be 65 and yet have the muscle tone of a 55-year-old, the kidney function of a 45-year-old, and the intellectual acuity of an 85-year-old. Or one can be 45 and have the body of a 70-year-old. See, e.g., Elizabeth W. Markson, *Physiological Changes, Illness, and Health Care Use in Later Life,* in *Growing Old in America* 173, at 174 (Beth B. Hess and Elizabeth W. Markson, eds., 4th ed., 1991); Steven M. Albert and Maria G. Cattell, *Old Age in Global Perspective* 19 (1994): "Chronological age is not the same as biologic age. In fact, the two are only moderately correlated."

55. See, e.g., Jeffrie G. Murphy, *Book Review, The Coming of Age,* 17 Ariz. L. Rev. 546, at 549 (1975); see also Carolyn G. Heilbrun, *The Last Gift of Time* 75 (paperback ed. 1997), quoting May Sarton, *Plant Dreaming Deep* (1983): "It is only past the meridian of fifty that one can believe that the universal sentence of death applies to oneself."

Actually, life expectancy statistics show that death by natural causes is increasingly an unusual phenomenon for the young. In 1992, for males and females between ages 1 and 44, accidents were the single most common cause of death. The percentage of deaths attributable to accidents was 36.5 percent for children ages 1–4; for children ages 5–14 the figure was 41.3 percent; it was 39.5 percent for individuals ages 15–24, and 17.2 percent for adults ages 25–44. Russell O. Wright, *Life and Death in the United States* 119 (1997). Because the first year of life is a very dangerous one and thus deaths are much higher in that year than in subsequent decades, the death rate for babies younger than one year is not included in these data. Id. at 118.

To obtain greater accuracy regarding the incidence of death by nonnatural causes, one must add to the foregoing data the figures for deaths by homicide and by suicide. For homicide, the percentages of total deaths in 1992 were as follows: 6.4 percent of children ages 1–4 who died were the victims of a homicide; the figure was 7.1 percent for youngsters ages 5–14, 23.2 percent for individuals ages 15–24, and 7.9 percent for persons ages 25–44. Death by suicide accounted for 13.6 percent of the deaths of persons ages 15–24 and 8.1 percent of the deaths of adults ages 25–44. Thus, the totals for deaths by other than natural causes in 1992 were as follows: 42.9 percent for children ages 1–4, 48.4 percent for youngsters ages 5–14, 75.8 percent for persons ages 15–24, and 33.2 percent for adults ages 25–44. Id. at 119.

In contrast to the foregoing data, deaths by accident accounted in 1992 for only 3.8 percent of deceased persons ages 45–64 and 1.7 percent of deceased individuals ages 65 and up. For these age groups, death by disease was much more common: 36.3 percent of individuals ages 45–64 died due to cancer and another 28.4 percent died as a result of heart disease; for those ages 65 and up, 37.8 percent died due to heart disease and 23 percent due to cancer. Ibid.

56. Simone de Beauvoir, *The Coming of Age* 283 (1972).

57. In a study of 100 college undergraduates ranging in age from 17 to 23, it was found that the subjects either viewed their own aging negatively or were "not able to conceive of it." Peggy Golde and Nathan Kogan, *A Sentence Completion Procedure for Assessing Attitudes Toward Old People,* 14 J. of Gerontology 355, at 359 (1959). Even many individuals who others would say fit the images of older folks no doubt dismiss any suggestion that they in fact do so. See note 54 supra.

58. Malcolm Cowley, *The View From 80* 2–3 (1982). The motif of a journey through life, culminating in old age, is common throughout Western culture as a device for describing and summarizing the processes of growing up and growing old. See Cole, *The Journey of Life,* note 6 supra, at xxx–xxxiii.

59. Florida Scott-Maxwell, *The Measure of My Days* (1968), excerpted in *Songs of Experience* 25 (Margaret Fowler and Priscilla McCutcheon, eds. 1991).

60. In this vein, there is a very relevant and poignant poem written by a today-unknown resident of what has been variously identified as a geriatric ward in a hospital in Scotland, England, Ireland, or Canada that was found, so the story goes, in a locker after she died:

What do you see, nurse, what do you see?
What are you thinking when you are looking at me?
A crabbit old woman, not very wise,
Uncertain of habit, with far away eyes,

Who dribbles her food and makes not reply,
When you say in a loud voice, "I do wish you'd try!"
Who seems not to notice the things that you do,
And forever is losing a stocking or shoe.

Who, unresisting or not, lets you do as you will
With bathing and feeding, the long day to fill.
Is that what you're thinking, is that what you see?
Then open your eyes, you're not looking at me.

I'll tell you who I am as I sit here so still,
As I rise at your bidding, as I eat at your will.
I'm a small child of ten with a father and mother,
Brothers and sister who love one another.

A young girl of sixteen with wings on her feet,
Dreaming that soon now a lover she'll meet.
A bride soon at twenty, my heart gives a leap,
Remembering the vows that I promised I'd keep.

At twenty-five now, I have young of my own
Who need me to build a secure happy home.
A woman of thirty, my young now grown fast,
Bound to each other with ties that should last.

At forty my young now soon will be gone,
By my man's stands beside me to see I don't mourn.
At fifty once more babies play around my knee,
Again we know children, my loved one and me.

Dark days are upon me, my husband is dead,
I look at the future, I shudder with dread,
For my young are still rearing young of their own,
And I think of the years and the love that I've known.

I'm now an old woman and nature is cruel;
'Tis her jest to make old age look a fool?
The body, it crumbles, grace and vigor depart,
And now there is a stone, where I once had a heart.

But inside this old carcass, a young girl still dwells,
And now and again my battered heart swells.
I remember the joys, I remember the pain,
And I am loving and living life over again.

I think of the years all too few, gone so fast,
And accept the stark fact that nothing can last.
So open your eyes, nurse, open and see,
Not a crabbit old woman; Look closer—see ME!
    http://www.seniorsnetwork.co.uk/features/poetry/mattiespoem.htm (March 2004).
    61. One could cite hundreds of literary sources, Shakespeare among them, for sorry
depictions of old age:
    Crabbéd age and youth cannot live together:
    Youth is full of pleasance, age is full of care.
    Youth like summer morn, age like winter weather;
    Youth like summer brave, age like winter bare.

Youth is full of sport, age's breath is short;
    Youth is nimble, age is lame;
Youth is hot and bold, age is weak and cold;
    Youth is wild, and age is tame;
Age, I do abhor thee; youth, I do adore thee;
    Oh, my love, my love is young!
Age, I do defy thee. O, sweet shepherd, hie thee
    For methinks thou stay'st too long.

William Shakespeare, *The Passionate Pilgrim XII*, in G. B. Harrison, ed., *Shakespeare: The Complete Works* 1586 (1952).

62. Jensen and Oakley, *Ageism Across Cultures and in Perspective of Sociobiologic and Psychodynamic Theories*, note 39 supra, at 24.

63. Discrimination based on race has generated an enormous body of scholarly literature. The primary theory that neoclassical economists use to explain how racism will be eradicated—a theory that has garnered currency among legal scholars who look to economic analysis as affording insights into the operation of legal systems—was first articulated by Professor Gary Becker. He starts with the premise that people who engage in race discrimination have a "taste" for avoiding association with people of another race. Gary Becker, *The Economics of Discrimination* 14 (2d ed. 1971). Discriminatory acts are the manifestations of efforts by such individuals to avoid that association. Becker makes the argument that an unrestricted marketplace eventually will drive out discriminatory acts when it becomes economically unprofitable—as it ultimately will—for an individual to satisfy his or her taste for nonassociation. Professor Becker's analysis is unhelpful here (and generally) because he fails to explain from whence a "taste" for nonassociation originates: "In economics . . . conventional theorists take 'tastes' as a given. In other words, macroeconomics does not consider how motives grow and change in people." Robert D. Cooter, *Comment on Article by Professor Jones*, 8 J. of Contemporary Legal Issues 209, at 210 (1997).

64. Louis Harris and Associates, *The Myth and Reality of Aging in America* 30 (1976). With regard to the survey, 4,254 in-person household interviews overall were conducted by Louis Harris and Associates. For data derived from the general public, the surveyors relied upon a representative cross-section of Americans 18 years of age and over. These people were selected by random probability sampling techniques. For data attributed to those individuals who were 65 and over, the surveyors relied upon a representative sample of the public fitting into that age category. Id. at v.

65. Indeed, the percentage of older women in the workforce has steadily risen over the past several decades. See note 26 supra.

66. See generally Richard G. Rogers, Robert A. Hummer, and Charles B. Nam, *Living and Dying in the USA* (2000).

67. See, e.g., Yntema, ed., *Americans 55 & Older*, note 40 supra, at 95:
Although the incidence of acute conditions diminishes as people enter the 45-plus age groups, chronic illnesses begin to emerge. People aged 45 or older account for the majority of victims of most chronic conditions. Some of the exceptions are acne, migraines, asthma, and hay fever.

The prevalence of chronic conditions rises sharply in the older age groups. The most prevalent chronic condition among 45- to 64-year-olds is arthritis (experienced by 232.9 per 1,000 persons in the age group, or 23 percent), followed by high blood pressure (22 percent). Arthritis is also the most prevalent chronic condition among people aged 65 or older, affecting 45 percent of 65- to 74-year-olds and 55 percent of people aged 75 or older. High blood pressure is also common, experienced by 39 percent of people aged 65 to 74 and by 42 percent of those aged 75 or older. Thirty-five percent of people aged 75 or older have hearing impairments. See also Palmore, *Ageism: Negative and Positive,* note 6 supra, at 19: "More persons over 65 have chronic illnesses that limit their activity (43%) than do younger persons (10%)."

68. John W. Rowe and Robert L. Kahn, *Breaking Down the Myths of Aging,* in *Aging in America* 119, at 123 (Olivia J. Smith, ed. 2000), excerpted from John W. Rowe and Robert L. Kahn, *Successful Aging* (1998). One finds some inconsistency in specifics among different researchers, likely because different questions elicit somewhat different answers. For example, in contrast to the percentages set forth in the quoted passage, another expert has written as follows:

Only 20 percent of those sixty-five to seventy-four find one or more home-management activities (shopping, household chores, preparing meals, or handling their own money) difficult, [although] by age eighty-five or over 55 percent [do] report that one or more home-management activities are difficult.

Elizabeth W. Markson, *Physical Changes, Illness, and Health Care Use in Later Life,* in *Growing Old in America* 173, at 178 (Beth B. Hess and Elizabeth W. Markson, eds., 4th ed., 1991).

69. Louis Harris and Associates, *The Myth and Reality of Aging in America,* note 64 supra, at 30.

70. Yntema, ed., *Americans 55 & Older,* note 40 supra, at 68. Different sources provide similar, but not entirely consistent, data. For example, two leading experts on the aging process have written as follows:

Research finds that older people have a quite positive view of their own health. In one major study, older people were asked to rate their health as excellent, very good, good, fair, or poor. In 1994, 39 percent of individuals over the age of sixty-five viewed their health as very good or excellent, while only 29 percent considered their health to be fair or poor. Even among those over age eighty-five, 31 percent viewed themselves to be in very good or excellent health, while 36 percent viewed themselves as in poor health. Men and women were equally positive, but there were some racial differences—for instance, older African Americans were more likely than Caucasians to rate their health as poor.

Rowe and Kahn, *Breaking Down the Myths of Aging,* note 68 supra, at 124.

71. Rowe and Kahn, *Breaking Down the Myths of Aging,* note 68 supra, at 125. Self-rated health assessments are good predictors of mortality. See Dorly J. H. Heeg and Peter A. Balt, *Self-Rated Health, Gender, and Mortality in Older Persons: Introduction to a Special Section,* 43 Gerontologist 369, at 369 (2003); see also Ellen L. Idler, *Discussion: Gender in Self-Rated Health, in Mortality, and in the Relationship Between the Two,* 43 Gerontologist 372, at 372 (2003) ("a consistent finding [based on dozens of studies is] that respondents to health surveys who rated their health as 'poor,' 'fair,' or sometimes just 'good' had a significantly higher risk of mortality than those who considered their health 'excellent' or the equivalent, even when other measures of health were considered").

72. Rowe and Kahn, *Breaking Down the Myths of Aging,* note 68 supra, at 125.

73. Ibid.

74. See chapter 5.

75. See, e.g., Palmore, *Ageism: Negative and Positive,* note 6 supra, at 81–82, 189–198; Kathleen M. Dillon and Barbara S. Jones, *Attitudes toward aging portrayed by birthday cards,* 13 International J. of Aging & Human Development 79 (1981); Leland Davies, *Attitudes Toward Old Age and Aging as Shown by Humor,* 17 Gerontologist 220 (1977); Joseph Richman and Margot Tallmer, *The Foolishness and Wisdom of Age: Attitudes Toward the Elderly as Reflected in Jokes,* 17 Gerontologist 210 (1977).

76. See, e.g., Connie Lauerman, "Remember: Memory loss comes with getting older," *Chicago Tribune,* Nov. 18, 2001, Sec. 13, pp. 1, 4, at p. 1: "Quite a few people in their 40s and 50s complain about having 'senior moments,' a popular euphemism for the transient inability to quickly recall a fact, name or word."

77. Rowe and Kahn, *Breaking Down the Myths of Aging,* note 68 supra, at 123.

78. See, e.g., Joan T. Erber and Sharon T. Rothberg, *Here's Looking at You: The Relative Effect of Age and Attractiveness on Judgments about Memory Failure,* 46 J. of Gerontology: Psychological Sciences 116, at 117 (1991); A. Daniel Yarmey, *The Older Eyewitness,* in *Elders, Crime, and the Criminal Justice System* 127, at 130–131 (Max B. Rothman, Burton D. Dunlop, and Pamela Entzel, eds. 2000).

79. Linda D. Chrosniak, *Aging and Source Monitoring,* 4 Psychology & Aging 106, at 109 (1989).

80. Ibid.

81. Rowe and Kahn, *Breaking Down the Myths of Aging,* note 68 supra, at 127.

82. Robert H. Binstock, Stephen G. Post, and Peter J. Whitehouse, eds., *Dementia and Aging* 2 (1992).

83. See chapter 1 regarding this and related nomenclature.

84. Richard Mayeux and Mary Sano, *Drug Therapy Treatment of Alzheimer's Disease,* 341 New England J. Med. 1670, at 1670 (1999). There are also non-Alzheimer's dementias, and so the number of the afflicted must be increased to reflect their incidence.

85. Ibid. See also Howard A. Crystal et al., *The Relative Frequency of "Dementia of Unknown Etiology" Increases with Age and is Nearly 50% in Nonagenarians,* 57 Archives Neurology 713 (2000).

86. "Older people can significantly improve their short-term memory by making lists and training their memory with practice games. Admittedly, similarly trained young people do still better, but trained elders often do better than trained young people." Rowe and Kahn, *Breaking Down the Myths of Aging,* note 68 supra, at 127.

87. Id. at 126.

88. Chrosniak, *Aging and Source Monitoring,* note 79 supra, at 110.

89. See Paul B. Baltes and K. Warner Schaie, *Aging and IQ: The Myth of the Twilight Years,* Psychology Today 35 (March 1974); Note, *Age Discrimination in Employment,* 50 New York University L. Rev. 924, at 935 n. 64 (1975); Whitton, *Ageism: Paternalism and Prejudice,* 46 DePaul L. Rev. 453, note 16 supra, at 466–467; John B. McHugh, *The Constitutional Challenge to Mandatory Retirement Statutes,* 49 St. John's L. Rev. 748, at 775 (1975).

90. Paul B. Baltes and R. Kliege, *On the Dynamics Between Growth and Decline in the Aging of Intelligence and Memory,* in *Neurology: Proceedings of the XIIIth World Congress of Neurology, Hamburg, Sept. 1–6, 1985* (Klaus Poeck, ed., Berlin and Heidelberg: Springer-Verlag, 1986), quoted in Betty Friedan, *The Fountain of Age* 102 (paperback ed. 1993).

91. See, e.g., Erber and Rothberg, *Here's Looking at You,* note 78 supra.

92. See generally Whitton, *Ageism,* note 16 supra, at 467 and 467 n. 82; see also Markson, *Physiological Changes, Illness, and Health Care Use in Late Life,* note 54 supra, at 184.

93. This is a wrong to which I confess guilt. In writing a book of this nature, one necessarily engages in generalizations. That does not make their use praiseworthy.

94. Robert N. Butler, *Why Survive? Being Old in America* 7 (1975).

95. Louis Harris and Associates, *The Myth and Reality of Aging in America,* note 64 supra, at 30.

96. Rogers, Hummer, and Nam, *Living and Dying in the USA,* note 66 supra, at 221–222.

97. Id. at 222.

98. Yntema, ed., *Americans 55 & Older,* note 40 supra, at 6. Data were developed by the National Opinion Research Center, University of Chicago, in the course of a 1996 survey in which respondents were asked: "'Taken all together, how would you say things are these days—would you say that you are very happy, pretty happy, or not too happy?'" Id. at 7. The responses were as follows:

People Total	very happy 30%	pretty happy 57%	not too happy 12%
Ages 18–24	24%	62%	13%
Ages 25–34	30%	59%	10%
Ages 35–44	27%	59%	13%
Ages 45–54	29%	58%	13%
Ages 55–64	37%	50%	11%
Ages 65–74	39%	51%	10%
Ages 75+	32%	53%	16%

(Some respondents answered "Don't know," and so no answer is shown, the result being that the percentages may not always add up to 100 percent for a given age group.) See also Susan Krauss Whitbourne and Joel R. Sneed, *The Paradox of Well-Being, Identity Processes, and Stereotype Threat: Ageism and Its Potential Relationships to the Self in Later Life,* in *Ageism* 246, at 250–251 (Todd D. Nelson, ed. 2002).

99. From age 30 on, the risk of death doubles every eight years. Thus, a 40-year-old man is twice as likely to die as a 32-year-old, and only half as likely to do so as a 48-year-old. S. Jay Olshansky, Bruce A. Carnes, and Christine K. Cassell, *The Aging of the Human Species,* 268 Sci. Am. 46, at 46 (Apr. 1993). It should be noted that there is some fuzziness about the numbers: two of the three foregoing authors wrote elsewhere that the death rate doubles every *eight to nine years,* and this paradigm commences in the *second decade* of life, rather than starting at the end of the third decade. Bruce A. Carnes and S. Jay Olshansky, *Evolutionary Perspectives on Human Senescence,* 19 Population & Development Rev. 793, at 802 (Dec. 1993).

100. David Lowenthal, *The Past Is a Foreign Country* 131 (1985); see also Jensen and Oakley, *Ageism Across Cultures and in Perspective of Sociobiologic and Psychodynamic Theories,* note 39 supra, at 24: "For persons who equate aging and old age with death, one would predict consequent negativism and avoidance of the aged."

101. In this regard, one might recall (with tongue somewhat in cheek) that Patrick Henry identified death as his second choice when he uttered the famous phrase, in a speech he delivered on March 23, 1775, "Give me liberty or give me death."

102. See generally Jeff Greenberg, Jeff Schimel, and Andy Martens, *Ageism: Denying the Face of the Future*, in *Ageism* 27 (Todd D. Nelson, ed. 2002).

103. See generally Anthony G. Amsterdam and Jerome Bruner, *Minding the Law* 19–53 (2000); Gordon W. Allport, *The Nature of Prejudice* 20–23 (paperback ed. 1994).

104. Eleanor Rosch, *Human Categorization*, in *Studies in Cross-Cultural Psychology* 1, at 1–2 (Neil Warren, ed. 1977–1980).

105. See, e.g., Donald C. Nugent, *Judicial Bias*, 42 Cleveland St. L. Rev. 1, at 10–11 (1994):

> Our aim in using schemata is to reduce the quantity and complexity of incoming information by abstracting its main gist, but to avoid oversimplification which sacrifices too much of the information. Schemata guide this selective filtering of incoming information by providing a model of what to expect; they tell the brain what information to pay attention to and what information to ignore. For example, when evaluating a drug offender case, invocation of a "drug offender" schema would probably contain information (suppositions) about the personality of the criminal, the kinds of crimes likely to be in the record, reasons why those crimes are committed, reasons why the individual got involved with drugs, prognosis for treatment, social history, and so forth. The brain then notices, selects, and organizes incoming information within this general framework.

106. David L. Hamilton and Tina K. Trolier, *Stereotypes and Stereotyping: An Overview of the Cognitive Approach*, in *Prejudice, Discrimination, and Racism* 127, at 143 (John F. Davidio and Samuel L. Gaertner, eds. 1986).

107. Linda Hamilton Krieger, *The Content of Our Categories: A Cognitive Bias Approach to Discrimination and Equal Employment Opportunity*, 47 Stanford L. Rev. 1161, at 1188 (1995); see also Charles R. Lawrence III, *The Id, the Ego, and Equal Protection: Reckoning with Unconscious Racism*, 39 Stanford L. Rev. 317, at 335 (1987).

108. Krieger, *The Content of Our Categories*, note 107 supra, at 1188.

109. It has been noted:

> In the case of social perception the identification of . . . [easily identifiable] features is not a difficult problem, for numerous cues are readily available that can be used to classify people into categories whose members thereby share some common property. A person's gender, race, and age group are almost immediately obvious to any perceiver.

Hamilton and Trolier, *Stereotypes and Stereotyping*, note 106 supra, at 128–129.

110. Georgia M. Barrow and Patricia A. Smith, *Aging, Ageism and Society* 73 (1979).

111. Hamilton and Trolier, *Stereotypes and Stereotyping*, note 106 supra, at 153. By "motivational processes" the authors mean "the intrapsychic needs of the perceiver," id. at 127; by "social learning" process, the authors are referring to "socialization, media influence, and the like," as well as "social reinforcements obtained from significant others and important reference groups." Ibid.

112. Allport, *The Nature of Prejudice*, note 103 supra, at 73. Allport's work clearly is focused on racial and ethnic prejudice, see id. at 17, and so his insights—while useful—unfortunately do not take us all the way insofar as an understanding of age bias is concerned.

113. Id. at 19.

114. Ibid.

115. Id. at 39.

116. See generally Robert J. Havighurst, Bernice L. Neugarten, and Sheldon S. Tobin, *Disengagement and Patterns of Aging,* in *Middle Age and Aging* 161–172 (Bernice L. Neugarten, ed. 1968).

117. See Lawrence, *The Id, the Ego, and Equal Protection,* note 107 supra, at 332.

118. See generally Joe R. Feagin and Clairece Booher Feagin, *Racial and Ethnic Relations* 15 (1986).

119. Theodor W. Adorno, Else Frenkil-Brunswik, Daniel J. Levinson, and Sanford Levinson, *The Authoritarian Personality* 971 (1950).

120. See note 128 infra.

121. See Palmore, *Ageism: Negative and Positive* 54 (1990).

122. George Eaton Simpson and M. Milton Yinger, *Racial and Cultural Minorities* 73 (1985).

123. Ibid.

124. Ibid.

125. Ibid. See also Feagin and Feagin, *Racial and Ethnic Relations,* note 118 supra, at 16.

126. See generally Wayne Ewing, Dasha Wright Ewing, and Dorothy Ives, *Tears in God's Bottle: Reflections on Alzheimer's Caregiving* (1999); Rose Oliver and Francis A. Bock, *Coping with Alzheimer's* (1987); Lyn Roche, *Coping With Caring: Daily Reflections for Alzheimer's Caregivers* (1996).

127. Simpson and Yinger, *Racial and Cultural Minorities,* note 122 supra, at 77; see also Allport, *The Nature of Prejudice,* note 103 supra, at 371–372; Richard McAdams, *Cooperation and Conflict: The Economics of Group Status Production and Race Discrimination,* 108 Harv. L. Rev. 1003, at 1045 and 1045 n. 166 (1995). Professor McAdams argues that race discrimination is best understood as a means "by which people who share certain roughly similar and observable traits that come to be known as 'race' produce social status for themselves."

128. Anecdotes often are the struggling scholar's substitute for good data. Even so, I will venture to recount an incident in support of my discussion.

During the summer of 2001 I happened to witness a bitter argument that grew out of a gentleman about age 60 allegedly going out of turn in ordering ice cream at the local Dairy Queen. Another man, about age 35 years of age, took great umbrage at this perceived unfairness. Yelling ensued; the young man grabbed and tore the older man's shirt, and the situation was moving toward an actual fist fight. The young man apparently did not want to engage in a physical fight, however, so the tack he took was to repeatedly yell at the older man, "You're old; you're old; you're old." My reading of this virtual mantra, which must have been uttered 15 or 20 times over a 10-minute period, was that from the younger man's perspective this phrase constituted an insult. Accusing his rival of being old was a way for the younger man to demean the older man and thereby to assert his dominance and superiority over him.

It occurs to me that indeed the young in some measure do treasure their youth as a weapon that enables them to feel superior to their older colleagues, rivals, etc.—an edge that takes the sting out of facts such as the older person being richer, having a nicer car, etc. In other words, "I have something you don't have and can't have—youthfulness!!! Ha ha."

129. See, e.g., Jensen and Oakley, *Ageism Across Cultures and in Perspective of Sociobiologic and Psychodynamic Theories,* note 39 supra, at 24.

130. Georgia M. Barrow, *Aging, the Individual, and Society* 38 (5th ed. 1992) (citations omitted).

131. There are some data supporting the proposition that perceptions of individuals' ages are present even in very young infants. See, e.g., Joanne M. Montepare and Leslie A. Zebrowitz, *A Social Developmental View of Ageism*, in *Ageism* 77, at 77–81 (Todd D. Nelson, ed. 2002).

132. Sociobiology has been a controversial field of scientific inquiry and theorizing. For an engrossing recounting of the dispute and the disputants, see Ullica Segerstrale, *Defenders of the Truth* (2000). See generally Timothy H. Goldsmith, *The Biological Roots of Human Nature: Forging Links Between Evolution and Behavior* (1991); Owen D. Jones, *Law, Emotions, and Behavioral Biology*, 39 Jurimetrics J. 283 (1999); Owen D. Jones, *Sex, Culture, and the Biology of Rape: Toward Explanation and Prevention*, 87 Cal. L. Rev. 827 (1997); Russell Korobkin, *A Multi-Disciplinary Approach to Legal Scholarship: Economics, Behavioral Economics, and Evolutionary Psychology*, 41 Jurimetrics J. 177 (2001). Certainly not all scholars deem evolutionary biology a useful touchstone for analyzing legal issues. See, e.g., Jeffrey F. Rachlinski, *Comment: Is Evolutionary Analysis of Law Science or Storytelling?* 41 Jurimetrics J. 365 (2001).

133. Sarah Blaffer Hrdy, *Mother Nature* 283 (1999); see also Jensen and Oakley, *Ageism Across Cultures and in Perspective of Sociobiologic and Psychodynamic Theories*, note 39 supra, at 21–22. Today, it is technologically possible to implant a young woman's ovum in a postmenopausal woman, who then can bear a healthy baby. See Gina Kolata, "A Record and Big Questions as Woman Gives Birth at 63," *New York Times*, April 24, 1997, p. A1. This technological feat, however, has nothing to do with changing genetically programmed attitudes.

134. See, e.g., Dean Hamer and Peter Copeland, *Living with Our Genes* 274 (1998): "Once the organism has survived past the age of reproduction, it is useless as far as evolution is concerned."

135. See, e.g., James W. Wood, Stephen C. Weeks, Gillian R. Bentley, and Kenneth M. Weiss, *Human Population Biology and the Evolution of Aging*, in *Biological Anthropology and Aging* 19, at 49 (Douglas E. Crews and Ralph M. Garruto, eds. 1994).

136. See chapter 2.

137. In earlier times few men and women survived to what today we would deem old age or even middle age. See note 138 infra; see also Barbara Myerhoff, *Remembered Lives* 110 (1992):

> Part of a culture's conceptualization of a stage of "old age" involves its notions of "over-age" or senescence and death. Senescence is widely recognized culturally as the time of maximum dependence and minimum social utility, a universally pathetic and hopeless period of the life cycle. It is a time remarkable in our own culture because our technological competence has transformed it into a social problem by preserving substantial numbers of such people. At no other time and place has this been true. In simpler societies these dying embers may be regarded as anomalies who are too few to require special institutions or elaborate conceptualizations.

Thus, the drain on resources posed by superannuated tribe members arguably was not significant, and accordingly there was no genetic imperative to program early death into humans as a means of disposing of these individuals, who met early death through disease, accident, conflict, and/or starvation.

Even if the foregoing assessment is accurate, however, there likewise was no genetic basis for *permitting* long life. Moreover, in marginal societies whose members barely survived from year to year, even one extra mouth might tip the scales from communal success to disaster, and so while there may have been fewer people surviving into old age, each one of them could pose a threat to the community's survival.

As for data regarding survival into old age in colonial times in what is now the United States, see chapter 7.

138.

For the 100,000 years that humans have inhabited the earth, intense mortality selection pressures have produced a consistent long-term pattern of high unstable death rates that resulted in very high attrition at younger ages. Historically, only a small but robust subgroup of the human population has been able to survive into older age.

Carnes and Olshansky, *Evolutionary Perspectives on Human Senescence,* note 99 supra, at 793. It has been estimated that the average life expectancy for Stone Age farmers, as well as medieval Europeans, was about 25 years. Of course, life expectancy is only an average, and so one would be mistaken if one understood these data to mean that there were no early humans who survived into their 30s, 40s, and beyond. Indeed, "long postreproductive survival of humans evidently dates back to the Paleolithic period. As a result of improved living conditions and medical advances, there have been very significant reductions in the last two centuries in infant, child, and maternal death rates. Medical technology also has brought about major declines in deaths caused by infectious diseases. Accordingly, survival into older age has become commonplace throughout much of the world." Albert and Cattell, *Old Age in Global Perspective,* note 54 supra, at 27.

139. See generally Robert Arking, *Biology of Aging* 279–372 (1991).

140. Id. at 283.

141. Ibid.

142. Ibid.

143. Leonard Hayflick, *How and Why We Age* 228 (1994).

144. Ibid.

145. Ibid.

146. It has been observed:

Each chromosome is just a giant, supercoiled, foot-long DNA molecule.... [A]t the end of the chromosome there occurs a repeated stretch of meaningless 'text': the 'word' TTAGGG repeated again and again about two thousand times. This stretch of terminal tedium is known as a telomere. Its presence enables the DNA-copying devices to get started without cutting short any sense-containing 'text.' ...

But every time the chromosome is copied, a little bit of the telomere is left off. After a few hundred copyings, the chromosome is getting so short at the end that meaningful genes are in danger of being left off. In your body the telomeres are shortening at the rate of about thirty-one 'letters' a year—more in some tissues. That is why cells grow old and cease to thrive beyond a certain age. It may be why bodies, too, grow old—though there is fierce disagreement on this point.

Mark Ridley, *Genome* 197 (2000).

147. Arking, *Biology of Aging,* note 139 supra, at 304–315.

148. See, e.g., August Weismann, *Essays Upon Heredity and Kindred Biological Problems, Volume 1* (1891).

149. Wood, Weeks, Bentley, and Weiss, *Human Population Biology and the Evolution of Aging*, note 135 supra, at 64.

150. It has been argued that denominating a basis of aging as being either programmed or stochastic is misleading:

No aspect of an organism's physiology can be wholly determined by a genetic program, while no form of random damage can be wholly independent of [an] organism's repair and replacement capacities. The use of the terms *programmed* and *stochastic* fosters obscurity rather than clarity.

Michael R. Rose, *Evolutionary Biology of Aging* 172 (1991).

151. See generally id. at 62–78; George C. Williams, *Pleiotropy, natural selection, and the evolution of senescence,* 11 Evolution 398 (1957).

152. Richard Dawkins, *The Selfish Gene* 41 (paperback ed. 1999) (describing the theory of aging attributed to Sir Peter Medawar).

153. Ridley, *Genome*, note 146 supra, at 372.

154. See Wood, Weeks, Bentley, and Weiss, *Human Population Biology and the Evolution of Aging,* note 135 supra, at 32; see also Trudy R. Turner and Mark L. Weiss, *The Genesis of Longevity in Humans,* in Douglas E. Crews and Ralph M. Garruto, eds., *Biological Anthropology and Aging* 76, at 85 (1994).

155. In addressing the roles of older people in primitive and agrarian societies, note should be made of sex differentiations:

In general, a favorable cultural milieu for aged men has existed within a patriarchal type of family organization, where herding and agriculture have been the chief means of subsistence; where residence has been more or less permanent, the food supply constant, and the political system well regulated; and when property rights in land, crops, herds, goods, and even women are deeply intrenched. Aged women, on the other hand, have seemed to gain relatively more prestige in simple societies characterized by collection, hunting and fishing, particularly under matriarchal forms of family organizations. Their position also has appeared to be higher among farmers than herders. Old men have been able to achieve considerable prestige, even under circumstances normally conducive to elevating the rights of women; but aged women have been at a distinct disadvantage where cultural factors are weighted in favor of old men. Wherever women have been respected in old age, men are rarely without honor, but prestige for aged men has been no assurance of a similar status for women.

Leo F. Simmons, *Aging in Preindustrial Societies,* in *Handbook of Social Gerontology* 62, 84 (Clark Tibbitts, ed. 1960); see also Judith K. Brown, *Cross-Cultural Perspectives on Middle-Aged Women,* 23 Current Anthropology 123 (1982); Catherine Coles, *The Older Woman in Hausa Society: Power and Authority in Urban Nigeria,* in *The Cultural Context of Aging* 57 (Jay Sokolovsky, ed. 1990).

156. See Hrdy, *Mother Nature,* note 133 supra, at 282–283; Edward O. Wilson, *Sociobiology: The New Synthesis* 95 (25th anniversary ed. 2000).

157. See, e.g., Steven M. Albert and Maria G. Cattell, *Old Age in Global Perspective,* note 54 supra, at 28 (1994), quoting an unpublished manuscript by P. W. Turke, entitled "Evolution of the 100 Year Lifespan": "The increase in the reproductive value of the elderly [resulted in natural selection favoring] . . . delayed senescence, eventually extending the maximum lifespan."

158. Typically, one thinks of grandparents as being individuals in their 50s, 60s, and

70s, although, to be sure, there are men and women who first become grandparents both when they are in their 40s and in their 80s. Indeed, the average age for first-time grandparents at the beginning of the twenty-first century was 47. Leslie Mann, "Boomers put their own mark on grandparenting," *Chicago Tribune,* March 20, 2002, Prime Time, pp. 1, 14, at p. 1

Arguably, the grandparent thesis does not entirely hold up in explaining how natural selection over time could lead to longevity. This is because the prime reproductive years occur in the second and third decades and so 50,000 years ago "30–40 years . . . represents a time frame for humans when our ancestors could have been grandparents (i.e., when the reproductive success of offspring would have been determined)." Carnes and Olshansky, *Evolutionary Perspectives on Human Senescence,* note 99 supra, at 802. Thus, one might conclude that an analysis that seeks to explain the absence of a negative view of aging vis-à-vis 60- and 70-year-olds is not supported by the positive role played by grandparents because in the millennia during which natural selection was inducing change, grandparents were much younger, e.g., in their 30s and early 40s. But the point is that for the young, i.e., those of breeding age, the assistance of their elders was beneficial, no matter that an elderly person 50,000 years ago was a 35-year-old rather than a 67-year-old. Moreover, even thousands of years ago some people did live to more advanced ages. See note 138 supra.

159. Professor Sarah Blaffer Hrdy argues that extended years of life after menopause are integrally related to the extended period of time it takes for a human child to mature. Slow maturation, she reasons, is a "luxury." This luxury is "primarily available to those, like elephants, who can count on staying alive for a long time." Hrdy, *Mother Nature,* note 133 supra, at 284. And she reasons further:

> The metabolic clock that programs humans to mature slowly could have evolved only in a primate-like species in which mothers were *already* under selection pressure to live longer. This would occur if mothers were [naturally] selected first to live long enough to get their last offspring to independence and thereafter selected because their altruism [as manifested through providing food and caregiving for their grandchildren] produced increased survival of close kin.

Id. at 285.

As to the heritability of altruism, see generally Wilson, *Sociobiology: The New Synthesis,* note 156 supra, at 106–129; see also William D. Hamilton, *The Genetical Evolution of Social Behavior II,* 7 J. of Theoretical Biology 17, at 21 (1964). Hamilton, in illustrating the existence of genetically generated altruism, explained a study involving moths with a particular identifiable coloration. The moths endeavored to die immediately after reproduction, lest a predator learn—by killing and eating one of them—that they tasted good and so it would seek out other similarly marked moths. On the other hand, another moth—also with identifiable markings—was bad tasting; it continued to live past its reproductive period for at least a period equaling the time other moths were mating and laying eggs, because if such a postreproductive moth were to be killed and eaten by a predator, the predator would discover its foul taste and thus avoid seeking out the other, still breeding moths.

160. See Albert and Catell, *Old Age in Global Perspective,* note 157 supra, at 28, citing, *inter alia,* William D. Hamilton, *The Moulding of senescence by natural selection* 12–45 (1966); Solomon H. Katz and David F. Armstrong, *Cousin Marriage and the X-Chromosome: Evolution of Longevity and Language,* in *Biological Anthropology and Aging* 101, at 115–116 (Douglas E. Crews and Ralph M. Garruto, eds. 1994). But see Carnes and

Olshansky, *Evolutionary Perspectives on Human Senescence,* note 99 supra, at 797: "The force (effectiveness) of natural selection is strongest before reproduction begins, diminishes as the cumulative reproductive potential of individuals is achieved, and is weak or nonexistent after the reproductive period ends."

Hamilton noted that both women and men live beyond their reproductive years, and that by so doing they (or at least women) enhance the survival potential of their genetic lines. But he seemed to refuse to ascribe this phenomenon to the consequences of natural selection, whereby breeding individuals who carried some genetic propensity for long life would come to dominate through natural selection. Rather, Hamilton wrote as follows:

> The vigour of the post-reproductive adult can be attributed to beneficial effects of continued survival on the survival and reproduction of descendants. In fact, the 15 or so years of comparatively healthy life of the post-reproductive woman is so long in itself and so conspicuously better than the performance of the male that it suggests a special value of the old woman as a mother or grandmother during a long ancestral period, a value which was for some reason comparatively little shared by the old male. In view of the weakness of selection on nonreproductives, however, no good weight is attached to this indication; it seems quite possible that the effect is non-adaptive and a mere side effect of differences in sexual physiology established by the more powerful selection on young age groups.

Hamilton, *The Moulding of Senescence by Natural Selection,* supra, at 36; see also Ridley, *Genome,* note 146 supra, at 201. Ridley asserts that "natural selection cannot weed out genes that damage the body in post-reproductive old age, because there is no reproduction of the successful [those who avoid succumbing to harmful genes in old age] in old age."

My analysis assumes that the effects of older family or clan members can for some period of time enhance the survival of the young, their own inability to reproduce notwithstanding. And so natural selection should favor longevity to the extent that longevity promotes survival of the young into breeding age. Admittedly, I am presumptuous in questioning the analyses of major figures in the fields of genetics and sociobiology. Even so, it seems to me that Carnes and Olshansky, as well as Ridley and Hamilton, fail to recognize that natural selection can and should favor those who, in their reproductive years, carry with them the genetic disposition for living into their later, parent-assisting years without being afflicted early on by chronic diseases or decline that would make them burdens on the family or tribe.

161. Mark Ridley asserts: "Natural selection has designed all parts of our bodies to last just long enough to see our children into independence, [and] no more." Ridley, *Genome,* note 146 supra, at 202. Were the word *children* changed to *grandchildren,* Ridley's position would be more palatable.

There is also the complicated matter of religion. Given that every society devises some means of explaining the world and the group's role in it by creating some sort of scheme involving supernatural forces, one might conclude that religiosity (in the broadest sense) is genetically driven. In any event, whatever the source of human beings' need to explain the world and their place in it by resorting to external mysterious or supernatural forces, typically there will follow a need for intermediaries—people who will mediate between the tribe and these forces, who will intercede with those forces, and who will know how to appease them. Here, too, is a role often seen as fit for elders (although not exclusively so). Older men and women can be seen as having the experience to be able to better intercede with these forces, or gods. Moreover, the very fact of their long survival may be seen as evidence that these oldsters are the gods' favored, else they otherwise would have died earlier. See generally Nancy Foner, *Ages in Conflict* 26–37 (1984).

162. A like analysis has been suggested with regard to homosexuals. If one posits that homosexuality is a heritable trait, one is called upon to ask how it is that homosexuality as a human trait has survived over time, inasmuch as homosexuals are much less likely than heterosexuals to reproduce and thereby transmit the homosexuality gene from generation to generation. Edward O. Wilson presents a hypothesis explaining how such genes survived:

> The homosexual members of primitive societies may have functioned as helpers, whether while hunting in company with other men or in more domestic occupations at the dwelling sites. Freed from the special obligations of parental duties, they could have operated with special efficiency in assisting close relatives. Genes favoring homosexuality could then be sustained at a high equilibrium level by kin selection alone.

Wilson, *Sociobiology: The New Synthesis,* note 156 supra, at 555.

163. See generally Wilson, *Sociobiology: The New Synthesis,* note 156 supra.

164. John Noble Wilford, "When Humans Became Human," *New York Times,* Feb. 26, 2002, Science Times, pp. D1, D5, quoting archaeologist Dr. Mary C. Stiner.

165. Wilson, *Sociobiology: The New Synthesis,* note 156 supra, at 560.

166. See chapter 3. That the elderly in preindustrial societies often had considerable prestige and power should not lead to the conclusion that there were no negative feelings and/or actions directed toward older men and women in such societies. Quite the contrary, as Nancy Foner has written:

> All is not smooth sailing for old men at the top [in preindustrial societies]. They may cherish their privileges, but, as in any system of inequality, relations with the less advantaged are frequently marked by strain. While old men are piling up rewards, young men, at least for the time being, are often on the losing end. Old men want to preserve their advantages. And the young, subject to their elders' authority and deprived of valued resources and roles, often resent old men's prerogatives and the restraints under which they themselves labor.

Foner, *Ages in Conflict,* note 161 supra, at 39; see generally id. at 39–66.

167. Montepare and Zebrowitz, *A Social-Developmental View of Ageism,* note 131 supra, at 93.

168. Myerhoff, *Remembered Lives,* note 137 supra, at 102.

169. Dawkins, *The Selfish Gene,* note 152 supra, at 3; see also Katherine K. Baker, *Biology for Feminists,* 75 Chi.-Kent L. Rev. 805, at 806 (2000); Jones, *Law, Emotions, and Behavioral Biology,* note 132 supra, at 285:

> Behavioral biology takes no side in the "Nature versus Nurture" debate. This is principally because, news headlines to the contrary [notwithstanding], there is no such debate within relevant scientific communities. . . . Nature and nurture are inseparably intertwined. Neither makes sense without the other. All biological processes, including normal brain development, ultimately depend on environmental inputs. Similarly, all environmental influences can only be perceived, sorted, analyzed, and understood through biological, evolved processes.

170. Leo Simmons writes:

> One may state with confidence that all primitive and agrarian societies have accorded some considerable respect to old people—often remarkable deference—*at*

least until they have reached such "over-age" that they are obviously powerless and incompetent. Under close analysis, respect for old age has been, as a rule, accorded to persons on the basis of some special assets possessed by them. They may receive some consideration for their usefulness in the performance of economic, camp, or household chores. They may be regarded highly for their skill in crafts, games, dances, songs, storytelling, and the care of small children. They may be respected and needed because of their control of property rights and the exercise of family prerogatives. They may be accorded great homage for their extensive knowledge, seasoned experience, good judgment, gifts in magic, and functions in religious rites and practices.

Simmons, *Aging in Preindustrial Societies,* note 155 supra, at 84 (emphasis added).

171. See generally Anthony D. Glascock, *By Any Other Name, It Is Still Killing: A Comparison of the Treatment of the Elderly in America and Other Societies,* in *Culture, Aging, and Society* 43 (Jay Sokolovsky, ed. 1990).

172. See chapter 2; see also Foner, *Ages in Conflict,* note 161 supra, at 107–108.

173. Actually, "older persons commit disproportionately more suicides than other age groups, with males over the age of sixty-five having the highest suicide rate in this country." William E. Adams Jr., *The Intersection of Elder Law and Criminal Law: More Traffic Than One Might Assume,* 30 Stetson L. Rev. 1331, at 1342 (2001), citing Edith Elisabeth Flynn, *Elders as Perpetrators,* in *Elders, Crime, and the Criminal Justice System* 43, at 70 (Max B. Rothman, Burton D. Dunlop, and Pamela Entzel, eds. 2000).

174. When the federal Age Discrimination in Employment Act of 1967, as amended, 29 U.S.C. §§ 621–634, was first enacted, it only afforded protection from discrimination to individuals between the ages of 40 and 64. Upon attainment of age 65, an employee could be subjected to age-based mandatory retirement. In 1978 the statute was amended so as to extend protection through age 69 for nonfederal employees, and until death for federal employees, Age Discrimination in Employment Act Amendments of 1978, Pub. L. No. 95-256, 92 Stat. 189, amending 29 U.S.C. § 631. In 1986 the age ceiling for employees in the private sector was removed, subject to only a couple of exceptions. Age Discrimination in Employment Amendments of 1986, Pub. L. No. 99-592, § 2(c), 100 Stat. 3342, at 3342. Still, employers with less than 20 employees are free to impose age-based retirement on their employees, unless a local or state fair employment practices statute extends protection to such individuals. 29 U.S.C. § 630(b).

175. See generally Howard Eglit, 1–3 *Age Discrimination* (2d ed. 1994 and annual supps.).

176. See chapter 2.

177. I do not want to unduly emphasize this assertion. While there are about 2.5 million men and women living in nursing homes today, the large majority of persons who claim to be in need of long-term care in fact are not residing in such facilities:

> In contrast to the traditional notions of long-term care, the vast majority of all those who say they need long-term care services do not live in nursing homes or other institutions. About 2.4 million live in institutions, and most of these individuals are over 65 years old. The remaining 10.4 million individuals live at home or in small community residential settings, such as group homes or supervised apartments.

U.S. General Accounting Office, Report to the Chairman, Special Committee on Aging, U.S. Senate, *Long-Term Care—Current Issues and Future Directions* 8, GAO/HEHS (Apr. 1995).

178. Board and care facilities and their roles have been described in the following manner:

Board and care homes for many years have been an integral part of the formal and informal systems of residential care for disabled and elderly populations. Board and care homes are distinguished from rooming houses or boarding homes in that they provide personal care and protective oversight for their residents in addition to room and board. These facilities are usually owned and operated by the private sector; residents, for the most part, pay for their care from personal resources.

Nancy D. Dittmar, *Facility and Resident Characteristics of Board and Care Homes for the Elderly,* in *Preserving Independence, Supporting Needs* 1, at 1 (Marilyn Moon, George Gaberlavage, Sandra J. Newman, eds. 1989). "[A]s many as one million older Americans (and at least two million others) live in such homes." Marilyn Moon, *Introduction,* in *Preserving Independence, Supporting Needs,* at vii.

179. Assisted living facilities have been defined as follows:

Broadly defined, an assisted living facility is a residential setting where some level of assistance with daily living, sometimes including health care, is provided to persons who can no longer live independently. . . . Most [such facilities] offer restaurant-style dining, common spaces for socializing, handicapped-accessible facilities in units, and two-way voice communication with staff. . . . [T]he most common unit offered is a one-bedroom apartment or single occupancy living space. Services offered . . . range from medication management and personal care to housekeeping, laundry, transportation, and special dietary needs management. They also include health-related and nursing care. The typical . . . resident is an 83-year-old woman, frail but mobile, who needs help with two or more activities of daily living . . . such as bathing or dressing.

Current estimates of the numbers of assisted living beds across the country range from 800,000 to 1.5 million.

Sue Seeley, *Assisted Living: Federal and State Options for Affordability, Quality of Care, and Consumer Protection,* 23 BIFOCAL 1, at 1 (Fall 2001); see generally Stephanie Edelstein, *Assisted Living: Recent Developments and Issues for Older Consumers,* 9 Stanford L. & Policy Rev. 373 (1998).

180. See chapter 1.

181. Cole, *The Journey of Life,* 229 (paperback ed. 1993).

Chapter 5. The Main Actors: Plaintiffs, Defendants, and Witnesses

The epigraphs are from the following sources: Hermann Hesse, *On Old Age,* quoted in Thomas R. Cole and Mary G. Winkler, *The Oxford Book of Aging* 56 (1994); *The Tragedy of King Lear,* Act II, Scene 4, in G. B. Harrison, *Shakespeare—the Complete Works* (1952).

1. For example, a complaint must be sufficiently informative to put the defendant on notice of what it is that the plaintiff is complaining. See, e.g., Swierkiewicz v. Sorema, NA, 534 U.S. 506 (2002).

2. For example, for a federal court to have jurisdiction as to a matter there must be a case or controversy, which means that for a plaintiff to have standing to sue she must have suffered some injury of a more or less tangible nature, rather than only an affront to her ideological position; the plaintiff's grievance must be live rather than a matter that has been resolved and is therefore moot; and her grievance must be in a sufficiently advanced

form—i.e., ripe—such that a judicial decision would not be premature. See generally John E. Nowak and Ronald D. Rotunda, *Constitutional Law* 69–106 (6th ed. 2000).

3. E. Allan Farnsworth, *Contracts,* § 4.4 (3d ed. 1999).

4. See, e.g., Hughes v. State, 198 N.W.2d 348, 55 Wis.2d 477 (1972) (a child under the statutory age—i.e., under age 13 in the case of first degree sexual assault and under age 16 in the case of second degree sexual assault—cannot consent to sexual intercourse). See also Carter v. State, 121 Tex. Crim. 493, 51 S.W.2d 316 (1932).

5. 29 U.S.C. §§ 621–634.

6. 29 U.S.C. § 631(b).

7. See generally Victor E. Flango and David B. Rottman, *Court Data on the Elderly and Persons with Disabilities,* in American Bar Association Commission on Legal Problems of the Elderly, American Bar Association Commission on the Mentally Disabled, and National Judicial College, *Court-Related Needs of the Elderly and Persons with Disabilities* 203 (1991).

8. By nonparty witness I mean a witness who is called to testify but who is not a plaintiff or defendant in the case in which she testifies.

9. See chapter 2.

10. See note 43 and accompanying text infra.

11. Unavoidably, there is some mixing of issues here. A lawyer's client also may appear in the role of a plaintiff or a defendant—individuals addressed in this chapter—if a given matter winds up in court. And a plaintiff or a defendant is likely to be a witness, a role that also is a separate subject of this chapter.

12. Often the two terms—*guardian* and *conservator*—are used interchangeably. As a formal matter, a guardian typically serves as the legal representative of the ward and thereby has the authority to provide direction and control regarding a ward's health, maintenance, and care needs, although in many states the guardian will be vested with control of the ward's finances and assets, as well. A conservator is an appointee who serves as a legal representative of a ward with regard to the ward's property or estate. See Hal Fliegelman and Debora C. Fliegelman, *Giving Guardians the Power to Do Medicaid Planning,* 32 Wake Forest L. Rev. 341, at 342–343 n. 7 (1997).

13. See Lawrence Friedman and Mark Savage, *Taking Care: The Law of Conservatorship in California,* 61 S. Cal. L. Rev. 273, 279 (1988). It was estimated that in 1990 there were 500,000 to 1 million older people in the United States who had been adjudicated to be wards pursuant to guardianship or conservatorship proceedings. Lawrence Frolik, *Elder Abuse and Guardians of Elderly Incompetents,* 2 J. of Elder Abuse & Neglect 31 (1990).

14. See Lauren Barritt List and Saidy Barinaga-Burch, *National Study of Guardianship Systems: Summary of Findings and Recommendations,* 29 Clearinghouse Rev. 643, 645 (1995) ("76 percent of guardianship petitions and 71 percent of conservatorship petitions were filed by a family member or friend of the respondent, usually the children of the respondent.")

15. 29 U.S.C. § 631.

16. The number of administrative charges filed with the U.S. Equal Employment Opportunity Commission under the ADEA was on the rise in the opening years of the twenty-first century. Admittedly, inasmuch as the ADEA applies not only to the elderly but to anyone over age 39, these data lack important specificity insofar as identifying older versus younger complainants is concerned. The data as to charges are as follows: FY 1992—

19,753; FY 1993—19,809; FY 1994—19,618; FY 1995—17,416; FY 1996—15,719; FY 1997—15,785; FY 1998—15,191; FY 1999—14,141; FY 2000—16,008; FY 2001—17,405; FY 2002—19,921; FY 2003—19,124. U.S. Equal Employment Opportunity Commission, Age Discrimination in Employment Act (ADEA) Charges, FY 1992–FY 2000. www. EEOC.gov. (2004). (The federal fiscal year runs from October 1 through September 30.)

17. There are a variety of reasons why the fairly limited number of published decisions does not provide an accurate portrayal of the actual larger incidence of age discrimination in the workplace. See Howard Eglit, *The Age Discrimination in Employment Act at Thirty: Where It's Been, Where It Is Today, Where It's Going,* 31 U. of Richmond L. Rev. 579, at 591–596 (1997).

18. Id. at 599.

19. The age breakdown, year by year, is set forth in id. at 600.

20. Actually, there was one case involving 431 plaintiffs, all age 55 and over; the author excluded all but one of these individuals, and to that individual he assigned the age of 55, inasmuch as there was no way of identifying the age of each individual in this massive case.

21. Id. at 602–603.

22. Id. at 603.

23. Id. at 614.

24. Id. at 614–615.

25. See generally Howard Eglit, 1–3 *Age Discrimination* (2d. ed. 1994 and annual supps.).

26. Rosalie S. Wolf, *Elders as Victims of Crime, Abuse, Neglect, and Exploitation,* in *Elders, Crime, and the Criminal Justice System* 19, at 24 (Max B. Rothman, Burton D. Dunlop, and Pamela Entzel, eds. 2000).

27. Id. at 22.

28. Ibid.

29. Id. at 23.

30. Ibid.

31. Id. at 20–23.

32. See notes 60–64 and accompanying text infra.

33. See generally Edith Elisabeth Flynn, *Elders as Perpetrators,* in *Elders, Crime, and the Criminal Justice System* 43 (Max B. Rothman, Burton D. Dunlop, and Pamela Entzel, eds. 2000); see also William E. Adams Jr., *The Intersection of Elder Law and Criminal Law: More Traffic Than One Might Assume,* 30 Stetson L. Rev. 1331, at 1343–1346 (2001). Some older data were addressed in Victoria K. Kidman, *The Elderly Offender: A New Wrinkle in the Criminal Justice System,* 14 J. of Contemporary Law 131, at 131 (1988).

34. Flynn, *Elders as Perpetrators,* note 33 supra, at 47–48.

35. Id. at 54.

36. Ibid. Index crimes "consist of major felony offenses and include murder and nonnegligent manslaughter, forcible rape, robbery, aggravated assault, burglary, larceny/ theft, auto theft, and arson." Id. at 48.

37. Id. at 74–76.

38. Data obtained from the Uniform Crime Reports regarding total arrests in calendar years 1995–1999 for 30 types of offenses, ranging from murder at the serious end of the violence spectrum to running away at the nonserious end of the nonviolence spectrum showed virtually no percentage increase for older individuals:

	Total arrests	50–54 years	55–59 years	60–64 years	65+ years	Total % for 50+
1995	100%	2.0%	1.0%	0.6%	0.7%	4.3%
1996	100%	2.1%	1.1%	0.6%	0.7%	4.5%
1997	100%	2.1%	1.1%	0.6%	0.6%	4.4%
1998	100%	2.3%	1.1%	0.6%	0.6%	4.6%
1999	100%	2.5%	1.2%	0.6%	0.7%	5.0%

In terms of absolute numbers there was a decline from 1995 to 1999 in arrests of older individuals. This was consistent with a general decrease in arrests across the board:

	Total arrests	50–54 years	55–59 years	60–64 years	65+ years	Total for for 50+
1995	11,416,346	226,410	119,031	68,039	75,542	489,012
1996	11,093,211	228,682	119,917	65,842	72,755	487,196
1997	10,544,624	225,172	112,845	60,116	67,261	465,394
1998	10,295,129	233,717	116,199	59,619	63,627	473,162
1999	9,141,201	224,755	109,867	54,514	59,983	449,119

Source for 1999 data: U.S. Dept. of Justice, Federal Bureau of Investigation, *Crime in the United States, 1999* 222, 223 (2000).

39. Flynn, *Elders as Perpetrators,* note 33 supra, at 56.

40. Ibid.

41. Dr. Flynn writes:

Elder liquor law violations increased by 13%, while they decreased by the same amount for the whole population. Offenses against family and children increased by 70% for elders and even more for the total population (79%). Drug abuse violations for elders increased by 11%. For the population as a whole it increased by 6%. White-collar crime (forgery and counterfeiting, fraud, and embezzlement) grew by 5% for older persons and 10% for the total population.

Id. at 57–59.

42. *Chicago Daily Law Bulletin* (June 27, 2000), p. 3.

43. See, e.g., 42 Pa. Cons. Stat. Ann. § 6302 (2000) (defining "child" as person under age 18); Va. Code Ann. § 16.1-228 (Michie 1999) (id.)

44. There may be, however, case law or statutory language barring prosecution of the very young, let us say, those 10 years of age and under, and knowledge of that datum at least will give the observer an age floor as to those who can be in the juvenile courtroom.

45. See, e.g., Ky. Rev. Stat. § 635.020(4) (Michie 1999); 42 Pa. Cons. Stat. Ann. § 6355 (2000); Va. Code Ann. § 16.1-269.1 (Michie 1999).

46. American Bar Association Commission on Legal Problems of the Elderly, et al., *Court Related-Needs,* note 7 supra, at 181–183.

47. Mary Helen McNeal, *Redefining Attorney-Client Roles: Unbundling and Moderate-Income Elderly Clients,* 32 Wake Forest L. Rev. 295, at 301 (1997); see also id. at 299–300:

Typical legal problems faced by the elderly for which discrete-task representation might be employed include traditional "general practice" problems in the areas of family, consumer, and housing law; health-related issues, including advance directives, advice on decision making for an incapacitated spouse, Medicare reimbursement issues, and Medicaid eligibility; and income and asset protection issues, such as employment and pension concerns, estate planning issues, and eligibility for various benefit programs. Other legal needs of the elderly, sometimes characterized as "quasi-legal," include having documents reviewed by an attorney, guidance in making decisions, and assistance in completing paperwork for Medicare and Medigap reimbursement.

48. See 1-3 Eglit, *Age Discrimination,* note 25 supra.

49. Eglit, *The Age Discrimination in Employment Act at Thirty,* note 17 supra, at 666.

50. Id. at 599.

51. It is true, however, that it is unlikely that such claims will be pursued by individuals who will be in their late 60s or older. See text accompanying note 22 supra. The small numbers of such claimants in the reported case law no doubt is due to the fact that increasing numbers of American men have been retiring at relatively early ages over the past several decades. See chapter 4. Absent some dramatic economic changes compelling potential retirees to stay on the job, this trend should continue. (One factor that may play some role in curbing this trend is the very gradual increase up to age 67 as the age of eligibility for full Social Security benefits, pursuant to 42 U.S.C. § 4161(l)(1).)

52. But see Louis Uchitelle, "Older Workers Are Thriving Despite Recent Hard Times," *New York Times,* Sept. 8, 2003, pp. A1, A15. (At least in the short term, older workers were not experiencing a disproportionate incidence of job losses during the employment downturn of the first years of the twenty-first century; rather, they were doing better than younger workers in retaining their jobs during a period of job layoffs.)

53. "'Of the chief executives who run Fortune 500 companies, just six are women.'" Alex Kuczynski, "They Conquered, They Left," *New York Times,* March 24, 2002, Sunday Styles, pp. 1, 7, at p. 7, quoting Sheila Wellington, president of Catalyst, a New York-based group working to advance the interests of women in business. "'That's a whopping 1.2 percent.'" Id.

54. The world of large law firms, however, has been particularly resistant to welcoming women into the ranks of partners. See, e.g., Claudia H. Deutsch, "Women Lawyers Strive for Chance to Make it Rain," *New York Times,* May 21, 1996, Business Day, pp. D1, D7, at D7:

> According to the *National Law Journal,* 13.6 percent of all partners in the country's 250 largest law firms are women, up from 11.1 percent in 1991. But only 54 percent of those women are equity partners who share in the firm's profits; 74 percent of the men are. Another cut at the same numbers: while women make up 23 percent of nonequity partners, they represent only 1 percent of equity partners.

55. See notes 17–24 and accompanying text supra.

56. See Eglit, *The Age Discrimination in Employment Act at Thirty,* note 17 supra, at 609.

57. U.S. General Accounting Office, Report to the Honorable William S. Cohen, Special Committee on Aging, U.S. Senate, *Long-Term Care—Projected Needs of the Aging Baby Boom Generation* 2, GAO/HRD-91-86 (1991).

58. See generally chapter 4. In a national survey of guardianship systems, it was determined that "[s]ixty-eight percent of petitioners characterized the respondent as having moderate to severe problems with conversation, 76 percent reported moderate to severe memory problems, and 91 percent reported that the respondents were having moderate to severe difficulties handling financial affairs." Lauren Barritt List and Saidy Barinaga-

Burch, *National Study of Guardianship Systems: Summary of Findings and Recommendations,* note 14 supra, at 645 (footnotes omitted). In the same survey it was further determined that "[i]n general, the respondents were less impaired in performing daily physical activities, such as bathing, dressing, using the toilet, doing household chores, and feeding themselves" Id. (footnote omitted).

59. See generally Richard J. Bonnie and Robert B. Wallace, eds., *Elder Mistreatment* (2003); Mark S. Lachs and Karl Pillemer, *Abuse and Neglect of Elderly Persons,* 332 New England J. of Med 437 (Feb. 16, 1995).

60. See, e.g., Vicki Gottlich, *Beyond Granny Bashing: Elder Abuse in the 1990s,* Clearinghouse Rev. Special Issue 371, at 372 (1994) (footnote omitted):

Despite a push toward mandatory reporting of elder abuse cases, the exact number of older people, nationally, who fall within the broad definition of abuse is unknown. First, as with abuse generally, not all elder abuse cases are reported. Older people are even less likely to report the abuse than other victims. . . .

Second, variations in state law definitions of abuse affect the number of cases reported. For example, not all states include self-neglect in their definition of abuse. States also have different age cutoffs for consideration as "elderly." . . . Third, state data collection practices also may influence the number of cases reported. States may not keep separate data on institutional and noninstitutional abuse, on elderly and other adult abuse victims, or on substantiated and unsubstantiated reports of abuse.

61. Marcia Libes Simon, *An Exploratory Study of Adult Protective Services Programs' Repeat Elder Abuse Clients* 4 (1992) (footnotes omitted).

62. Wolf, *Elders As Victims of Crime, Abuse, Neglect, and Exploitation,* note 26 supra, at 29. Data from Canada, Great Britain, and Finland are in accord. See Seymour H. Moskowitz, *Reflecting Reality: Adding Elder Abuse and Neglect to Legal Education,* 47 Loyola L. Rev. 191, at 201 n. 39 (2001).

63. Moskowitz, *Reflecting Reality,* note 62 supra, at 201 n. 39, citing National Center for Elder Abuse, *Understanding the Nature and Extent of Elder Abuse in Domestic Settings* (1997). In Illinois the number of reported cases of elder abuse rose from 2,503 in 1991 to 7,415 in 2001, according to the state's Department on Aging; about half involved alleged financial abuse. Tom McCann and Mickey Ciokajlo, "Rise in elder abuse overwhelms system," *Chicago Tribune,* March 26, 2002, pp. 1, 18, at p. 1.

64. Wolf, *Elders As Victims of Crime, Abuse, Neglect, and Exploitation,* note 26 supra, at 29–30.

65. See, e.g., Gottlich, *Beyond Granny Bashing,* note 60 supra, at 374:

In 1980, when legislation which would have required mandatory reporting of elder abuse was first introduced [in the Congress], only 16 states had laws which required reporting of elder abuse. Ten years later, forty-two states and the District of Columbia had mandatory elder abuse reporting laws. The remaining eight states made reporting voluntary.

66. Simon, *An Exploratory Study of Adult Protective Services Programs' Repeat Elder Abuse Clients,* note 61 supra, at 6 table 2.

67. Ibid.

68. See generally Lee Beneze and Ann Neighbors, *Elder Abuse and Neglect Cases: An Attorney's Guide,* 79 Ill. B.J. 390 (Aug. 1991); Gottlich, *Beyond Granny Bashing,* note 60 supra, at 377–380.

69. See generally Beneze and Neighbors, *Elder Abuse and Neglect Cases,* note 68 supra.

70. See, e.g., Gottlich, *Beyond Granny Bashing,* note 60 supra, at 374 n. 15.

71. See chapter 6.

72. Clearly, the matter of deciding to report or not can raise significant issues for the conscientious attorney. An elderly person who appears to be the possible victim of abuse may not want that abuse reported, and there is no basic reason why her autonomy should not be respected. After all, there are no laws requiring the reporting of suspected abuse of young adults, such as women caught up in abusive marriages. Why should older people be treated differently in terms of respect for their privacy and their freedom to choose whether or not to seek help?

Autonomy issues aside, the victim may not wish to have any report made because the abuser is a relative or a friend whom the victim loves and/or whom she does not want to end up in trouble with the law. Or the abuser may be the only person in the victim's life, and while the relationship is a dysfunctional one, it may be better than none. Moreover, removal of the abuser from the scene may result in the victim being divested of her rights by virtue of being declared a ward pursuant to a guardianship petition, or being placed in a nursing home or board and care facility, where her care may be better, but her emotional isolation may well be worse.

The right answer, notwithstanding the problems associated with it, is that where physical and/or psychological abuse of a serious nature is occurring the lawyer should report that abuse. But where the abuse is of a mild nature, whether physical and/or psychological, the correct response is a more elusive matter. Moreover, there is another problem: attorney-client confidentiality. If the victim discloses her plight but insists that it not be revealed, the lawyer may have no choice but to remain silent. See chapter 6. If it is the perpetrator who discloses the wrongdoing, the lawyer has more flexibility: the ethical rules governing attorneys do not require an attorney to remain silent in the face of the commission, or suspected commission, of a crime. See American Bar Association, *Model Rules of Professional Conduct,* Rule 1.6(b)(1) (1994): "A lawyer may reveal . . . information to the extent the lawyer reasonably believes necessary: (1) to prevent the client from committing a criminal act that the lawyer believes is likely to result in imminent death or substantial bodily harm."

73. See, e.g., Elder Abuse and Neglect Act, 320 Ill. Comp. Stat. 20/1 *et seq.*

74. Ways in which the legal system can better respond to elder abuse are detailed in a report issued in 1995 by the American Bar Association's Commission on Legal Problems of the Elderly. Lori A. Stiegel, *Recommended Guidelines for State Courts Handling Cases Involving Elder Abuse* (1995).

75. See notes 86–87 and accompanying text infra.

76. See, e.g., Robert B. Fleming, *Elder Law Answer Book* (2001); Joan M. Krauskopf, Robert N. Brown, Karen L. Tokarz, and Allan D. Bogutz, *Elderlaw: Advocacy for the Aging* (2d ed. 1993); John J. Regan, Rebecca C. Morgan, and David M. English, *Tax, Estate & Financial Planning for the Elderly* (1997 and periodic supps.); Peter J. Strauss, Robert Wolf, and Dana Shilling, *Aging and the Law* (1990).

77. Not all long-term care residents are elderly, although of the 2.4 million or so people living in long-term care facilities in the 1990s, most were over 65 years of age. U.S. General Accounting Office, Report to the Chairman, Special Committee on Aging, U.S. Senate, *Long-Term Care—Current Issues and Future Directions* 8, GAO/HEHS-95-109 (Apr. 1995). These data, while published in a 1995 report, unquestionably hold true for the entire decade.

Many different types of physical and mental conditions can give rise to a need for long-term care. Physical conditions include paraplegia, heart diseases, asthma, arthritis, and many others. Mental conditions include severe and persistent mental illness, dementia, traumatic brain injuries, and mental retardation and other developmental disabilities. Among the elderly, arthritis and heart disease are the two most common causes of long-term care for individuals. For nonelderly adults, the most common causes of long-term care need are arthritis, heart disease, and mental retardation. In children, the most common chronic conditions limiting activity are respiratory disorders, such as asthma, mental retardation, and other mental or nervous system conditions such as cerebral palsy.

Id. at 4–5.

78. U.S. General Accounting Office, *Long-Term Care—Projected Needs of the Aging Baby Boom Generation,* note 57 supra, at 8. Even higher figures have been projected by some. See *id.*

79. See Robert Pear, "9 of 10 Nursing Homes Lack Adequate Staff, a Government Study Finds," *New York Times,* Feb. 18, 2002, p. A11; U.S. General Accounting Office, Report to the Special Committee on Aging, U.S. Senate, *California Nursing Homes—Care Problems Persist Despite Federal and State Oversight,* GAO/HEHS-98–202 (July 1998).

80. See, e.g., Toby S. Edelman, *The Nursing Home Reform Law: Issues for Litigation,* 24 Clearinghouse Rev. 545, at 549 (Oct. 1990); David R. Hoffman, *Ensuring Quality Care Through the Use of the Federal False Claims Act,* 17 BIFOCAL 1 (Spring 1996); John F. Romano, *Nursing Home and Elderly Care Facility Cases, Part 1: Initial Client Interview, Investigation, Case Workup, and Experts,* 17 Trial Diplomacy J. 1 (Jan./Feb. 1994).

81. In the American courts prevailing plaintiffs cannot recover the costs of litigation absent some law specifically authorizing such recovery. Typically, no such laws exist with regard to personal injury claims.

82. A survey of the country's 75 most populous counties as of 1992 found that the state courts in these counties had disposed of 762,000 cases. See Richard C. Reuben, *Plaintiffs Rarely Win Punitives, Study Says,* 81 ABA J. 26 (Oct. 1995).

83. See Equal Employment Opportunity Commission Alternative Dispute Resolution Statement, EEOC Notice No. 915.002 (July 17, 1995), www.eeoc.gov/docs/adrstatement. html (Sept. 2003).

84. Divorce rate data are rare:

It is true that the divorce rate for older couples apparently is on the rise. "'Substantially more senior citizens are divorcing today than in the past,' says Donald C. Schiller, a partner at Schiller, DuCanto & Fleck, the nation's largest matrimonial-law firm. Most states don't keep track of divorces by age; in Maryland, one of the states that do, the divorce rate among men 65 and older increased 11 percent in the past two decades."

http:/www.oomo.org/50_year_itch.htm (2003); see also *The old grey divorce,* http://www.divorcemag.com/news/senior divorce.shtm/ (2003); William Grady, "Lawyers see more divorces among elderly," *Chicago Tribune,* Nov. 6, 1992, Sec. 1, p. 20. However, in terms of absolute numbers, the total of 65+ divorcees in no way even approaches the numbers of divorced young and middle-aged men and women. As reported in 2003, the median age of divorce in the United States is 35.6 for males and 33.2 for women; as of 1993 people ages 25 to 39 made up 60 percent of all divorcees. http:/www.divorces.com/ stats.html (Aug. 18, 2003). Child custody issues, in any event, are very rarely going to be relevant in divorce disputes involving older couples. See generally Ellen Widen Kessler, *The Financial Impact of Divorces for Older Clients,* 12 Experience 24 (Winter 2002).

The issue of grandparents' visitation rights vis-à-vis their grandchildren has attracted considerable attention in the press, as well as from politicians and academics. See, e.g., Edward M. Burns, *Grandparent Visitation Rights: Is It Time for the Pendulum to Fall?* 25 Family L. Q. 59 (1991); Select Committee on Aging, U.S. House of Representatives, *Grandparents: New Roles and Responsibilities,* Comm. Pub. No. 102-876, 102d Cong., 2d Sess. (1991). Indeed, by 1991 all 50 states had adopted statutes granting grandparents visitation rights in some instances, over parents' objections. See Burns, *Grandparent Visitation Rights,* at 60. Disputes arising out of barriers imposed to such visitation, typically by parents, in the 1980s and 1990s generated a number of legal rulings. See, e.g., Bronstein v. Bronstein, 434 So.2d 780 (Ala. 1983); Hawkins v. Hawkins, 102 Ill. App.3d 1037, 430 N.E.2d 652 (1981); *In re* Carl B., 142 Misc.2d 406, 537 N.Y.S.2d 456 (1989). Such disputes, however, should be seen much less often in the courts in the future in light of the Supreme Court more or less resolving this issue (in favor of parents) in Troxel v. Granville, 530 U.S. 57 (2000). See generally Ellen Marrus, *Over the Hills and Through the Woods to Grandparents' House We Go, or Do We, Post-Troxel?* 43 Ariz. L. Rev. 751 (2001).

85. Older drivers have a higher accident rate per miles driven than any other group, save males between the ages of 18 and 24, see chapter 3, although older drivers tend to drive fewer miles than do younger men and women. See Jennifer L. Klein, *Elderly Drivers: The Need for Tailored License Renewal Procedures,* 3 Elder L. J. 309, at 314 (1995). There are data showing significant increases over the next several decades in both the numbers of older drivers and the miles driven. For example, "[t]he number of drivers age 85 and over in 2030 will be from four to five times greater than today." Http:// www.seniorcitizens.com/k/maturedrivers.html. (2003).

Between 1990 and 2020, the total annual mileage driven by male older drivers will increase by 465 percent—and this estimate is conservative. For female elderly drivers, the total annual vehicle miles driven will increase almost 500 percent (again based on conservative estimates). The proportion of the total mileage for elderly drivers to the total miles driven by all drivers is also steadily increasing. In 1990, elderly drivers accounted for 6.7 percent of all miles driven. By 2030, according to our conservative estimate, elderly drivers will account for 18.9 percent of all vehicle miles driven, almost triple the 1990 figure.

Ibid.

86. As to Medicaid coverage of nursing home costs, see Fliegelman and Fliegelman, *Giving Guardians the Power to Do Medicaid Planning,* note 12 supra, at 354–358 (1997). As to divestiture of assets so as to make an individual eligible for Medicaid, see id. at 359–364; see also Lisa Schreiber Joire, *After* New York State Bar Association v. Reno: *Ethical Problems in Limiting Medicaid Estate Planning,* 12 Georgetown J. of Legal Ethics 789 (1999); Shawn Patrick Regan, *Medicaid Estate Planning: Congress' Ersatz Solution for Long-Term Health Care,* 44 Catholic U. L. Rev. 1217 (1995).

87. The legality of attorneys providing counsel for the transfer of assets has been a matter of considerable debate, as well as an object of legislative action, as described by the court that decided New York State Bar Association v. Reno, 999 F. Supp. 710 (N.D.N.Y. 1998):

Before Congress enacted section 217 of the Health Insurance Portability and Accountability Act of 1996 [42 U.S.C. § 1320a-7b(a)], certain transfers of assets up to 36 months prior to an application for Medicaid benefits and certain transfers to trusts up to 60 months prior to application, could result in a period of ineligibility for Medicaid benefits. In enacting section 217, Congress left the ineligibility period intact, but added certain criminal penalties. Essentially, section 217 made it a crime to dispose of assets in order to become eligible for Medicaid benefits if the disposition of assets "resulted in the imposition of a period of ineligibility." § 1320a-7b(a)(6) (sometimes referred to as the "Granny Goes to Jail Act"). Violators were subject to fines of up to $25,000 or imprisonment for up to 5 years, or both. . . .

A number of organizations lobbied for the repeal of section 217. . . . Rather than repeal [it], Congress amended section 217 by enacting section 4734 of the Balanced Budget Act of 1997. Section 4734, which became effective August 5, 1997, struck the former language and added a provision making it illegal to counsel or assist an individual to dispose of certain assets to qualify for Medicaid.

999 F. Supp. at 712. Subsequently, Attorney General Janet Reno informed Congress that in light of the First Amendment and due process problems raised by the amended 42 U.S.C. § 1320a-7(b)(a)(6), the Department of Justice would not enforce the provision, which criminalized the professional activities of attorneys and financial counselors. 999 F. Supp. at 713. Notwithstanding Reno's representation that the provision would not be enforced, thereby seemingly making judicial action unnecessary, the federal district court for the Northern District of New York went ahead and issued a preliminary injunction barring any federal officer from commencing, maintaining, or otherwise taking action to enforce the provision. Id. at 716.

88. See generally Regan, Morgan, and English, *Tax, Estate, & Financial Planning for the Elderly,* note 76 supra.

89. While older adults may be more likely than young men and women to experience incapacity, and thus elder law attorneys often identify the drafting of advance directives as constituting one of their particular areas of professional concern, the fact is that such directives should be executed by every adult. Consequently, no lawyer should regard the matter of advance directives as being one of exclusive or even just particular concern for the elderly.

90. In fact, there is no way of knowing what the real percentage is.

91. A number of law schools offer courses on elder law. See chapter 6. Unfortunately, the very existence of such courses may tend to erect and to reinforce the notion that the elderly are different from younger folks and that their legal concerns are unlike those of younger people. It is useful, therefore, to emphasize that legal problems involving older people can arise in a variety of legal settings and that one does not have to segregate their legal issues from those of the rest of the populace. See generally Symposium, *Elder Law Across the Curriculum,* 30 Stetson L. Rev. 1265–1468 (2001).

92. Hearing before the Select Comm. on Aging, U.S. House Representatives, *Crime: Violence and the Elderly* 39, Comm. Pub. No. 99-547, 99th Cong., 1st Sess., Oct. 22, 1985 (1986). An anecdote of recent vintage that is somewhat corroborative of Ms. Hetherington's position involves the reported devaluation of the out-of-court statements of an elderly attorney, Jeremiah Gutman, regarding an interview he had conducted in 2002 with a client, a Mr. Faneuil. Attorney Gutman later was himself interviewed by investigators for the prosecution in a federal securities fraud case involving Martha Stewart, but the document recording the investigators' meeting with Mr. Gutman was not turned over, as it should have been, to Ms. Stewart's attorneys. In defending this lapse, the assistant U.S.

attorney discounted the significance of that unrevealed investigatorial document by pointing to Mr. Gutman's age: "Ms. Seymour (the assistant U.S. attorney) said that when the investigators interviewed Mr. Gutman, he did not have notes from his 2002 meeting with [his then-client] Mr. Fanueil, and consequently 'we are depending on Mr. Gutman, who is in his 80's, to recall what Mr. Fanueil said.'" Constance L. Hays, "Setback for Prosecutors in Martha Stewart Trial," *New York Times* (Jan. 30, 2004), pp. C1, C4, at C4. In other words, whatever Mr. Gutman might have said during his interview with the investigators, it was not worth much, in any event, given his age.

93. See Brian H. Bornstein, *Memory Processes in Elderly Eyewitnesses: What We Know and What We Don't Know,* 13 Behavioral Sciences and the Law 337 (1995); A. Daniel Yarmey, *Accuracy and Credibility of the Elderly Witness,* 3 Canadian J. on Aging 79 (1984); A. Daniel Yarmey, Hazel P. Tressillian Jones, and Sohail Rashid, *Eyewitness Memory of Elderly and Young Adults,* in *Psychology and Law* 215 (Dave J. Muller, Derek E. Blackman, and Antony J. Chapman, eds. 1984).

94. Yarmey, *Accuracy and Credibility of the Elderly Witness,* note 93 supra, at 88.

95. C. A. Elizabeth Brinacombe, Sandy Jung, Lynn Garrioch, and Meredith Allison, *Perceptions of Older Adult Eyewitnesses: "Will You Believe Me When I'm 64,"* 27 Law & Human Behavior 507, at 518 (Oct. 2003).

96. David F. Ross, David Dunning, Michael P. Toglia, and Stephen J. Ceci, *The Child in the Eyes of the Jury,* 14 Law & Human Behavior 5, at 10 (1990). While the testimony of the child eyewitness was rated most positively, the gap between that rating and the rating of the elderly eyewitness was relatively small (55.4 for the child; 52.9 for the elderly witness); the gap between the elderly eyewitness's rating and that of the young adult was much larger (52.9 for the elderly eyewitness versus 46.8 for the young adult). Ibid.

97. The researchers rationalized this result in the following way:
One explanation for the lack of an age effect on guilt ratings is that the testimony in this case was weighted heavily in favor of the defense. . . . If the evidence in the case was more evenly balanced, perhaps a judgment concerning the credibility of the prosecution's key witness would have produced a greater impact on the outcome of the trial.
Ross, Dunning, Toglia, and Ceci, *The Child in the Eyes of the Jury,* note 96 supra, at 14–15.

98. Id. at 11–13. The gap between the ratings for the child eyewitness and the elderly eyewitness was much less than the gap between the rating of the elderly eyewitness and that of the young adult—52.3 for the child; 50.61 for the elderly witness, and 44.3 for the young adult. Id. at 13; see also note 96 supra.

The question of the competence of children as witnesses has generated a considerable body of literature. Clearly, there are bases for calling into question children's testimony, but in so doing one must take account of the child's age, the type of testimony being offered, the child's maturity, and other factors. Neither general unalloyed rejection nor uncritical embrace of testimony of children is in order. See generally Pamela Coxon and Tim Valentine, *The Effects of the Age of Eyewitness[es] on the Accuracy and Suggestibility of Their Testimony,* 11 Applied Cognitive Psychology 415 (1997); Michael R. Leippe and Ann Romanczyk, *Reactions to Child (Versus Adult) Eyewitnesses,* 13 Law & Human Behavior 103 (1989); David Frank Ross, J. Don Read, and Michael P. Toglia, *Adult Eyewitness Testimony* 46–48 (1994).

99. Ross, Dunning, Toglia, and Ceci, *The Child in the Eyes of the Jury,* note 96 supra, at 13.

100. Id. at 16. A contrary result was obtained in another study, in which the subjects—introductory psychology students—rated the 70-year-old witnesses in the experiment as less honest than the 20-year-old witnesses. C. A. Elizabeth Brinacombe, Nyla Quinton, Natalie Nance, and Lynn Garrioch, *Is Age Irrelevant? Perceptions of Young and Old Adult Eyewitnesses,* 21 Law & Human Behavior 619, at 628–630 (1997). The researchers expressed perplexity as to this result:

> We are . . . perplexed as to why the seniors were seen as less honest than the younger adults, particularly in light of the fact that we did not anticipate our participants having any reason to question the honesty of our witnesses. They were all dispassionate observers of a crime, not suspected perpetrators or accomplices. Perhaps future research will yield a better understanding of how eyewitness honesty is communicated and evaluated.

Id. at 630.

101. In terms of total scores, the 6-year-old received 13.42, the 8-year-old 16.32, the 21-year-old 22.32, and the 74-year-old 19.64. Ross, Dunning, Toglia, and Ceci, *The Child in the Eyes of the Jury,* note 96 supra, at 16. In another study of eyewitness testimony, the college students who were asked to rate the witnesses again ranked the oldsters as less cognitively capable than the younger adult witnesses. Brinacombe, Quinton, Nance, and Garrioch, *Is Age Irrelevant?* note 100 supra, at 625–627.

102. A like criticism, or at least cautionary note, was articulated in Carole S. Slotterback and David A. Saarnio, *Attitudes Toward Older Adults Reported by Young Adults: Variation Based on Attitudinal Task and Attribute Categories,* 11 Psychology & Aging 563, at 568 (1996). See also Brinacombe, Jung, Garrioch, and Allison, *Perceptions of Older Adult Eyewitnesses,* note 95 supra, at 520–521.

103. Bornstein, *Memory Processes in Elderly Eyewitnesses,* note 93 supra, at 339.

104. Brinacombe, Quinton, Nance, and Garrioch, *Is Age Irrelevant?* note 100 supra, at 630.

105. See A. Daniel Yarmey, *The Older Eyewitness,* in *Elders, Crime, and the Criminal Justice System* 127, at 128 (Max B. Rothman, Burton D. Dunlop, and Pamela Entzel, eds. 2000):

> [O]lder adults compared to young adults are less reliable eyewitnesses, on average, in selected situations. This conclusion, however, must be qualified by the fact that the cognitive and social processes that accompany adult aging, when applied to comparisons of performance of younger and older eyewitnesses, have not been extensively examined. Furthermore, the accuracy and credibility of reports from some older persons can be equal to or superior to some younger persons.

106. Yarmey, *Accuracy and Credibility of the Elderly Witness,* note 93 supra, at 88.

107. Bornstein, *Memory Processes in Elderly Eyewitnesses,* note 93 supra, at 341; see also Ross, Read, and Toglia, *Adult Eyewitness Testimony,* note 98 supra, at 47.

108. Brinacombe, Quinton, Nance, and Garrioch, *Is Age Irrelevant?* note 100 supra, at 624.

109. Bornstein, *Memory Processes in Elderly Eyewitnesses,* note 93 supra, at 346.

110. Ibid. In fact, this latter statement is belied by other data. See notes 122–124 and accompanying text infra.

111. See Carolyn Adams-Price, *Eyewitness Memory and Aging: Predictors of Accuracy in Recall and Person Recognition,* 7 Psychology & Aging 602 (1992).

112. See Eileen W. Mello and Ronald P. Fisher, *Enhancing Older Adult Eyewitness Memory with the Cognitive Interview,* 10 Applied Cognitive Psychology 403, at 410–412 (1996).

113. Daniel L. Schacter, Alfred W. Kaszniak, John F. Kihlstrom, and Michael Valdiserri, *The Relation Between Source Memory and Aging,* 6 Psychology & Aging 559 (1991).

114. Brinacombe, Jung, Garrioch, and Allison, note 95 supra, at 521.

115. Linda D. Chrosniak, *Aging and Source Monitoring,* 4 Psychology & Aging 106, at 110 (1989).

116. There were two groups of elderly subjects, one made up of individuals ages 60–68 and the other consisting of people ages 72–83. The third group consisted of individuals ranging in age from 24 to 39.

117. Gillian Cohen and Dorothy Faulkner, *Age Differences in Source Forgetting: Effects on Reality Monitoring and on Eyewitness Testimony,* 4 Psychology & Aging 10, at 17 (1989).

118. Schacter, Kaszniak, Kihlstrom, and Valdiserri, *The Relation Between Source Memory and Aging,* note 113 supra.

119. Id. at 16.

120. Id. at 17.

121. Ibid.

122. Coxon and Valentine, *The Effects of the Age of Eyewitness[es] on the Accuracy and Suggestibility of Their Testimony,* note 98 supra, at 428.

123. Brian H. Bornstein, Christy J. Witt, Katie E. Cherry, and Edith Greene, *The Suggestibility of Older Witnesses,* in *Elders, Crime, and The Criminal Justice System* 149, at 157 (Max B. Rothman, Burton D. Dunlop, and Pamela Entzel, eds. 2000).

124. Id. at 159.

125. Katie E. Cherry and Denny C. LeCompte, *Age and Individual Differences Influence Prospective Memory,* 14 Psychology & Aging 60, at 60 (1999).

126. Id. at 73.

127. Ibid.

128. An effort to treat the testimony of elderly witnesses differently than that of the nonelderly–albeit not because there was a perception that older persons' testimony was in some way unreliable—was essayed unsuccessfully in Florida with the enactment of a statute creating an exception to the usual exclusion of hearsay evidence so as to allow out-of-court statements made by elderly individuals. Fla. Stat. § 90.803(24) (1995). Such individuals were defined as persons 60 years of age or older who were "suffering from the infirmities of age as manifested by advanced age or organic brain damage, or other physical, mental, or emotional dysfunctioning, to the extent that the ability of the person to provide adequately for the person's own care or protection is impaired." Fla. Stat. § 825.101(6) (1995) (later recodified at Fla. Stat. Ann. § 825.101(5).)

This statutory exception provided that the out-of-court statement of an elderly person who had been subjected to abuse, neglect, exploitation, a battery or aggravated battery, a sexual battery, an assault, or any other violent act would be admissible in court if it was determined by the court that the "time, content, and circumstances of the statement provide[d] sufficient safeguards of reliability." Fla. Stat. § 90.803(24) (1995). The Florida Supreme Court held this exception to be unconstitutional under both the federal and

Florida constitutions because it violated an accused's right of confrontation, inasmuch as a defendant would have no ability to confront the out-of-court declarant and subject him or her to examination. Conner v. State, 748 So.2d 950 (Fla. Sup. Ct. 1999).

129. "Memory is one domain in which age stereotypes are overwhelmingly negative." Sherrie Bieman-Copland and Ellen Bouchard Ryan, *Age-Biased Interpretation of Memory Successes and Failures in Adulthood,* 53B J. of Gerontology P105, at P105 (1998). In other words, a memory lapse by an older person is more likely to be interpreted by an observer as a sign of mental impairment than is a comparable memory lapse by a young person. Such biased interpretations are indulged in by both young and old observers (as well as by study participants themselves).

130. Studies establish that a witness's hesitancy, stumbling, and lack of confidence are regarded as signaling lack of credibility, but in fact these factors do not correlate with inaccurate testimony. See Adams-Price, *Eyewitness Memory and Aging,* note 111 supra, at 602.

131. Yarmey, *The Older Eyewitness,* note 105 supra, at 141.

132. See Adams-Price, *Eyewitness Memory and Aging,* note 111 supra.

133. Bornstein, *Memory Processes in Elderly Eyewitnesses,* note 93 supra, at 346.

134. Professor Yarmey wrote as follows:

One way to improve eyewitnesses' recall would be to structure the investigative interview in an interviewee-friendly, memory-enhancing manner, such as the cognitive interview. . . . The cognitive interview is based on the theoretical principle that a memory is composed of a collection of features or details. The effectiveness of retrieval cues is related to the amount of overlap of the cue with the encoded witnessed event. Furthermore, there are several retrieval paths to memory for an event and information not accessible with one technique may be accessible with another. Following these principles of memory, witnesses are told: (1) to mentally reconstruct the physical and personal contexts that existed at the time of the witnessed event; (2) to report everything in detail without screening information that may be considered irrelevant or for which there is only partial memory; (3) to recall the event in different orders; and (4) to recall from a variety of different perspectives.

Yarmey, *The Older Eyewitness,* note 105 supra, at 138–139 (citations omitted).

135. Mello and Fisher, *Enhancing Older Adult Eyewitness Memory with the Cognitive Interview,* note 112 supra, at 404.

136. Id. at 412.

137. Ibid.

138. The possible drawbacks following from the error rate were addressed as follows:

Although accuracy rate may be the appropriate measure theoretically, the additional errors elicited by the . . . [cognitive interview] may be detrimental legally if they contribute to falsely arresting or convicting innocent people or to exonerating guilty people. This is an empirical issue, and we have no relevant data to support or refute the belief that the additional errors, in the context of additional correct recollections, will increase the number of incorrect legal decisions. If anything, we expect just the opposite to occur, that decision-makers (police, judges, jurors) will be able to make better decisions because of the additional information. Decisions based on 100 units of high-accuracy information should be more accurate that those based on 10 units of equally accurate information.

Id. at 413.

Chapter 6. Lawyers and Clients

The epigraphs are from the following sources: Gerard W. Gawalt, Introduction, in *The New High Priests* vii (Gerard W. Gawalt, ed., 1984); Mark Twain, Letter to James R. Osgood, Jan. 25, 1876, in *The Quotable Mark Twain* 157 (R. Kent Rasmussen, ed. 1997); American Bar Association, Preamble: A Lawyer's Responsibilities, *Model Rules of Professional Conduct* (1994).

1. See I. F. Ehrlich, P. Ehrlich and R. Dreher, *The Law and the Elderly: Where is the Legal Profession? A Challenge and a Response,* 31 J. of Legal Education 452 (1981); Howard Gelt, *Psychological Considerations in Representing the Aged Client,* 17 Ariz. L. Rev. 293, at 303–304 (1975). As to evidence of ageism in another professional field, i.e., health care delivery, see Linda S. Whitton, *Ageism: Paternalism and Prejudice,* 46 DePaul L. Rev. 453, at 472–476 (1997).

2. See generally Lawrence A. Frolik, *The Developing Field of Elder Law: A Historical Perspective,* 1 Elder L. J. 1 (1993). The National Academy of Elderlaw Attorneys, Inc., based in Tucson, Arizona, is an organization of approximately 4,000 attorneys who practice in this field. Overall, there were 681,000 men and women working as attorneys (or at least licensed to practice) in 2000. U.S. Bureau of Labor Statistics, U.S. Department of Labor, Occupational Outlook Handbook 211 (2002–2003), at http:/www.bls.gov./oco/pdf/ocos)053pdf (2004).

3. But see Gelt, *Psychological Considerations in Representing the Aged Client,* note 1 supra, at 301 (stereotypes and ageist attitudes "are prevalent, not only among the population at large, but also among people who have self-selected themselves as potential workers with the aged").

4. See chapter 8.

5. See notes 54–65, 70–80, 126–130, 142–150, and 154 and accompanying text infra.

6. William Shakespeare, *Henry VI, Part II,* act IV, scene II, in G. B. Harrison, *Shakespeare: The Complete Works* 170 (1952). Dick the Butcher was one of the conspirators who belonged to a gang run by Jack Cade, a pretender to the English throne.

7. Marc Galanter, *"Old and in the Way": The Coming Demographic Transformation of the Legal Profession and its Implications for the Provision of Legal Services,* 1999 Wis. L. Rev. 1081, at 1083. (In 1960 about 3 percent of these lawyers were women; by 1999 women constituted about 25 percent of the lawyer population, and it has been predicted that they will make up 40 percent of all attorneys by 2020 and 50 percent by 2050. Id. at 1084.)

8. Id. at 1084.

9. Using the assumptions that attorneys in their 50s constitute the senior lawyers who occupy the top positions in the profession, and that attorneys in their 30s constitute the young men and women working their way up, Professor Marc Galanter has graphically depicted this development:

> [W]e see the number of older lawyers for each 100 younger lawyers fall dramatically from 79 in 1970 to just 35 in 1985 before it starts to rise again to 50 in 1995. And ... barring a major increase in law school enrollment, this ratio will continue to rise to 79 in 2005—the 1970 figure—and to an unprecedented 97 in 2020. After a generation during which older lawyers were relatively scarce compared to the abundance of younger lawyers, the profession is entering an era in which older lawyers will be equally plentiful.

Id. at 1085.

10. Mike McKee, *State Lawyers Older, More Diverse,* http://www.law.com/regionals/ca/stories/edt1030b.shtml (Oct. 30, 2001).

11. Because law firm partners are not deemed to be employees, they cannot invoke the protection of the federal Age Discrimination in Employment Act of 1967, as amended (ADEA), 29 U.S.C. §§ 621–634, which prohibits discrimination against employees on the basis of age. If the evidence warrants, however, a court will be willing to look more deeply to inquire as to whether someone who ostensibly is denominated a partner is really an employee, after all. See, e.g., Wheeler v. Hurdman, 825 F.2d 257 (10th Cir.), *cert. denied,* 484 U.S. 986 (1987). *Cf.* Clackamas Gastroenterology Associates v. Wells, 538 U.S. 140 (2003) (case arising under the Americans with Disabilities Act, 42 U.S.C. § 12101 *et seq.*).

12. See, e.g., Claudia H. Deutsch, "Women Lawyers Strive for Chance to Make it Rain," *New York Times,* May 21, 1996, Business Day, pp. D1, D7, at D1:

> More than anything else, getting business—what lawyers whimsically call "making rain"—is the barometer of success in the legal profession today. . . .
>
> "Ten years ago, I'd be asked to find lawyers with expertise," said Lynn Mestel, a New York recruiter. "Today, firms will hire a mediocre lawyer who can bring $5 million in business."

13. In an article about the efforts of women attorneys to rise to the top in their firms, the reporter quoted a senior partner in a firm whose locale was not identified: "Law is not a profession anymore," agreed Eugene R. Anderson, a name partner in Anderson Kill Olick & Oshinsky. "It is a business in which making rain is the primary criterion for promotion." Deutsch, "Women Lawyers Strive for Chance to Make it Rain," note 12 supra, at D1; see generally Galanter, "*Old and in the Way,*" note 7 supra, at 1094–1096.

14. See generally Adam Liptak, "Stop the Clock? Critics Call the Billable Hour a Legal Fiction," *New York Times,* Oct. 29, 2002, p. 7:

> Larger firms now generally expect at least 2,000 to 2,200 billable hours from the associates, and billing 2,500 to 3,000 hours is not unusual. Earlier this month, associates at the New York office of Clifford Chance, the British law firm that is the world's largest, sent the partners an anguished memorandum. Its primary complaint was that the firm required 2,400 billable hours annually to qualify for a bonus. The requirement is, their memorandum said, "profoundly unrealistic," "dehumanizing," and "verging on an abdication of our professional responsibilities." It encourages, they said, "padding of hours, inefficient work, repetition of tasks and other problems."
>
> Associate salaries, which start at around $125,000 for new associates at big firms in New York and easily top $200,000 for more senior associates, create few options for firms. Partners at such firms, whose hourly rates have been approaching $700, often make more than $1 million.
>
> "The salary wars have only made things worse," said Susan Saab Fortney, a law professor at Texas Tech University in Lubbock. "Where is the money going to come from? It's going to come from the sweat of associates."

The percentage of associates who are promoted to partners in large firms varies from location to location. In New York City—the financial capital of the United States and the home base for many of the country's premier large firms—the percentage already is low and indeed has been for some years. According to the Association of the Bar of the City of New York, 21.5 percent of male associates and 15.25 percent of women associates hired between 1973 and 1981 made partner. For associates hired after 1981 the rate for men declined to 17 percent and for women to 5 percent. Amy Bach, "Nolo Contendere," *New York Magazine* 49, at 50 (Dec. 11, 1995). It would seem that the rates for elevation to partner really cannot go much, if at all, lower.

15. See, e.g., Galanter, "*Old and in the Way,*" note 7 supra, at 1094–1096.

16. Ibid. In 1999 one of the United States' largest firms, Chicago-based Sidley and Austin (now known as Sidley, Austin, Brown, and Wood), took action with regard to 32 partners by either demoting them to "counsel" or "senior counsel" or by terminating them. The firm also changed its mandatory retirement policy, which provided for retirement at age 65, by introducing a sliding scale for retirement with the age of departure ranging from 60 to 65. T. Shawn Taylor, "'Partners' put law firms in labor bind," *Chicago Tribune*, Apr. 7, 2002, Business, pp. 1, 6. It was reported as follows regarding the changes' effects:

> An unnamed partner at Sidley told the EEOC [Equal Employment Opportunity Commission] the demotions were the product of age discrimination, according to John Hendrickson, regional attorney for the EEOC's Chicago district office. He said the agency also was concerned about statements attributed to managing partner Charles Douglas in business and legal publications that the partners affected by the demotions "were mostly in their mid-50s and early 60s," and that the firm's strategy "will expand opportunities for younger partners and associates."

Id. at 1, 6.

17. See note 12 supra.

18. Galanter, "*Old and in the Way,*" note 7 supra, at 1097 (footnotes omitted). Of course, one cannot assume that all older attorneys who leave do so involuntarily. Ample pension benefits, boredom, a desire for new challenges, and other reasons can help a given lawyer to willingly depart the profession.

19. John P. Heinz and Edward O. Laumann, *Chicago Lawyers* (1982).

20. The authors also surveyed their subject audience with regard to lawyers' views concerning the local Chicago Bar Association (CBA). While there were age-identifiable differences regarding various activities engaged in by the Association, most of these do not offer much that is relevant here. Generally, in those instances where there was a significant difference between age groups in terms of their ratings of various CBA activities and/or objectives, "older age groups and higher income groups consistently gave the CBA higher effectiveness ratings than did younger or lower income groups." Id. at 258.

21. Id. at 153.

22. Id. at 161.

23. Id. at 163. The authors set forth the data in a table. On the economic liberalism scale, lawyers through age 31 registered a mean score of 3.37 for practitioners in the conservative fields, while attorneys who practiced in other areas had a mean score of 3.38. But for the age group made up of persons 53 and older, the practitioners in the conservative fields of law registered a mean score of 2.80, while those in the other fields had a mean score of 3.16. Thus, for all practitioners there was an increase in conservatism; but for practitioners in conservative areas the divergence between them and practitioners in nonconservative area grew from .01 to .36.

On the civil libertarian scale, lawyers under age 32 who practiced in conservative law fields registered a mean score of 3.75, while those in other fields had a mean score of 3.55. For attorneys 43 and older, the mean score was 3.24 for lawyers practicing in the conservative fields and 2.81 for those lawyers practicing in other fields. Thus, the divergence grew from .20 (3.75 minus 3.55) to .43 (3.24 minus 2.81). Id. at 162, Table 5.4.

24. Id. at 163 n. 41, citing, *inter alia,* Angus Campbell, Philip E. Converse, Warren E. Miller, and Donald Stokes, *The American Voter* (1960); Norman H. Nie, Sidney Verba, and John R. Petrocik, *The Changing American Voter* (1976). Professors Heinz and Laumann cautioned, however, that it does not necessarily follow that age produces the conservatism. "It could be the case that different cohorts of individuals—in commonly experiencing major social events of peace or war, prosperity or depression in their formative years—were more or less likely to acquire certain social attitudes." Heinz and Laumann, *Chicago Lawyers,* note 19 supra, at 174.

25. Heinz and Laumann, *Chicago Lawyers,* note 19 supra, at 166.

26. John P. Heinz, Kathleen E. Hull, and Ava A. Harter, *Lawyers and Their Discontents: Findings from a Survey of the Chicago Bar,* 74 Indiana L. J. 735, at 735 (1999).

27. Id. at 736. For a more downbeat view, see Bach, "Nolo Contendere," note 14 supra.

28. Heinz, Hull, and Harter, *Lawyers and Their Discontents,* note 26 supra, at 736.

29. Ibid.

30. Id. at 737.

31. Id. at 743.

32. Ibid.

33. *Report of the Special Committee on Gender to The D.C. Circuit Task Force on Gender, Race, and Ethnic Bias,* 84 Georgetown L. J. 1657 (1996).

34. Id. at 1709–1710.

35. Ibid.

36. Thus, it was explained as follows:

For example, an attorney's age affected the degree to which attorneys were questioned about their status as attorneys. . . . Younger attorneys were more likely to report having been questioned about their status as attorneys than were older attorneys. Within each age group, however, women were more likely to report being questioned than were men. For example, in the group of "younger attorneys" (those with a birth date after 1950), 15% of the women as compared with 3% of the men reported having been questioned about their status as attorneys by a federal judge. In the group of "older attorneys" 6% of the women and 1% of the men reported having been questioned about their status. . . . [W]hile older women were less likely than their younger counterparts to be questioned about their status by a judge, they still were significantly more likely to be questioned than their male colleagues of similar age.

Id. at 1714.

37. Id. at 1715.

38. Ibid.; accord *The Effects of Gender in the Federal Courts: Final Report of the Ninth Circuit Gender Bias Task Force* 71–72 and Table 4.9 (July 1993), reprinted in 67 S. Cal. L. Rev. 745 (1994).

39. See chapter 2.

40. Daniel G. Linz and Steven Penrod, *Increasing Attorney Persuasiveness in the Courtroom,* 8 Law & Psychology Rev. 1, at 37 (1984).

41. Ibid.; see also Joan T. Erber and Sharon T. Rothberg, *Here's Looking at You: The*

Relative Effect of Age and Attractiveness on Judgments About Memory Failure, 46 J. of Gerontology, Psychological Sciences P116, at P116 (1991).

42. Linz and Penrod, *Increasing Attorney Persuasiveness in the Courtroom,* note 40 supra, at 40–41.

43. Id. at 41.

44. See notes 51–53 and accompanying text infra. Cf. the strategy of the Arthur Andersen accounting firm as the Enron debacle expanded in the latter part of 2001 and through 2002. Arthur Andersen Co., one of the Big Five accounting firms, had been Enron's auditor and thus apparently was heavily implicated in the financial intricacies that appeared to account for Enron's downfall. As a result, Arthur Andersen found itself under attack in the courts, in the media, and in the court of public opinion. One response was its naming in early 2002 of former Federal Reserve Board Chairman Paul Volcker to conduct a review of Andersen's practices. Mr. Volcker, age 74, subsequently recruited two other eminent individuals to assist him—former Merck & Co. chief executive P. Roy Vagelos, age 72, and Charles A. Bowsher, the 70-year-old chairman of the accounting profession's Public Oversight Board. A *Chicago Tribune* columnist commented upon these developments as follows:

> The Arthur Andersen accounting firm has deployed one of the oldest techniques in the annals of damage control. Andersen has recruited a "wise old man" to help fix its problems.
>
> The "wise old man" strategy is fairly simple. A troubled enterprise taps someone beyond reproach. Working alone or with a small posse of similarly clean characters, he swoops in. The wise person cleans up the mess, throws out the bad actors, reforms the bad practices, and sets a new, cleaner, and more upright course for the future.
>
> Sort of like Gary Cooper in "High Noon," but with more gray hair and a lot less gunplay.

David Greising, "Volcker needs help; we know just the person," *Chicago Tribune,* March 3, 2002, Sec. 5, p. 1.

45. The earlier noted District of Columbia study, see notes 33–38 and accompanying text supra, is just one of many that have been conducted in recent years. See, e.g., *Report of the First Circuit Gender, Race and Ethnic Bias Task Forces,* 9 Boston U. Public Interest L. J. 173 (2001), and the reports listed therein at 184 n. 1.

46. See, e.g., *Panel Discussion,* 49 U. of Kansas L. Rev. 847, at 858 (2001) (panelist in a discussion about women in the law stated: "I've actually been patted on the rear end by some older attorneys").

47. See Cynthia Fuchs Epstein, Robert Saute, Bonnie Oglensky, and Martha Gever, *Glass Ceilings and Open Doors: Women's Advancement in the Legal Profession,* 64 Fordham L. Rev. 291, at 417 (1995); *Third Circuit Task Force on Equal Treatment in the Courts,* 42 Vill. L. Rev. 1345, at 1424 (1997).

48. Tennessee v. John Scopes (Tenn. 1925).

49. Jerome Lawrence and Robert E. Lee, *Inherit the Wind* (1950).

50. In a message to Congress dated February 5, 1937, President Roosevelt proposed a plan to add to the federal courts one judge for each judge who was age 70 and had held office for at least 10 years. See Kathleen M. Sullivan and Gerald Gunther, *Constitutional Law* 135 (14th ed. 2001). At the time six justices of the U.S. Supreme Court were over age 70.

51. Clifford was described in his obituary in the *New York Times* as "the silver-haired Brahmin of the nation's political establishment who advised four presidents across half a century of American history." Marilyn Berger, "Clark Clifford, a Major Advisor to Four Presidents, is Dead at 91," *New York Times,* Oct. 11, 1998, pp. 1, 46, at p. 1.

52. Strauss served under President George H. W. Bush as U.S. ambassador to the Soviet Union and to the subsequent Russian Federation in the early 1990s. He earlier had served as special representative for trade negotiations under President Jimmy Carter. He also served as the national chairman of the Democratic Party.

53. Cutler served as special counsel to the president on ratification of the SALT II Treaty in 1979–1980, and he was senior consultant to the President's Commission on Strategic Forces in 1983–1984. He served, as well, in a variety of other high-level presidentially appointed positions.

54. According to a 1997 article, 38 states and the District of Columbia had at that point adopted the rules in substantial part. Mary Helen McNeal, *Redefining Attorney-Client Roles: Unbundling and Moderate-Income Elderly Clients,* 32 Wake Forest L. Rev. 295, at 305 (1997). However, "Illinois, New York, North Carolina, Oregon and Virginia follow codes that rely to varying extents on both the Model Code and Model Rules." Joseph A. Rosenberg, *Adapting Unitary Principles of Professional Responsibility to Unique Practice Contexts: A Reflective Model for Resolving Ethical Dilemmas in Elder Law,* 31 Loyola U. Chicago L. Rev. 403, at 424 (2000).

55. Rosenberg, *Adapting Unitary Principles of Professional Responsibility to Unique Practice Contexts,* note 54 supra, at 424.

56. Ibid.

57. The Illinois Supreme Court possesses the exclusive authority to regulate the admission and discipline of attorneys in Illinois. It has delegated its authority to the Commission and has authorized the Commission to devise rules for the conducting of disciplinary proceedings. Illinois Supreme Court Rule 751 (2001).

58. American Bar Association, *Code of Professional Responsibility,* Canon 6 (1969).

59. American Bar Association, *Code of Professional Responsibility,* DR 6-101 (1969).

60. American Bar Association, *Model Rules of Professional Conduct,* Rule 1.1 (1994).

61. See Edmund B. Spaeth Jr., *To What Extent Can a Disciplinary Code Assure the Competence of Lawyers?* 61 Temple L. Rev. 1211, at 1221 (1988).

62. See, e.g., Hinton v. Judicial Retirement and Removal Comm'n, 854 S.W.2d 756 (Ky. 1993); *In re* Johnson, 395 A.2d 1319, 1326 (Pa. 1978). Judges are not free to do whatever they wish; they can be held accountable for abuse of the contempt power. See generally Jeffrey M. Shaman, Steven Lubet, and James J. Alfini, *Judicial Conduct and Ethics* 38–42 (2d ed. 1995).

63. Virginia Canons of Judicial Conduct, Canon 3, Section A(3), reprinted in Shaman, Lubet, and Alfini, *Judicial Conduct and Ethics,* note 62 supra, at 548.

64. Wyoming Code of Judicial Conduct, Section 3B(6) (1990), reprinted in Shaman, Lubet, and Alfini, *Judicial Conduct and Ethics,* note 62 supra, at 559. The provision goes on to articulate an exception to the prohibition quoted in the text: "This Section 3B(6) does not preclude legitimate advocacy when race, sex, religion, national origin, disability, age, sexual orientation or socioeconomic status, or other similar factors, are issues in the proceeding."

65. *Illinois Rules of Professional Conduct,* Rule 8.4, as amended (March 26, 2001).

66. Between 50 and 75 percent of all disciplinary cases in Georgia in the recent past

involved substance abuse. George Edward Bailey, *Impairment, the Profession, and Your Law Partner,* 11 No. 1 Prof. Law.2, at 1, 2 n. 14 (1999).

67. Peter H. Geraghty, *Ask Ethicsearch,* 9 No. 2 Prof. Law 22 (Feb. 1998).

68. See generally American Bar Association Standing Committee on Professional Discipline, *Model Rules for Lawyer Disciplinary Enforcement,* Rule 23 (1989).

69. Illinois Supreme Court Rule 758(a) (2001).

70. Illinois Supreme Court Rule 758(c), (e) (2001).

71. American Bar Association Standing Committee on Ethics and Professional Responsibility, Formal Opinion 03-429 (June 11, 2003), reprinted at *ABA/BNA Lawyer's Manual on Professional Conduct* 1201:133, at 135 (1984–).

72. American Bar Association, *Model Rules of Professional Conduct,* Rule 8.3 (1994).

73. ABA Formal Opinion 03-429, note 71 supra, at 136.

74. It was thought, on the basis of a physician's letter, that this memory impairment was not due to age, but rather was the result of the attorney's having fallen ill with viral encephalitis.

75. American Bar Association, *Model Rules of Professional Conduct,* Rule 7.3 (1994).

76. Pennsylvania Bar Association Committee on Legal Ethics & Professional Responsibility, Informal Opinion No. 98-124 (Dec. 7, 1998), reprinted at *ABA/BNA Lawyers' Manual on Professional Conduct* 1001:7320 (1984–). But see Illinois State Bar Association, Opinion No. 92-12 (Jan. 21, 1993), reprinted at *ABA/BNA Lawyer's Manual on Professional Responsibility* 1001:3011 (1984–). This latter opinion involved a doctor who consulted with his legal counsel about his view that a patient—also a lawyer—was irreversibly senile and thus not competent to practice. The Illinois State Bar Association took the position that because of the doctor-patient privilege, the doctor could not disclose any information about his patient (save to the doctor's own attorney). The doctor's attorney in turn could not disclose the information because it had been given to him in the context of a lawyer-client relationship, and the client had not consented to its disclosure (and the client, i.e., the doctor, could not give such consent because of the doctor-patient privilege). The Opinion further observed that there was no issue as to the healthy lawyer's duty to report under Illinois' version of Model Rule of Professional Conduct 8.3—which requires a lawyer to report professional misconduct—because there was no indication of such misconduct on the part of the senile attorney (and, in any event, the healthy lawyer's knowledge was obtained in confidence). American Bar Association, *Model Rules of Professional Conduct,* Rule 8.3 (1994). The only courses open were for the healthy attorney to advise his doctor/client to suggest to the family of the senile attorney that a guardian be sought for the attorney, and/or the family could report its concerns regarding their family member's fitness to practice law to the state disciplinary authority.

77. Philadelphia Bar Association Professional Guidance Committee, Ethics Opinion 2000-12 (2000), reprinted in *ABA/BNA Lawyers' Manual on Professional Conduct* 1001:7320 (1984–), discussed in Elizabeth Cohen, *Walking a Fine Line,* 87 ABA J. 62 (2001).

78. American Bar Association Standing Committee on Ethics and Professional Responsibility, Formal Opinion 03-429, note 71 supra, at 136.

79. Ibid.

80. Id. at 137.

81. American Bar Association, *Model Rules of Professional Conduct,* Rule 1.2 (1994), provides as follows:

(a) A lawyer shall abide by a client's decision concerning the objectives of representation . . . and shall consult with the client as to the means by which they are to be pursued.

82. American Bar Association, *Model Rules of Professional Conduct*, Rule 1.3 (1994).

83. American Bar Association, *Model Rules of Professional Conduct*, Rule 1.7 (1994), entitled "Conflict of Interest: General Rule," provides as follows:

(a) A lawyer shall not represent a client if the representation of that client will be directly adverse to another client, unless:

(1) the lawyer reasonably believes the representation will not adversely affect the relationship with the other client; and

(2) each client consents after consultation.

(b) A lawyer shall not represent a client if the representation of that client may be materially limited by the lawyer's responsibilities to another client or to a third person, or by the lawyer's own interest, unless

(1) the lawyer reasonably believes the representation will not be adversely affected; and

(2) the client consents after consultation. When representation of multiple clients in a single matter is undertaken, the consultation shall include explanation of the implications of the common representation and the advantages and risks involved.

84. See generally Monroe H. Freedman, *Understanding Lawyers' Ethics* 7 (1990); Rosenberg, *Adapting Unitary Principles of Professional Responsibility to Unique Practice Contexts*, note 54 supra, at 427–428.

85. "[I]n the context of everyday lawyer-client interaction, concern for the senior citizen's welfare and her autonomy interact." Peter Margulies, *Access, Connection, and Voice: A Contextual Approach to Representing Senior Citizens of Questionable Capacity*, 62 Fordham L. Rev. 1073, at 1076 (1994).

86. See, e.g., Michael Smyer, K. Warner Schaie, and Marshall B. Kapp, eds., *Older Adults' Decision-Making and the Law* (1996); William E. Adams and Rebecca C. Morgan, *Representing the Client Who is Older in the Law Office and in the Courtroom*, 2 Elder L. J. 1 (1994); Jacqueline Allee, *Representing Older Persons: Ethical Dilemmas*, 8 BIFOCAL (Spring 1987); Edwin M. Boyer, *Representing the Client With Marginal Capacity: Challenges for the Elder Law Attorney—A Resource Guide*, 12 NAELA Quarterly 3 (Spring 1999); Gelt, *Psychological Considerations in Representing the Aged Client*, note 1 supra; Marshall B. Kapp, *Representing Older Persons: Ethical Challenges*, 53 Fla. B. J. 25 (June 1989); Margulies, *Access, Connection, and Voice*, note 85 supra, at 1074; Jan Ellen Rein, *Clients with Destructive and Socially Harmful Choices—What's An Attorney to Do? Within and Beyond the Competency Construct*, 62 Fordham L. Rev. 1101 (1994); Jan Ellen Rein, *Ethics and the Questionably Competent Client: What the Model Rules Say and Don't Say*, 9 Stanford L. & Policy Rev. 241 (1998); Rosenberg, *Adapting Unitary Principles of Professional Responsibility to Unique Practice Contexts*, note 54 supra; Robert Rubinson, *Constructions of Client Competence and Theories of Practice*, 31 Ariz. St. L. J. 121 (1999); Charles P. Sabatino, *Assessing Clients with Diminished Capacity*, 22 BIFOCAL 1 (Summer 2001); Linda F. Smith, *Representing the Elderly Client and Addressing the Question of Competence*, 14 J. Contemp. L. 61 (1988); Paul R. Tremblay, *On Persuasion and Paternalism: Lawyer Decisionmaking and the Questionably Competent Client*, 1987 Utah L. Rev. 515 (1987).

87. See notes 115–151 and accompanying text infra.

88. Cf. Erdman B. Palmore, *Ageism: Negative and Positive* 133 (1990): "All studies of health professionals' attitudes toward elders agree that they tend to have the same ageist attitudes that the rest of our society shares."

89. Seymour Wishman, *Anatomy of a Jury* 30 (1986).

90. Michael Francis Gilbert, *The Oxford Book of Legal Anecdotes* 101 (1986).

91. Boyer, *Representing the Client With Marginal Capacity,* note 86 supra, at 8; see also Gelt, *Psychological Considerations in Representing the Older Client,* note 1 supra, at 293–294.

92. Margulies, *Access, Connection, and Voice,* note 85 supra, at 1074.

93. Rubinson, *Constructions of Client Competence and Theories of Practice,* note 86 supra, at 131.

94. Rubinson explains:

[O]ne assumption about the elderly is especially preeminent: aging entails a "progressive decline in health or competence." This view conceptualizes health and competence as an "inverted U" over time, with a steadily increasing level of competence from childhood until adulthood, with a steadily decreasing level thereafter until reaching, once again, a level comparable to that of a child.

Ibid. (footnote omitted).

95. Id. at 134–135 (footnote omitted).

96. Id. at 135.

97. See, e.g., Rein, *Preserving Dignity and Self-Determination of the Elderly in the Face of Competing Interests and Grim Alternatives: A Proposal for Statutory Refocus and Reform,* 60 Geo. Washington L. Rev. 1818, 1835 (1992). It also has been noted that there may be physiological reasons having nothing to do with intellectual decline for what are mistakenly taken to be signs of intellectual deterioration:

A range of common problems among the elderly might hamper their ability to communicate. Decreased tongue maneuverability, dry mouth, and hearing loss all may impede communication. Given the homogenizing influence of the idea of decrement, it is likely that such symptoms—entirely unrelated to mental competence—might lead to an utterly unfounded conclusion of mental impairment.

Rubinson, *Constructions of Client Competence and Theories of Practice,* note 86 supra at 136 (footnotes omitted).

98. See generally chapter 4.

99. Gelt, *Psychological Considerations in Representing the Older Client,* note 1 supra, at 294 n. 3.

100. Ibid.

101. Boyer, *Representing The Client With Marginal Capacity: Challenges For The Elder Law Attorney—A Resource Guide,* note 86 supra, at 8. A much older study reported less than adequate vision in 9 percent of the subjects between 65 and 80 years of age and in 20 percent of the subjects who were over 80. Howard Gelt, *Psychological Considerations in Representing the Older Client,* 17 Ariz. L. Rev. 293, at 294 n. 3 (1975).

102. See chapter 4.

103. See generally Marc Charmatz, *Eliminating Communication Barriers in the Courtroom,* in American Bar Association Commission on Legal Problems of the Elderly, American Bar Association Commission on the Mentally Disabled, and National Judicial College, *Court-Related Needs of the Elderly and Persons with Disabilities* 85 (1991).

A checklist of suggestions applicable for attorneys representing elderly clients has been devised by four experts in the field of elderlaw:

1. Make Yourself Physically Accessible. . . .
2. Develop Your Client's Confidence and Trust in a Thoughtful Way. . . .
3. Sharpen Your Active Listening Skills. . . .
4. Do Not Assume Hearing or Vision Loss in Older Clients. . . .
5. Compensate for Hearing Loss. . . .
6. Compensate for Vision Loss. . . .
7. Organize Sessions Carefully, Allowing Sufficient Time for All Tasks. . . .
8. Actively Involve the Client and Maintain Regular Contact. . . .
9. Learn Techniques for Closing an Interview with the Client Who Wants to Stay Longer. . . .
10. Fully Explore the Problems Your Client May (or May Not) Have Before Initiating Any Action. . . .
11. Learn About Available Community Resources for Older People. . . .
12. Confront Your Own Pre-Existing Perceptions and Values About Aging. . . .

Joan M. Krauskopf, Robert N. Brown, Karen L. Tokarz, and Allan D. Bogutz, *Elderlaw: Advocacy for the Aging* 42–43 (2d ed. 1993) (emphasis deleted).

104. Adams and Morgan, *Representing the Client Who is Older,* note 86 supra, at 27.

105. Id. at 26.

106. Krauskopf, Brown, Tokarz, and Bogutz, *Elderlaw: Advocacy for the Aging,* note 103 supra, at 30.

107. Gelt, *Psychological Considerations in Representing the Older Client,* note 101 supra, at 296 (footnote omitted); see also chapter 3. To the credit of Gelt, who is the most-often cited source for admonitions regarding the psychological needs of older clients, he himself emphasized the need to debunk the stereotypes of the elderly as being psychologically fragile and intellectually on the wane. Id. at 293–294.

108. Id. at 296.

109. See id. at 296–298.

110. Id. at 298.

111. Id. at 298–300.

112. Id. at 300.

113. Ibid., quoting Anthony Lenzer, *Sociocultural Influences on Adjustment to Aging,* 16 Geriatrics 631, at 636 (1961).

114. Gelt, *Psychological Considerations in Representing the Older Client,* note 101 supra, at 301.

115. See Panel Discussion, *The Best Interest Role Versus the Advocate Role in Representing the Elderly Client,* comments of DaCosta Mason, Senior Legal Program Coordinator, American Association of Retired Persons, in *Exploring Ethical Issues in Meeting the Legal Needs of the Elderly* 26, at 26 (1987):

I feel a little disappointed that the elderly have been separated out as requiring certain ethical considerations that are different than other individuals.

Traditionally, the elderly have been treated as any other clients by attorneys. An attorney was required to provide competent representation for the client and to advocate the client's interest. I don't think that it is any different necessarily for elderly persons. Probably the most important thing for attorneys who deal with elderly persons is not to look at the elderly person as an individual who is 50, 60, or

70 years of age but to look at them as a normal client. The attorney should make a determination of the kind of decision that [the] particular individual is capable of making, and then represent that person as they would represent any other client, as a zealous advocate.

116. See chapter 5.

117. See, e.g., Krauskopf, Brown, Tokarz, and Bogutz, *Elderlaw: Advocacy for the Aging,* note 103 supra; Lawrence A. Frolik and Alison McChrystal Barnes, *Elderlaw–Cases and Materials* (2d ed. 1999); Thomas P. Gallanis, A. Kimberley Dayton, and Molly M. Wood, *Elder Law—Readings, Cases and Materials* (2000); Peter J. Strauss, Robert Wolf, and Dana Shilling, *Aging and the Law* (1990). For more intensive analysis of particular issues involving older men and women, see Howard Eglit, 1–3 *Age Discrimination* (2d ed. 1994 and annual supps.); Marshall B. Kapp, *Geriatrics and the Law* (3d ed. 1999); John J. Regan, Rebecca Morgan, and David M. English, *Tax, Estate & Financial Planning for the Elderly* (1997 and periodic supps.); Max B. Rothman, Burton D. Dunlop, and Pamela Entzel, eds., *Elders, Crime, and the Criminal Justice System* (2000).

118. Of particular concern here are capacity and the matter of determining who the client is. The matter of confidentiality also is briefly touched on. Another context in which ethical concerns can particularly come to the fore entails the role of the attorney in guardianship proceedings. Should the attorney unqualifiedly represent a person who is the resistant subject of a guardianship petition, even if he thinks that the client indeed would be better off as a ward rather than as an independent actor? Or should the attorney adopt a *best interests* model of representation, whereby he advocates for what he deems to be the best interest of the client, even if that means appointment of a guardian whom the client opposes? See the articles cited in note 86 supra.

Actually, in many instances individuals who are the subjects of guardianship petitions are unrepresented. Indeed, in a key study it was found that "[o]nly 17–20 percent of . . . respondents were represented by court-appointed attorneys" while an "additional 9 percent had retained private counsel." Lauren Barritt List and Saidy Barinaga-Burch, *National Study of Guardianship Systems: Summary of Findings and Recommendations,* 29 Clearinghouse Rev. 643, at 649 (1995) (footnote omitted). In states with statutes requiring legal counsel for respondents, however, it was reported "that 80–93 percent of respondents were represented by attorneys." Ibid. (footnote omitted). Most significantly, perhaps, "over half of respondents who had some objection to the proceeding were unrepresented." Id. at 650.

119. Margulies, *Access, Connection, and Voice,* note 85 supra, at 1082.

120. This difficulty has been aptly delineated by Professor Jan Ellen Rein:

Capacity is a flexible, elusive, and ultimately, undefinable concept. Like beauty, capacity or incapacity may exist only in the eye of the beholder. No single test has succeeded in capturing the boundary between capacity and incapacity because capacity is not a reified concept. All of us are in varying states of incapacity at different times. There is always someone who could manage better and there are periods of our lives when we don't manage well at all.

Rein, *Ethics and the Questionably Competent Client,* note 86 supra, at 242.

121. National Conference of Commissioners of Uniform State Laws, Uniform Guardianship and Protective Proceedings Act (1997).

122. President's Commission for the Study of Ethical Problems in Medicine and Biomedical and Behavioral Research, *Vol. 1, Report: Making Health Care Decisions: The*

Ethical and Legal Implications of Informed Consent in the Patient-Practitioner Relationship 57 (1982).

123. Boyer, *Representing the Client With Marginal Capacity: Challenges for the Elder Law Attorney–A Resource Guide,* note 86 supra, at 5 (footnote omitted) (describing Fla. Stat., Ch. 744.012(10)).

124. See, e.g., Walter T. Burke, *Ethical and Psychological Aspects of Representing the Elderly,* 13 Experience 5, at 8 (Summer 2003); Rein, *Ethics and the Questionably Competent Client,* note 86 supra, at 242 (quoted in note 120 supra); see also Panel Discussion, *The Best Interest Role Versus the Advocate Role in Representing the Elderly Client,* in *Exploring Ethical Issues in Meeting the Legal Needs of the Elderly* 17, note 115 supra, at 22 (comments of Nancy Neveloff Dubler):

> [C]onsider a phenomenon recognized in geriatric medicine called "sundowning," meaning that a patient can be absolutely fine at 10:00 in the morning, know his nurse and his family, recognize his surroundings and be able to participate in discussions, and yet be totally disoriented at 6:00 at night. Why? Well, the why is unclear. Some experts think it has to do with light deprivation in increasing levels of darkness. Some think that it has to do with fatigue and with the inability to maintain a consistent level of functioning. Notwithstanding the theory, there's no question that there are many elderly persons whose abilities vary markedly over even a short period of time.

125. See, e.g., Garcia v. Borelli, 129 Cal. App.3d 24, 180 Cal. Rptr. 768 (1982); Stowe v. Smith, 184 Conn. 194, 441 A.2d 81 (1981); Arnold v. Carmichael, 524 So.2d 464 (Fla. App.), *rev. denied,* 531 So.2d 1352 (Fla. 1988); Ogle v. Fuiten, 102 Ill.2d 356, 466 N.E.2d 224 (1984). See generally Joan Teshima, Annotation, *Attorney's Liability, to One Other Than Immediate Client, for Negligence in Connection with Legal Duties,* 61 ALR4th 615 (1988).

126. American College of Trust and Estate Counsel, *Commentaries on the Model Rules of Professional Conduct* (3rd ed. 1999).

127. American Bar Association, *Model Rules of Professional Conduct,* Rule 1.14 (1994). In contrast, Canon 7 of the Model Code of Professional Responsibility does not authorize an attorney to seek the appointment of a guardian for a client whom she believes to be incapacitated. American Bar Association, *Code of Professional Responsibility,* Canon 7 (1969).

128. American Bar Association, *Model Rules of Professional Conduct,* Rule 1.14, Comment [1] (Feb. 27, 2002), reprinted at *ABA/BNA Lawyer's Manual on Professional Conduct* 1201:142 (1984–).

129. Ibid.

130. American Bar Association, *Model Rules of Professional Conduct,* Rule 1.14, Comment [6] (Feb. 27, 2002), reprinted at *ABA/BNA Lawyers' Manual on Professional Conduct* 1201:143 (1984–).

131. Margulies, *Access, Connection, and Voice,* note 85 supra, at 1082; see also Kapp, *Representing Older Persons: Ethical Challenges,* note 86 supra, at 28.

132. Margulies, *Access, Connection, and Voice,* note 85 supra, at 1082.

133. Ibid.

134. Id. at 1083.

135. Ibid.

136. Ibid.

137. Sabatino, *Assessing Clients with Diminished Capacity,* note 86 supra, at 4. If the individual is unable to give such consent, the existence of incapacity is pretty much resolved at this juncture.

138. Id. at 5.

139. Id. at 5–6.

140. Id. at 6–7

141. Margulies, *Access, Connection, and Voice,* note 85 supra, at 1085.

142. American Bar Association, *Model Rules of Professional Conduct,* Rule 1.14, Comment [2] (1994) (rescinded).

143. Rein, *Ethics and the Questionably Competent Client,* note 86 supra, at 252.

144. Ibid. (footnote omitted). For a more positive view, see Margulies, *Access, Connection, and Voice,* note 85 supra, at 1093–1096.

145. American Bar Association, *Model Rules of Professional Conduct,* Rule 1.14, Comment [5] (Feb. 27, 2002), reprinted at *ABA/BNA Lawyers' Manual on Professional Conduct* 01:144 (1984–), provides as follows:

> If a lawyer reasonably believes that a client is at risk of substantial physical, financial or other harm unless action is taken, and that a normal client-lawyer relationship cannot be maintained . . . (a) because the client lacks sufficient capacity to communicate or to make adequately considered decisions in connection with the representative, then paragraph (b) [of Rule 1.14] permits the lawyer to take protective measures deemed necessary. Such measures could include: consulting with family members, using a reconsideration period to permit clarification or improvement of circumstances, using voluntary surrogate decision-making tools such as durable powers of attorney or consulting with support groups, professional services, adult-protective agencies or other individuals or entities that have the ability to protect the client.

146. American Bar Association, *Model Rules of Professional Conduct,* Rule 1.14 (b) (1994).

147. American Bar Association, *Model Rules of Professional Conduct,* Rule 1.14, Comment [7] (Feb. 27, 2002), reprinted at *ABA/BNA Lawyer's Manual on Professional Conduct* 1201:143 (1994–).

148. With regard to taking protective action short of seeking appointment of a legal representative, Comment [5] provides as follows:

> In taking any protective action, the lawyer should be guided by such factors as the wishes and values of the client to the extent known, the client's best interests and the goals of intruding into the client's decisionmaking autonomy to the least extent feasible, maximizing client capacities and respecting the client's family and social connections.

American Bar Association, *Model Rules of Professional Conduct,* Rule 1.14, Comment [5] (Feb. 27, 2002), reprinted at *ABA/BNA Lawyers' Manual on Professional Conduct* 1201:143 (1984–).

149. American Bar Association, *Model Rules of Professional Conduct,* Rule 1.14, Comment [8] (Feb. 27, 2002), reprinted at *ABA/BNA Lawyers' Manual on Professional Conduct* 1201:143 (1984–) provides as follows:

> Disclosure of the client's diminished capacity could adversely affect the client's interests. For example, raising the question of diminished capacity could, in some circumstances, lead to proceedings for involuntary commitment. Information relat-

ing to the representation is protected by Rule 1.6. Therefore, unless authorized to do so, the lawyer may not disclose such information. When taking protective action pursuant to paragraph (b), the lawyer is impliedly authorized to make the necessary disclosures, even when the client directs the lawyer to the contrary. Nevertheless, given the risks of disclosure, paragraph (c) limits what the lawyer may disclose in consulting with other individuals or entities or seeking the appointment of a legal representative. At the very least, the lawyer should determine whether it is likely that the person or entity consulted with will act adversely to the client's interests before discussing matters related to the client. The lawyer's position in such cases is an unavoidably difficult one.

Professor Rein points out that in California disclosure of information is absolutely barred: In contrast to the ABA and consistent with the California bar's absolute prohibition against divulging information learned during the representation, the California Ethics Committee rejects the notion that an attorney can initiate conservatorship proceedings: "By instituting conservatorship proceedings, the attorney will not only be disclosing such client secrets to the court, but also to any necessary third parties (including family members) called upon to act in the conservatorship role." The committee concluded that "[a]n attorney is *absolutely forbidden* from divulging the client's secrets gained during the attorney-client relationship, and from acting in any manner whereby the attorney is forced to use such secrets to the client's disadvantage."

Rein, *Ethics and the Questionably Competent Client,* note 86 supra, at 251, quoting California State Bar Standing Comm. on Professional Responsibility and Conduct, Formal Opinion 1989-112, at 1–2 (1989).

150. Perhaps the most comprehensive effort was that undertaken several years ago by the members of the Conference on Ethical Issues in Representing Older Clients. The proceedings of this conference, including the conferees' recommendations and a number of articles, were published in *Proceedings of the Conference on Ethical Issues in Representing Older Clients,* 62 Fordham L. Rev. 961-1516 (1994).

151. According to Rule 1.8(f) of the Model Rules of Professional Conduct, even if the son or daughter is paying the fee, it does not automatically follow that it is the adult child, rather than the parent, who is the client. The Rule provides as follows:

(f) A lawyer shall not accept compensation for representing a client from one other than the client unless:

(1) the client consents after consultation;

(2) there is no interference with the lawyer's independence of professional judgment or with the client-lawyer relationship; and

(3) information relating to representation of a client is protected as required by Rule 1.6 [which concerns confidentiality].

152. See generally Margulies, *Access, Connection, and Voice,* note 85 supra, at 1080–1082 (1994); Panel Discussion, *Ethical Issues in Dealing with Elderly Clients,* in *Exploring Ethical Issues in Meeting the Legal Needs of the Elderly,* note 115 supra, at 39–65.

153. Rule 1.7 of the Model Rules of Professional Conduct provides as follows:

(a) Except as provided in paragraph (b), a lawyer shall not represent a client if the representation involves a concurrent conflict of interest. A concurrent conflict of interest exists if:

(1) the representation of one client will be directly adverse to another client, or

(2) there is a significant risk that the representation of one or more clients will be materially limited by the lawyer's responsibility to another client, a former client or a third person or by a personal interest of the lawyer.

(b) Notwithstanding the existence of a concurrent conflict of interest under paragraph (a), a lawyer may represent a client if:

(1) the lawyer reasonably believes that the lawyer will be able to provide competent and diligent representation to each affected client,

(2) the representation is not prohibited by law,

(3) the representation does not involve the assertion of a claim by one client against another client represented by the lawyer in the same litigation or other proceeding before a tribunal, and

(4) each affected client gives informed consent, confirmed in writing.

154. Adams and Morgan, *Representing the Client Who is Older,* note 86 supra, at 14 n. 75.

155. Id. at 14.

156. Paul Nathanson, Paul L. Hain, and L. Lane Horder, *Lawyers, Legal Services, and the Elderly* (unpublished, c. 1987) (manuscript on file with the author). Questionnaires were sent to 1,356 attorneys, including 356 who participated in the New Mexico bar's Lawyer Referral for the Elderly Project ["Project"]. Of the one-third of the Project attorneys who responded, over 50 percent were between ages 31 and 40 and over 70 percent were male. For the other 1,000 attorneys who received questionnaires, the response rate was 16 percent; their age and gender distributions reflected those of the state bar generally, which at the time was 84 percent male and of whom approximately 45 percent were between ages 31 and 40.

Questionnaires also were distributed to the 336 law students then attending the University of New Mexico Law School. One-third responded; over half of these respondents were between ages 20 and 30, and they were split about evenly between men and women.

All of the survey subjects were presented with a list of advantages and disadvantages possibly associated with working with elderly clients. The responses established that over half of all three groups felt that older clients were more appreciative than were other clients. Over half of the law students and Project attorneys, as well as 46 percent of the other attorneys, indicated that older clients were more interesting, because of their life experiences, than were younger clients. Over one-third of the respondents from each sample group felt that they had better rapport with older clients than with younger ones.

There was one disadvantage of working with older clients that received a fairly large affirmative response: 35 percent of the law students, 29 percent of the Project attorneys, and 31 percent of the other attorneys perceived older clients as being more rigid and resistant to change than were younger persons. More generally, there were some negative feelings revealed by additional written comments made by 60 of the attorneys (both Project and other attorneys). They expressed frustration with the fact that many of the problems confronting older clients were not really legal problems that lent themselves to legal solutions. Obviously, this frustration was generated by circumstance and not by the clients themselves. On a more personal level, several of the lawyers asserted that elderly clients seemed to be obsessed with their cases and perceived minor issues as being major ones. The authors of the study suggested that these characterizations "perhaps were due to the fact that these particular elderly clients were not working and so had chunks of free time which they filled in by frequently calling their attorneys to talk about their cases" (manuscript, pp. 23–24).

All in all, the researchers concluded "that many in the legal profession in Mew Mexico see elderly clients as being appreciative and interesting. Most importantly, many attorneys and law students derived a sense of satisfaction from working with elderly clients." Id. at 22. Another conclusion also was drawn: "Lawyers apparently do not want to be seen as having stereotyped views about aged persons." Ibid.

157. Thus, for example, studies of court systems such as those that have been pursued regarding race and gender issues, see note 45 supra, should be undertaken with age as the focus of inquiry.

158. In this latter regard, see Symposium, *Elder Law Across the Curriculum,* 30 Stetson L. Rev. 1265–1468. Professor Rebecca C. Morgan organized this excellent symposium to demonstrate how elder law issues can be infused into a wide range of law school courses. Actually, a number of law schools report offering courses in elder law; however, many of these supposed elder law courses actually are traditional offerings, such as Estates and Trusts. See Legal Counsel for the Elderly, Inc., *1993 Elderlaw Directory of Seminars, Courses, and Clinics in U.S. Law Schools* (1993). In these latter courses, there almost certainly is little or no attention directed to the psychological and physical characteristics of older clients.

159. See chapter 5.

160. Panel Discussion, *Ethical Issues in Dealing with Elderly Clients,* comments of Professor Linda Smith, in *Exploring Ethical Issues in Meeting the Legal Needs of the Elderly* 71, note 115 supra, at 72.

161. Rosenberg, *Adapting Unitary Principles of Professional Responsibility to Unique Practice Contexts,* note 54 supra, at 412–413.

162. As to theories regarding how changed beliefs may be effectuated, see David L. Hamilton and Tina K. Trolier, *Stereotypes and Stereotyping: An Overview of the Cognitive Approach,* in *Prejudice, Discrimination, and Racism* 127, at 147 (John F. Dovidio and Samuel L. Gaertner, eds. 1986).

163. See, e.g., Diane C. Ray, Kelly A. McKinney, and Charles V. Ford, *Differences in Psychologists' Ratings of Older and Younger Clients,* 27 Gerontologist 82 (1987). The authors noted that one study of 220 health care providers reported that 80 percent preferred not to work with the elderly. Id. at 82. As for psychiatrists' negative views, see Diane C. Ray, Michael A. Raciti, and Charles V. Ford, *Ageism in Psychiatrists: Associations with Gender, Certification, and Theoretical Orientation,* 25 Gerontologist 496 (1985).

164. See, e.g., Dawn Warren, Albert Painter, and John Rudisell, *Effects of Geriatric Education on the Attitudes of Medical Students,* 31 J. of American Geriatrics Society 435 (1983); Mary J. White and Dale M. Johnson, *Changes in Nursing Students' Stereotypic Attitudes Toward Old People,* 25 Nursing Research 430 (Nov./Dec. 1976). Cf. Michael J. Lichtenstein, Linda A. Pruski, Carolyn E. Marshall, Cheryl L. Blalock, Douglas L. Murphy, Rosemarie Plaetke, and Shuko Lee, *The Positive Aging Teaching Materials Improve Middle School Students' Images of Older People,* 41 Gerontologist 322 (2001) (training materials can improve attitudes of middle school students); Josephine A. Allen and N. Yolanda Burwell, *Ageism and Racism: Two Issues in Social Work Education and Practice,* 16 J. of Educ. for Social Work 71, at 72 (Spring 1980) ("A more positive orientation toward . . . [the minority aged] can be propagated by proposing strategies that make students and practitioners aware of the strengths and coping techniques of the Black and other minority aged, as well as their particular social needs").

165. See, e.g., J. Wilson and E. Hafferty, *Long-Term Effects of A Seminar on Aging and Health for First-Year Medical Students,* 3 Gerontologist 319 (1983). More equivocal data are provided by a later study at the University of Wyoming of 152 subjects, most of whom

244 / Notes to Pages 113–14

were under age 21. The investigators sought to determine whether negative attitudes regarding older people could be changed by providing to the subjects correct information as to aging and as to what old people are like. Some subjects subsequently received reinforcement by way of discussion of the information provided. The researchers found that the initial information indeed did effectuate more positive attitudes, but four weeks later the subjects who had not received the reinforcement had reverted back to their negative attitudes. On the other hand, those subjects who had engaged in the discussion session retained their heightened positive views. Amie M. Ragan and Anne M. Bowen, *Improving Attitudes Regarding the Elderly Population: The Effects of Information and Reinforcement for Change,* 41 Gerontologist 511 (2001).

Chapter 7. Judges

The epigraphs are from the following sources: Richard A. Posner, *Aging and Old Age* 180 (1995); Cicero, *On Old Age,* in Frank O. Copley, translator, Cicero, *On Old Age and On Friendship* 1, at 13 (1967); Archibald MacLeish, "With Age, Wisdom," in *New and Collected Poems 1917–1976* (1976).

1. As to the settling of legal claims generally, see Samuel R. Gross and Kent D. Syverud, *Don't Try: Civil Jury Verdicts in a System Geared to Settlement,* 44 UCLA L. Rev. 1, at 2–3 (1996). In the employment discrimination context (a context that generates a tremendous number of federal cases), most claims that have some merit are settled, as is the case in other areas of the law, as well. In this regard, in a survey of 651 employment discrimination lawyers, the defense attorneys estimated that 79 percent of their cases were settled prior to final adjudication, while the plaintiffs' attorneys gave an estimate of 84 percent. William J. Howard, *Arbitrating Claims of Employment Discrimination,* 50 Disp. Resol. J. 40, at 43–44 (1995).

2. For example, only about 8 percent of criminal cases are decided by juries. Valerie P. Hans and Neil Vidmar, *Judging the Jury* 9 (1986). As for tort cases, it has been reported that only 2.7 percent are resolved by juries. Brian J. Ostrom, David B. Rottman, and John A. Goerdt, *A step above anecdote: a profile of the civil jury in the 1990s,* 79 Judicature 233, at 234 (March–Apr. 1996).

3. In a civil case involving a suit in which money damages are sought, the judge can conclude that the jury has awarded an excessive amount. By a process known as remittitur, she then affords the prevailing party two options: either accept a reduced amount that the judge deems to be appropriate, or pursue a new trial with the hope that (1) the jury in that trial will come in with an award comparable to (or even higher than) the award made by the first jury, and (2) the judge the second time around will change her mind and allow that new award. For a rare instance in which that scenario, i.e., upholding of an even higher award in the retrial, occurred, see Weinberg v. Johnson, 518 A.2d 985 (D.C. 1986).

4. The figure in the text is based on data current as of May 15, 2000. Diana R. Irvine, *The American Bench* v (11th ed. 2000).

5. See chapter 2.

6. When President Franklin Delano Roosevelt in 1936 proposed what is popularly known as the "court packing plan," which would have allowed for the appointment of a new federal judge (including Supreme Court justices) for each individual who was 70 or older, there were six justices whose ages would have triggered additional vacancies under the plan: Louis D. Brandeis (77), Pierce Butler (70), Charles Evans Hughes (71), James C. McReynolds (71), George Sutherland (71), and Willis Van Devanter (74).

7. See L. A. Powe Jr., *Old People and Good Behavior,* 12 Constitutional Commentary 195, at 196 (1995):

> [L]ife-tenured [Supreme Court] Justices enjoy a job that has good pay, high prestige, manageable hours, great vacation opportunities, and no heavy lifting, so they can last longer and longer. And as they age, their formative experiences grow ever more distant from those of the 250,000,000 people whose Constitution they interpret and whose lives they periodically affect.

See also Sanford Levinson, *Contempt of Court: The Most Important Contemporary Challenge to Judging,* 49 Wash. & Lee L. Rev. 339, at 341 (1992).

8. See, e.g., Sheldon Goldman, *Voting Behavior on the United States Courts of Appeals Revisited,* 75 American Political Sci. Rev. 491, at 505 (1975):

> The age variable presents a special challenge for judicial behavior. The variable, after all, is a dynamic one, and the age hypothesis seems to suggest that judges grow more conservative as they grow older. This proposition deserves closer scrutiny using the voting records of individual judges. The challenge to the analyst is to be able to demonstrate that, for example, Justice Hugo Black's more conservative voting behavior in his last decade on the Supreme Court can best be explained by the aging process. . . . [T]he age variable is likely to be troublesome even as scholars undertake painstaking analysis of actual changes in the voting behavior of individual judges over time.

Id. at 505.

9. Richard A. Posner, *Aging and Old Age* 199 (1995).

10. Ibid., quoting Henry J. Friendly, *Book Review* (of Marvin Schick, *Learned Hand's Court*), 86 Political Sci. Q. 470, at 471 (1971).

11. Posner, *Aging and Old Age,* note 9 supra, at 182–184.

12. Russell Smyth and Mita Bhattacharya, *How fast do old judges slow down? A life cycle study of aging and productivity in the Federal Court of Australia,* 23 International Rev. of Law and Economics 141 (2003).

13. Mita Bhattacharya and Russell Smyth, *The Aging and Productivity Among Judges: Some Empirical Evidence from the High Court of Australia,* 40 Australian Economic Papers 199 (2001).

14. Smyth and Bhattacharya, *How fast do old judges slow down?* note 12 supra, at 162.

15. During congressional committee hearings on nominees for federal judgeships, examination of prior rulings is commonly undertaken, even as the examiners, that is, senators and Senate staffers, disingenuously disclaim any partisanship in their so doing.

16. It is conceivable that a decision by a lower court judge could be four-square in conflict with a clear Supreme Court precedent. For example, a federal district court judge might, let us hypothesize, hold that the separation of children on the basis of race in public schools is satisfied by the separate-but-equal doctrine. That doctrine, however, was jettisoned by the Supreme Court in Brown v. Board of Education, 347 U.S. 483 (1954), and thus the hypothetical lower court decision is clearly, unequivocally wrong. There would be little reason in this instance, therefore, to reach anything but a totally negative judgment about the legal acumen (or at least integrity) of the district court judge. In fact, however, such perverse lower court rulings hardly ever are rendered.

17. Some local bar associations, such as the Chicago Council of Attorneys, conduct

periodic surveys of attorneys in which the respondents are asked to rate local federal court judges on just such criteria. The value of such surveys is open to question.

18. See Page's Ohio Rev. Code Ann. § 2907.04 (2002) (sexual contact by person 18 or older with person whom he or she knows to be between 13 and 15 constitutes "unlawful sexual conduct").

19. See 720 Illinois Compiled Statutes 5/12-2(1)(12) (2002); see also chapter 1. For an interesting article concerning old age as a defense in criminal cases, see Fred Cohen, *Old Age as a Criminal Defense*, 21 Crim. L. Bull. 5 (1985).

20. Writing in 1972, Professors George Alexander and Travis H. D. Lewin reported as follows:

> An increasing number of states have enacted statutes which specifically recognize old age as a possible factor causing incompetency to manage personal and property matters, thus requiring the appointment of a guardian or conservator. The statutes enumerate conditions such as "old age," "senility," "extreme old age," "physical and mental weakness on account of old age," or "mental infirmities of old age," as the requirements for appointment of guardians in such cases.

George J. Alexander and Travis H. D. Lewin, *The Aged and the Need for Surrogate Management* 17 (1972). In recent years the impropriety of using age per se as a proxy for incapacity in the context of judicial decisions concerning guardianships has been increasingly recognized. "In the 1980's, the category of age was deleted from the Uniform Probate Code, and from many state statutes." Lawrence A. Frolik and Alison Patrucco Barnes, *Elderlaw* 791 (1992); but see Linda S. Whitton, *Ageism: Paternalism and Prejudice*, 46 DePaul L. Rev. 453, at 477 (1997), regarding the continuing existence of a number of such statutes:

> [As recently as 1997, a] survey of [all] adult protection legislation revealed that twelve state statutes listed "age," "old age," or "advanced age" as an independent basis for considering a person to be "impaired," "incapacitated," "disabled," or "vulnerable" and in need of protection. Similarly, ten guardianship and conservatorship statutes currently list "advanced" age as an independent basis for imposition of guardianship or conservatorship, and at least fourteen states had ageist language in their guardianship and conservatorship statutes until recently amended or repealed.

21. See Todd D. Peterson, *Studying the Impact of Race and Ethnicity in the Federal Courts*, 64 Geo. Wash. L. Rev. 173 (1996); *Report of the First Circuit Gender, Race and Ethnic Bias Task Forces,* 9 Boston U. Public Interest L. J. 173, at 184 n. 1 (2000); Deborah Ruble Round, *Gender Bias in the Judicial System*, 61 Southern California L. Rev. 2193 (1988).

22. The First Circuit courts are those sitting in Maine, New Hampshire, Massachusetts, Rhode Island, and Puerto Rico.

23. *Report of the First Circuit Gender, Race and Ethnic Bias Task Forces,* note 21 supra, at 228.

24. Id. at 277.

> A negative experience entailed not having one's opinions or views taken seriously, or being subjected to (a) an unwillingness on the part of the court personage to accommodating the lawyer's scheduling needs; (b) inaccurate assumptions regarding the attorney's professional status; (c) inappropriate comments or advances of a sexually suggestive nature; (d) inappropriate comments about physical appearance or cloth-

ing; (e) inappropriate comments about the presumed foreign origin or citizenship of the attorney; and/or (f) demeaning or derogatory comments. Id. at 276.

25. Id. at 319.

26. Id. at 320. The actual numbers were not large: 26 respondents complained that their opinions or views were not taken seriously by a judge; 19 complained of rude treatment at the hands of a judge.

27. Sherrilyn A. Ifill, *Judging the Judges: Racial Diversity, Impartiality, and Representation on State Trial Courts,* 39 Boston C. L. Rev. 95, at 102–103 (1997).

28. Sheldon Goldman, *Voting Behavior on the United States Courts of Appeals Revisited,* note 8 supra, at 499.

29. Ibid.

30. Id. at 505.

31. U.S. Const., amend. XIV, § 1.

32. Theodore Eisenberg and Sherri Lynn Johnson, *The Effects of Intent: Do We Know How Legal Standards Work?* 76 Cornell L. Rev. 1151, at 1190 (1991). The authors also found that judges with prior prosecutorial experience, judges with prior judicial experience in state courts, black judges, and women judges responded most favorably to plaintiffs. Ibid.

33. Peter David Blanck, Robert Rosenthal, and LaDoris Hazzard Cordell, *The Appearance of Justice: Judges' Verbal and Nonverbal Behavior in Criminal Jury Trials,* 38 Stanford L. Rev. 89, at 124– 26 (1985).

34. Donald C. Nugent, *Judicial Bias,* 42 Cleveland State L. Rev. 1, at 18 (1994), citing Lorenzo A. Arredondo, Helen V. Collier, and Gary J. Scrimgeour, *To Make a Good Decision . . . Law and Experience Alone Are Not Enough,* 1988 Judges J. 23, at 24 (Fall 1988) (emphasis added).

35. Robert A. Wenke, *The Art of Selecting a Jury* 84–85 (1979). It is conceivable that the observations of this judge are correct, but absent study, there is no way of assessing the validity of his contentions.

36. Walter E. Jordan, *Jury Selection* 302–303 (1980).

37. 66 American Bar Association J. 134 (Feb. 1980) (no title).

38. Darrell Steffensmeier and Mark Motivans, *Older Men and Older Women in the Arms of Criminal Law: Offending Patterns and Sentencing Outcomes,* 55B Journals of Gerontology: Social Sciences S141 (2000).

39. These differences could not be explained away by statutory guidelines or other rules dictating such results; while such guidelines did exist, Steffensmeier and Motivans noted that these structured, but did not eliminate, sentencing discretion. Id. at S143.

40. Id. at S148–S149.

41. Because of the data regarding the offender's age group—18–20—the investigators limited their comparative analysis regarding the treatment of older offenders to adults ages 21 and older.

42. However, they provided hardly any supporting data—such as interviews with judges—regarding their suppositions.

43. Steffensmeier and Motivans, note 38 supra, at S143.

44. Ibid.

45. Ibid. (Citation omitted).

46. Steffensmeier and Motivans explain:

Time for older offenders is more likely to be seen as a diminishing, exhaustible resource in which the future becomes increasingly valuable. A year of imprisonment given to an offender in his or her 60s takes a considerably larger proportion of that person's remaining years than the same punishment imposed on a 20-year-old.

Ibid.

47. See Darrell Steffensmeier and Mark Motivans, *Sentencing the Older Offender: Is there an 'Age Bias'?* in *Elders, Crime, and the Criminal Justice System* 185, at 189–190 (Max B. Rothman, Burton D. Dunlop, and Pamela Entzel, eds. 2000).

48. Kevin Clancy, John Bartolomeo, David Richardson, and Charles Wellford, *Sentencing Decision Making: The Logic of Sentence Decisions and the Extent and Sources of Sentence Disparity,* 72 Crim. L. & Criminology 524, at 539 (1981).

49. Peter David Blanck, *Calibrating the Scales of Justice: Studying Judges' Behavior in Bench Trials,* 68 Ind. L. J. 1119, at 1179 (1993).

50. Id. at 1146.

51. Ibid.

52. Gary Feinberg and Dinesh Khosla, *Sanctioning Elder Delinquents,* 21 Trial 46 (Sept. 1985).

53. The judges were asked to respond to the following two statements: "The elderly have paid their dues and ought to be looked after by society if they need help," and "The elderly suffer more than the general population during hard economic times." Id. at 47.

54. Ibid. Feinberg and Khosla noted, however, that "older judges with less experience manifest almost the same attitudinal patterns toward the elderly as younger judges with more experience"; the researchers opined that "[i]t is as if age may be substituted for experience, and vice versa." Ibid.

55. Ibid.

56. Ibid.

57. Id. at 49. The researchers set forth some thoughtful and useful recommendations for dealing with elderly offenders, but these did not really have much, if anything, to do with the survey data that had been collected.

58. Donald C. Nugent, *Judicial Bias,* note 34 supra, at 14; see also Robert McCoun, *Inside the Black Box: What Empirical Research Tells Us about Decisionmaking by Civil Juries,* in *Verdict: Assessing the Civil Jury System* 127, at 180 n. 160 (Robert E. Litan, ed. 1993).

59. See chapter 2.

60. Blanck, Rosenthal, and Cordell, *The Appearance of Justice,* note 33 supra, at 121. According to the authors, every defendant was the subject of at least one charge or count. Fifteen of the 34 defendants were the subjects of two or more charges or counts. Typically, the first and second charges did not differ substantively. Id. at 120 n. 98.

Perhaps to the researchers' dismay, the data did not support the ultimate conclusion that judges' expectations influenced jurors' verdicts:

The tendency for judges' expectations for trial outcome *not* to be related to actual trial outcome runs counter to our basic hypothesis that jurors' decisionmaking processes may be importantly influenced by, and [be] consistent with, judges' expectations for trial outcome.

As Kalven and Zeisel argue in *The American Jury,* however, the judge and the jury might not be "deciding the same case." Exclusionary rules of evidence keep some information about the case from the jury which is only available to the judge.

Id. at 133, citing Harry Kalven and Hans Zeisel, *The American Jury* (1966).

61. See Cleveland Board of Education v. LaFleur, 414 U.S. 632 (1972).

62. 29 U.S.C. §§ 621–634.

63. Since the beginning of 1969, Republican presidents have occupied the White House for 24 years (1969–1976, 1981–1992, 2001–2004), and thus have had an opportunity to appoint a majority of the sitting federal court judges, almost none of whom had been appointed, as of 2003, prior to 1969. Some studies of appellate-level federal court judges find Democratic judges to be more liberal than Republican judges, with the former more often tending to rule in favor of civil rights claimants, labor unions, and governmental agencies in business regulation cases. See Orley Ashenfelder, Theodore Eisenberg, and Stephen J. Schwab, *Politics and the Judiciary: The Influence of Judicial Background in Case Outcomes*, 24 J. of Legal Studies 257, at 260–261 (1995); see also Jilda M. Aliotta, *Combining Judges' Attributes and Case Characteristics: An Alternative Approach to Explaining Supreme Court Decisionmaking*, 71 Judicature 277, at 280 (1988). What is more, "[e]vidence . . . exists of a correlation between the president appointing a judge and case outcomes." *Politics and the Judiciary: The Influence of Judicial Background in Case Outcomes* at 161; see also Robert A. Carp and C. K. Rowland, *Policymaking and Politics in the Federal District Courts* 34–36, 51–83, 150–152 (1983) (addressing correlation between appointing president and district court judges' decisions).

64. The U.S. Sentencing Commission Guidelines, enacted pursuant to the Sentencing Reform Act of 1984, as amended, 18 U.S.C. §3551 *et seq.*, and 28 U.S.C. §§ 991–998, generally preclude federal sentencing judges from taking age into account except in extraordinary cases. Section 5H1.1 of the Guidelines provides that "[a]ge is not ordinarily relevant in determining whether a sentence should be outside the guidelines," and the same provision further allows judges to consider departing from the Guidelines only where "the offender is elderly and infirm and where a form of punishment (e.g., home confinement) might be equally efficient as and less costly than incarceration." See generally United States v. Carey, 895 F.2d 318, 324 (7th Cir. 1990).

65. The age proxy argument, i.e., the argument that condemns the use of a decision-making criterion that is nothing more than a stand-in for age itself, has been gutted of force by the Supreme Court in another setting, i.e., employment discrimination cases. See Hazen Paper Co. v. Biggins, 507 U.S. 604 (1993); see generally Howard Eglit, *The Age Discrimination in Employment Act at Thirty: Where It's Been, Where It Is Today, Where It's Going,* 31 U. of Richmond L. Rev. 579, at 693–696 (1997).

66. See, e.g., Fla. Const., Art. 5, § 8 (age 70 cap). Approximately 30 states have enacted mandatory retirement statutes applicable to judges. See Christopher R. McFadden, *Judicial Independence, Age-Based BFOQs, and the Perils of Mandatory Retirement Policies for Appointed State Judges,* 52 Southern California L. Rev. 81, at 83 n. 10 (2000).

67. It is not beyond doubt that a state might want to impose an age minimum as a precondition to election to, or selection for, the bench. In Humphrey v. Walls, 169 Md. 292, 181 A. 735 (1935), the court held that a Maryland law prescribing a minimum age requirement for judicial officers was invalid because it was preempted by the state constitution. The court determined that the constitution's single condition of eligibility for the office of justice of the peace, i.e., scrutiny and approval by the state senate, was the maximum qualification that could be imposed upon candidates for the office. The *Humphrey* court did not reach the merits of the age issue.

In another case involving judicial officers, a state statute setting age 35 as the minimum age for magistrates was upheld by the Pennsylvania Supreme Court. Kelly v. Keiser, 340 Pa.

59, 16 A.2d 307 (1940). The court determined that the state constitution's silence on the matter did not indicate an intent to allow all adult citizens to hold the office. The court held that the legislature's power to prescribe an age qualification for a given office only could be restricted if its action was so manifestly arbitrary and capricious as to amount to an abuse of discretion. To be unreasonable and capricious, the court explained, either an age qualification would have to so limit the electorate's field of choice that it would prevent the filling of the office, or it would have to bear no rational relationship to the functions and duties of the office. Id. at 63, 16 A.2d at 309.

Minimum age requirements for other public offices almost always have been upheld. Indeed, attacks made under the U.S. Constitution's Equal Protection Clause, U.S. Const., amend. XIV, §1, uniformly have been unsuccessful. See, e.g., Manson v. Edwards, 482 F.2d 1076 (6th Cir. 1973) (city councilman); Whitehead v. Westbrook, Civ. No. F-74-41-C (W.D. Ark. 1975), affd. memorandum, 423 U.S. 962 (1975) (city director); Blassman v. Markworth, 359 F. Supp. 1 (N.D. Ill. 1973) (school board); Raza Unida Party v. Bullock, 349 F. Supp. 1272 (W.D. Tex. 1972), affd. in part & vacated and remanded in part on other grounds sub nom. American Party of Texas v. White, 415 U.S. 767 (1974) (governor and lieutenant governor); Meyers v. Roberts, 310 Minn. 358, 246 N.W.2d 186 (1976), app. dismissed, 429 U.S. 1083 (1977) (local governmental board); Opatz v. St. Cloud, 293 Minn. 379, 196 N.W.2d 298 (1972) (city alderman); Wurzel v. Falcey, 69 N.J. 401, 354 A.2d 617 (1976) (state legislature); Spencer v. Board of Educ., 39 A.D.2d 399, 334 N.Y.S.2d 783 (1972), affd. memorandum, 31 N.Y.2d 810, 291 N.E.2d 585, 339 N.Y.S.2d 461 (1972) (school board).

Likewise, attacks based on a claimed infringement of the rights of voters and/or office-holders under the U.S. Constitution's First Amendment, U.S. Const., amend. I, have failed. See, e.g., Blassman v. Markworth, supra; Meyers v. Roberts, supra; Opatz v. St. Cloud, supra; Spencer v. Board of Educ., supra. There is no reason to believe a result more favorable to a plaintiff challenging an age restriction for judicial office would obtain. Attacks based on state constitutional provisions likewise have been unsuccessful, save in Humphrey v. Walls, supra, and in Canavan v. Messina, 31 Conn. Supp. 447, 334 A.2d 237 (1973), in which the court held invalid a town charter provision on state constitutional preemption grounds. See, e.g., Quinn v. Marsh, 141 Neb. 436, 3 N.W.2d 892 (1972); Mengelkamp v. List, 88 Nev. 542, 501 P.2d 1032 (1972); Kelly v. Keiser, supra.

68. See, e.g., Sabo v. Casey, 757 F. Supp. 587 (E.D. Pa.) rev'd in part & dismissed in part without opinion, 968 F.2d 14 (3d Cir. 1991); United States Equal Employment Opportunity Comm'n v. Illinois, 721 F. Supp 156 (N.D. Ill. 1989); Apkin v. Treasurer & Receiver Gen., 401 Mass. 427, 517 N.E.2d 141 (1988); Diamond v. Cuomo, 70 N.Y.2d 338, 514 N.E.2d 1356, 520 N.Y.S.2d 732 (1987), app. dismissed, 486 U.S. 1028 (1988); In re Stout, 521 Pa. 571, 559 A.2d 489 (1989); but see Equal Employment Opportunity Comm'n v. Vermont, 904 F.2d 794 (2d Cir. 1990).

69. See generally Howard Eglit, 1–3 Age Discrimination (2d ed. 1994 and annual supps.).

70. See, e.g., Zielasko v. Ohio, 873 F.3d 967 (6th Cir. 1989); Hatten v. Rains, 854 F.2d 687 (5th Cir. 1988), cert. denied, 490 U.S. 1106 (1989); Malmed v. Thornburgh, 621 F.2d 565 (3d Cir.), cert. denied, 449 U.S. 955 (1980); Trafelet v. Thompson, 594 F.2d 623 (7th Cir.), cert. denied, 444 U.S. 906 (1979); Rubino v. Ghezzi, 512 F.2d 431 (2d Cir.), cert. denied, 423 U.S. 891 (1975); Boughton v. Price, 70 Idaho 243, 215 P.2d 286 (1950); O'Neil v. Baine, 568 S.W.2d 761 (Mo. 1978); Grinnell v. State, 121 N.H. 823, 435 A.2d

523 (1981); Diamond v. Cuomo, 130 A.D.2d 292, 519 N.Y.S.2d 691, *affd.*, 70 N.Y.2d 338, 514 N.E.2d 1356, 520 N.Y.S.2d 732, *app. dismissed*, 486 U.S. 1028 (1988); Dolan v. Secretary of State, 55 Ohio App.3d 157, 563 N.E.2d 745 (1988), *dismissed*, 41 Ohio St.3d 725, 535 N.E.2d 1370 (1989); *In re* Stout, 521 Pa. 571, 559 A.2d 489 (1989); Nelson v. Miller, 25 Utah2d 277, 480 P.2d 467 (1971); Aronstam v. Cashman, 132 Vt. 538, 325 A.2d 361 (1974); but see Gondelman v. Commonwealth, 120 Pa. Commw. 624, 550 A.2d 814 (1988), *dismissed*, 520 Pa. 451, 554 A.2d 896, *cert. denied*, 493 U.S. 849 (1989).

71. 501 U.S. 452 (1991).

72. Id. at 461.

73. See, e.g., Vance v. Bradley, 440 U.S. 93 (1979); Massachusetts Board of Retirement v. Murgia, 427 U.S. 307 (1976); see generally chapter 3.

74. 568 S.W.2d 761 (Mo. 1978).

75. 501 U.S. at 471–472. The *Vance* decision that is referred to in the excerpt involved the sustaining of a federal law imposing age-based mandatory retirement upon federal foreign service officers.

76. Id. at 472–473.

77. The *Gregory* Court so observed:
[A] State "'does not violate the Equal Protection Clause merely because the classifications made by its laws are imperfect.'" [*Massachusetts Board of Retirement v.*] *Murgia*, 427 U.S. [307,] at 316 [(1976)]. . . . "In an equal protection case . . . [not involving a suspect classification or a fundamental right] . . . those challenging the . . . judgment [of the people] must convince the court that the . . . facts on which the classification is apparently based could not reasonably be conceived to be true by the . . . decisionmaker." [*Vance v.*] *Bradley*, 440 U.S. [93,] at 111 [(1979)].
Id. at 473.

78. Ibid.

79. See generally Howard Eglit, *Of Age and the Constitution*, 57 Chi-Kent L. Rev. 859 (1981).

80. 427 U.S. 307 (1976). *Murgia* is discussed in chapter 3.

81. See, e.g., Kimel v. Florida Board of Regents, 528 U.S. 62 (2000); Cleburne v. Cleburne Living Center, Inc., 473 U.S. 432 (1989); Vance v. Bradley, 440 U.S. 93 (1979).

82. U.S. Constitution, Article III, § 1 provides: "The Judges, both of the supreme and inferior Courts, shall hold their Offices during good Behavior."

83. No formal record of the deliberations of the members of the Constitutional Convention was maintained. Thus, we have only bits and pieces of debates that were recorded by various members from time to time. See Max Farrand, *The Records of the Federal Convention of 1787* (rev. ed. 1966).

84. The Constitution only expressly creates one court: the Supreme Court. The creation of lower federal courts is left to the discretion of the Congress by Article III, § 1. This tack reflected a compromise between those who wanted a fully functioning federal judicial branch as part of a strong new federal government and those who feared a too-powerful federal establishment and so opposed a federal judiciary. Obviously, then, there was in the minds of some at the Constitutional Convention, i.e., the proponents of a federal court system, the vision of a federal judiciary larger than just the members of the Supreme Court (who totaled six in the Court's very early years). But there is nothing to tell us what these men thought about the possibility of that judiciary being staffed by superannuated judges. We do know that the very first Congress proceeded to enact the Judiciary Act of 1789,

which, *inter alia,* created a small number of federal courts subordinate to the Supreme Court.

85. David Hackett Fischer, *Growing Old in America* 3 (expanded paperback ed. 1978).

86. Id. at 27.

87. The matter of life expectancy is a complicated one because the data are not complete and because different analysts have arrived at different conclusions. Moreover, there are variations as to the data for the various colonies and early states. The following data are taken from Fischer, *Growing Old in America,* note 85 supra, but are certainly not the last word on the subject. Fischer reported information as to survival rates for 20-year-olds, as well as data regarding life expectancy at birth. These data confirm that if one survived to adulthood, one had a much better chance of living to age 50, 60, or 70 than did a newborn:

Place	Year	% surviving from age 20 to		
		age 50	60	70
Philadelphia	1768–1790	38.3	24.5	11.2
Salem, Mass.	1782–1790	35.9	27.4	20.0
American colonies	1650–1700	58.5	39.5	20.8
United States	1840	73.0	59.6	38.8

Id. at 275, Table IV.

If one looks to life expectancy at birth, one finds much smaller percentage figures:

Place	Year	% surviving from birth to age		
		60	65	70
Philadelphia	1770–1790	11.4–14.0	—	5.2–6.2
Salem, Mass.	1782–1790	12.9–17.8	—	9.4–12.6
United States	1840	36.4	30.7	23.8

Id. at 278, Table V. See generally id. at 272–279, Tables I–VI.

88. The *Federalist Papers* were a series of newspaper essays written in the late 1780s by John Jay, James Madison, and Alexander Hamilton defending the proposed Constitution, the merits of which were at issue in the context of the ratification fight then being waged in the state of New York.

89. *Federalist* Paper No. 78. As Hamilton indicated, life tenure was commonly afforded to higher state court judges. For example, John Adams in 1779 drafted the constitution of the Commonwealth of Massachusetts; therein, he provided for a life-tenured judiciary. David McCullough, *John Adams* 222 (2001). However, life tenure in later years was abolished in those states that in earlier days had extended this privilege to their judiciary.

90. See Julius Goebel Jr., *History of the Supreme Court of the United States, Vol. 1, Antecedents and Beginnings to 1801,* at 225 (1971).

91. *Federalist* Paper No. 78. While it might be argued, and often is, that life tenure is necessary to ensure judicial independence, the fact is that a fixed term, let us say of 15 or 20 years, would go a considerable way toward ensuring independence, even though such a term would entail departure from the bench upon its expiration. Thus, the independence claim, although powerful, is not necessarily dependent upon judges having life tenure. (On the other hand, it must be conceded that the need or desire of a given judge to find new employment upon expiration of her term of office arguably could cause her to trim her

judicial sails so as to curry favor with potential postexpiration employers.) As to recent attention to the perennially discussed issue of judicial independence, see *Judicial Independence and Accountability Symposium*, 72 S. Cal. L. Rev. 311–810 (1999); *Symposium*, 61 S. Cal. L. Rev. 1555–2073 (1988).

92. *Federalist* Paper No. 78.

93. See, e.g., Neil A. Lewis, "Unmaking the G.O.P. Court Legacy," *New York Times*, Aug. 23, 1993, p. A9:

There are 828 Federal judgeships. Between them, Mr. Reagan and Mr. Bush named more than 60 percent of the nation's current sitting judges, and almost 70 percent of those at the appeals court level. Mr. Reagan appointed 371 judges; Mr. Bush appointed 187.

Mr. Bush's choices, like those of Mr. Reagan, were mostly white, male, wealthy and, most striking of all, relatively young. The Republicans sought to insure a lasting legacy by appointing many judges in their 40's.

See also Stephen Wermiel, "Reagan Choices Alter the Makeup and Views of the Federal Courts," *Wall St. J.*, Feb. 1, 1988, pp. 1, 17, at p. 17:

Compared with other judges, says Prof. [Sheldon] Goldman [of the University of Massachusetts], the Reagan appointees are . . . somewhat younger, especially the appeals-court judges, and therefore likely to serve longer."

94. See Howard Eglit, 1 *Age Discrimination* 3–14 n. 7 (1981).

95. H.R. Res. 693, 96th Cong., 2d Sess (1980); S. Res. 374, 96th Cong., 2d Sess. (1980). The ABA committee in that same year discontinued the use of age guidelines. See "ABA Panel Stops Age Blackball," *Legal Times of Washington*, Dec. 22, 1980, p. 28.

According to the now-defunct guidelines, a nominee for initial appointment who was 60 or over would not be deemed qualified by reason of age "unless in excellent health" and unless evaluated as "well qualified" or "exceptionally well qualified." Furthermore, "[i]n no event . . . [would] persons 64 years of age or older [be] found qualified for initial appointment." In addition, a district court judge over 67 would not be found qualified for elevation to an appellate court.

Eglit, 1 *Age Discrimination,* note 94 supra, at 3–14.

96. 28 U.S.C. § 372(a).

97. Ibid.

98. 28 U.S.C. § 371.

99. Kelly J. Baker, Note, *Senior Judges: Valuable Resources, Partisan Strategists, or Self-Interested Maximizers?* 16 J. of Law & Politics 139, at 144 n. 35 (2000).

100. 28 U.S.C. § 371(e).

101. 28 U.S.C. § 372(b).

102. 28 U.S.C. § 372(c).

103. Ibid.

104. It has been noted:

Senior status is a popular option among District Court judges; well over one-third the number of authorized judgeships are occupied by senior judges. Furthermore, the workload shouldered by senior judges is increasing each year, and they are now viewed as indispensable to the federal system plagued [as it is] with high vacancy rates.

Baker, Note, *Senior Judges,* note 99 supra, at 139; see also Jerry Markon, "Elderly Judges Handle 20% of U.S. Caseload," *Wall St. J.*, Oct 8, 2001, Marketplace, pp. A15, A20, at p.

A15: "Nearly 40 percent of the nation's more than 1,200 working federal judges are on senior status. . . . These senior judges handle nearly 20 percent of the federal judiciary's work."

105. See, e.g., *In re* Assignment of Justices and Judges, 222 So.2d 22 (Fla. Sup. Ct. 1969).

106. For an extensive analysis and condemnation of mandatory retirement being imposed on state court judges, see McFadden, *Judicial Independence, Age-Based BFOQs, and the Perils of Mandatory Retirement Policies for Appointed State Judges*, note 66 supra.

107. A critical concern for those who have studied racial, ethnic, and gender bias in the judicial process is the matter of diversity. An absence of judges who are members of racial and ethnic minorities has been identified as a failing that at the least may contribute to the perception that the courts are unfair (insofar as minorities are concerned), see, e.g., Min W. Chin, *Keynote Address: "Fairness or Bias? A Symposium on Racial and Ethnic Composition and Attitudes in the Judiciary,"* 4 Asian L. J. 181, at 187–192 (1997), and at worst may account for bias in the ways in which the courts actually operate. The suggestions also have been made that the lack of diversity of court personnel can produce perceptions by users of the legal system that the judiciary is biased, and that a more diverse judiciary will result in a more diverse court staff:

> If our bench becomes more diverse, other areas of the judiciary are inevitably affected. This, in turn, may instill more confidence in the judiciary in the public's mind. For example, public perception of bias in the judiciary extends not only to the judges, but also to the personnel throughout the legal system. Statistics support this view. Caucasians, for example, hold 78 percent of the court reporter positions, 68 percent of the courtroom clerk positions, and 81 percent of the official and manager positions in the state superior courts [in California]. Again, this does not indict our judges for intentional bias; it is, however, the public's perception, based on what they see in our courts. If the bench becomes more diverse, however, the chances are likely to increase that these judges will, in turn, contribute to more diversity in their appointment of court personnel. This, of course, will also help to improve the perception of bias in the courts.

Id. at 192.

108. American Bar Association, *Model Code of Judicial Conduct* (1990).

> Before 1990, the 1972 Code had been adopted, in whole or in large part, by forty-seven states, the District of Columbia, and the Federal Judicial Conference. Since the enactment of the 1990 version, twenty-five of these states, plus Rhode Island, the District of Columbia, and the Federal Judicial Conference have partially or completely repealed the 1972 version of the code. These jurisdictions have adopted all or part of the 1990 Code, a slight variation of it, or a combination of the two Codes. . . . [Thus,] [t]he vast majority of judges, both state and federal, are subject to a code of conduct with uniform general principles and relatively specific rules, some of which are uniform and others of which vary from jurisdiction to jurisdiction.

Jeffrey M. Shaman, Steven Lubet, and James J. Alfini, *Judicial Conduct and Ethics* 4–5 (2d ed. 1995).

109. Illinois Supreme Court Rule 63, as amended (March 26, 2001).

110. *Illinois Rules of Professional Conduct*, Rule 8.4, as amended (March 26, 2001).

111. Judicial Conference of the United States, *Code of Conduct for United States Judges* (1996).

112. See, e.g., *In re* Charge of Judicial Misconduct, 62 F. 3d 320, 322 (9th Cir. 1995).

113. Judicial Conference of the United States, *Code of Conduct*, note 111 supra, Canon 2.

114. Ibid.

115. Judicial Conference of the United States, *Code of Conduct*, note 111 supra, Canon 2, Commentary.

116. In 1994 it was reported that the "majority of states have statutory provisions that enable litigants to disqualify judges for bias or prejudice by filing an affidavit with the state's supreme court." Donald C. Nugent, *Judicial Bias*, note 34 supra, at 93.

117. See id. at 30.

118. Parrish v. Board of Commissioners, 524 F.2d 98, 100 (5th Cir. 1975) (en banc), quoting United States v. Thompson, 483 F.2d 527, 528 (3d Cir. 1973), *cert. denied*, 425 U.S. 944 (1976).

119. Donald C. Nugent, *Judicial Bias*, note 34 supra, at 26, quoting Hughes v. United States, 899 F.2d 1495, 1501 (6th Cir.), *cert. denied*, 498 U.S. 980 (1990); United States v. Sammons, 918 F.2d 592, 599 (6th Cir. 1990); *In re* M. Ibrahim Khan, 751 F.2d 162, 164 (6th Cir. 1984).

120. See, e.g., United States v. Sibla, 624 F.2d 864, 868 (9th Cir. 1980).

121. See, e.g., United States v. Grinnell, 384 U.S. 563, 583 (1966); *In re* Corrugated Container Antitrust Litigation, 614 F.2d 958, 964 (5th Cir.), *cert. denied*, 449 U.S. 888 (1980); United States v. Carignan, 600 F.2d 762 (9th Cir. 1979); King v. United States, 576 F.2d 432 (2d Cir. 1978), *cert. denied*, 439 U.S. 850 (1978).

122. 510 U.S. 540 (1994).

123. Id. at 550.

124. Ibid.

125. Ibid.

126. Id. at 555–556.

127. See Donald C. Nugent, *Judicial Bias*, note 34 supra, at 4–20.

128. *In re* Union Leader Corp., 292 F.2d 381, 388 (1st Cir. 1961), *cert. denied*, 368 U.S. 927 (1961); see also Knapp v. Kinsey, 232 F.2d 458, 466 (6th Cir. 1956), *cert. denied*, 352 U.S. 892 (1956) ("Nor is it sufficient [to disqualify a judge] that the alleged bias or prejudice arises out of the judge's background and associations"); Andrews, Mosburg, Davis, Elam & Bixler, Inc. v. General Insurance Co. of America, 418 F. Supp. 304, 307 (W.D. Okla. 1976) (disqualification not warranted on basis of "an impersonal prejudice which goes to the judge's background and associations or experiences"). The court that decided Duplan Corp. v. Derking Milliken, Inc., 400 F. Supp. 497 (D. S.C. 1975), put the matter nicely:

> Bias and partiality . . . cannot be defined as the total absence of preconceptions; instead, it must be recognized that all individuals, including trial judges, have preconceptions and prejudices:
>
> > Interests, points of view, preferences, are the essence of living. Only death yields complete dispassionateness, for such dispassionateness signifies utter indifference. . . . An "open mind," in the sense of a mind containing no preconceptions whatever, would be a mind incapable of learning anything.

Id. at 511, quoting *In re* J. P. Linahan, 138 F.2d 650, 651–652 (2d Cir. 1983).

129. 510 U.S. at 550.

130. United States v. Kimball, 73 F.3d 269, 273 (10th Cir. 1995).

131. Sato v. Plunkett, 154 F.R.D. 189, 191 (N.D. Ill 1994).

132. See, e.g., *In re* Chevron U.S.A., Inc., 121 F.3d 163 (5th Cir. 1997); Phillips v. Joint Legislative Committee on Performance and Expenditure Review of the State of Miss., 637 F.2d 1014, 1019–1021 (5th Cir. 1981), *cert. denied,* 456 U.S. 690 (1982); Blank v. Sullivan & Cromwell, 418 F. Supp. 1, 4–5 (S.D.N.Y. 1975). There appears to be one case in which the motion to recuse was denied. See Barkan v. United States, 362 F.2d 158 (7th Cir.), *cert. denied,* 385 U.S. 882 (1966) (judge correctly refused to recuse himself where there was no showing of bias or prejudice save a mere statement by petitioner that judge was anti-Semitic).

133. In *In re* Chevron U.S.A., Inc., 121 F.3d 163 (5th Cir. 1997), the appellate court addressed a trial court denial of a motion to disqualify, the motion being based on various comments of a racial (and arguably racist) nature. Ultimately, the appellate court upheld the denial of the motion, and it refused to issue an order removing the lower court judge from the case, reasoning that the trial had proceeded so far that it was too late to start over. In addressing the judge's comments that gave rise to the motion to disqualify, the court offered the following observations as to the judge's conduct and as to the matter of judicial bias generally:

> [W]e must conclude that a reasonable person could believe that some of the judge's rulings might be impacted by beliefs or feelings, conscious or unconscious, underlying the quoted [racially tinged] statements. Despite the assurance of counsel present when the statements were made that they were made either in jest or purposely were outrageous or sarcastic and used by the judge to emphasize his point in explaining his position, and that no harm was intended, we must consider more. Regardless of intent, it is totally unacceptable for a federal judge—irrespective of the judge's color—to make racially insensitive statements or even casual comments of same during the course of judicial proceedings. Such are not to be tolerated in any litigation and most decidedly are verboten in litigation in which racial or ethnic considerations are relevant to an issue before the court. When they occur, the risk of creating a public perception that the judge has a bias or prejudice which might affect the outcome crosses the proscribed threshold. This is especially true in a racially charged case such as the instant one.

Id. at 166–167.

134. Shaman, Lubet, and Alfini, *Judicial Conduct and Ethics,* note 108 supra, at 105.

135. Ibid. See Gonzalez v. Commission on Judicial Performance, 33 Cal.3d 359, 188 Cal. Rptr. 880, 657 P.2d 372 (Cal. 1983), *app. dismissed,* 464 U.S. 1033 (1984) (racial and ethnic slurs); *In re* Stevens, 31 Cal.3d 403, 183 Cal. Rptr. 48, 645 P.2d 99 (Cal. 1982) (censure of judge for engaging in conduct that was deemed prejudicial to the administration of justice and that was deemed to bring the judicial office into disrepute, where judge repeatedly and persistently used racial and ethnic epithets and made comments embodying racial stereotypes to lawyers and court personnel).

136. See David N. Atkinson, *Leaving the Bench* (1999).

137. See, e.g., Nixon v. United States, 506 U.S. 224 (1993) (upholding impeachment, followed by conviction in the Senate, of a federal district court judge who had made false

statements before a federal grand jury that was investigating reports that he had accepted a bribe).

138. See Posner, *Aging and Old Age* 195 (1995).

139. 347 U.S. 483 (1954).

140. Granted, the *Brown* decision was so incendiary for most white Southerners that the ages of the Justices no doubt had no positive effect in quieting the Court's critics.

141. See chapter 5.

142. See Darrell Steffensmeier and Mark Motivans, *Older Men and Older Women in the Arms of Criminal Law: Offending Patterns and Sentencing Outcomes,* 55B of Gerontology: Social Sciences S141, at S151 (2000).

On the one hand, in view of the emphasis on equality before the law in our justice system, it is reasonable to expect that judges will sentence strictly on the basis of what defendants have allegedly done, not on who they are or how old they are. Older offenders should receive sentences as severe (or lenient) as younger offenders convicted of identical offenses and with similar prior records. On the other hand, it is arguable that age-based differences in crime propensity, blameworthiness, and even factors such as the "costs" to the justice/correctional system of jailing older offenders are legitimate considerations in judges' sentencing decisions. If so, then the overall pattern of less severe punishing of women and older offenders may still be viewed as warranted. Whatever is advocated, these two positions represent conflicting views of fairness and constitute value judgments not readily resolved by empirical inquiry.

143. See chapter 5.

144. See generally Jack B. Weinstein, *Limits on Judges Learning, Speaking, and Acting—Part I—Tentative First Thoughts: How May Judges Learn?* 36 Ariz. L. Rev. 539, at 543–56 (1994).

Chapter 8. Juries

The epigraphs are from the following sources: Thomas Jefferson, Letter to Thomas Paine (1789), in Julian Boyd, ed., 15 *The Papers of Thomas Jefferson* 269 (1950–); Deirdre McCloskey, *Crossing: A Memoir* 16 (1999); William O. Douglas, *We, The Judges* 389 (1956).

1. "Most observers of legal culture recognize that most potential grievances never become lawsuits and that more than 90–95 percent of lawsuits never reach the jury." Robert McCoun, *Inside the Black Box: What Empirical Research Tells Us About Decisionmaking by Civil Juries,* in *Verdict: Assessing the Civil Jury System* 127, at 139 (Robert E. Litan, ed. 1983). In 1995 an article in the *American Bar Association Journal* summarized the findings of a report, entitled *Civil Jury Cases and Verdicts in Large Counties,* that was produced by the U.S. Department of Justice's Bureau of Justice Statistics and the National Center for State Courts. In the report, which was based on a survey of most of the state court dockets in the country's 75 most populous counties as of 1992, it was reported that 762,000 cases had been disposed of by settlement, trial, or otherwise in 1992, but that only 2 percent of these, i.e., about 15,000, were decided by juries. Richard C. Reuben, *Plaintiffs Rarely Win Punitives, Study Says,* 81 ABA J. 26 (Oct. 1995).

More recently, a significant decline was reported in the number of jury trials in the federal courts, notwithstanding a very significant increase in the number of cases filed. The percentage of cases resolved by federal juries dropped from 4.3 percent in 1970 to 1.5 percent in 2001, even as the number of civil and criminal case filings rose from 127,280 in 1970 to 313,615 in 2001. It was further reported that the percentage of civil cases going to either bench or jury trial dropped in 16 of 22 reporting states. Hope Viner Sanborn, *The Vanishing Trial,* 88 ABA J. 25, at 27 (2002). The decline in jury trial percentages likely is due not to disinterest on the part of the litigants, but rather to the surge in case filings, with these increased numbers resulting in pressure both on judges and litigants to dispose of cases expeditiously. This pressure militates against trials, given that trials take more time on average than cases that, with or without judicial encouragement, are settled or that are resolved by judicial rulings on motions to dismiss and motions for summary judgment.

2. See note 1 supra. Then, too, settlement negotiations occur "in the shadow of the jury," inasmuch as litigants attempt to anticipate how a jury would deal with their dispute were it to go forward. Marc Galanter, *Jury Shadows: Reflections on the Civil Jury and the "Litigation Explosion,"* in Marc Galanter, John Guinther, and Morris Arnold, *The American Civil Jury: Final Report of the 1986 Chief Justice Earl Warren Conference on Advocacy in the United States* 15, at 17 (1987).

3. A recent study produced data supporting the conclusion that there is a negative correlation between advancing age and confidence in the court system (of which the jury is, of course, a part). According to the researchers, "[T]he older the court user, the lower the level of confidence in courts." Sara C. Benesh and Susan E. Howell, *Confidence in the Courts: A Comparison of Users and Non-Users,* 19 Behavioral Sciences & the Law 199, 211 (2001). The authors, who conducted their study in Louisiana, suggested the following by way of possible explanations for this finding:

[O]ne explanation might be that users who are older have had more interactions with the Louisiana courts. If that is the case, we have some evidence that the number of experiences one has may have some cumulative negative effect on confidence. Another explanation may be that a court experience is simply more traumatic for an older person, thus producing a negative reaction.

Ibid.

4. Perhaps the most famous fictional depiction of a jury in action is Reginald Rose's 1955 play, *Twelve Angry Men.* In this drama the testimony of an elderly witness is a central focus of the jurors' deliberations, but neither his age nor stereotypes associated with age are the bases for the jurors' questioning of his testimony.

5. Joanne Doroshow, *The Case for the Civil Jury* 1 (1992). In a February 2000 survey conducted by the *Dallas Morning News* and the *Southern Methodist Law Review,* 594 U.S. district court judges were queried regarding the jury system. Asked whether they had ever seen a jury use its verdict to send a broader political or social message, 40.4 percent responded affirmatively and 59.4 percent responded in the negative. When asked, "Which most closely characterizes the proper role of a jury?" the judges responded as follows: fact finders—23.8 percent; truth seekers—46.1 percent; conscience of the community—15.5 percent; arbiters of justice—11.6 percent. Mark Curriden, *Power of 12,* 87 ABA J. 36, at 41 (2001).

6. For a comprehensive review of a number of issues involving the American civil jury system, see Litan, ed., *Verdict: Assessing the Civil Jury System,* note 1 supra.

7. See chapter 5.

8. Joseph M. Fitzgerald, *Younger and Older Jurors: The Influence of Environmental Supports on Memory Performance and Decision Making in Complex Trials*, 55B Journals of Gerontology: Psychological Sciences P323 (2000).

9. "Although note taking is more prevalent than it has ever been, note taking is still not permitted in all courtrooms, even though the decision whether to permit it is usually left to the trial judge's discretion." Nancy S. Marder, *The Technological Juror*, Judges J. 34, at 35 (Fall 2001).

10. It has been explained:

[T]he judge in both versions began with general instructions about the role of the judge and jurors. In the preinstruction condition, the judge then delivered several minutes of liability instructions before the opening arguments and liability evidence were heard. In the standard version, the same liability instructions followed the evidence. After the liability portion of the trial was completed, the compensation phase was presented. Again, in the preinstructed version the judge's instructions preceded the evidence and in the standard condition the instructions were presented after the evidence.

Fitzgerald, *Younger and Older Jurors*, note 8 supra.

11. Id. at P329.

12. Ibid.

13. Ibid.

14. A *lure* is a statement that is partially true and partially false.

15. Fitzgerald, *Younger and Older Jurors*, note 8 supra, at P330. "Similar but nonsignificant patterns were noted for the defense and plaintiff facts." Ibid.

16. Ibid.

17. Ibid.

18. Amy Singer, *Focusing on Jury Focus Groups*, 19 Trial Diplomacy J. 321, at 322 (Nov./Dec. 1996); accord Shari Seidman Diamond, Michael J. Saks, and Stephen Landsman, *Juror Judgments About Liability and Damages: Sources of Variability and Ways to Increase Consistency*, 48 DePaul L. Rev. 301, at 306–307 (1998).

19. Rita Simon, *The Jury: Its Role in American Society* 40–41 (1980).

20. Diamond, Saks, and Landsman, *Juror Judgments About Liability and Damages*, note 18 supra, at 307–308; see also Robert J. McCoun, *Getting Inside the Black Box: Toward a Better Understanding of Civil Jury Behavior* 18 (1987).

21. Michael J. Saks, *What Do Jury Experiments Tell Us About How Juries (Should) Make Decisions?*, 6 Southern California Interdisciplinary L. J. 1, at 10 (1997).

22. Id. at 10–11.

23. Phoebe C. Ellsworth, *Some steps between attitudes and verdicts*, in *Inside the Juror* 42, at 61 (Reid Hastie, ed. 1993). Ellsworth's focus on the fact that the jury rarely is unanimous when the first vote is taken is derived from the data reported in a seminal jury study by Harry Kalven and Hans Zeisel: *The American Jury* (1966). (Empirical studies also verify that the final verdict typically mirrors the position initially taken by a majority of the jurors. *The American Jury*, at 488; Hans Zeisel and Shari Seidman Diamond, *The Effect of Peremptory Challenges on Jury and Verdict: An Experiment in a Federal District Court*, 30 Stanford L. Rev. 491, at 504 (1978).) As Ellsworth points out, the initial disagreement cannot be attributed to the jury members hearing different evidence: the evidence pre-

sented is the same for all of them. Accordingly, it follows that "[t]he differences in juror reaction must stem from pre-existing differences among the jurors that affect juror responses to the evidence." Shari Seidman Diamond, *Scientific jury selection: what social scientists know and do not know,* 73 Judicature 178, at 178 (Dec./Jan. 1990).

24. See generally Walter F. Abbott, Flora Hall, and Elizabeth Linville, *Jury Research: A Review and Bibliography* (1993); Paul Lermack, *Materials on Juries and Jury Research* (1977); see also Valerie P. Hans and Neil Vidmar, *The American Jury at Twenty-Five Years,* 16 Law & Social Inquiry 323 (Spring 1991).

25. Two leading investigators described four models that have been devised to explain and analyze jury decision making:

> *Information integration* models . . . describe the juror's decision process as a series of independent evaluations of evidence items on a single dimension of culpability, culminating in a calculation in which all of the item values are weighted and summed to determine a final judgment of probability of guilt. *Bayesian probability* models . . . describe the decision process as a sequence of multiplicative products of the prior opinion and diagnosticity of each evidence item. Most applications of the Bayesian model treat the evidence items as independent sources of information. . . . *Poisson process* models . . . describe the decision as a constant accumulation of the weight of evidence until a critical stochastic event occurs that fixes the weight of a final value. The final value is compared to a decision criterion and a decision is made to convict or acquit. *Sequential weighting* models . . . describe the process as a series of opinion revision, where each revision is the weighted average of the previous judgment and the value of the current evidence item.

Nancy Pennington and Reid Hastie, *Explanation-based decision making: Effects of memory structure on judgment,* in *Research on Judgment and Decision Making* 454, at 457–58 (William M. Goldstein and Robin M. Hogarth, ed. 1997) (citations omitted).

26. See Robert G. Boatright, *Generational and Age-Based Differences in Attitudes Towards Jury Service,* 19 Behavioral Sciences and the Law 285, at 303 (2001):

> Age is a demographic variable that is often placed into empirical studies of human behavior of all sorts, not least of which is jury participation. Careful theoretical considerations of the impact of generational differences on any decisionmaking practice, however, are somewhat more rare. This is particularly so in the case of jury service. Observations of biases in the jury pool toward the elderly are frequent in anecdotes about the jury system, but empirical studies of this phenomenon are rare, and considerations of the effect of this bias are even more rare. Future research should address generational differences in jury selection, in jury deliberations, and in verdicts.

27. Donald E. Vinson, *Jury Trials: The Psychology of Winning Strategy* 88 (1986).

28. 29 U.S.C. §§ 621–634.

29. See Howard Eglit, *The Age Discrimination in Employment Act at Thirty: Where It's Been, Where It Is Today, Where It's Going,* 31 U. of Richmond L. Rev. 579, at 599–606 (1997).

30. See id. at 650–657.

31. Vinson, *Jury Trials,* note 27 supra, at 58–59. In another nonemployment context, United States *ex rel.* Hawthorne v. Cowan, 224 F. Supp.2d 1178 (N.D. Ill. 2002), a man convicted of criminal sexual assault on an 81-year-old woman argued, in a postconviction habeas corpus action, that he had been wrongly convicted in state court by virtue of two

of the jurors being biased in favor of the victim on account of her age. The federal court judge who ruled on the habeas corpus petition rejected the contention, concluding that there was no evidence to support it. Thus, the judge did not address the age claim per se.

32. Eric Oliver, *Jury See, Jury Decide: Courtroom Behavior and Juror Judgments,* 19 Trial Diplomacy J. 299, at 301–302 (Nov./Dec. 1996).

33. See, e.g., Michael G. Efran, *The Effect of Physical Appearance on the Judgment of Guilt, Interpersonal Attraction, and Severity of Recommended Punishment In a Simulated Jury Task,* 8 J. of Research in Personality 45 (1974); Ronald M. Friend and Michael Vinson, *Leaning Over Backwards: Jurors' Response to Defendants' Attractiveness,* 24 J. of Communication 124 (Summer 1974); Cookie Stephan and Judy C. Tully, *The Influence of Physical Attractiveness of a Plaintiff on the Decisions of Simulated Jurors,* 101 J. of Social Psychology 149 (1977); Harold Sigall and Nancy Ostrove, *Beautiful But Dangerous: Effects of Offender Attractiveness and Nature of the Crime on Juridic Judgment,* 31 J. of Personality and Social Psychology 410 (1975).

34. See David E. Reynolds and Mark S. Sanders, *Effect of Defendant Attractiveness, Age, and Injury on Severity of Sentence Given by Simulated Jurors,* 96 J. of Social Psychology 149 (1975).

35. See chapter 2.

36. See note 33 supra; see also note 64 and accompanying text infra.

37. See Benjamin I. Page and Robert Y. Shapiro, *The Rational Public* 302–305 (1992). These authors conclude that "[i]n general, . . . there is little evidence of basically differing patterns of opinion *trends* among different age groups, even when one contrasts the youngest (eighteen to twenty-nine) group with the oldest (over sixty-five) group." Id. at 304; accord Erdman B. Palmore, *Ageism: Negative and Positive* 68–70 (1990).

38. See Elizabeth A. Foley, *The Changing Face of Juries: Understanding Generation X,* 14 Chicago Bar Association Record 28 (Nov. 2000).

39. 22 Cal. 3d 258, 148 Cal. Rptr. 890, 583 P.2d 748, 755 (1978).

40. Mitchell S. Zuklie, *Rethinking the Fair Cross-Section Requirement,* 84 Cal. L. Rev. 101, at 137 (1996) (footnotes omitted).

41. Jon M. Van Dyke, *Jury Selection Procedures* 37(1977).

42. Id. at 38 (footnote omitted). On a slightly different note, there are data to the effect that authoritarian tendencies rise with age. See, e.g., George Eaton Simpson and J. Milton Yinger, *Racial and Cultural Minorities* 79 (1985). For discussion of the so-called authoritarian personality, see chapter 4.

43. Peggy S. Sullivan, Roger G. Dunham, and Geoffrey P. Alpert, *Attitude Structures of Different Ethnic and Age Groups Concerning Police,* 78 J. of Crim. Law & Criminology 177, at 191 (1987); see also Andrew D. Leipold, *Constitutionalizing Jury Selection in Criminal Cases: A Critical Examination,* 86 Georgetown L. J. 945, at 969 (1998): "Scholarly research and common sense (categories that occasionally overlap) suggest that twenty-one-year-olds see the world quite differently than do their elders."

44. Pew Research Center for the People and the Press, news release, *Young, Old Differ on Using Surplus to Fix Social Security,* p. 1 (Jan. 28, 1998). Gay rights is another issue that will rarely manifest itself in a litigated courtroom context. Even so, it is useful to note that here too one sees significant differences in attitudes that are age correlated, with particularly strong contrasts between the views of the youngest interviewees and the oldest. In a *New York Times*-CBS poll of 1,057 adults, conducted between December 10 and 13,

2003, the following responses were elicited as to the question of whether homosexual relations should be legal:

Respondents' Age Ranges	Yes	No
18–29	58%	39%
30–44	43%	48%
45–64	38%	52%
65 and older	24%	61%

As to the question of whether the respondent favored a law allowing homosexuals to marry, the responses—showing again a strong contrast between the youngest group of interviewees and the oldest—were as follows:

Respondents' Age Ranges	Yes	No
18–29	56%	40%
30–44	34%	62%
45–64	30%	65%
65 and older	14%	79%

Katherine Q. Seelye and Janet Elder, "Strong Support is Found for Ban on Gay Marriage," *New York Times* (Dec. 21, 2003), pp. 1, 26, at 26.

45. 42 U.S.C. § 12101 *et seq.*

46. Dan R. Gallipeau, *Juror Perceptions and the ADA,* 5 Employment Rights and Responsibilities Newsletter 2 (Fall 2000).

47. Ibid.

48. Ibid. The respondents also were asked their view as to whether "[c]ompanies will do anything they can to not pay for special equipment that an employee with a disability needs to do the job." The responses were as follows:

Over 45
Disagree   30%
Neutral   24%
Agree   46%
Under 45
Disagree   62%
Neutral   30%
Agree   8%

49. Carol J. Mills and Wayne E. Bohannon, *Juror characteristics: to what extent are they related to jury verdicts?,* 64 Judicature 22, at 30 (June–July 1980).

50. Ibid.

51. Simon, *The Jury,* note 19 supra, at 33.

52. Ibid.

53. Robert A. Wenke, *The Art of Selecting a Jury* 65 (1979). The complete rankings were as follows (with the first four being described by the subjects as "extremely important," and the next five as "important"):

1. Personal characteristics. (For example, has the individual suffered an injury, or does he have an infirmity; is he intelligent, educated, strong-minded, etc., or is he the opposite of these?)

2. Occupation.
3. Personality.
4. Race.
5. Physical signs.
6. Nationality.
7. Body language.
8. Sex.
9. Age.
10. Marital status.

Id. at 64–65. Judge Wenke also set forth his own generalizations regarding the differences between young and elderly jurors. Id. at 84–85; see also Walter E. Jordan, *Jury Selection* 302–303 (1989).

54. Seymour Wishman, *Anatomy of a Jury* 30, 272 n. 27 (1986); see also Mark Hansen, *Reaching Out to Jurors*, 88 ABA J. 33, at 35 (Feb. 2002) (Miami criminal defense attorney quoted as stating that "'Age is one thing you have to take into consideration,' . . . but that 'you have to look at the totality of circumstances.'")

55. Hansen, *Reaching Out to Jurors*, note 54 supra, at 35.

56. Ibid.

57. See id. at 34–35.

58. See, e.g., Walter F. Abbott, *Analytic Juror Rater* 50 (1987); Cathy E. Bennett and Robert Hirshhorn, *Bennett's Guide to Jury Selection and Trial Dynamics in Civil and Criminal Litigation* 270 (1993); Farrald G. Belote, *Jury Research: Spotting Jurors Who Can Hurt,* 12 American Bar Association J. of Litigation 17, at 18 (1986); Hansen, *Reaching Out to Jurors,* note 54 supra, at 35 (quoting a personal injury attorney who discounted the significance of the age factor).

59. Nancy S. Marder, *Justice and Multiculturalism,* 75 Southern California L. Rev. 659, at 692 (2002).

60. Here, in fact, is how one judge ruefully described her (undesired) exalted status and jurors' transference reactions to her (without, in this instance, her age being a factor addressed by the judge):

Judges are, almost universally, held in high esteem and accorded special status. The psychological exaltation of my role as judge is cleverly reflected in my physical exaltation. My bench (my throne) is several feet higher than the seats of the litigants, jurors, and spectators. It is placed at the head of the room, dead center. My unique status is enhanced by the black robe and the appellation, "Your Honor." Within the confines of my courtroom, surrounded by all of the accoutrements of power, I am the supreme and ultimate voice. My regal trappings and my control of the courtroom may be perceived as evidence that I am all knowing and above reproach. It should come as no surprise, however, that, in fact, my knowledge is severely limited, and no one with whom I am acquainted has ever accused me of being above reproach. I am left to conclude, therefore, that the jurors' responses to me have only little to do with who I am, and a lot to do with who they are. Such is the wonderful power of transference.

Transference, which describes the tendency of people to endow the present with significant emotional residues of the past, is a central notion in psychodynamic theory. Its effects are most clearly visible in psycho-therapy. . . . Wherever people participate in significant events, transference occurs. When jurors encounter the

drama of the courtroom, they predictably undergo two experiences. First, they bring emotions of the past into the present and, therefore, construe the judge in terms colored by their histories. Second, they attend very carefully to the judge, ascribing to her most casual behaviors meanings that had never been intended.
LaDoris H. Corsell and Florence O. Keller, *Pay No Attention to the Woman Behind the Bench: Musings of a Trial Court Judge,* 68 Indiana L. J. 1199, at 1204–1205 (1993).

61. Boatright, *Generational and Age-Based Differences in Attitudes Towards Jury Service,* note 26 supra, at 293.

62. Just think of all the lawyer jokes, most of them reflecting unflattering views of attorneys.

63. Boatright, *Generational and Age-Based Differences in Attitudes Towards Jury Service,* note 26 supra, at 293.

64. Ann T. Greeley, Karen Kaplowitz, and Vicki Stone, *What's In A Face?* Corporate Counsel Magazine 64, at 68–69 (October 1998). The significance of the attorney's gender has been studied through the use of mock juries on several occasions. See Barbara A. Curran, *American Lawyers in the 1980s: A Profession in Transition,* 20 Law & Society Rev. 19 (1986); Shari Hodgson and Bert Pryor, *Sex Discrimination in the Courtroom: Attorney's Gender and Credibility,* 55 Psychol. Rep. 483, at 483 (1984) (as opposed to male college students, female college students rated male attorneys higher than female attorneys on 6 of 12 credibility scales); Mary V. McGuire and Gordon Bermant, *Individual and Group Decisions in Response to a Mock Trial: A Methodological Note,* 7 J. of Applied Social Psychology 220, at 224 (1974) (mock jurors more supportive of male defense attorneys than females).

65. The Constitution has been interpreted to condemn practices that discriminate against individuals who are identifiable in terms of race or national origin in the creation of jury pools and jury venires. See Castaneda v. Partida, 430 U.S. 482 (1977). Further, the voir dire process, discussed below in the text, can be used to try to identify the racist bigot and thence remove him for cause. See Ham v. South Carolina, 409 U.S. 524 (1973). And the Constitution further condemns the use of peremptory challenges to fashion race-defined juries. Batson v. Kentucky, 476 U.S. 79 (1986).

66. There are going to be some times when the age factor is directly relevant to the jury's decision making by virtue of the nature of the cause of action. For example, if an individual is seeking relief under the Age Discrimination in Employment Act of 1967, as amended, 29 U.S.C. §§ 621–634 (ADEA), which protects individuals over age 39 from discrimination in workplaces in which 20 or more employees are employed for 20 or more weeks of the current or preceding calendar year, the success or failure of a claim of discrimination made by a terminated plaintiff will turn, sometimes dispositively, on proof as to the age of her replacement. If the defendant shows that the plaintiff was replaced by someone who was older, or of the same age, or even just a couple of years younger than the plaintiff, the claimant's case will be fatally undercut. See, e.g., Munoz v. St. Mary-Corwin Hospital, 221 F.3d 1160 (2d Cir. 2000); Williams v. Raytheon Co., 220 F.3d 16 (1st Cir. 2000). On the other hand, if the plaintiff shows that she was replaced by someone 15 years younger, that will be important evidence in support of her discrimination claim. See generally Howard Eglit, 1 *Age Discrimination* § 7.18 (2d ed. 1994 and annual supps.).

67. See Stephanie Nickerson, Clara Mayo, and Althea Smith, *Racism in the Courtroom,* in *Prejudice, Discrimination, and Racism* 259, at 264 (John F. Dovidio and Samuel L. Gaertner, eds. 1986).

68. In United States *ex rel*. Hawthorne v. Cowan, 228 F. Supp.2d 1178 (N.D. Ill 2002), the defendant pursued a postconviction habeas corpus petition following his conviction in state court for criminal sexual assault on an 81-year-old woman. He contended that two of the state court jurors had been biased in favor of the victim because of her age. The federal judge adjudicating the petition noted that in conducting voir dire the state court judge, twice had asked each of the allegedly biased jurors if he or she would be unable to be impartial. Both affirmed their impartiality. Based on this voir dire, the federal court judge rejected the petitioner's claim.

69. Typically, each litigant only will have a limited number of peremptory challenges to exercise, so these challenges must be utilized with some caution. The courts have upheld peremptory challenges based on the age of the prospective juror. See notes 81 and 89, and accompanying text infra.

70. Nickerson, Mayo, and Smith, *Racism in the Courtroom*, note 67 supra, at 265.

71. Id. at 266.

72. Ibid.

73. See chapter 3.

74. See, e.g., Local Rule 16.1, U.S. District Court for the Northern District of Illinois (1999); see also the Final Pretrial Order Form to which Local Rule 16.1 makes reference. This form provides, *inter alia,* that the parties must submit, as an appendix to the completed form, "an agreed statement or statements by each party of the contested issues of fact and law and a statement or statements of contested issues of fact or law not agreed to." Form LR16.1.1, Final Pretrial Order Form, § 2(b) (1999).

75. John Guinther, *The Jury in America* 58 (1988).

76. As to various methods for compiling such lists, see *Developments in the Law: The Civil Jury,* 110 Harv. L. Rev. 1408, at 1452–1454 (1997).

77. See generally Van Dyke, *Jury Selection Procedures,* note 41 supra, at 35–39; Donald H. Ziegler, *Young Adults as a Cognizable Group in Jury Selection,* 76 Mich. L. Rev. 1045 (1978). A study of federal and state courts in eight cities, published in 1991, revealed this maldistribution:

City	18–19	20–29	30–39	40–49	50–59	60–69	70+
Bismarck, North Dakota							
State court	1%	10%	31%	22%	18%	12%	6%
Federal court	1%	11%	27%	19%	21%	17%	4%
Boston, Massachusetts							
State court	1%	19%	28%	23%	17%	11%	1%
Federal court	1%	20%	20%	25%	20%	12%	1%
Dallas, Texas							
State court	—	15%	28%	26%	23%	8%	—
Federal court	—	15%	25%	26%	16%	16%	1%
Denver, Colorado							
State court	1%	14%	26%	21%	18%	14%	6%
Federal court	—	12%	26%	27%	21%	10%	4%
Montgomery, Alabama							
State court	2%	13%	16%	28%	18%	15%	8%
Federal court	2%	16%	26%	21%	17%	16%	2%
Phoenix, Arizona							
State court	2%	12%	23%	22%	18%	16%	6%

Federal court	—	9%	18%	23%	25%	23%	2%
Seattle, Washington							
State court	—	13%	25%	25%	18%	14%	5%
Federal court	1%	9%	23%	30%	20%	12%	3%
Washington, D.C.							
Local court	1%	14%	24%	23%	17%	15%	7%
Federal court	—	16%	22%	28%	15%	13%	5%

Janet T. Munsterman, *The Relationship of Juror Fees and Terms of Service to Jury System Performance* D-10 (1991). (Different geographical areas are used for the selection of federal and state juries. For example, the Denver federal court draws prospective jurors from the whole state, and so only 15 percent come from Denver County, whereas the local Denver state court draws from a much smaller area.)

As the foregoing data show, while the percentage of jurors between 18 and 39 in a given jurisdiction generally exceeded the percentage of those 50 and up, older jurors still were disproportionately overrepresented, given their percentage of the total jury-eligible population.

In a study made of Dallas courts, which was later discussed in a law journal article, two newspaper reporters found that while 37 percent of Dallas County residents were 18 to 34 years of age, only 8 percent of those called to report as prospective jurors were in that age group. Ted M. Eades, *Revisiting the Jury System in Texas: A Study of the Jury Pool in Dallas County,* 54 Southern Methodist Univ. L. Rev. 1813, at 1815 (2001).

78. "The minimum age for jury service . . . varies by state; four states have a minimum age other than 18. In Missouri and Mississippi, citizens must be 21, and in Nebraska and Alabama they must be 19." Boatright, *Generational and Age-Based Differences in Attitudes Towards Jury Service,* note 26 supra, at 290 n. 4. For a dated listing of state laws setting age minima, see Van Dyke, *Jury Selection Procedures,* note 41 supra, at app A. In Carter v. Jury Commission, 396 U.S. 320, 333 n. 9 (1970), the Court noted, with no expression of disapproval, several such statutes, including two that set age 25 as the minimum.

79. Most common have been attacks on statutes that exclude individuals ages 18 to 20. The courts regularly have ruled that such persons have no constitutional right to serve on juries. See, e.g., United States v. Test, 550 F.2d 577 (10th Cir. 1976); United States v. Owen, 492 F.2d 1100 (5th Cir.), *cert. denied,* 419 U.S. 965 (1974); United States v. Osborne, 482 F.2d 1354 (8th Cir. 1973); United States v. Ross, 468 F.2d 1213 (9th Cir. 1972), *cert. denied,* 410 U.S. 989 (1973); United States v. Gast, 457 F.2d 141 (7th Cir.), *cert. denied,* 406 U.S. 969 (1972).

80. See Chestnut v. Criminal Court, 442 F.2d 611, 614 n. 3 (2d Cir.), *cert. denied,* 404 U.S. 856 (1971) (exclusion of persons under age 35 from grand juries).

81. Students often are excused. See People v. Attica Bros., 79 Misc.2d 492, 495–496, 359 N.Y.S.2d 699, 704 (Sup. Ct. 1974); People v. Marr, 67 Misc.2d 113, 115, 324 N.Y.S.2d 608 (Just. Ct. 1971). The same is true for parents caring for young children. See, e.g., United States v. Test, 550 F.2d 577 (10th Cir. 1976); United States v. Eskew, 460 F.2d 1028, 1029 (9th Cir. 1972); United States v. Sciences Corp., 511 F. Supp. 1125 (E.D. Va. 1981).

82. See Van Dyke, *Jury Selection Procedures,* note 41 supra, at 36; Ziegler, *Young Adults as a Cognizable Group in Jury Selection,* note 77 supra, at 1046 n. 8; Cynthia A. Williams, Note, *Jury Source Representativeness and the Use of Voter Registration Lists,* 65

N.Y.U. L. Rev. 590 (1990). Dramatic illustration of this phenomenon was provided by a news story coming out of Decatur, Georgia, that was printed in 1998 in the *Chicago Tribune:*

Any young man is going to have a hard time finding a jury of his peers in this Atlanta suburb, which is so desperate for 18- to 24-year-old male jurors that court officials have placed newspaper ads begging for volunteers.

It hasn't helped much. Not one volunteer has called since the ads ran last month, and defendants still face juries made up primarily of women and older men. . . .

The county, the state's second most populous, uses voter registration lists to randomly summon about 7,000 jurors a month. But males in that age group make up only 3 percent of registered voters in DeKalb County.

Associated Press, "In these courts, jurors Are wanted," *Chicago Tribune,* Oct. 18, 1998, Sec. 1, p. 12.

83. See Hamling v. United States, 418 U.S. 87 (1974).

84. See, e.g., United States v. Maxwell, 160 F.3d 1071, 1075 (6th Cir. 1998).

85. See Munsterman, *The Relationship of Juror Fees and Terms of Service to Jury System Performance,* note 77 supra, at D-10.

86. Ibid.; see also Leigh R. Bienen, *Helping Jurors Out: Post-Verdict Debriefing for Jurors in Emotionally Disturbing Trials,* 68 Ind. L. J. 1333, at 1343 (1993) (emphasis added):

In state capital trials in the jurisdiction with which I am most familiar, New Jersey, the people who serve on juries are people who do not work in offices or people whose employers are required to pay them while on jury duty. Consequently, certain groups are overrepresented: *the retired,* employees of state or federal government, employees of a few large organizations and corporations, the self-employed, people in the arts, *older women,* and people with marginal jobs.

See also Boatright, *Generational and Age-Based Differences in Attitudes Towards Jury Service,* note 26 supra, at 290.

87. In the national study of 16 jurisdictions discussed in the text, it was found that the percentages of jurors 70 and over ranged from 1 percent in the federal courts in Boston and Dallas and the state court in Boston, to 2 percent in the federal courts in Phoenix and Montgomery, Ala., up to 8 percent in the Montgomery state court. See Munsterman, *The Relationship of Juror Fees and Terms of Service to Jury System Performance,* note 77 supra, at D-10.

88. See, e.g., Fla. Stat. Ann. § 40.013(8) (persons 70 years of age and older excused upon request); Official Code of Ga. § 15-12-1 (persons age 70 and older may request removal from jury lists); Mass. Ann. Laws, ch. 234, § 1 (same); Mich. Stat. Ann. §§ 27.3935(4), 27.3936(5), 27A.1307(1) (persons ages 71 and older can choose to be excused); Rev. Stat. of Neb. § 25-1601 (persons age 65 and older may request exemption from service on grand and petit juries); Code of S.C. Ann. § 14-7-840 (same). "Twenty-six states allow jurors to request an excusal on the basis of age; in these states the age at which citizens may be excused ranges from 65 to 75." Boatright, *Generational and Age-Based Differences in Attitudes Towards Jury Service,* note 26 supra, at 290 n. 3.

89. See, e.g., United States District Court, S.D. Cal. Local Rule 83.10 (persons over age 70 may be excused upon their request); United States District Court, S.D. Ill., Appendix 1 (same); United States District Court, D. Kan. Rule 38.1(B)(1) (same).

90. In the 1970s three investigators found a striking absence of jurors older than 70.

Whereas such individuals made up 11.9 percent of the adult population, only 4.6 percent appeared on venire lists. The investigators attributed this to the self-excusal of these individuals when they were called for jury duty. Hayward R. Alker Jr., Carl Hosticka, and Michael Mitchell, *Jury Selection as a Biased Social Process,* 11 Law & Society Rev. 9, 35 (1976). In a more recent study of state and federal courts in eight cities, the data revealed that 40.8 percent of persons between 18 and 39 requested excusal, while 36.5 percent of those ages 50 and over did so. As for jurors actually excused (and these were not necessarily the same persons as those requesting excusal), 44.5 percent were between ages 18 and 39, while 43.4 percent were ages 50 and over. Munsterman, *The Relationship of Juror Fees and Terms of Service to Jury System Performance,* note 77 supra, at 52–53 (1991).

91. See, e.g., Mitchell v. Ward, 150 F. Supp.2d 1194, 1256 (W.D. Okla 1999); Trice v. State, 853 P.2d 203, 208 (Okl. Ct. Crim. App. 1993).

92. See, e.g., Weber v. Strippit, Inc., 186 F.3d 907, 911 (8th Cir. 1999); United States v. Clemons, 941 F.2d 321, 325 (5th Cir. 1991); State v. Sanders, 949 P.2d 1084, 1090–1091 (Kan. Sup. Ct. 1997); cf. State v. Kelly, 885 S.W.2d 730, 735 (Mo. App. 1994) (age-based peremptory challenges upheld, without court clarifying whether those challenged were old or young).

93. See, e.g., Letson v. State, 215 Ala. 229, 110 So. 21 (1926) (over age 65); Mack v. State, 375 So.2d 476 (Ala. App. 1979) (id.); Gardner v. Baker, 40 Ala. App. 374, 113 So.2d 695 (1959) (id.); Reddock v. State, 23 Ala. App. 290, 124 So. 398 (1929) (id.); Burroughs v. State, 33 Ga. 403 (1863); Cohron v. State, 20 Ga. 752 (1856) (over age 60); People v. Scott, 17 Ill. App.3d 1026, 309 N.E.2d 257 (1974); North Chicago Elec. Ry. v. Moosman, 82 Ill. App. 172 (1899) (over age 60); State v. Brooks, 92 Mo. 542, 5 S.W. 257 (1887) (over age 65).

94. The argument was made in King v. Leach, 131 F.2d 8 (5th Cir. 1942), that the appellant had been denied a fair trial in a civil suit because one of the jurors was over 60 years of age and accordingly was unable to perform her duties adequately. In response the court asserted: "Advanced age alone is not ground for disqualification of a juror." Id. at 9; accord Trotter v. State, 237 Ark. 820, 377 S.W.2d 14, *cert. denied,* 379 U.S. 890 (1964); see also State v. Willis, 33 Ohio Misc. 159, 293 N.E.2d 895 (1972). Other courts, speaking to arguments that juries were tainted by the participation of older jurors who by virtue of their age had the option under state law to excuse themselves but did not do so, responded that such individuals were not disqualified if they chose to serve. See Williams v. State, 67 Ala. 183 (1880); Smith v. State, 225 Ga. 328, 168 S.E.2d 587 (1969), *cert. denied,* 396 U.S. 1045 (1970); Thomas v. State, 144 Ga. 298, 87 S.E. 7 (1915); Carter v. Georgia, 75 Ga. 747 (1885); Caswell v. State, 27 Ga. App. 76, 107 S.E. 560 (1921); Staten v. State, 141 Ga. 82, 80 S.E. 850 (1913); Albany Phosphate Co. v. Hugger Bros., 4 Ga. App. 771, 62 S.E. 533 (1908); Davison v. People, 90 Ill. 221 (1878); Davis v. People, 19 Ill. 74 (1857); State v. Clark, 249 La. 914, 192 So.2d 122 (1962); State v. Anderson, 384 S.W.2d 591 (Mo. 1964).

95. U.S. Const., amend. VI. The Sixth Amendment provides in relevant part: "In all criminal prosecutions, the accused shall enjoy the right to a speedy and public trial, by an impartial jury of the state and district wherein the crime shall have been committed." In Duncan v. Louisiana, 391 U.S. 145 (1968), the Court held that the Sixth Amendment's jury trial guarantee applies to the states through the Due Process Clause of the Fourteenth Amendment. U.S. Const., amend. XIV, § 1.

96. Taylor v. Louisiana, 419 U.S. 522, 536 (1975) (Sixth Amendment); cf. Smith v.

Texas, 311 U.S. 128, 130 (1940) (Equal Protection Clause). The fair cross-section principle is reinforced by 28 U.S.C. § 1861, which makes the principle applicable to both federal criminal and civil juries.

97. See Thiel v. Southern Pacific, 328 U.S. 217 (1946).

98. Taylor v. Louisiana, 419 U.S. 522, 530 (1975).

99. The fact that the "ideal" jury may be one that reflects the heterogeneity of the population does not lead to the conclusion that if the jury members as a group indeed were reflective of the age distribution of the adult population, the result in any given case would differ from what it would have been with another, nonrepresentative jury. In other words, there is no empirically established basis for concluding that the mere fact of the inclusion of a 70-year-old on a jury would, in and of itself, cause the jury to arrive at a verdict other than that which it would have rendered absent any 70-year-olds. While one might reason that the 70-year-old, who hypothetically might entertain more sympathetic views as to, let us say, mercy killing, could hold out and prevent a conviction, that is very unlikely. Studies of jury dynamics suggest that one or two dissenting jurors are not likely to hold out against a majority vote and cause a hung jury. Donna J. Meyer, *A New Peremptory Inclusion to Increase Representativeness and Impartiality in Jury Selection,* 45 Case Western Reserve L. Rev. 251, 281 n. 218 (1994), citing Solomon E. Asch, *Effects of Group Pressure Upon the Modification and Distortion of Judgments,* in *Basic Studies in Social Psychology* 393 (Harold Proshansky and Bernard Seidenberg, eds. 1965). On the other hand, the presence of one or two 70-year-olds on the jury arguably might affect the jury's dialogue during deliberations. In this regard, the following observations have been made:

[I]n any group the single hold out, because of peer pressure to conform, hardly ever maintains his or her position at the end when a unanimous vote is required. However, when at least two people hold a minority position, the possibility of eventual unanimity drastically decreases, even in large groups.

Guinther, *The Jury in America,* note 75 supra, at 82.

100. Batson v. Kentucky, 476 U.S. 79, 85 n. 6 (1986) (emphasis added), quoting Taylor v. Louisiana, 419 U.S. 522, 538 (1975).

101. See Holland v. Illinois, 493 U.S. 474, 477 (1990).

102. See Carter v. Jury Commission, 396 U.S. 320 (1970).

103. See Taylor v. Louisiana, 419 U.S. 522, 526 (1975); Peters v. Kiff, 407 U.S. 493 (1972).

104. 439 U.S. 357 (1979).

105. Id. at 364.

106. United States v. Guzman, 337 F. Supp. 140, 143–144 (S.D.N.Y.), *affd. on other grounds,* 468 F.2d 1245 (2d Cir. 1972), *cert. denied,* 410 U.S. 937 (1973).

107. U.S. Const., amend. XIV, § 1.

108. See McGinnis v. M. I. Harris, Inc., 486 F. Supp. 750 (N.D. Tex. 1980); Simmons v. Jones, 317 F. Supp. 397 (S.D. Ga. 1970), *rev'd. on other grounds,* 478 F.2d 321 (5th Cir. 1973), *modified,* 519 F.2d 52 (5th Cir. 1975).

109. As to criminal grand juries, see Castaneda v. Partida, 430 U.S. 482 (1977); Alexander v. Louisiana, 405 U.S. 625, 626 n. 3 (1972); King v. United States, 346 F.2d 123 (1st Cir. 1965).

110. J.E.B. v. Alabama, 511 U.S. 127, 128 (1994).

111. See Castaneda v. Partida, 430 U.S. 482 (1977).

112. See, e.g., United States v. DiTommaso, 405 F.2d 385 (4th Cir. 1968), *cert. denied,*

394 U.S. 934 (1969); United States v. Armsbury, 408 F. Supp. 1130 (D. Or. 1976); Cobbs v. State, 244 Ga. 344, 260 S.E.2d 60 (1979); Commonwealth v. Bastarache, 382 Mass. 86, 100, 414 N.E.2d 984 (1980); People v. Redwine, 50 Mich. App. 593, 213 N.W.2d 841 (1973).

113. In Hamling v. United States, 418 U.S. 87 (1974), the Court assumed—but did not actually decide—that the young are a cognizable group; it went on to rule that systematic exclusion had not been proved. Subsequent lower court case law directly addressing the issue makes clear, however, that the young are not deemed to be a cognizable group, after all. See, e.g., McQueen v. Scroggy, 99 F.3d 1302, 1333 (6th Cir. 1996) ("young people" or "young adults"); United States v. Fletcher, 965 F.2d 781, 782 (9th Cir. 1992) ("young adults"); Davis v. Greer, 675 F.2d 141, 146 (7th Cir.), cert. denied, 459 U.S. 975 (1982) (persons 18–21); United States v. Test, 550 F.2d 577 (10th Cir. 1976) (persons 21–39); United States v. Kirk, 534 F.2d 1262 (8th Cir. 1976), cert. denied, 430 U.S. 906 (1977) (persons 18–20); United States v. Diggs, 522 F.2d 1310 (D.C. Cir. 1975), cert. denied, 429 U.S. 852 (1976) (young people); United States v. Geelan, 509 F.2d 737 (8th Cir. 1974), cert. denied, 421 U.S. 999 (1975) (persons 18–20); United States v. Gooding, 473 F.2d 686 (5th Cir.), cert. denied, 412 U.S. 928 (1973) (persons 18–21.3); United States v. Lewis, 472 F.2d 252 (3d Cir. 1973) (persons 18–20); United States v. Ross, 468 F.2d 1213 (9th Cir. 1972), cert. denied, 410 U.S. 989 (1973) (persons 18–20, 21–24); Chase v. United States, 468 F.2d 141 (7th Cir. 1972) (young adults); United States v. Kuhn, 441 F.2d 179 (5th Cir. 1971) (persons 21–23); King v. United States, 346 F.2d 123 (1st Cir. 1965) (persons under 25 and over 70); United States v. Pleier, 849 F Supp. 1321, 1324 (D. Alaska 1994) (persons 18–30); United States v. Briggs, 366 F. Supp. 1356 (N.D. Fla. 1973) (persons 21–29); Williamson v. State, 562 Ala. App. 617, 296 So.2d 241 (1974) (persons under 36); but see United States v. Butera, 420 F.2d 564 (1st Cir. 1970); United States v. Deardorff, 343 F. Supp. 1033, 1043 (S.D.N.Y. 1971); State v. Holmstrom, 43 Wis.2d 465, 168 N.W.2d 574 (1969).

114. 346 F.2d 123, 124 (1st Cir. 1965).

115. See, e.g., Romano v. State, 847 P.2d 368, 377 (Okl. Ct. Crim. App. 1993); Trice v. State, 853 P.2d 203, 208 (Okl. Ct. Crim App. 1993).

116. United States v. Butera, 420 F.2d 564 (1st Cir. 1970).

117. See generally Howard Eglit, 1 Age Discrimination § 4.07 (1st ed. 1982 and annual supps.).

118. See, e.g., Johnston v. Bowersox, 119 F. Supp.2d 971, 980–981 (E.D. Mo. 2000); Skaggs v. Parker, 27 F. Supp.2d 952, 1002 (W.D. Ky. 1998).

119. See Vikram David Amar, Jury Service as Political Participation Akin to Voting, 80 Cornell L. Rev. 203, at 216–217 (1995). The Twenty-sixth Amendment, U.S. Const., amend. XXVI, sets age 18 for voting for federal officials.

120. See Bill Carter and Jim Rutenberg, "With no Knockouts, NBC's Champ Faces Jabs," New York Times, Sept. 15, 2003, Business Day, pp. 1, 6, at p. 6: "NBC still leads [in viewer audience] in the 18–49 audience that three of the four networks regard as the only rating measurement that counts, because of the advertising premiums that are tied to ratings for that group."

121. Admittedly, this same line of reasoning could be used to challenge the case law that demands that the jury selection process be premised on seeking a fair cross-section of persons in terms of race and gender.

122. See generally Nancy S. Marder, *Juries and Technology: Equipping Jurors for the Twenty-First Century,* 66 Brooklyn L. Rev. 1257, at 1276–1277 (2001).

123. Id. at 1278.

124. See Erica Wood, *Toward a Barrier-Free Courthouse: Equal Access to Justice for Persons with Physical Disabilities,* in American Bar Association Commission on Legal Problems of the Elderly, American Bar Association Commission on the Mentally Disabled, and National Judicial College, *Court-Related Needs of the Elderly and Persons with Disabilities* 69, at 71 (1991).

125. See Marc Charmatz, *Eliminating Communication Barriers in the Courtroom,* in American Bar Association Commission on Legal Problems of the Elderly, American Bar Association Commission on the Mentally Disabled, and National Judicial College, *Court-Related Needs of the Elderly and Persons with Disabilities* 85 (1991).

126. See William E. Adams Jr., *Elders in the Courtroom,* in *Elders, Crime, and the Criminal Justice System* 87, at 96–98 (Max B. Rothman, Burton D. Dunlop, and Pamela Entzel, eds. 2000).

Bibliography

Books, Book Chapters, Monographs, Plays, Speeches, Poetry, and Aphorisms

Abbott, Walter F., *Analytic Juror Rater*. Philadelphia: ALI-ABA Committee on Continuing Professional Education, 1987.

Abbott, Walter F., Flora Hall, and Elizabeth Linville, *Jury Research: A Review and Bibliography*. Philadelphia: ALI-ABA Committee on Continuing Professional Education, 1993.

Achenbaum, W. Andrew, *Old Age in the New Land*. Baltimore: Johns Hopkins University Press, 1978.

Adams, William E., Jr., "Elders in the Courtroom," in *Elders, Crime, and the Criminal Justice System*, edited by Max B. Rothman, Burton D. Dunlop, and Pamela Entzel. New York: Springer, 2000.

Adorno, Theodor W., Else Frenkil-Brunswick, Daniel J. Levinson, and Sanford R. Levinson, *The Authoritarian Personality*. New York: Harper, 1950.

Albert, Steven M., and Maria G. Cattell, *Old Age in Global Perspective*. New York: G. K. Hall, 1994.

Alexander, George J., and Travis H. D. Lewin, *The Aged and the Need for Surrogate Management*. Syracuse, N.Y.: Syracuse University Press, 1972.

Allport, Gordon W., *The Nature of Prejudice*. Reading, Mass.: Addison-Wesley, paperback ed., 1994.

American Association of Retired Persons, *Valuing Older Workers*. Washington, D.C.: n.d.

American Bar Association/Bureau of National Affairs, *Lawyer's Manual on Professional Conduct*. Washington, D.C.: American Bar Assn. and Bureau of National Affairs, 1984–.

American Bar Association Commission on Legal Problems of the Elderly and American Bar Association Commission on the Mentally Disabled, *Court-Related Needs of the Elderly and Persons with Disabilities*. Washington, D.C.: American Bar Assn., 1991.

Amsterdam, Anthony G., and Jerome Bruner, *Minding the Law*. Cambridge: Harvard University Press, 2000.

Arking, Robert, *Biology of Aging*. Englewood Cliffs, N.J.: Prentice-Hall, 1991.

Augarde, Tony, ed., *The Oxford Dictionary of Modern Quotations*. New York: Oxford University Press, 1991.

Asch, Solomon E., "Effects of Group Pressure Upon the Modification and Distortion of Judgments," in *Basic Studies in Social Psychology* 393, edited by Harold Proshansky and Bernard Seidenberg. New York: Holt Rinehart & Winston, 1965.

Atkinson, David N., *Leaving the Bench*. Lawrence: University Press of Kansas, 1999.

Baltes, Paul B., and R. Kliege, "On the Dynamics Between Growth and Decline in the Aging of Intelligence and Memory," in *Neurology: Proceedings of the XIIIth World Congress of Neurology, Hamburg, Sept. 1–6, 1985*, edited by Klaus Poeck. Berlin and Heidelberg: Springer, 1986.

Barrow, Georgia M., *Aging, the Individual, and Society*. St. Paul, Minn.: West, 5th ed., 1992.

Barrow, Georgia M., and Patricia A. Smith, *Aging, Ageism and Society.* St. Paul, Minn.: West, 1979.

Becker, Gary, *The Economics of Discrimination.* Chicago: University of Chicago Press, 2d ed., 1971.

Bennett, Cathy E., and Robert Hirshhorn, *Bennett's Guide to Jury Selection and Trial Dynamics in Civil and Criminal Litigation.* St. Paul, Minn.: West, 1993.

Berkowitz, Monroe, "Functioning Ability and Job Performance as Workers Age," in *The Older Worker* 87, edited by Michael S. Borus, Herbert S. Parnes, Steven H. Sandell, and Bert Seidman. Madison, Wisc.: Industrial Relations Research Assn., 1988.

"The Best Interest Role Versus the Advocate Role in Representing the Elderly Client," panel discussion, in *Exploring Ethical Issues in Meeting the Legal Needs of the Elderly* 17. Washington, D.C.: American Bar Association, 1987.

Binstock, Robert H., "Aging, Politics, and Public Policy," in *Growing Old in America* 325, edited by Beth B. Hess and Elizabeth W. Markson. New Brunswick, N.J.: Transaction, 4th ed., 1991.

Binstock, Robert H., and Stephen G. Post, eds., *Too Old for Health Care?* Baltimore: Johns Hopkins University Press, 1991.

Binstock, Robert H., Stephen G. Post, and Peter J. Whitehouse, eds., *Dementia and Aging.* Baltimore: Johns Hopkins University Press, 1992.

Binstock, Robert H., and Linda K. George, eds., *Handbook of Aging and the Social Sciences.* San Diego: Academic Press, 1990.

Binstock, Robert H., and Ethel Shanas, eds., *Handbook of Aging and the Social Sciences.* New York: Van Nostrand Reinhold, 1976.

Bluestone, Irving, Rhonda J. V. Montgomery, and John D. Owen, eds., *The Aging of the American Work Force.* Detroit: Wayne State University Press, 1990.

Bluh, Bonnie, *The "Old" Speak Out.* New York: Horizon Press, 1979.

Bonnie, Richard J., and Robert B. Wallace, eds., *Elder Mistreatment.* Washington, D.C.: National Academic Press, 2003.

Bornstein, Brian H., Christy J. Witt, Katie E. Cherry, and Edith Greene, "The Suggestibility of Older Witnesses," in *Elders, Crime, and The Criminal Justice System* 149, edited by Max B. Rothman, Burton D. Dunlop, and Pamela Entzel. New York: Springer, 2000.

Borus, Michael E., Herbert S. Parnes, Steven Sandell, and Bert Seidman, eds., *The Older Worker.* Madison, Wisc.: Industrial Relations Research Assn., 1988.

Boyd, Julian, ed., 15 *The Papers of Thomas Jefferson.* Princeton, N.J.: Princeton University Press, 1950–.

Breen, Leonard Z., "The Aging Individual," in *Handbook of Social Gerontology* 145, edited by Clark Tibbitts. Chicago: University of Chicago Press, 1974.

Browning, Robert, "Rabbi Ben-Ezra" (1864), in *The Oxford Book of Aging* 306, edited by Thomas R. Cole and Mary G. Winkler. New York: Oxford University Press, 1994.

Burgess, Ernest W., "Western Experience in Aging as Viewed by an American," in *Social Welfare of the Aging* 349, edited by Jerome Kaplan and Gordon J. Aldridge. New York: Columbia University Press, 1962.

Butler, Robert A., *Why Survive? Being Old in America.* New York: Harper & Row, 1975.

Callahan, Daniel, *Setting Limits.* New York: Simon & Schuster, 1987.

Campbell, Angus, Philip E. Converse, Warren E. Miller, and Donald Stokes, *The American Voter.* New York: Wiley, 1960.

Carp, Robert A., and C. K. Rowland, *Policymaking and Politics in the Federal District Courts*. Knoxville: University of Tennessee Press, 1983.

Charmatz, Marc, "Eliminating Communication Barriers in the Courtroom," in *Court-Related Needs of the Elderly and Persons with Disabilities* 85, by American Bar Association Commission on Legal Problems of the Elderly, American Bar Association Commission on the Mentally Disabled, and National Judicial College. Washington, D.C.: American Bar Association, 1991.

Chudacoff, Howard P., *How Old Are You?* Princeton, N.J.: Princeton University Press, 1989.

Cicero, *Cato Maior de Senectute (On Old Age)*. New York: Cambridge University Press, 1998.

Cicero, *On Old Age*, in *Cicero—On Old Age and On Friendship* 1, translated by Frank O. Copley. Ann Arbor: University of Michigan Press, 1967.

Cohen, Wilbur, *Retirement Policies Under Social Security*. Berkeley: University of California Press, 1957.

Cole, Thomas R., *The Journey of Life*. Cambridge: Cambridge University Press, paperback ed., 1993.

Cole, Thomas R., and Mary G. Winkler, eds., *The Oxford Book of Aging*. New York: Oxford University Press, 1994.

Coles, Catherine, "The Older Woman in Hausa Society: Power and Authority in Urban Nigeria," in *The Cultural Context of Aging* 57, edited by Jay Sokolovsky. New York: Bergin & Garvey, 1990.

Cowley, Malcolm, *The View From 80*. New York: Penguin Books, 1982.

Cox, Oliver C., *Caste, Class, and Race*. Garden City, N.Y.: Doubleday, 1948.

Crews, Douglas E., and Ralph M. Garruto, eds., *Biological Anthropology and Aging*. New York: Oxford University Press, 1994.

Cuddy, Amy J. C., and Susan T. Fiske, *Doddering but Dear: Process, Content, and Function in Stereotyping of Older Persons*, in *Ageism* 3, edited by Todd D. Nelson. Cambridge: MIT Press, 2002.

Davis, Richard H., *Television and the Aging Audience*. Los Angeles: Ethel Percy Andrus Gerontology Center, University of Southern California, 1980.

Dawkins, Richard, *The Selfish Gene*. Oxford: Oxford University Press, paperback ed., 1999.

De Beauvoir, Simone, *The Coming of Age*. New York: G. P. Putnam's Sons, 1972.

Demos, John, "Old Age in Early New England," in *Aging, Death, and the Completion of Being* 115, edited by David D. Van Tassel. Philadelphia: University of Pennsylvania Press, 1979.

Dittmar, Nancy D., "Facility and Resident Characteristics of Board and Care Homes for the Elderly," in *Preserving Independence, Supporting Needs* 1, edited by Marilyn Moon, George Gaberlavage, and Sandra J. Newman. Washington, D.C.: Public Policy Institute, American Association of Retired Persons, 1989.

Doroshow, Joanne, *The Case for the Civil Jury*. Washington, D.C.: Center for the Study of Responsive Law, 1992.

Douglas, William O., *We The Judges*. Garden City, N.Y.: Doubleday, 1956.

Dovidio, John F., and Samuel L. Gaertner, "Prejudice, Discrimination, and Racism: Historical Trends and Contemporary Approaches," in *Prejudice, Discrimination, and*

Racism 1, edited by John F. Dovidio and Samuel L. Gaertner. Orlando: Academic Press, 1986.

Dovidio, John F., and Samuel L. Gaertner, eds., *Prejudice, Discrimination, and Racism.* Orlando: Academic Press, 1986.

Eglit, Howard, 1–3 *Age Discrimination.* St. Paul, Minn.: West Group, 2d ed., 1994, and annual supps.

———, 1, 2, 4 *Age Discrimination.* Colorado Springs: Shepard's/McGraw-Hill, 1981, and annual supps.

Eisenhandler, Susan A., "The Asphalt Identikit: Old Age and the Driver's License," in *Growing Old in America* 107, edited by Beth B. Hess and Elizabeth W. Markson. New Brunswick, N.J.: Transaction, 4th ed.,1991.

Eliot, T. S., *Collected Poems, 1909–1962.* New York: Harcourt Brace & World 1963.

———, "The Love Song of J. Alfred Prufrock," in *T. S. Eliot, Collected Poems, 1909–1962.* New York: Harcourt Brace & World, 1963.

Ellsworth, Phoebe C., *Some steps between attitudes and verdicts*, in *Inside the Juror* 42, edited by Reid Hastie. Cambridge: Cambridge University Press, 1993.

Euripides, *Suppliants*, in *Euripides: Plays, Vol. 1*, translated by A. S. Way. London: J. M. Dent & Sons, 1956.

Ewing, Wayne, Dasha Wright Ewing, and Dorothy Ives, *Tears in God's Bottle: Reflections on Alzheimer's Caregiving.* Tucson: Whitestone Circle Press, 1999.

Exploring Ethical Issues in Meeting the Legal Needs of the Elderly. Washington, D.C.: American Bar Association, 1987.

Farnsworth, E. Allan, *Contracts.* New York: Aspen Business & Law, 3d ed., 1999.

Farrand, Max, ed., *The Records of the Federal Convention of 1787.* New Haven: Yale University Press, rev. ed., 1966.

Feagin, Joe R., and Clairece Booker Feagin, *Racial and Ethnic Relations.* Upper Saddle River, N.J.: Prentice-Hall, 1996.

Federalist Paper No. 78. New York: Westvaco, 1995.

Fischer, David Hackett, *Growing Old in America.* New York: Oxford University Press, expanded paperback edition, 1978.

Flango, Victor E., and David B. Rottman, "Court Data on the Elderly and Persons with Disabilities," in *Court-Related Needs of the Elderly and Persons with Disabilities* 203, by American Bar Association Commission on Legal Problems of the Elderly, American Bar Association Commission on the Mentally Disabled, and National Judicial College. Washington, D.C.: American Bar Association, 1991.

Fleming, Robert B., *Elder Law Answer Book.* New York: Aspen, 2001.

Flynn, Edith Elisabeth, "Elders as Perpetrators," in *Elders, Crime, and the Criminal Justice System* 43, edited by Max B. Rothman, Burton D. Dunlop, and Pamela Entzel. New York: Springer, 2000.

Foner, Nancy, *Ages in Conflict.* New York: Columbia University Press, 1984.

Foster, Wayne F., annotation, *Validity, Construction, and Application of Age Requirements for Licensing of Motor Vehicle Operators*, 86 A.L.R. 3d 475. Rochester, N.Y.: Lawyers Co-operative, 1978.

Fowler, Margaret, and Priscilla McCutcheon, eds., *Songs of Experience.* New York: Ballantine Books, 1991.

Freedman, Monroe H., *Understanding Lawyers' Ethics.* New York: Matthew Bender, 1990.

Friedan, Betty, *The Fountain of Age*. New York: Simon & Schuster, 1993.

Frolik, Lawrence A., and Alison McChrystal Barnes, *Elderlaw—Cases and Materials*. Charlottesville, Va.: Lexis, 2d ed., 1999.

Frolik, Lawrence A., and Alison Patrucco Barnes, *Elderlaw*. Charlottesville, Va.: Michie, 1992.

Galanter, Marc, "Jury Shadows: Reflections on the Civil Jury and the 'Litigation Explosion,'" in *The American Civil Jury: Final Report of the 1986 Chief Justice Earl Warren Conference on Advocacy in the United States*, by Marc Galanter, John Guinther, and Morris Arnold. Washington, D.C.: The Foundation, 1987.

Galanter, Marc, John Guinther, and Morris Arnold, *The American Civil Jury: Final Report of the 1986 Chief Justice Earl Warren Conference on Advocacy in the United States*. Washington, D.C.: The Foundation, 1987.

Gallanis, Thomas P., A. Kimberley Dayton, and Molly M. Wood, *Elder Law—Readings, Cases, and Materials*. Cincinnati: Anderson, 2000.

Gawalt, Gerard W., ed., *The New High Priests*. Westport, Conn.: Greenwood Press, 1984.

Gibson, Rose C., "Children: Treasured Resource or Forgotten Minority?" in *Our Aging Society* 161, edited by Alan Pifer and Lydia Bronte. New York: Houghton Mifflin, 1986.

Gilbert, Michael Francis, *The Oxford Book of Legal Anecdotes*. New York: Oxford University Press, 1986.

Glascock, Anthony D., "By Any Other Name, It Is Still Killing: A Comparison of the Treatment of the Elderly in America and Other Societies," in *Culture, Aging, and Society* 43, edited by Jay Sokolovsky. Boston: Bergin, 1990.

Goebel, Julius, Jr., *History of the Supreme Court of the United States, Vol. 1, Antecedents and Beginnings to 1801*. New York: Macmillan, 1971.

Goldsmith, Timothy H., *The Biological Roots of Human Nature: Forging Links Between Evolution and Behavior*. New York: Oxford University Press, 1991.

Goldstein, William M., and Robin M. Hogarth, eds., *Research on Judgment and Decision Making*. Cambridge: Cambridge University Press, 1997.

Greenberg, Jeff, Jeff Schimel, and Andy Martens, "Ageism: Denying the Face of the Future," in *Ageism* 27, edited by Todd D. Nelson. Cambridge: MIT Press, 2002.

Guinther, John, *The Jury in America*. New York: Facts on File Publications, 1988.

Haber, Carole, *Beyond Sixty-Five*. New York: Cambridge University Press, paperback ed., 1983.

Hamer, Dean, and Peter Copeland, *Living with Our Genes* 274. New York: Anchor Books, 1998.

Hamilton, David L., and Tina K. Trolier, *Stereotypes and Stereotyping: An Overview of the Cognitive Approach*, in *Prejudice, Discrimination, and Racism* 127, edited by John F. Dovidio and Samuel L. Gaertner. Orlando: Academic Press, 1986.

Hamilton, Edith, and Huntington Cairns, eds., *Plato: The Collected Dialogues*. New York: Bollingen Series LXXI, Pantheon Books, 1966.

Hans, Valerie P., and Neil Vidmar, *Judging the Jury*. New York: Plenum Press, 1986.

Harlan, William H., "Social Status of the Aged in Three Indian Villages," in *Middle Age and Aging* 469, edited by Bernice Neugarten. Chicago: University of Chicago Press, 1968.

Harris, Diana K., ed., *Sociology of Aging*. New York: Harper & Row, 2d ed.,1992.

Harris, Diana K., and William E. Cole, *Sociology of Aging*. Boston: Houghton Mifflin, 1980.

Harris, Louis, and Associates, *The Myth and Reality of Aging in America: A Study for the National Council on the Aging, Inc.*. Washington, D.C.: National Council on the Aging, 1976.

Harrison, G. B., ed., *Shakespeare: The Complete Works*. New York: Harcourt, Brace, 1952.

Hastie, Reid, ed., *Inside the Juror*. New York: Cambridge University Press, 1993.

Havighurst, Robert J., Bernice L. Neugarten, and Sheldon S. Tobin, "Disengagement and Patterns of Aging," in *Middle Age and Aging* 161, edited by Bernice L. Neugarten. Chicago: University of Chicago Press, 1968.

Hayflick, Leonard, *How and Why We Age*. New York: Ballantine Books, 1994.

Heilbrun, Carolyn G., *The Last Gift of Time*. New York: Ballantine Books, paperback ed., 1997.

Heinz, John P., and Edward O. Laumann, *Chicago Lawyers*. New York: Russell Sage Foundation, 1982.

Hess, Beth B., and Elizabeth W. Markson, eds., *Growing Old in America*. New Brunswick, N.J.: Transaction, 4th ed., 1991.

Hesse, Hermann, "On Old Age," in Hermann Hesse, *My Belief: Essays on Life and Art*, edited by Theodore Ziolkowski. New York: Farrar, Straus & Giroux, 1974.

Hommel, Penelope A., "Guardianship Reform in the 1980s: A Decade of Substantive and Procedural Change," in *Older Adults' Decision-Making and the Law* 225, edited by Michael Smyer, K. Warner Schaie, and Marshall B. Kapp. New York: Springer, 1996.

Horowitz, Irwin A., and Thomas Willging, *The Psychology of Law: Integrations and Applications*. Boston: Little, Brown, 1984.

Hrdy, Sarah Blaffer, *Mother Nature*. New York: Pantheon Books, 1999.

Hudson, Robert B., and Robert H. Binstock, "Political Systems and Aging," in *Handbook of Aging and the Social Sciences* 369, edited by Robert H. Binstock and Ethel Shanas. New York: Van Nostrand Reinhold, 1976.

Hume, Sally Balch, ed., *1993 Elderlaw Directory of Seminars, Courses, and Clinics in U.S. Law Schools*. Washington, D.C.: Legal Counsel for the Elderly, 1993.

Irvine, Diana R., *The American Bench*. Sacramento, Calif.: Forster-Long, 11th ed., 2000.

Jacobs, Bruce, "Aging and Politics," in *Handbook of Aging and the Social Sciences* 349, edited by Robert H. Binstock and Linda K. George. San Diego: Academic Press, 1990.

Johnson, Paul, and Pat Thane, *Old Age From Antiquity to Post-Modernity*. London: Routledge, 1998.

Jordan, Walter E., *Jury Selection*. Colorado Springs: Shepard's/McGraw-Hill, 1980.

Kalven, Harry, and Hans Zeisel, *The American Jury*. Boston: Little, Brown, 1966.

Kaplan, Jerome, and Gordon J. Aldridge, eds., *Social Welfare of the Aging*. New York: Columbia University Press, 1962.

Kapp, Marshall B., *Geriatrics and the Law*. New York: Springer, 3d ed., 1999.

Kerbs, John J., "The Older Prisoner: Social, Psychological, and Medical Considerations," in *Elders, Crime, and the Criminal Justice System* 207, edited by Max B. Rothman, Burton D. Dunlop, and Pamela Entzel. New York: Springer, 2000.

Kiefer, Christie W., "The Elderly in Modern Japan: Elite Victims or Plural Players?" in *The*

Cultural Context of Aging 181, edited by Jay Sokolovsky. New York: Bergin & Garvey, 1990.

Kilner, John F., *Who Lives? Who Dies?* New Haven: Yale University Press, 1990.

Kite, Mary E., and Lisa Smith Wagner, "Attitudes Toward Older Adults," in *Ageism* 129, edited by Todd D. Nelson. Cambridge: MIT Press, 2002.

Krauskopf, Joan M., Robert N. Brown, Karen L. Tokarz, and Allan D. Bogutz, *Elderlaw: Advocacy for the Aging*. St. Paul, Minn.: West, 2d ed., 1993.

Kreuzer, Arthur, and Ulrike Grasberger, "Elders and the Criminal Justice System in Germany," in *Elders, Crime, and the Criminal Justice System* 273, edited by Max B. Rothman, Burton D. Dunlop, and Pamela Entzel. New York: Springer, 2000.

Lancaster, Lynn C., and David Stillman, *When Generations Collide*. New York: HarperBusiness, 2002.

Lawrence, Jerome, and Robert E. Lee, *Inherit the Wind*. New York: Random House, 1955.

Lermack, Paul, *Materials on Juries and Jury Research*. Chicago: American Judicature Society, 1977.

Levin, Jack, and William C. Levin, *Ageism, Prejudice and Discrimination Against the Elderly*. Belmont, Calif.: Wadsworth, 1980.

Levy, Becca R., and Mahzarin R. Banaji, "Implicit Ageism," in *Ageism* 49, edited by Todd D. Nelson. Cambridge: MIT Press, 2002.

Litan, Robert E., ed., *Verdict: Assessing the Civil Jury System*. Washington, D.C.: Brookings Institution, 1983.

Longman, Phillip, *Born to Pay*. Boston: Houghton Mifflin, 1987.

Lowenthal, David, *The Past is a Foreign Country*. New York: Cambridge University Press, 1985, 1999.

MacLeish, Archibald, "With Age, Wisdom," in Archibald MacLeish, *New and Collected Poems, 1917–1976*. Boston: Houghton Mifflin, 1976.

Markson, Elizabeth W., "Physiological Changes, Illness, and Health Care Use in Later Life," in *Growing Old in America* 173, edited by Beth B. Hess and Elizabeth W. Markson. New Brunswick, N.J.: Transaction, 4th ed., 1991.

McCann, Robert, and Howard Giles, "Ageism in the Workplace: A Communication Perspective," in *Ageism* 163, edited by Todd D. Nelson. Cambridge: MIT Press, 2002.

McCloskey, Deirdre, *Crossing: A Memoir*. Chicago: University of Chicago Press, 2000.

McCoun, Robert J., *Getting Inside the Black Box: Toward a Better Understanding of Civil Jury Behavior*. Washington, D.C.: Brookings Institution, 1987.

———, *Inside the Black Box: What Empirical Research Tells Us About Decisionmaking by Civil Juries*, in *Verdict: Assessing the Civil Jury System* 127, edited by Robert E. Litan. Washington, D.C.: Brookings Institution, 1983.

McCullough, David, *John Adams*. New York: Simon & Schuster, 2001.

Mendelson, Mary Adelaide, *Tender Loving Greed*. New York: Vintage Books, paperback ed., 1974.

Minois, Georges, *History of Old Age*. Chicago: University of Chicago Press, 1989.

Montepare, Joanne M., and Leslie A. Zebrowitz, "A Social Developmental View of Ageism," in *Ageism* 77, edited by Todd D. Nelson. Cambridge: MIT Press, 2002.

Moon, Marilyn, George Gaberlavage, and Sandra J. Newman, eds., *Preserving Independence, Supporting Needs*. Public Policy Institute, American Association of Retired Persons, 1989.

Muller, Dave J., Derek E. Blackman, and Anthony J. Chapman, eds., *Psychology and Law*. New York: Wiley, 1984.

Munsterman, Janet T., *The Relationship of Juror Fees and Terms of Service to Jury System Performance*. Arlington, Va.: National Center for State Courts, Washington Project Office, 1991.

Myerhoff, Barbara, *Remembered Lives*. Ann Arbor: University of Michigan Press, 1992.

Nahemow, Lucille, Kathleen A. McClusky-Fawcett, and Paul E. McGhee, eds., *Humor and Aging*. Orlando: Academic Press, 1986.

National Center on Elder Abuse, *Understanding the Nature and Extent of Elder Abuse in Domestic Settings*. Washington, D.C.: National Center on Elder Abuse, 1997.

Nelson, Todd D., ed., *Ageism*. Cambridge: MIT Press, 2002.

Neugarten, Bernice L., "The Middle Generation," in *Aging Parents* 258, edited by Pauline K. Ragan. Los Angeles: Ethel Percy Andrus Gerontology Center, University of Southern California, 1979.

———, "Policy for the 1980s: Age or Need Entitlement?" in *Age or Need? Public Policies for Older People* 21, edited by Bernice L. Neugarten. Beverly Hills: Sage Publications, 1982.

Neugarten, Bernice L., ed., *Age or Need? Public Policies for Older People*. Beverly Hills: Sage Publications, 1982.

———, ed., *Middle Age and Aging*. Chicago: University of Chicago Press, 1968.

Neugarten, Bernice L., and Gunhild Hagestad, "Age and the Life Course," in *Handbook of Aging and the Social Sciences* 35, edited by Robert H. Binstock and Ethel Shanas. New York: Van Nostrand Reinhold, 1976.

Neugarten, Bernice L., Joan W. Moore, and John C. Lowe, "Age Norms, Age Constraints, and Adult Socialization," in *Middle Age and Aging* 22, edited by Bernice L. Neugarten. Chicago: University of Chicago Press, 1968.

Neugarten, Bernice L., and Dail A. Neugarten, "Changing Meanings of Age in the Aging Society," in *Our Aging Society* 33, edited by Alan Pifer and Lydia Bronte. New York: W. W. Norton, 1986.

Newman, Evelyn S., Donald J. Newman, and Mindy L. Gewirtz, eds., *Elderly Criminals*. Cambridge, Mass.: Oelge Schlager, Gunn & Hain, 1984.

Ng, Sik Hung, "Will Families Support Their Elders? Answers From Across Cultures," in *Ageism* 295, edited by Todd D. Nelson. Cambridge: MIT Press, 2002.

Nickerson, Stephanie, Clara Mayo, and Althea Smith, "Racism in the Courtroom," in *Prejudice, Discrimination, and Racism* 259, edited by John F. Dovidio and Samuel L. Gaertner. Orlando: Academic Press, 1986.

Nie, Norman H., Sidney Verba, and John R. Petrocik, *The Changing American Voter*. Cambridge: Harvard University Press, 1976.

Nowak, John E., and Ronald D. Rotunda, *Constitutional Law*. St. Paul, Minn.: West Group, 6th ed., 2000.

Oliver, Rose, and Francis A. Bock, *Coping with Alzheimer's*. New York: Dodd, Mead, 1987.

Olson, Philip, "The Elderly in the People's Republic of China," in *The Cultural Context of Aging* 143, edited by Jay Sokolovsky. New York: Bergin & Garvey, 1990.

Page, Benjamin I., and Robert Y. Shapiro, *The Rational Public*. Chicago: University of Chicago Press, 1992.

Palmore, Erdman B., *Ageism: Negative and Positive*. New York: Springer, 1990.

————, "Attitudes Toward Aging as Shown by Humor: A Review," in *Humor and Aging* 101, edited by Lucille Nahemow, Kathleen A. McClusky-Fawcett, and Paul E. McGhee. Orlando: Academic Press, 1986.

Palmore, Erdman B., and Daisaku Maeda, "The Honorable Elders," in *Sociology of Aging* 105, edited by Diana K. Harris. New York: Harper & Row, 2d ed., 1992.

Parkin, Tim G., "Aging in Antiquity: Status and Participation," in *Old Age From Antiquity to Post-Modernity* 19, edited by Paul Johnson and Pat Thane. London: Routledge, 1998.

Parnes, Herbert S., and Steven H. Sandell, "Introduction and Overview," in *The Older Worker* 1, edited by Michael E. Borus, Herbert S. Parnes, Steven H. Sandell, and Bert Seidman. Washington, D.C.: Industrial Relations Research Association, 1988.

Pennington, Nancy, and Reid Hastie, "Explanation-based decision making: Effects of memory structure on judgment," in *Research on Judgment and Decision Making* 454, edited by William M. Goldstein and Robin M. Hogarth. Cambridge: Cambridge University Press, 1997.

Pifer, Alan, and Lydia Bronte, eds., *Our Aging Society*. New York: W. W. Norton, 1986.

Plato, *The Republic*, in *Plato: The Collected Dialogues*, edited by Edith Hamilton and Huntington Cairns. New York: Bollingen Series LXXI, Pantheon Books, 1966.

Poeck, Klaus, ed., *Neurology: Proceedings of the XIIIth World Congress of Neurology, Hamburg, Sept. 1–6, 1985*. Berlin and Heidelberg: Springer, 1986.

Posner, Richard A., *Aging and Old Age*. Chicago: University of Chicago Press, 1995.

Proshansky, Harold, and Bernard Seidenberg, eds. *Basic Studies in Social Psychology*. New York: Holt, Rinehart & Winston, 1965.

Ragan, Pauline K., ed., *Aging Parents*. Los Angeles: Ethel Percy Andrus Gerontology Center, University of Southern California, 1979.

Rasmussen, R. Kent, ed., *The Quotable Mark Twain*. Lincolnwood, Ill.: Contemporary Books, 1997.

Regan, John J., Rebecca C. Morgan, and David M. English, *Tax, Estate, & Financial Planning for the Elderly*. New York: Matthew Bender, 1997, and periodic supps.

Ridley, Mark, *Genome*. New York: Perennial, 2000.

Riley, Matilda White, Marilyn Johnson, and Anne Foner, 3 *Aging and Society*. New York: Russell Sage Foundation, 1972.

Rix, Sara E., ed., *Older Workers: How Do They Measure Up?*. Washington, D.C.: Public Policy Institute, American Association of Retired Persons, 1994.

Roche, Lyn, *Coping With Caring: Daily Reflections for Alzheimer's Caregivers*. Forest Knolls, Calif.: Elder Books, 1996.

Rogers, Richard G., Robert A. Hummer, and Charles B. Nam, *Living and Dying in the USA*. San Diego: Academic Press, 2000.

Rosch, Eleanor, "Human Categorization," in *Studies in Cross-Cultural Psychology* 1, edited by Neil Warren. New York: Academic Press, 1977–1980.

Rose, Arnold M., "The Subculture of the Aging: A Topic for Sociological Research," in *Middle Age and Aging* 29, edited by Bernice L. Neugarten. Chicago: University of Chicago Press, 1968.

Rose, Michael R., *Evolutionary Biology of Aging*. New York: Oxford University Press, 1991.

Rose, Reginald, *Twelve Angry Men: A Play in Three Acts*. Chicago: Dramatic, 1955.

Ross, David Frank, J. Don Read, and Michael P. Toglia, *Adult Eyewitness Testimony*. New York: Press Syndicate of the University of Cambridge, 1994.

Rothman, Max B., Burton D. Dunlop, and Pamela Entzel, eds., *Elders, Crime, and the Criminal Justice System*. New York: Springer, 2000.

Rowe, John W., and Robert L. Kahn, "Breaking Down the Myths of Aging," in *Aging in America* 119, edited by Olivia Smith. New York: H. W. Wilson, 2000.

———, *Successful Aging*. New York: Pantheon Books, 1998.

Sarton, May, *Plant Dreaming Deep*. New York: W. W. Norton, 1983.

Scott-Maxwell, Florida, *The Measure of My Days, 1968*, excerpted in *Songs of Experience* 25, edited by Margaret Fowler and Priscilla McCutcheon. New York: Ballantine Books, 1991.

Segerstrale, Ullica, *Defenders of the Truth*. New York: Oxford University Press, 2000.

Shakespeare, William, *Henry VI*, Part II, in *Shakespeare: The Complete Works* 142, edited by G. B. Harrison. New York: Harcourt, Brace, 1952.

———, *The Passionate Pilgrim XII*, in *Shakespeare: The Complete Works* 1586, edited by G. B. Harrison. New York: Harcourt, Brace, 1952.

———, *The Tragedy of King Lear*, in *Shakespeare: The Complete Works* 1136, edited by G. B. Harrison. New York: Harcourt, Brace, 1952.

Shaman, Jeffrey M., Steven Lubet, and James J. Alfini, *Judicial Conduct and Ethics*. Charlottesville, Va.: Michie, 2d ed., 1995.

Simmons, Leo W., "Aging in Preindustrial Societies," in *Handbook of Social Gerontology* 87, edited by Clark Tibbits. Chicago: University of Chicago Press, 1960.

———, *The Role of the Aged in Primitive Society*. New Haven: Yale University Press, 1945.

Simon, Marcia Libes, *An Exploratory Study of Adult Protective Services Programs' Repeat Elder Abuse Clients*. Washington, D.C.: American Association of Retired Persons, 1992.

Simon, Rita, *The Jury: Its Role in American Society*. Lexington, Mass.: Lexington Books, 1980.

Simpson, George Eaton, and J. Milton Yinger, *Racial and Cultural Minorities*. New York: Plenum Press, 1985.

Smith, Daniel Scott, "Old Age and the 'Great Transformation': A New England Case Study," in *Aging and the Elderly: Humanistic Perspectives in Gerontology* 285, edited by Stuart F. Spicker, Kathleen M. Woodward, and David D. Van Tassel. Atlantic Highlands, N.J.: Humanities Press, 1978.

Smith, Olivia, ed., *Aging in America*. New York: H. W. Wilson, 2000.

Smyer, Michael, K. Warner Schaie, and Marshall B. Kapp, eds., *Older Adults' Decision-Making and the Law*. New York: Springer, 1996.

Sokolovsky, Jay, ed., *The Cultural Context of Aging*. New York: Bergin & Garvey, 1990.

Spence, Alexander P., *Biology of Human Aging*. Englewood Cliffs, N.J.: Prentice Hall, 1989.

Spicker, Stuart F., Kathleen M. Woodward, and David D. Van Tassel, eds., *Aging and the Elderly: Humanistic Perspectives in Gerontology*. Atlantic Highlands, N.J.: Humanities Press, 1978.

Stearns, Peter N., *Old Age in European Society: The Case of France*. New York: Holmes & Meier, 1976.

Steffensmeier, Darrell, and Mark Motivans, "Sentencing the Older Offender: Is there an

'Age Bias'?" in *Elders, Crime, and the Criminal Justice System* 185, edited by Max B. Rothman, Burton D. Dunlop, and Pamela Entzel. New York: Springer, 2000.

Stiegel, Lori A., *Recommended Guidelines for State Courts Handling Cases Involving Elder Abuse*. Washington, D.C.: American Bar Association, 1995.

Strauss, Peter J., Robert Wolf, and Dana Shilling, *Aging and the Law*. Chicago: Commerce Clearing House, 1990.

Streib, Gordon F., "Traditional Cultural Patterns: China and the United States," in *Sociology of Aging* 87, edited by Diana K. Harris. New York: Harper & Row, 2d ed., 1990.

Sullivan, Kathleen M., and Gerald Gunther, *Constitutional Law*. New York: Foundation Press, 14th ed., 2001.

Tallmer, Margot, ed., *Questions and Answers About Sex in Later Life*. Philadelphia: Charles Press, 1996.

Teshima, Joan, annotation, *Attorney's Liability, to One Other Than Immediate Client, for Negligence in Connection with Legal Duties,* 61 ALR4th 615. Rochester, N.Y.: Lawyers Co-Operative, 1988.

Thoreau, Henry David, *Walden*, edited by J. Lyndon Shanley. Princeton, N.J.: Princeton University Press, 1971.

Tibbitts, Clark, ed., *Handbook of Social Gerontology*. Chicago: University of Chicago Press, 1960, 1974.

Townsend, Clair, *Old Age: The Last Segregation*. New York: Bantam Books, paperback ed., 1971.

Turke, P. W., "Evolution of the 100 Year Lifespan," unpublished, n.d.

Turner, Trudy R., and Mark L. Weiss, "The Genesis of Longevity in Humans," in *Biological Anthropology and Aging* 76, edited by Douglas E. Crews and Ralph M. Garruto. New York: Oxford University Press, 1994.

Twain, Mark, Letter to James R. Osgood, Jan. 25, 1876, in *The Quotable Mark Twain* 157, edited by R. Kent Rasmussen. Lincolnwood, Ill.: Contemporary Books, 1997.

Van Dyke, Jon M., *Jury Selection Procedures*. Cambridge, Mass.: Ballinger, 1977.

Van Tassel, David, ed., *Aging, Death, and the Completion of Being*. Philadelphia: University of Pennsylvania Press, 1979.

Vinson, Donald E., *Jury Trials: The Psychology of Winning Strategy*. Charlottesville, Va.: Michie, 1986.

Vladeck, Bruce C., *Unloving Care*. New York: Basic Books, 1980.

Wachs, Martin, *Transportation for the Elderly*. Berkeley: University of California Press, 1979.

Warren, Neil, ed., *Studies in Cross-Cultural Psychology*. New York: Academic Press, 1977.

Way, A. S., trans., *Euripides: Plays, Vol. 1*. London: J. M. Dent & Sons, 1956.

Weismann, August, *Essays Upon Heredity and Kindred Biological Problems*. Oxford: Clarendon Press, 1891–1892.

Wenke, Robert A., *The Art of Selecting a Jury*. Los Angeles: Parker, 1979.

Whitbourne, Susan Krauss, and Joel R. Sneed, "The Paradox of Well-Being, Identity Processes, and Stereotype Threat: Ageism and Its Potential Relationships to the Self in Later Life," in *Ageism* 247, edited by Todd D. Nelson. Cambridge: MIT Press, 2002.

Wilson, Edward O., *Sociobiology: The New Synthesis* 553. Cambridge: Belknap Press of Harvard University, 25th anniversary ed., 2000.

Wishman, Seymour, *Anatomy of a Jury*. New York: Times Books, 1986.

Wolf, Rosalie S., "Elders as Victims of Crime, Abuse, Neglect, and Exploitation," in *El-*

ders, Crime, and the Criminal Justice System 19, edited by Max B. Rothman, Burton D. Dunlop, and Pamela Entzel. New York: Springer, 2000.

Wood, Erica, "Toward a Barrier-Free Courthouse: Equal Access to Justice for Persons with Physical Disabilities," in Court-Related Needs of the Elderly and Persons with Disabilities 69 by American Bar Association Commission on Legal Problems of the Elderly, American Bar Association Commission on the Mentally Disabled, and National Judicial College. Washington, D.C.: American Bar Association, 1991.

Wood, James W., Stephen C. Weeks, Gillian R. Bentley, and Kenneth M. Weiss, "Human Population Biology and the Evolution of Aging," in Biological Anthropology and Aging 19, edited by Douglas E. Crews and Ralph M. Garruto. New York: Oxford University Press, 1994.

Wright, Russell O., Life and Death in the United States. Jefferson, N.C.: McFarland, 1997.

Yarmey, A. Daniel, "The Older Eyewitness," in Elders, Crime, and the Criminal Justice System 127, edited by Max B. Rothman, Burton D. Dunlop, and Pamela Entzel. New York: Springer, 2000.

Yarmey, A. Daniel, Hazel P. Tressillian Jones, and Sohail Rashid, "Eyewitness Memory of Elderly and Young Adults," in Psychology and Law 215, edited by Dave J. Muller, Derek E. Blackman, and Antony J. Chapman. New York: Wiley, 1984.

Yntema, Sharon, ed., Americans 55 & Older. Ithaca, N.Y.: New Strategist Publications, 1999.

Zemke, Ron, Claire Raines, and Bob Filipczak, Generations at Work. New York: AMACOM, 2000.

Ziolkowski, Theodore, ed., Hermann Hesse, My Belief: Essays on Life and Art. New York: Farrar, Straus & Giroux, 1974.

Journal, Internet, and Magazine Articles

Adams, William E., Jr., The Incarceration of Older Criminals: Balancing Safety, Cost, and Humanitarian Concerns, 19 Nova Law Review 465 (1994).

———. The Intersection of Elder Law and Criminal Law: More Traffic Than One Might Assume, 30 Stetson Law Review 1331 (2001).

Adams, William E., Jr., and Rebecca C. Morgan, Representing the Client Who is Older in the Law Office and in the Courtroom, 2 Elder Law Journal 1 (1994).

Adams-Price, Carolyn, Eyewitness Memory and Aging: Predictors of Accuracy in Recall and Person Recognition, 7 Psychology & Aging 602 (1992).

Aliotta, Jilda M., Combining Judges' Attributes and Case Characteristics: An Alternative Approach to Explaining Supreme Court Decisionmaking, 71 Judicature 277 (1988).

Alker, Hayward R., Jr., Carl Hosticka, and Michael Mitchell, Jury Selection as a Biased Social Process, 11 Law & Society Review 9 (1976).

Allee, Jacqueline, Representing Older Persons: Ethical Dilemmas, 8 BIFOCAL (Spring 1987).

Allen, Josephine A., and N. Yolanda Burwell, Ageism and Racism: Two Issues in Social Work Education and Practice, 16 Journal of Education for Social Work 71 (Spring 1980).

Amar, Vikram David, Jury Service as Political Participation Akin to Voting, 80 Cornell Law Review 203 (1995).

American Bar Association Commission on the Mentally Disabled and American Bar Association Commission on Legal Problems of the Elderly, Guardianship: An Agenda for Reform, 13 Mentally & Physically Disabled Rptr. 271 (1989).

Arluke, Arnold, and Jack Levin, *Another Stereotype: Old Age As A Second Childhood,* Aging 7 (Aug./Sept. 1994).

Arredondo, Lorenzo A., Helen V. Collier, and Gary J. Scrimgeour, *To Make a Good Decision . . . Law and Experience Alone Are Not Enough,* 1988 Judges Journal 23 (Fall 1988).

Ashenfelder, Orley, Theodore Eisenberg, and Stephen J. Schwab, *Politics and the Judiciary: The Influence of Judicial Background in Case Outcomes,* 24 Journal of Legal Studies 257 (1995).

Austin, David R., *Attitudes Toward Old Age: A Hierarchical Study,* 25 Gerontologist 431 (1985).

Bailey, George Edward, *Impairment, the Profession, and Your Law Partner,* 11 No. 1 Prof. Law. 2 (1999).

Bach, Amy, "Nolo Contendere," New York Magazine 49 (Dec. 11, 1995).

Baker, Katherine K., *Biology for Feminists,* 75 Chicago-Kent Law Review 805 (2000).

Baker, Kelly J., Note, *Senior Judges: Valuable Resources, Partisan Strategists, or Self-Interested Maximizers?* 16 Journal of Law & Politics 139 (2000).

Baltes, Paul B., and K. Warner Schaie, "Aging and IQ: The Myth of the Twilight Years," Psychology Today 35 (March 1974).

Barbato, Carole A., and Jerry D. Feezel, *The Language of Aging in Different Age Groups,* 27 Gerontologist 527 (1987).

Barnes, Alison Patrucco, *Florida Guardianship and the Elderly: The Paradoxical Right to Unwanted Assistance,* 40 University of Florida Law Review 949 (1988).

Belote, Farrald G., *Jury Research: Spotting Jurors Who Can Hurt,* 12 American Bar Association Journal of Litigation 17 (1986).

Benesh, Sara C., and Susan E. Howell, *Confidence in the Courts: A Comparison of Users and Non-Users,* 19 Behavioral Sciences & the Law 199 (2001).

Beneze, Lee, and Ann Neighbors, *Elder Abuse and Neglect Cases: An Attorneys' Guide,* 79 Illinois Bar Journal 390 (Aug. 1991).

Bhattacharya, Mita, and Russell Smyth, *Aging and Productivity Among Judges: Some Empirical Evidence from the High Court of Australia,* 40 Australian Economic Papers 199 (2001).

Bieman-Copland, Sherrie, and Ellen Bouchard Ryan, *Age-Biased Interpretation of Memory Successes and Failures in Adulthood,* 53B Journal of Gerontology P105 (1998).

Bienen, Leigh R., *Helping Jurors Out: Post-Verdict Debriefing for Jurors in Emotionally Disturbing Trials,* 68 Indiana Law Journal 1333 (1993).

Bishop, James M., and Daniel R. Krause, *Depictions of Aging and Old Age on Saturday Morning Television,* 24 Gerontologist 91 (1984).

Blanck, Peter David, *Calibrating the Scales of Justice: Studying Judges' Behavior in Bench Trials,* 68 Indiana Law Journal 1119 (1993).

Blanck, Peter David, Robert Rosenthal, and LaDoris Hazzard Cordell, *The Appearance of Justice: Judges' Verbal and Nonverbal Behavior in Criminal Jury Trials,* 38 Stanford Law Review 89 (1995).

Boatright, Robert G., *Generational and Age-Based Differences in Attitudes Towards Jury Service,* 19 Behavioral Sciences & the Law 285 (2001).

Bohm, David A., *Striving for Quality Care in America's Nursing Homes: Tracing the History of Nursing Homes and Noting the Effect of Recent Federal Government Initia-*

tives to Ensure Quality Care in the Nursing Home Setting, 4 DePaul Journal of Health Care 316 (2001).

Bornstein, Brian H., *Memory Processes in Elderly Witnesses: What We Know and What We Don't Know,* 13 Behavioral Sciences & the Law 337 (1995).

Boyer, Edwin M., *Representing the Client With Marginal Capacity: Challenges for the Elder Law Attorney—A Resource Guide,* 12 National Academy of Elder Law Attorneys Quarterly 3 (Spring 1999).

Brinacombe, C. A. Elizabeth, Nyla Quinton, Natalie Nance, and Lynn Garrioch, *Is Age Irrelevant? Perceptions of Young and Old Adult Eyewitnesses,* 21 Law & Human Behavior 619 (1997).

Brown, Judith K., *Cross-Cultural Perspectives on Middle-Aged Women,* 23 Current Anthropology 143–165 (1982).

Burke, Walter T., *Ethical and Psychological Aspects of Representing the Elderly,* 13 Experience 5 (Summer 2003).

Burns, Edward M., *Grandparent Visitation Rights: Is It Time for the Pendulum to Fall?* 25 Family Law Quarterly 59 (1991).

Carnes, Bruce A., and S. Jay Olshansky, *Evolutionary Perspectives on Human Senescence,* 19 Population & Development Review 793 (Dec. 1993).

Cherry, Katie E., and Denny C. LeCompte, *Age and Individual Differences Influence Prospective Memory,* 14 Psychology & Aging 60 (1999).

Chin, Min W., *Keynote Address; "Fairness or Bias?": A Symposium on Racial and Ethnic Composition and Attitudes in the Judiciary,* 4 Asian Law Journal 181 (1997).

Chrosniak, Linda D., *Aging and Source Monitoring,* 4 Psychology & Aging 106 (1989).

Clancy, Kevin, John Bartolomeo, David Richardson, and Charles Wellford, *Sentencing Decision Making: The Logic of Sentence Decisions and the Extent and Sources of Sentence Disparity,* 72 Criminal Law & Criminology 524 (1981).

Cohen, Elizabeth, *Walking a Fine Line,* 87 American Bar Association Journal 62 (2001).

Cohen, Fred, *Old Age as a Criminal Defense,* 21 Criminal Law Bulletin 5 (1985).

Cohen, Gillian, and Dorothy Faulkner, *Age Differences in Source Forgetting: Effects on Reality Monitoring and on Eyewitness Testimony,* 4 Psychology & Aging 10 (1989).

Condominas, Georges, *Aines anciens et ancetres en Asie du Sud-Est,* 37 Communications 63 (1983).

Cooter, Robert D., *Comment on Article by Professor Jones,* 8 Journal of Contemporary Legal Issues 209 (1997).

Corsell, LaDoris H., and Florence O. Keller, *Pay No Attention to the Woman Behind the Bench: Musings of a Trial Court Judge,* 68 Indiana Law Journal 1199 (1993).

Coxon, Pamela, and Tim Valentine, *The Effects of the Age of Eyewitness[es] on the Accuracy and Suggestibility of Their Testimony,* 11 Applied Cognitive Psychology 415 (1997).

Crystal, Howard A., et al., *The Relative Frequency of "Dementia of Unknown Etiology" Increases with Age and is Nearly 50% in Nonagenarians,* 57 Archives Neurology 713 (2000).

Curran, Barbara A., *American Lawyers in the 1980s: A Profession in Transition,* 20 Law & Society Review 19 (1986).

Curran, Nadine, *Blue Hairs in the Bighouse: The Rise in the Elderly Inmate Population, Its Effect on the Overcrowding Dilemma, and Solutions to Correct It,* 26 New England Journal on Criminal & Civil Confinement 225 (2000).

Curriden, Mark, *Power of 12*, 87 American Bar Association Journal 36 (2001).

Dann, B. Michael, *"Learning Lessons" and "Speaking Rights": Creating Educated and Democratic Juries*, 68 Indiana Law Journal 1229 (1993).

Davies, Leland, *Attitudes Toward Old Age and Aging as Shown by Humor*, 17 Gerontologist 220 (1977).

Developments in the Law—The Civil Jury, 110 Harvard Law Review 1408 (1997).

Diamond, Shari Seidman, *Scientific jury selection: What social scientists know and do not know*, 73 Judicature 178 (Dec./Jan. 1990).

Diamond, Shari Seidman, Michael J. Saks, and Stephen Landsman, *Juror Judgments About Liability and Damages: Sources of Variability and Ways to Increase Consistency*, 48 DePaul Law Review 301 (1998).

Dillon, Kathleen M., and Barbara S. Jones, *Attitudes toward Aging Portrayed by Birthday Cards*, 13 International Journal of Aging & Human Development 79 (1981).

Doremus, Mark E., *Wisconsin's ElderLinks Initiative: Using Technology to Provide Legal Services to Older Persons*, 32 Wake Forest Law Review 545 (1997).

Eades, Ted M., *Revisiting the Jury System in Texas: A Study of the Jury Pool in Dallas County*, 54 Southern Methodist Univ. L. Rev. 1813, at 1815 (2001).

Edelman, Toby S., *The Nursing Home Reform Law: Issues for Litigation*, 24 Clearinghouse Review 545 (Oct. 1990).

Edelstein, Stephanie, *Assisted Living: Recent Developments and Issues for Older Consumers*, 9 Stanford Law & Policy Review 373 (1998).

The Effects of Gender in the Federal Courts: Final Report of the Ninth Circuit Gender Bias Task Force, 67 Southern California Law Review 745 (1994).

Efran, Michael G., *The Effect of Physical Appearance on the Judgment of Guilt, Interpersonal Attraction and Severity of Recommended Punishment in a Simulated Jury Task*, 8 Journal of Research in Personality 45 (1974).

Eglit, Howard, *The Age Discrimination in Employment Act at Thirty: Where It's Been, Where It Is Today, Where It's Going*, 31 University of Richmond Law Review 579 (1997).

———, *Health Care Allocation for the Elderly: Age Discrimination by Another Name?* 26 Houston Law Review 813 (1989).

———, *Of Age and the Constitution*, 57 Chicago-Kent Law Review 859 (1981).

Ehrlich, Ira F., Phyllis Ehrlich, and Robert Dreher, *The Law and the Elderly: Where is the Legal Profession? A Challenge and a Response*, 31 Journal of Legal Education 452 (1981).

Eisenberg, Theodore, and Sherri Lynn Johnson, *The Effects of Intent: Do We Know How Legal Standards Work?* 76 Cornell Law Review 1151 (1991).

Elder Law Across the Curriculum, Symposium, 30 Stetson Law Review 1265–1468 (2001).

Epstein, Cynthia Fuchs, Robert Saute, Bonnie Oglensky, and Martha Gever, *Glass Ceilings and Open Doors: Women's Advancement in the Legal Profession*, 64 Fordham Law Review 291 (1995).

Erber, Joan T., and Sharon T. Rothberg, *Here's Looking at You: The Relative Effect of Age and Attractiveness on Judgments About Memory Failure*, 46 Journal of Gerontology, Psychological Sciences P116 (1991).

Ethical Issues in Dealing with Elderly Clients, panel discussion, in *Exploring Ethical Issues in Meeting the Legal Needs of the Elderly* 39. American Bar Association, 1987.

Feinberg, Gary, and Dinesh Khosla, *Sanctioning Elder Delinquents,* 21 Trial 46 (Sept. 1985).

Fischer, David Hackett, and Lawrence Stone, *Growing Old: An Exchange,* New York Review of Books 47 (Sept. 15, 1977).

Fitzgerald, Joseph M., *Younger and Older Jurors: The Influence of Environmental Supports on Memory Performance and Decision Making in Complex Trials,* 55B Journals of Gerontology: Psychological Sciences P323 (2000).

Fliegelman, Hal, and Debora C. Fliegelman, *Giving Guardians the Power to Do Medicaid Planning,* 32 Wake Forest Law Review 341 (1997).

Foley, Elizabeth A., *The Changing Face of Juries: Understanding Generation X,* 14 Chicago Bar Association Record 28 (Nov. 2000).

Friedman, Lawrence, and Mark Savage, *Taking Care: The Law of Conservatorship in California,* 61 Southern California Law Review 273 (1988).

Friend, Ronald M., and Michael Vinson, *Leaning Over Backwards: Jurors' Response to Defendants' Attractiveness,* 24 Journal of Communication 124 (Summer 1974).

Friendly, Henry J., *Book Review,* 86 Political Science Quarterly 470 (1971).

Frolik, Lawrence A., *The Developing Field of Elder Law: A Historical Perspective,* 1 Elder Law Journal 1 (1993).

———, *Elder Abuse and Guardians of Elderly Incompetents,* 2 Journal of Elder Abuse & Neglect 31 (1990).

———, *Guardianship Reform: When the Best is the Enemy of the Good,* 9 Stanford Law & Policy Review 347 (1998).

Galanter, Marc, *"Old and in the Way": The Coming Demographic Transformation of the Legal Profession and its Implications for the Provision of Legal Services,* 1999 Wisconsin Law Review 1081.

Gallipeau, Dan R., *Juror Perceptions and the ADA,* 5 Employment Rights and Responsibilities Newsletter 2 (Fall 2000).

Gelt, Howard, *Psychological Considerations in Representing the Aged Client,* 17 Arizona Law Review 293 (1975).

Geraghty, Peter H., *Ask Ethicsearch,* 9 No. 2 Prof. Law 22 (Feb. 1998).

Gerbner, George, Larry Gross, Nancy Signorielli, and Michael Morgan, *Aging with Television: Images In Television Drama and Conceptions of Social Reality,* 30 Journal of Communication 30 (1980).

A Global View of Age and Productivity, 3 Global Aging Report 3 (May/June 1998).

Golde, Peggy, and Nathan Kogan, *A Sentence Completion Procedure for Assessing Attitudes Toward Old People,* 14 Journal of Gerontology 355 (1959).

Goldman, Sheldon, *Voting Behavior on the United States Courts of Appeals Revisited,* 75 American Political Science Review 491 (1975).

Gottlich, Vicki, *Beyond Granny Bashing: Elder Abuse in the 1990s,* Clearinghouse Review Special Issue 371 (1994).

Greeley, Ann T., Karen Kaplowitz, and Vicki Stone, *What's In A Face?* Corporate Counsel Magazine 64 (Oct. 1998).

Gross, Samuel R., and Kent D. Syverud, *Don't Try: Civil Jury Verdicts in a System Geared to Settlement,* 44 University of California in Los Angeles Law Review 1 (1996).

Hamilton, William D., *The Genetical Evolution of Social Behavior II,* 7 Journal of Theoretical Biology 17 (1964).

Hans, Valerie P., and Neil Vidmar, *The American Jury at Twenty-Five Years,* 16 Law & Social Inquiry 323 (Spring 1991).

Hansen, Mark, *Reaching Out to Jurors,* 88 American Bar Association Journal 33 (Feb. 2002).

Heeg, Dorly J. H., and Peter A. Balt, *Self-Rated Health, Gender, and Mortality in Older Persons: Introduction to a Special Section,* 43 Gerontologist 369 (2003).

Heinz, John P., Kathleen E. Hull, and Ava A. Harter, *Lawyers and Their Discontents: Findings from a Survey of the Chicago Bar,* 74 Indiana Law Journal 735 (1999).

Hess, Thomas H., Corinne Auman, Stanley J. Colcombe, and Tamara A. Rahhal, *The Impact of Stereotype Threat on Age Differences in Memory Performance,* 58B Journal of Gerontology P3 (2003).

Hodgson, Shari, and Bert Pryor, *Sex Discrimination in the Courtroom: Attorney's Gender and Credibility,* 55 Psychology Reports 483 (1984).

Hoffman, David R., *Ensuring Quality Care Through the Use of the Federal False Claims Act,* 17 BIFOCAL 1 (Spring 1996).

Housman, Peter M., *Protective Services for the Elderly: The Limits of Parens Patriae,* 40 Missouri Law Review 215 (1975).

Howard, William J., *Arbitrating Claims of Employment Discrimination,* 50 Dispute Resolution Journal 40 (1995).

Idler, Ellen L., *Discussion: Gender in Self-Rated Health, in Mortality, and in the Relationship Between the Two,* 43 Gerontologist 372 (2003).

Ifill, Sherrilyn A., *Judging the Judges: Racial Diversity, Impartiality and Representation on State Trial Courts,* 39 Boston College Law Review 95 (1997).

Jensen, Gordon D., and Fredricka B. Oakley, *Ageism Across Cultures and in Perspective of Sociobiologic and Psychodynamic Theories,* 15 International Journal of Aging & Development 17 (1982–1983).

Joire, Lisa Schreiber, *After New York State Bar Association v. Reno: Ethical Problems in Limiting Medicaid Estate Planning,* 12 Georgetown Journal of Legal Ethics 789 (1999).

Jones, Owen D., *Law, Emotions, and Behavioral Biology,* 39 Jurimetrics Journal 283 (1999).

———, *Sex, Culture, and the Biology of Rape: Toward Explanation and Prevention,* 87 California Law Review 827 (1997).

Judicial Independence and Accountability Symposium, 72 Southern California Law Review 311–810 (1999).

Kaplan, Richard L., *Top Ten Myths of Social Security,* 3 Elder Law Journal 191 (Fall 1995).

Kapp, Marshall B., *Representing Older Persons: Ethical Challenges,* 53 Florida Bar Journal 25 (June 1989).

Kessler, Ellen Widen, *The Financial Impact of Divorces for Older Clients,* 12 Experience 24 (Winter 2002).

Kidman, Victoria, *The Elderly Offender: A New Wrinkle in the Criminal Justice System,* 14 Journal of Contemporary Law 131 (1988).

Klein, Jennifer L., *Elderly Drivers: The Need for Tailored License Renewal Procedures,* 3 Elder Law Journal 309 (1995).

Knapp, James L., and Kenneth B. Elder, *Assessing Prison Personnel's Knowledge of the*

Aging Process, 4 Journal of the Oklahoma Criminal Justice Research Consortium (Aug. 1997/1998).

Korobkin, Russell, *A Multi-Disciplinary Approach to Legal Scholarship: Economics, Behavioral Economics, and Evolutionary Psychology,* 41 Jurimetrics Journal 177 (2001).

Krieger, Linda Hamilton, *The Content of Our Categories: A Cognitive Bias Approach to Discrimination and Equal Employment Opportunity,* 47 Stanford Law Review 1161 (1995).

Lachs, Mark S., and Karl Pillemer, *Abuse and Neglect of Elderly Persons,* 332 New England Journal of Medicine 437 (Feb. 16, 1995).

Lampman, David V., II, Comment, *Fun, Fun, Fun, 'Til Sonny (or the Government) Takes the T-Bird Away: Elder Americans and the Privilege to be Independent,* 12 Albany Law Journal of Science & Technology 863 (2002).

Lawrence, Charles R., III, *The Id, The Ego, and Equal Protection: Reckoning with Unconscious Racism,* 39 Stanford Law Review 317 (1987).

Leipold, Andrew D., *Constitutionalizing Jury Selection in Criminal Cases: A Critical Examination,* 86 Georgetown Law Journal 945 (1998).

Leippe, Michael R., and Ann Romanczyk, *Reactions to Child Versus Adult Eyewitnesses,* 13 Law & Human Behavior 103 (1989).

Lenzer, Anthony, *Sociocultural Influences on Adjustment to Aging,* 16 Geriatrics 631 (1961).

Levinson, Sanford, *Contempt of Court: The Most Important Contemporary Challenge to Judging,* 49 Washington & Lee Law Review 339 (1992).

Levy, Becca R., *Mind Matters: Cognitive and Physical Effects of Aging Self-Stereotypes,* 58B Journal of Gerontology P203 (2003).

Levy, David T., Joy S. Vernick, and Kim A. Howard, *Relationship Between Driver's License Renewal Policies and Fatal Crashes Involving Drivers 70 Years or Older,* 274 Journal of the American Medical Association 1026 (Oct. 4, 1995).

Lichtenstein, Michael J., Linda A. Pruski, Carolyn E. Marshall, Cheryl L. Blalock, Douglas L. Murphy, Rosemarie Plaetke, and Shuko Lee, *The Positive Aging Teaching Materials Improve Middle School Students' Images of Older People,* 41 Gerontologist 322 (2001).

Linz, Daniel G., and Steven Penrod, *Increasing Attorney Persuasiveness in the Courtroom,* 8 Law & Psychology Review 1 (1984).

List, Lauren Barritt, and Saidy Barinaga-Burch, *National Study of Guardianship Systems: Summary of Findings and Recommendations,* 29 Clearinghouse Review 643 (1995).

Lopez, Ian F. Haney, *The Social Construction of Race: Some Observations on Illusion, Fabrication, and Choice,* 29 Harvard Civil Rights–Civil Liberties Law Review 1 (1994).

Marder, Nancy S., *Juries and Technology: Equipping Jurors for the Twenty-First Century,* 66 Brooklyn Law Review 1257 (2001).

———, *Justice and Multiculturalism,* 75 Southern California Law Review 659 (2002).

———, *The Technological Juror,* Judges Journal 34 (Fall 2001).

Margulies, Peter, *Access, Connection, and Voice: A Contextual Approach to Representing Senior Citizens of Questionable Capacity,* 62 Fordham Law Review 1073 (1994).

Marrus, Ellen, *Over the Hills and Through the Woods to Grandparents' House We Go, or Do We, Post-Troxel?* 43 Arizona Law Review 751 (2001).

Mayeux, Richard, and Mary Sano, *Drug Therapy Treatment of Alzheimer's Disease,* 341 New England Journal of Medicine 1670 (1999).

McAdams, Richard, *Cooperation and Conflict: The Economics of Group Status Production and Race Discrimination,* 108 Harvard Law Review 1003 (1995).

McFadden, Christopher R., *Judicial Independence, Age-Based BFOQs, and the Perils of Mandatory Retirement Policies for Appointed State Judges,* 52 Southern California Law Review 81 (2000).

McGuire, Mary V., and Gordon Bermant, *Individual and Group Decisions in Response to a Mock Trial: A Methodological Note,* 7 Journal of Applied Social Psychology 220 (1974).

McHugh, John B., *The Constitutional Challenge to Mandatory Retirement Statutes,* 49 St. John's Law Review 748 (1975).

McNeal, Mary Helen, *Redefining Attorney-Client Roles: Unbundling and Moderate-Income Elderly Clients,* 32 Wake Forest Law Review 295 (1997).

Mello, Eileen W., and Ronald P. Fisher, *Enhancing Older Adult Eyewitness Memory with the Cognitive Interview,* 10 Applied Cognitive Psychology 403 (1996).

Meltzer, H., *Age Differences in Status and Happiness of Workers,* 17 Geriatrics 831 (Dec. 1962).

Menkel-Meadow, Carrie, *The Trouble With the Adversary System in a Post-Modern Multicultural World,* 38 William & Mary Law Review 5 (1996).

Meyer, Donna J., *A New Peremptory Inclusion to Increase Representativeness and Impartiality in Jury Selection,* 45 Case Western Reserve Law Review 251 (1994).

Meyer, Harris, *Senior Bashing,* Hospitals & Health Networks 29 (Dec. 5, 1996).

Miller, Dorothy A., *The "Sandwich" Generation: Adult Children of the Aging,* 26 Social Work 419 (1981).

Mills, Carol J., and Wayne E. Bohannon, *Juror characteristics: to what extent are they related to jury verdicts?* 64 Judicature 22 (June/July 1980).

Mnookin, Robert, and Lewis Kornhauser, *Bargaining in the Shadow of Law: The Case of Divorce,* 88 Yale Law Journal 950 (1979).

Montague, Ashley, *Don't be adultish!* Psychology Today 46 (1977).

Moskowitz, Seymour H., *Adult Children and Indigent Parents: Intergenerational Responsibilities in International Perspective,* 86 Marquette Law Review 402 (2002).

———, *Reflecting Reality: Adding Elder Abuse and Neglect to Legal Education,* 47 Loyola Law Review 191 (2001).

Murphy, Jeffrie G., *Book Review, The Coming of Age,* 17 Arizona Law Review 546 (1975).

Nathanson, Paul, Paul L. Hain, and L. Lane Horder, *Lawyers, Legal Services, and the Elderly.* Unpublished (c. 1987).

National Conference on Constitutional and Legal Issues Relating to Age Discrimination and the Age Discrimination Act, symposium, 57 Chicago-Kent Law Review 805–1116 (1981).

Nuessel, Frank, *The Language of Ageism,* 22 Gerontologist 243 (1982).

Nugent, Donald C., *Judicial Bias,* 42 Cleveland State Law Review 1 (1994).

Oliver, Eric, *Jury See, Jury Decide: Courtroom Behavior and Juror Judgments,* 19 Trial Diplomacy Journal 299 (Nov./Dec. 1996).

Olshansky, S. Jay, Bruce A. Carnes, and Christine K. Cassell, *The Aging of the Human Species,* 268 Scientific American 46 (Apr. 1993).

Ostrom, Brian J., David B. Rottman, and John A. Goerdt, *A step above anecdote: a profile of the civil jury in the 1990s,* 79 Judicature 233 (March/Apr. 1996).

Owsley, Cynthia, Gerald McGwin, Michael Sloane, Jennifer Wells, Beth T. Stalvey, and Scott Gauthreaux, *Impact of Cataract Surgery on Motor Vehicle Crash Involvement by Older Adults,* 288 Journal of the American Medical Association 841 (2002).

Palmore, Erdman B., *Attitudes Toward Aging as Shown by Humor,* 12 Gerontologist 181 (1971).

Passuth, Patricia M., and Fay Lomax Cook, *Effects of Television Viewing on Knowledge and Attitudes About Older Adults: A Critical Reexamination,* 25 Gerontologist 69 (1985).

Peterson, Todd D., *Studying the Impact of Race and Ethnicity in the Federal Courts,* 64 George Washington Law Review 173 (1996).

Powe, L. A., Jr., *Old People and Good Behavior,* 12 Constitutional Commentary 195 (1995).

Preston, Samuel, *Children and the Elderly in the U.S.,* 251 Scientific American 44 (Dec. 1984).

Proceedings of the Conference on Ethical Issues in Representing Older Clients, 62 Fordham Law Review 961–1516 (1994).

Rachlinski, Jeffrey F., *Comment: Is Evolutionary Analysis of Law Science or Storytelling?* 41 Jurimetrics Journal 365 (2001).

Ragan, Amie M., and Anne M. Bowen, *Improving Attitudes Regarding the Elderly Population: The Effects of Information and Reinforcement for Change,* 41 Gerontologist 511 (2001).

Ray, Diane C., Kelly A. McKinney, and Charles V. Ford, *Differences in Psychologists' Ratings of Older and Younger Clients,* 27 Gerontologist 82 (1987).

Ray, Diane C., Michael A. Raciti, and Charles V. Ford, *Ageism in Psychiatrists: Associations with Gender, Certification, and Theoretical Orientation,* 25 Gerontologist 496 (1985).

Regan, John, *Protective Services for the Elderly: Commitment, Guardianship, and Alternatives,* 13 William & Mary Law Review 569 (1972).

Regan, Shawn Patrick, *Medicaid Estate Planning: Congress' Ersatz Solution for Long-Term Health Care,* 44 Catholic University Law Review 1217 (1995).

Report of the First Circuit Gender, Race, and Ethnic Bias Task Forces, 9 Boston University Public Interest Law Journal 173 (2000).

Report of the Special Committee on Gender to The D.C. Circuit Task Force on Gender, Race, and Ethnic Bias, 84 Georgetown Law Journal 1657 (1996).

Rein, Jan Ellen, *Clients with Destructive and Socially Harmful Choices—What's An Attorney to Do?: Within and Beyond the Competency Construct,* 62 Fordham Law Review 1101 (1994).

———, *Ethics and the Questionably Competent Client: What the Model Rules Say and Don't Say,* 9 Stanford Law & Policy Review 241 (1998).

———, *Preserving Dignity and Self-Determination in the Face of Competing Interests and Grim Alternatives: A Proposal for Statutory Refocus and Reform,* 60 George Washington L. Rev. 1818 (1992).

Reuben, Richard C., *Plaintiffs Rarely Win Punitives, Study Says,* 81 American Bar Association Journal 26 (Oct. 1995).

Reynolds, David E., and Mark S. Sanders, *Effect of Defendant Attractiveness, Age, and*

Injury on Severity of Sentence Given by Simulated Jurors, 96 Journal of Social Psychology 149 (1975).

Richman, Joseph and Tallmer, Margot, *The Foolishness and Wisdom of Age: Attitudes Toward the Elderly as Reflected in Jokes,* 17 Gerontologist 210 (1977).

Romano, John F., *Nursing Home and Elderly Care Facility Cases, Part 1: Initial Client Interview, Investigation, Case Workup, and Experts,* 17 Trial Diplomacy Journal 1 (Jan./Feb. 1994).

Rosenberg, Joseph A., *Adapting Unitary Principles of Professional Responsibility to Unique Practice Contexts: A Reflective Model for Resolving Ethical Dilemmas in Elder Law,* 31 Loyola University of Chicago Law Review 403 (2000).

Ross, David F., David Dunning, Michael P. Toglia, and Stephen J. Ceci, *The Child in the Eyes of the Jury,* 14 Law & Human Behavior 50 (1990).

Round, Deborah Ruble, *Gender Bias in the Judicial System,* 61 Southern California Law Review 2193 (1988).

Rubinson, Robert, *Constructions of Client Competence and Theories of Practice,* 31 Arizona State Law Journal 120 (1999).

Sabatino, Charles P., *Assessing Clients with Diminished Capacity,* 22 BIFOCAL 1 (Summer 2001).

Saharsky, Nicole A., Note, *Consistency as a Constitutional Value: A Comparative Look at Age in Abortion and Death Penalty Jurisprudence,* 85 Minnesota Law Review 1119 (2001).

Saks, Michael J., *What Do Jury Experiments Tell Us About How Juries (Should) Make Decisions?* 6 Southern California Interdisciplinary Law Journal 1 (1997).

Sanborn, Hope Viner, *The Vanishing Trial,* 88 American Bar Association Journal 25 (2002).

Schacter, Daniel L., Alfred W. Kaszniak, John F. Kihlstrom, and Michael Valdiserri, *The Relation Between Source Memory and Aging,* 6 Psychology & Aging 559 (1991).

Schonfield, David, *Who is stereotyping whom and why?* 22 Gerontologist 267 (1982).

Seeley, Sue, *Assisted Living: Federal and State Options for Affordability, Quality of Care, and Consumer Protection,* 23 BIFOCAL 1 (Fall 2001).

Shichor, David, *An Exploratory Study of Elderly Probationers,* 32 International Journal of Offender Therapy and Comparative Criminology 163 (1988).

Sigall, Harold, and Nancy Ostrove, *Beautiful but Dangerous: Effects of Offender Attractiveness and Nature of the Crime on Juridic Judgment,* 31 Journal of Personality and Social Psychology 410 (1975).

Singer, Amy, *Focusing on Jury Focus Groups,* 19 Trial Diplomacy Journal 321 (Nov./Dec. 1996).

Slotterback, Carole S., and David A. Saarnio, *Attitudes Toward Older Adults as Reported by Young Adults: Variation Based on Attitudinal Task and Attribute Categories,* 11 Psychology & Aging 563 (1996).

Smith, Linda F., *Representing the Elderly Client and Addressing the Question of Competence,* 14 Journal of Contemporary Law 61 (1988).

Smyth, Russell, and Mita Bhattacharya, *How fast do old judges slow down? A life cycle study of aging and productivity in the Federal Court of Australia,* 23 International Review of Law and Economics 141 (2003).

Spaeth, Edmund B., Jr., *To What Extent Can a Disciplinary Code Assure the Competence of Lawyers?* 61 Temple Law Review 1211 (1988).

Steele, Claude M., and Joshua Aronson, *Stereotype Threat and the Intellectual Test Performance of African Americans,* 69 Journal of Personality & Social Psychology 797 (1995).

Steffensmeier, Darrell, and Mark Motivans, *Older Men and Older Women in the Arms of Criminal Law: Offending Patterns and Sentencing Outcomes,* 55B Journals of Gerontology: Social Sciences S141 (2000).

Stephan, Cookie, and Judy C. Tully, *The Influence of Physical Attractiveness of a Plaintiff on the Decisions of Simulated Jurors,* 101 Journal of Social Psychology 149 (1977).

Stone, Lawrence, *Walking over Grandma,* New York Review of Books 10 (May 12, 1977).

Sullivan, Peggy S., Roger G. Dunham, and Geoffrey P. Alpert, *Attitude Structures of Different Ethnic and Age Groups Concerning Police,* 78 Journal of Criminal Law & Criminology 177 (1987).

Third Circuit Task Force on Equal Treatment in the Courts, 42 Villanova Law Review 1345 (1997).

Thomas, Louis-Vincent, *La vieillesse en Afrique Noire,* 37 Communications 85 (1983).

Tibbits, Clark, *Can We Invalidate Negative Stereotypes in Aging?* 19 Gerontologist 10 (1979).

Tremblay, Paul R., *On Persuasion and Paternalism: Lawyer Decisionmaking and the Questionably Competent Client,* 1987 Utah Law Review 515.

Tripodis, Vasiliki L., Note, *Licensing Policies for Older Drivers: Balancing Public Safety with Individual Mobility,* 38 Boston College Law Review 1051 (1997).

USC Symposium on Judicial Election, Selection, and Accountability, 61 Southern California Law Review 1555–2073 (1988).

Warren, Dawn, Albert Painter, and John Rudisell, *Effects of Geriatric Education on the Attitudes of Medical Students,* 31 Journal of American Geriatrics Society 435 (1983).

Weinstein, Jack B., *Limits on Judges Learning, Speaking and Acting—Part I—Tentative First Thoughts: How May Judges Learn?* 36 Arizona Law Review 539 (1994).

Werick, Mark, and Guy J. Manaster, *Age and the Perception of Age and Attractiveness,* 24 Gerontologist 408 (1984).

White, Mary J., and Dale M. Johnson, *Changes in Nursing Students' Stereotypic Attitudes Toward Old People,* 25 Nursing Research 430 (Nov./Dec. 1976).

Whitton, Linda S., *Ageism: Paternalism and Prejudice,* 46 DePaul Law Review 453 (1997).

Wiatrowski, William J., *Changing retirement ages: ups and downs,* 124 Monthly Labor Review 3 (Apr. 2001).

Williams, Cynthia A., Note, *Jury Source Representativeness and the Use of Voter Registration Lists,* 65 New York University Law Review 590 (1990).

Williams, George C., *Pleiotropy, natural selection, and the evolution of senescence,* 11 Evolution 398 (1957).

Wilson, J., and E. Hafferty, *Long-Term Effects of a Seminar on Aging and Health for First-Year Medical Students,* 3 Gerontologist 319 (1983).

Withers, Irma R., *Some Irrational Beliefs about Retirement in the United States,* 1 Industrial Gerontology 23 (Winter 1974 New Series).

"Women in Law: A Panel Discussion," 49 University of Kansas Law Review 847 (2001).

Wood, Erica F., *State Guardianship Legislation: Directions of Reform,* 29 Clearinghouse Review 654 (1995).

Yarmey, A. Daniel, *Accuracy and Credibility of the Elderly Witness,* 3 Canadian Journal on Aging 79 (1984).

Zeisel, Hans, and Diamond, Shari Seidman, *The Effect of Peremptory Challenges on Jury and Verdict: An Experiment in a Federal District Court,* 30 Stanford Law Review 491 (1978).

Ziegler, Donald H., *Young Adults as a Cognizable Group in Jury Selection,* 76 Michigan Law Review 1045 (1978).

Zuklie, Mitchell S., *Rethinking the Fair Cross-Section Requirement,* 84 California Law Review (1996).

Newspaper, Newsletter, Internet, and Bulletin Articles

"ABA Panel Stops Age Blackball," *Legal Times of Washington,* Dec. 22, 1980, p. 28.

Adsit, Laury L., *Elder Promoting Law,* IX NAELA News 3 (Nov./Dec. 1997).

Angier, Natalie, "Do Races Differ? Not Really, Genes Show," *New York Times,* Aug. 22, 2000, Science Times, pp. 1, 6.

———, "Weighing the Grandma Factor," *New York Times,* Nov. 5, 2002, Science Times, pp. D1, D4.

Apple, R. W., Jr., "Political Issue for the Ages," *New York Times,* Nov. 3, 2002, pp. A1, A18.

Arenson, Karen, "Reading Statistical Tea Leaves," *New York Times,* Aug. 5, 2001, Education Life, Sec. 4A, p. 14.

Associated Press, "In These Courts, Jurors Are Wanted," *Chicago Tribune,* Oct. 18, 1998, Sec. 1, p. 12.

Astor, Gerald, "The Elderly as Television's Forgotten Men and Women," *New York Times,* Aug. 4, 1974, p. D15.

Berger, Marilyn, "Clark Clifford, A Major Advisor to Four Presidents, is Dead at 91," *New York Times,* Oct. 11, 1998, pp. 1, 46.

Brantley, Ben, "To Survive, Ma, Never Look Back," *New York Times,* Nov. 15, 2001, p. E5.

Brock, Fred, "For Older Authors, a Steeper Hill," *New York Times,* Nov. 5, 2000, Business, p. 11.

Carter, Bill, and Jim Rutenberg, "With No Knockouts, NBC's Champ Faces Jabs," *New York Times,* Sept. 15, 2003, Business Day, pp. 1, 6.

Chicago Daily Law Bulletin (June 27, 2000).

Curriden, Mark, and Allen Posey, "Number of minority, lower-income jurors doesn't mirror county population," *Dallas Morning News,* Oct. 22, 2000.

Deutsch, Claudia H., "Women Lawyers Strive for Chance to Make it Rain," *New York Times,* May 21, 1996, Business Day, pp. D1, D7.

Feuer, Alan, "High-Rise Colony of Workers Evolves for Their Retirement," *New York Times,* Aug. 5, 2002, pp. A1, A15.

Grady, William, "Lawyers see more divorces among elderly," *Chicago Tribune,* Nov. 6, 1992, Sec. 1, p. 20.

Greising, David, "Volcker needs help; we know just the person," *Chicago Tribune,* March 3, 2002, Sec. 5, p. 1.

Hays, Constance L., "Setback for Prosecutors in Martha Stewart Trial," *New York Times,* Jan. 30, 2004, pp. C1, C4.

Jacobs, Andrew, "Still Working Boomers 'Retire' to Resorts," *New York Times,* Aug. 26, 2001, pp. 1, 27.

Kolata, Gina, "A Record and Big Questions as Woman Gives Birth at 63," *New York Times,* Apr. 24, 1997, p. A1.

Kristof, Nicholas D., "Hanoi Journal: Bean Paste vs. Miniskirts: Generation Gap Grows," *New York Times,* May 5, 1999, p. A4.

Kuczynski, Alex, "They Conquered, They Left," *New York Times,* March 24, 2002, Sunday Styles, pp. 1, 7.

Lauerman, Connie, "Remember: Memory loss comes with getting older," *Chicago Tribune,* Nov. 18, 2001, Sec. 13, pp. 1, 4.

Leicester, John, "China Population Hurtles Toward Old Age; Pension Retiree Facilities Pushed as Crisis Nears," *Chicago Tribune,* March 19, 2000, Business, p. 7.

Lewis, Neil A., "Unmaking the GOP Court Legacy," *New York Times,* Aug. 23, 1993, p. A9.

Liptak, Adam, "Stop the Clock? Critics Call the Billable Hour a Legal Fiction," *New York Times,* Oct. 29, 2002, p. 7.

Magnier, Mark, "Confucian Respect for Elders Is Withering Away," *Herald Tribune,* Nov. 23, 2001.

Maio, Pat, "High noon for older writers," 42 *AARP Bulletin* 17 (June 2001).

Mann, Leslie, "Boomers put their own mark on grandparenting," *Chicago Tribune,* March 20, 2002, Prime Time, pp. 1, 14.

Markon, Jerry, "Elderly Judges Handle 20% of U.S. Caseload," *Wall Street Journal,* Oct. 8, 2001, Marketplace, pp. A15, A20.

McCann, Tom, and Mickey Ciokajlo, "Rise in elder abuse overwhelms system," *Chicago Tribune,* March 26, 2002, pp. 1, 18.

McKee, Mike, *State Lawyers Older, More Diverse,* http://www.law.com/regionals/ca/stories/edt1030b.shtml (Oct. 30, 2001).

Nichols, Peter M., "Some Keep Shining, but Most Just Fade to Gray," *New York Times,* Feb. 23, 1997, Art & Living, pp. 15, 23.

Nunn, Emily, "One for the ages," *Chicago Tribune,* Sept. 10, 2003, Tempo, pp. 1, 4.

O'Hallaren, Bill, "Nobody (in TV) Loves You When You're Old and Gray," *New York Times,* July 24, 1977, p. D21.

The old grey divorce, http://www.divorcemag.com/news/seniordivorce.shtm (2003).

Pear, Robert, "9 of 10 Nursing Homes Lack Adequate Staff, a Government Study Finds," *New York Times,* Feb. 18, 2002, p. A11.

Pew Research Center for the People & the Press, news release, *Young, Old Differ on Using Surplus to Fix Social Security,* Jan. 28, 1998.

Pogrebin, Robin, *At 40, They're Finished, Television Writers Say,* at www.SalaryExpert.com. Jan. 30, 2001.

Ramirez, Anthony, "Consumer Crusader Feels a Chill in Washington/ Nader Remains Unbent by Winds of Change," *New York Times,* Dec. 31, 1995, Sec. 3, pp. 1, 10.

Reich, Howard, "Borge's Chord," *Chicago Tribune,* July 28, 1996, Sec. 7, p. 6.

Researchers Say Educated U.S. Kids Respect Their Elders, University of Kansas Office of University Relations, http://www.ur.ku.edu/News/96N/MayNews/May14/elders.html. 2002.

Seelye, Katherine Q., and Janet Elder, "Strong Support is Found for Ban on Gay Marriage," *New York Times,* Dec. 21, 2003, pp. 1, 26.

Stock, Robert W., "Balancing the Needs and Risks of Older Drivers," *New York Times,* July 13, 1995, p. B5

Taylor, T. Shawn, "'Partners' put law firms in labor bind," *Chicago Tribune,* Apr. 7, 2002, Business, pp. 1, 6

Uchitelle, Louis, "Older Workers Are Thriving Despite Recent Hard Times," *New York Times,* Sept. 8, 2003, pp. A1, A15

Vinciguerra, Thomas, "Old Fires, New Sparks: Call Them Start-Over Dads," *New York Times,* Dec. 12, 1996, Living Arts, pp. B1–B2.

Wermiel, Stephen, "Reagan Choices Alter the Makeup and Views of the Federal Courts," *Wall Street Journal,* Feb. 1, 1988, pp. 1, 17.

Wheeler, David L., "A Growing Number of Scientists Reject the Concept of Race," *Chronicle of Higher Education,* Feb. 17, 1995, p. A8.

Whitaker, Barbara, "In Hollywood No One Gets A Casting Call for this Role," *New York Times,* March 12, 2000, Art & Living, p. 8.

Wilford, John Noble, "When Humans Became Human," *New York Times,* Feb. 26, 2002, Science Times, pp. D1, D5.

Government Reports and Issuances

Administration on Aging, U.S. Dept. of Health and Human Services, *A Profile of Older Americans: 2000* (n.d.).

Division for Social & Policy Development, United Nations, *The Aging of the World's Population* (June 11, 2002), http://www.un.org.esa/socdev/ageing/agewpop.html (2002).

Equal Employment Opportunity Commission, *Waiver of Rights and Claims Under the Age Discrimination in Employment Act (ADEA),* 63 Fed. Reg. 30631, 30627 (June 6, 1998).

Equal Employment Opportunity Commission Alternative Dispute Resolution Statement, EEOC Notice No. 915.002 (July 17, 1995), www.eeoc.gov/docs/adrstatement.html (Sept. 2003).

National Academy on Aging, *Old Age in the 21st Century: A Report to the Assistant Secretary for Aging,* U.S. Dept. of Health & Human Services (1994).

National Commission for Employment Policy, *Older Workers: Prospects, Problems and Policies,* 9th Annual Report (1995).

The Older American Worker—Age Discrimination in Employment, Report of the Secretary of Labor to the Congress Under Section 715 of the Civil Rights Act of 1964 (June 1965).

President's Commission for the Study of Ethical Problems in Medicine and Biomedical and Behavioral Research, *Vol. 1, A Report on Making Health Care Decisions: The Ethical and Legal Implications of Informed Consent in the Patient-Practitioner Relationship* (1982).

Select Committee on Aging, U.S. House of Representatives, *Age Stereotyping and Television,* Comm. Pub. No. 95-109, 95th Cong., 1st Sess. (1977).

Select Committee on Aging, U.S. House of Representatives, *Crime: Violence and the Elderly,* Comm. Pub. No. 99-547, 99th Cong., 1st Sess., Oct. 22, 1985 (1986).

Select Committee on Aging, U.S. House of Representatives, *Grandparents: New Roles and Responsibilities,* Comm. Pub. No. 102-876, 102d Cong., 2d Sess. (1991).

Select Committee on Aging, U.S. House of Representatives, *Surrogate Decisionmaking for*

Adults: Model Standards to Ensure Quality Guardianship and Representative Payeeship Services, Comm. Pub. No. 100-705, 100th Cong., 2d Sess. (1989).

Select Committee on Aging, U.S. House of Representatives, *Televised Advertising and the Elderly,* Comm. Pub. No. 95-128, 95th Cong., 2d Sess. (1978).

Special Committee on Aging, Subcommittee on Long-Term Care, U.S. Senate, *Nursing Home Care in the United States: Failure in Public Policy,* S. Rpt. No. 93-1420, 93d Cong., 2d Sess. (1974).

Special Committee on Aging, U.S. Senate, *Nursing Home Care: The Unfinished Agenda,* S. Rpt. 99-160, 99th Cong., 2d Sess. (1986).

Special Committee on Aging, U.S. Senate, *Protective Services for the Elderly—A Working Paper,* 95th Cong., 1st Sess. (1977).

Taenber, Cynthia M., U.S. Department of Commerce, Special Studies P23–178, *Sixty-Five Plus in America* (1992).

United States Bureau of the Census, *Projections of the Total Resident Population by 5-Year Age Groups, and Sex with Special Age Categories, Middle Series, 2001 to 2005* (Jan. 13, 2003).

United States Bureau of the Census, *Projections of the Total Resident Population by 5-Year Age Groups, and Sex with Special Age Categories: Middle Series, 2025–2045* (Jan. 13, 2003).

United States Bureau of the Census, *Statistics About Business Size,* http:/www.census.gov/epcd/www/smallbus.html (2002).

United States Bureau of Labor Statistics, U.S. Department of Labor, *Occupational Outlook Handbook* 211 (2002–2003), http:/www.bls.gov./oco/pdf/ocos.053pdf (2003).

United States Commission on Civil Rights, *The Age Discrimination Study* 76 (1977).

United States Department of Health and Human Services, Health Care Financing Administration, *2001 HCFA Statistics* (n.d.).

United States Department of Health, Education, and Welfare, 44 Federal Register 33774 (June 12, 1979).

United States Department of Justice, Federal Bureau of Investigation, *Crime in the United States, 1999* (2000).

United States Equal Employment Opportunity Commission, Age Discrimination in Employment Act (ADEA) Charges, FY 1992–FY 2003, www.EEOC.gov. (Aug. 16, 2004).

United States General Accounting Office, *An Aging Society—Meeting the Needs of the Elderly While Responding to Rising Federal Costs* (Sept. 1986).

United States General Accounting Office, Report to the Chairman, Special Committee on Aging, U.S. Senate, *Long-Term Care—Current Issues and Future Directions,* GAO/HEHS-95-109 (Apr. 1995).

United States General Accounting Office, Report to the Honorable William S. Cohen, Special Committee on Aging, U.S. Senate, *Long-Term Care—Projected Needs of the Aging Baby Boom Generation,* GAO/HRD-91-86 (1991).

United States General Accounting Office, Report to the Special Committee on Aging, U.S. Senate, *California Nursing Homes—Care Problems Persist Despite Federal and State Oversight,* GAO/HEHS-98-202 (July 1998).

United States Sentencing Commission Guidelines

United States Senate Special Committee on Aging, American Association of Retired Persons, Federal Council on the Aging, and U.S. Administration on Aging, *Aging America,*

Trends and Projections, 1991 Edition. Washington, D.C.: Department of Health and Human Services, n.d.

Judicial Decisions

Adarand Constructors, Inc. v. Pena, 515 U.S. 200 (1995).

Albany Phosphate Co. v. Hugger Bros, 4 Ga. App. 771, 62 S.E. 533 (1908).

Alexander v. Louisiana, 405 U.S. 625 (1972).

Andrews, Mosburg, Davis, Elam & Bixler, Inc. v. General Insurance Co. of America, 418 F. Supp. 304 (W.D. Okla. 1976).

Apkin v. Treasurer & Receiver General, 401 Mass. 427, 517 N.E.2d 141 (1988).

Arnold v. Carmichael, 524 So.2d 464 (Fla. App.), *rev. denied*, 531 So.2d 1352 (Fla. 1988).

Aronstam v. Cashman, 132 Vt. 538, 325 A.2d 361 (1974).

Barkan v. United States, 362 F.2d 158 (7th Cir.), *cert. denied*, 385 U.S. 882 (1966).

Batson v. Kentucky, 476 U.S. 79 (1986).

Blank v. Sullivan and Cromwell, 418 F. Supp. 1 (S.D.N.Y. 1975).

Blassman v. Markworth, 359 F. Supp. 1 (N.D. Ill. 1973).

Boughton v. Price, 70 Idaho 243, 215 P.2d 286 (1950).

Bowers v. Hardwick, 478 U.S. 186 (1986).

Bronstein v. Bronstein, 434 So.2d 780 (Ala. 1983).

Brown v. Board of Education, 347 U.S. 483 (1954).

Burroughs v. State, 33 Ga. 403 (1863).

Canavan v. Messina, 31 Conn. Supp. 447, 334 A.2d 237 (1973).

Carlson v. WPLG/TV-10, 70 FEP Cas. (BNA) 1596 (S.D. Fla. 1996).

Carter v. Georgia, 75 Ga. 747 (1885).

Carter v. Jury Commission, 396 U.S. 320 (1970).

Carter v. State, 121 Tex. Crim. 493, 51 S.W.2d 316 (1932).

Castaneda v. Partida, 430 U.S. 482 (1977).

Caswell v. State, 27 Ga. App. 76, 107 S.E. 560 (1921).

Chase v. United States, 468 F.2d 141 (7th Cir. 1972).

Chestnut v. Criminal Court, 442 F.2d 611 (2d Cir.), *cert. denied*, 404 U.S. 856 (1971).

City of Cleburne v. Cleburne Living Center, Inc., 473 U.S. 432 (1985).

Clackamas Gastroenterology Associates v. Wells, 538 U.S. 140 (2003).

Cleveland Board of Education v. LaFleur, 414 U.S. 632 (1972).

Coates v. National Cash Register Co., 433 F. Supp. 655 (W.D. Va. 1977).

Cobbs v. State, 244 Ga. 344, 260 S.E.2d 60 (1979).

Cohron v. State, 20 Ga. 752 (1856).

Colgan v. Fisher Scientific Co., 935 F.2d 1407 (3d Cir.), *cert. denied*, 502 U.S. 941 (1991).

Combes v. Griffin Television, Inc., 421 F. Supp. 841 (W.D. Okla. 1976).

Commonwealth v. Bastarache, 382 Mass. 86, 414 N.E.2d 984 (1980).

Conner v. State, 748 So.2d 950 (Fla. Sup. Ct. 1999).

Davis v. Greer, 675 F.2d 141 (7th Cir.), *cert. denied*, 459 U.S. 975 (1982).

Davis v. People, 19 Ill. 74 (1857).

Davison v. People, 90 Ill. 221 (1878).

Diamond v. Cuomo, 70 N.Y.2d 338, 514 N.E.2d 1356, 520 N.Y.S.2d 732 (1987), *app. dismissed*, 486 U.S. 1028 (1988).

Diamond v. Cuomo, 130 A.D.2d 292, 519 N.Y.S.2d 691, *affd.*, 70 N.Y.2d 338, 514 N.E.2d 1356, 520 N.Y.S.2d 732, *app. dismissed*, 486 U.S. 1028 (1988).

Dolan v. Secretary of State, 55 Ohio App.3d 157, 563 N.E.2d 745 (1988), *dismissed*, 41 Ohio St.3d 725, 535 N.E.2d 1370 (1989).

Duplan Corp. v. Derking Milliken, Inc., 400 F. Supp. 497 (D.S.C. 1975).

Duncan v. Louisiana, 391 U.S. 145 (1968).

Duren v. Missouri, 439 U.S. 357 (1979).

Equal Employment Opportunity Commission v. Vermont, 904 F.2d 794 (2d Cir. 1990).

Equal Employment Opportunity Commission v. Wyoming, 460 U.S. 226 (1983).

Esberg v. Union Oil Co., 47 P.3d 1069, 28 Cal.4th 262 (2002).

Garcia v. Borelli, 129 Cal. App.3d 24, 180 Cal. Rptr. 768 (1982).

Gardner v. Baker, 40 Ala. App. 374, 113 So.2d 695 (1959).

Gondelman v. Commonwealth, 120 Pa. Commw. 624, 550 A.2d 814 (1988), *dismissed*, 520 Pa. 451, 554 A.2d 896, *cert. denied*, 493 U.S. 849 (1989).

Gonzalez v. Commission on Judicial Performance, 33 Cal.3d 359, 188 Cal. Rptr. 880, 657 P.2d 372 (Cal. 1983), *app. dismissed*, 464 U.S. 1033 (1984).

Gregory v. Ashcroft, 501 U.S. 452 (1991).

Grinnell v. State, 121 N.H. 823, 435 A.2d 523 (1981).

Grutter v. Bollinger, 539 U.S. 306 2325 (2003).

Ham v. South Carolina, 409 U.S. 524 (1973).

Hamling v. United States, 418 U.S. 87 (1974).

Hammond v. Marx, 406 F. Supp. 853 (D. Me. 1975).

Hatten v. Rains, 854 F.2d 687 (5th Cir. 1988), *cert. denied*, 490 U.S. 1106 (1989).

Hawkins v. Hawkins, 102 Ill. App.3d 1037, 430 N.E.2d 652 (1981).

Hazen Paper Co. v. Biggins, 507 U.S. 604 (1993).

Hinton v. Judicial Retirement and Removal Commission, 854 S.W.2d 756 (Ky. 1993).

Holland v. Illinois, 493 U.S. 474 (1990).

Hughes v. State, 198 N.W.2d 348, 55 Wis.2d 477 (1972).

Hughes v. United States, 899 F.2d 1495 (6th Cir.), *cert. denied*, 498 U.S. 980 (1990).

Humphrey v. Walls, 169 Md. 292, 181 A. 735 (1935).

In re Assignment of Justices and Judges, 222 So.2d 22 (Fla. Sup. Ct. 1969).

In re Carl B., 142 Misc.2d 406, 537 N.Y.S.2d 456 (1989).

In re Charge of Judicial Misconduct, 62 F.3d 320 (9th Cir. 1995).

In re Chevron U.S.A., Inc., 121 F.3d 163 (5th Cir. 1997).

In re Corrugated Container Antitrust Litigation, 614 F.2d 958 (5th Cir.), *cert. denied*, 449 U.S. 888 (1980).

In re Johnson, 395 A.2d 1319 (Pa. 1978).

In re J. P. Linahan, 138 F.2d 650 (2d Cir. 1983).

In re M. Ibrahim Khan, 751 F.2d 162 (6th Cir. 1984).

In re Stevens, 31 Cal.3d 403, 183 Cal. Rptr. 48, 645 P.2d 99 (Cal. 1982).

In re Stout, 521 Pa. 571, 559 A.2d 489 (1989).

In re Union Leader Corp., 292 F.2d 381 (1st Cir. 1961), *cert. denied*, 368 U.S. 927 (1961).

Izquierdo Prieto v. Agustin Mercado Rosa, 894 F.2d 467 (1st Cir. 1990).

J.E.B. v. Alabama, 511 U.S. 127 (1994).

Johnston v. Bowersox, 119 F. Supp.2d 971 (E.D. Mo. 2000).

Karlen v. City Colleges of Chicago, 837 F.2d 314 (7th Cir.), *cert. denied*, 486 U.S. 1044 (1988).

Kelly v. Keiser, 340 Pa. 59, 16 A.2d 307 (1940).

Kimel v. Florida Board of Regents, 528 U.S. 62 (2000).

King v. Leach, 131 F.2d 8 (5th Cir. 1942).

King v. United States, 576 F.2d 432 (2d Cir. 1978), *cert. denied*, 439 U.S. 850 (1978).

King v. United States, 346 F.2d 123 (1st Cir. 1965).

Knapp v. Kinsey, 232 F.2d 458 (6th Cir. 1956), *cert. denied*, 352 U.S. 892 (1956).

Lawrence v. Texas, 123 S. Ct. 2472 (2003).

Letson v. State, 215 Ala. 229, 110 So. 21 (1926).

Liteky v. United States, 510 U.S. 540 (1994).

Loving v. Virginia, 388 U.S. 1 (1967).

Mack v. State, 375 So.2d 476 (Ala. App. 1979).

Maldini v. Ambro, 36 N.Y.2d 481, 330 N.E.2d 403, 369 N.Y.S.2d 385 (1973), *cert. denied*, 423 U.S. 993 (1975).

Malmed v. Thornburgh, 621 F.2d 565 (3d Cir.), *cert. denied*, 449 U.S. 955 (1980).

Manson v. Edwards, 482 F.2d 1076 (6th Cir. 1973).

Mason v. Lister, 562 F.2d 343 (5th Cir. 1977).

Massachusetts Board of Retirement v. Murgia, 427 U.S. 307 (1976).

McGinnis v. M.I. Harris, Inc., 486 F. Supp. 750 (N.D. Tex. 1980).

McQueen v. Scroggy, 99 F.3d 1302 (6th Cir. 1996).

Mengelkamp v. List, 88 Nev. 542, 501 P.2d 1032 (1972).

Meyers v. Roberts, 310 Minn. 358, 246 N.W.2d 186 (1976), *app. dismissed*, 429 U.S. 1083 (1977).

Mississippi University for Women v. Hogan, 458 U.S. 718 (1982).

Mitchell v. Ward, 150 F. Supp.2d 1194 (W.D. Okla. 1999).

Munoz v. St. Mary-Corwin Hospital, 221 F.3d 1160 (2d Cir. 2000).

Nelson v. Miller, 25 Utah2d 277, 480 P.2d 467 (1971).

New York State Bar Association v. Reno, 999 F. Supp. 710 (N.D.N.Y. 1998).

Nixon v. United States, 506 U.S. 224 (1993).

North Chicago Electric Railway v. Moosman, 82 Ill. App. 172 (1899).

Ogle v. Fuiten, 102 Ill.2d 356, 466 N.E.2d 224 (1984).

O'Neil v. Baine, 568 S.W.2d 761 (Mo. 1978).

Opatz v. St. Cloud, 293 Minn. 379, 196 N.W.2d 298 (1972).

Parrish v. Board of Commissioners, 524 F.2d 98, 100 (5th Cir. 1975).

People v. Attica Bros., 79 Misc.2d 492, 359 N.Y.S.2d 699 (Sup. Ct. 1974).

People v. Marr, 67 Misc.2d 113, 324 N.Y.S.2d 608 (Just. Ct. 1971).

People v. Redwine, 50 Mich. App. 593, 213 N.W.2d 841 (1973).

People v. Scott, 17 Ill. App.3d 1026, 309 N.E.2d 257 (1974).

People v. Wheeler, 22 Cal. 3d 258, 148 Cal. Rptr. 890, 583 P.2d 748 (1978).

Peters v. Kiff, 407 U.S. 493 (1972).

Phillips v. Joint Legislative Committee on Performance and Expenditure Review of the State of Mississippi, 637 F.2d 1014 (5th Cir. 1981), *cert. denied*, 456 U.S. 690 (1982).

Pierce v. Lafourche Parish Council, 762 So.2d 608 (La. 2000).

Powers v. Ohio, 499 U.S. 400 (1991).

Purdie v. University of Utah, 584 P.2d 831 (Utah 1978).

Quinn v. Marsh, 141 Neb. 436, 3 N.W.2d 892 (1972).

Raza Unida Party v. Bullock, 349 F. Supp. 1272 (W.D. Tex. 1972), *affd. in part & vacated and remanded in part on other grounds sub nom.* American Party of Texas v. White, 415 U.S. 767 (1974).

Re Adoption of Ann, 461 S.W.2d 338 (Mo. 1970).

Re Adoption of Shields, 4 Wis.2d 219, 89 N.W.2d 827 (1958).

Re T, 81 Misc.2d 535, 365 N.Y.S.2d 709 (1975).

Reddock v. State, 23 Ala. App. 290, 124 So. 398 (1929).

Romano v. State, 847 P.2d 368 (Okl. Ct. Crim. App. 1993).

Rubino v. Ghezzi, 512 F.2d 431 (2d Cir.), *cert. denied*, 423 U.S. 891 (1975).

Ryther v. KARE 11, 108 F.3d 832 (8th Cir.), *cert. denied*, 521 U.S. 1119 (1997).

Sabo v. Casey, 757 F. Supp. 587 (E.D. Pa.) *rev'd in part & dismissed in part without opinion*, 968 F.2d 14 (3d Cir. 1991).

Sato v. Plunkett, 154 F.R.D. 189 (N.D. Ill. 1994).

Sheahan v. CBS Inc., 1994 U.S. Dist. LEXIS 2623 (S.D.N.Y. 1994).

Simmons v. Jones, 317 F. Supp. 397 (S.D. Ga. 1970), *revd.*, 478 F.2d 321 (5th Cir. 1973), *modified*, 519 F.2d 52 (5th Cir. 1975).

Skaggs v. Parker, 27 F. Supp.2d 952 (W.D. Ky. 1998).

Smith v. State, 225 Ga. 328, 168 S.E.2d 587 (1969), *cert. denied*, 396 U.S. 1045 (1970).

Smith v. Texas, 311 U.S. 128 (1940).

Spencer v. Board of Education, 39 A.D.2d 399, 334 N.Y.S.2d 783 (1972), *affd. memorandum*, 31 N.Y.2d 810, 291 N.E.2d 585, 339 N.Y.S.2d 461 (1972).

State v. Anderson, 384 S.W.2d 591 (Mo. 1964).

State v. Brooks, 92 Mo. 542, 5 S.W. 257 (1887).

State v. Clark, 249 La. 914, 192 So.2d 122 (1962).

State v. Holmstrom, 43 Wis.2d 465, 168 N.W.2d 574 (1969).

State v. Kelly, 885 S.W.2d 730 (Mo. App. 1994).

State v. Sanders, 949 P.2d 1084 (Kan. Sup. Ct. 1997).

State v. Willis, 33 Ohio Misc. 159, 293 N.E.2d 895 (1972).

State *ex rel.* Oleson v. Graunke, 119 Neb. 440, 229 N.W. 329 (1930).

Staten v. State, 141 Ga. 82, 80 S.E. 850 (1913).

Stowe v. Smith, 184 Conn. 194, 441 A.2d 81 (1981).

Swierkiewicz v. Sorema, NA, 534 U.S. 506 (2002).

Taylor v. Louisiana, 419 U.S. 522 (1975).

Taylor v. Rancho Santa Barbara, 206 F.3d 932 (9th Cir. 2000).

Taxpayers Association of Weymouth Township, Inc. v. Weymouth Township, 71 N.J. 249, 364 A.2d 1016 (1976), *cert. denied*, 430 U.S. 977 (1977).

Tennessee v. John Scopes (Tenn. 1925).

Thiel v. Southern Pacific, 328 U.S. 217 (1946).

Thomas v. State, 144 Ga. 298, 87 S.E. 7 (1915).

Trafelet v. Thompson, 594 F.2d 623 (7th Cir.), *cert. denied*, 444 U.S. 906 (1979).

Troxel v. Granville, 530 U.S. 57 (2000).

Trice v. State, 853 P.2d 203 (Okl. Ct. Crim. App. 1993).

Trotter v. State, 237 Ark. 820, 377 S.W.2d 14, *cert. denied*, 379 U.S. 890 (1964).

United States v. Armsbury, 408 F. Supp. 1130 (D. Or. 1976).

United States v. Briggs, 366 F. Supp. 1356 (N.D. Fla. 1973).

United States v. Butera, 420 F.2d 564 (1st Cir. 1970).

United States v. Carey, 895 F.2d 318 (7th Cir. 1990).

United States v. Carignan, 600 F.2d 762 (9th Cir. 1979).

United States v. Carolene Products Co., 304 U.S. 144 (1938).

United States v. Clemons, 941 F.2d 321 (5th Cir. 1991).

United States v. Computer Sciences Corp., 511 F. Supp. 1125 (E.D. Va. 1981).

United States v. Deardorff, 343 F. Supp. 1033 (S.D.N.Y. 1971).

United States v. Diggs, 522 F.2d 1310 (D.C. Cir. 1975), *cert. denied*, 429 U.S. 852 (1976).

United States v. DiTommaso, 405 F.2d 385 (4th Cir. 1968), *cert. denied*, 394 U.S. 934 (1969).

United States v. Eskew, 460 F.2d 1028 (9th Cir. 1972).

United States v. Fletcher, 965 F.2d 781 (9th Cir. 1992).

United States v. Gast, 457 F.2d 141 (7th Cir.), *cert. denied*, 406 U.S. 969 (1972).

United States v. Geelan, 509 F.2d 737 (8th Cir. 1974), *cert. denied*, 421 U.S. 999 (1975).

United States v. Gooding, 473 F.2d 686 (5th Cir.), *cert. denied*, 412 U.S. 928 (1973).

United States v. Grinnell, 384 U.S. 563 (1966).

United States v. Guzman, 337 F. Supp. 140 (S.D.N.Y.), *affd.*, 468 F.2d 1245 (2d Cir. 1972), *cert. denied*, 410 U.S. 937 (1973).

United States v. Kimball, 73 F.3d 269 (10th Cir. 1995).

United States v. Kirk, 534 F.2d 1262 (8th Cir. 1976), *cert. denied*, 430 U.S. 906 (1977).

United States v. Kuhn, 441 F.2d 179 (5th Cir. 1971).

United States v. Lewis, 472 F.2d 252. (3d Cir. 1973).

United States v. Maxwell, 160 F.3d 1071 (6th Cir. 1998).

United States v. Osborne, 482 F.2d 1354 (8th Cir. 1973).

United States v. Owen, 492 F.2d 1100 (5th Cir.), *cert. denied*, 419 U.S. 965 (1974).

United States v. Pleier, 849 F Supp. 1321 (D. Alaska 1994).

United States v. Ross, 468 F.2d 1213 (9th Cir. 1972), *cert. denied*, 410 U.S. 989 (1973).

United States v. Sammons, 918 F.2d 592 (6th Cir. 1990).

United States v. Sibla, 624 F.2d 864 (9th Cir. 1980).

United States v. Test, 550 F.2d 577 (10th Cir. 1976).

United States v. Thompson, 483 F.2d 527 (3d Cir. 1973), *cert. denied*, 425 U.S. 944 (1976).

United States v. Virginia, 518 U.S. 515 (1996).

United States Equal Employment Opportunity Commission v. Illinois, 721 F. Supp 156 (N.D. Ill. 1989).

United States *ex rel.* Hawthorne v. Cowan, 224 F. Supp.2d 1178 (N.D. Ill. 2002).

Vance v. Bradley, 440 U.S. 93 (1979).

Weber v. Strippit, Inc., 186 F.3d 907 (8th Cir. 1999).

Wehrly v. American Motor Sales Corp., 678 F. Supp. 1366 (N.D. Ind. 1988).

Weinberg v. Johnson, 518 A.2d 985 (D.C. 1986).

Wheeler v. Hurdman, 825 F.2d 257 (10th Cir.), *cert. denied*, 484 U.S. 986 (1987).

White Egret Condominium v. Franklin, 379 So.2d 346 (Fla. 1979).

Whitehead v. Westbrook, Civ. No. F-74-41-C (W.D. Ark. (1975), *affd. memorandum*, 423 U.S. 962 (1975).

Williams v. Raytheon Co., 220 F.3d 16 (1st Cir. 2000).

Williams v. State, 67 Ala. 183 (1880).

Williamson v. State, 562 Ala. App. 617, 296 So.2d 241 (1974).

Wingfield v. United Technologies Corp., 678 F. Supp. 973 (D. Conn. 1988).

Wurzel v. Falcey, 69 N.J. 401, 354 A.2d 617 (1976).

Young v. General Foods Corp., 840 F.2d 825 (11th Cir. 1988), *cert. denied*, 488 U.S. 1004 (1989).

Zielasko v. Ohio, 873 F.3d 967 (6th Cir. 1989).

Constitutional and Statutory Provisions—Actual and Proposed

Federal Constitutional Provisions

U.S. Const., art. I, § 2
U.S. Const., art. I, § 3
U.S. Const., art. II, § 1
U.S. Const., art. III, §1
U.S. Const., amend. V
U.S. Const., amend. VI
U.S. Const., amend. XII
U.S. Const., amend. XIV, § 1
U.S. Const., amend XXVI

Federal Statutes and Public Laws

Age Discrimination in Employment Act Amendments of 1978, Pub. L. No. 95-256, 92 Stat. 189.
Age Discrimination in Employment Amendments of 1986, Pub. L. No. 99-592, § 2(c), 100 Stat. 3342.
Balanced Budget Act of 1997, § 4734.
Civil Rights Act of 1964, Pub. L. No. 88-352, § 715, 78 Stat. 287, 316.
15 U.S.C. §§ 1691–1691f (Equal Credit Opportunity Act).
18 U.S.C. §3551 *et seq.* (Sentencing Reform Act of 1984, as amended).
20 U.S.C. §§ 1681–1688 (Title IX of the Education Amendments of 1972, as amended).
21 U.S.C. § 859(a)
28 U.S.C. § 144
28 U.S.C. § 371
28 U.S.C. § 371(e)
28 U.S.C. § 372(a)
28 U.S.C. § 372(b)
28 U.S.C. § 372(c)
28 U.S.C. § 455(a)
28 U.S.C. § 455(b)(1).
28 U.S.C. §§ 991–998 (Sentencing Reform Act of 1984, as amended).
29 U.S.C. §§ 621–634 (Age Discrimination in Employment Act of 1967, as amended).
29 U.S.C. § 623(f)(2)(B)(ii).
29 U.S.C. § 630(b).
29 U.S.C. § 631(b).
42 U.S.C. § 1320a-7b(a)(6) (section 217 of the Health Insurance Portability and Accountability Act of 1996).
42 U.S.C. § 1320a-7b(a)(6) ("Granny Goes to Jail Act").
42 U.S.C. § 1395 *et seq.* (Medicare).
42 U.S.C. §§ 1395i-3(a)–(h), 1396r(a)–(h) (codifying Omnibus Reconciliation Act of 1987, Pub. L. No. 100-203, 101 Stat. 1330-175, 1330-179, 1330-182 [1987]).
Title VII of the Civil Rights Act of 1964, 42 U.S.C. §§ 2000e –2000e-17.
42 U.S.C. § 2000e(b).
42 U.S.C. § 2000e-2(e).

42 U.S.C.§ 3001 *et seq.*
42 U.S.C. § 3607 (Federal Fair Housing Act, as amended).
42 U.S.C. § 4161(l)(1).
42 U.S.C. §§ 6101–6107 (Age Discrimination Act of 1975).
42 U.S.C. Sec. 12101 *et seq.* (Americans with Disabilities Act).
Pub. L. No. 202, § 15, 81 Stat. 606–607.

Federal Proposed Legislation

H.R. Res. 693, 96th Cong., 2d Sess. (1980).
S. Res. 374, 96th Cong., 2d Sess. (1980).

State Constitutional Provisions

Fla. Const., Art. 5, § 8.

State Laws

Ariz. Rev. Stat. Ann. § 13-702.D12.
Fla. Stat. Ann. § 40.013(8).
Fla. Stat. Ann. § 90.803(24).
Fla Stat. Ann. Ch. 744.012(10).
Fla. Stat. Ann. § 825.101(5).
Fla Stat. Ann. § 825.101(6) (1995) (recodified at Fla. Stat. Ann. § 825.101(5).
Official Code of Ga. § 15-12-1.
320 Ill Comp. Stat. Ann. 20/1 *et seq.* (Elder Abuse and Neglect Act).
720 Ill. Comp. Stat. Ann. 5/12-2(1)(12).
753 Ill. Comp. Stat. Ann. § 5/2-1007.1.
Ky. Rev. Stat. § 635.020(4) (Michie 1999).
Mass. Ann. Laws, ch. 234, § 1.
Mich. Stat. Ann. § 27.3935(4).
Mich. Stat. Ann. § 27.3936(5).
Mich. Stat. Ann. Sec. 27A.1307(1).
Mo. Ann. Stat. §§ 565.180-184.
Page's Ohio Rev. Code Ann. § 2907.04 (2002).
Rev. Stat. of Neb. § 25-1601.
Nev. Rev. Stat. Ann. § 193.167.
42 Pa. Cons. Stat. Ann. § 6302 (2000).
42 Pa. Cons. Stat. Ann. § 6355 (2000).
Code of S.C. Ann. § 14-7-840.
Va. Code Ann. § 16.1-228 (Michie 1999).
Va. Code Ann. § 16.1-269.1 (Michie 1999).

Professional Conduct Rules and Court Rules

American Bar Association, *Code of Professional Responsibility*. Chicago: American Bar
    Association, 1969.
American Bar Association, *Model Code of Judicial Conduct*. Chicago: American Bar As-
    sociation, 1990.

American Bar Association, *Model Rules of Professional Conduct*. Chicago: American Bar Association, 1994.

American Bar Association, Model Rules of Professional Conduct Rule 1.14, Comments [1], [5], [6], [7], [8] (Feb. 27, 2002), reprinted in American Bar Association/Bureau of National Affairs *Manual on Professional Conduct*. Washington, D.C.: Bureau of National Affairs, 1994–.

American Bar Association Standing Committee on Ethics and Professional Responsibility, Formal Opinion 03-429 (June 11, 2003), reprinted in American Bar Association/Bureau of National Affairs *Manual on Professional Conduct* 1201:133. Washington, D.C.: Bureau of National Affairs, 1994–.

American Bar Association Standing Committee on Professional Discipline, *Model Rules for Lawyer Disciplinary Enforcement*. Chicago: American Bar Association, 1989.

American College of Trust and Estate Counsel, *Commentaries on the Model Rules of Professional Conduct*. 3rd ed. Los Angeles: ACTEC, 1999.

California State Bar Standing Committee on Professional Responsibility and Conduct, Formal Opinion 1989-112 (1989), reprinted in American Bar Association/Bureau of National Affairs *Lawyers' Manual on Professional Conduct* 901: 1601. Washington, D.C.: Bureau of National Affairs, 1994–.

Form LR16.1.1, Final Pretrial Order Form, § 2(b) (1999). U.S. District Court, Northern District of Illinois.

Illinois Rules of Professional Conduct, as amended (March 26, 2001), Ill. Comp. Stat. Annot. St. Paul, Minn.: West, 1993, and 2003 supp.

Illinois State Bar Association, Opinion No. 92-12 (Jan. 21, 1993), reprinted in American Bar Association/Bureau of National Affairs *Lawyer's Manual on Professional Responsibility* 1001:3011. Washington, D.C.: Bureau of National Affairs, 1994–.

Illinois Supreme Court Rules, as amended (2001), Ill. Comp. Stat. Annot. St. Paul, Minn.: West, 1993, and 2003 supp.

Judicial Conference of the United States, *Code of Conduct for United States Judges*. Washington, D.C.: Judicial Conference of the United States, 1996.

Judicial Conference of the United States, *Code of Conduct for United States Judges*, Canon 2, Commentary to Canon 2. Washington, D.C.: Judicial Conference of the United States, 1996.

Local Rule 16.1, United States District Court for the Northern District of Illinois (1999), reprinted in *Sullivan's Law Directory, 2002–2003*, Vol. 2. Chicago: Law Bulletin, 2003.

Pennsylvania Bar Association Committee on Legal Ethics and Professional Responsibility, Informal Opinion Number 98-124 (Dec. 7, 1998), reprinted in American Bar Association/Bureau of National Affairs Lawyers' Manual on Professional Conduct 1001:7320. Washington, D.C.: Bureau of National Affairs, 1994–.

Philadelphia Bar Association Professional Guidance Committee Ethics Opinion 2000-12 (2000), reprinted in American Bar Association/Bureau of National Affairs *Lawyers' Manual on Professional Conduct* 1101:7511. Washington, D.C.: Bureau of National Affairs, 1994–.

United States District Court, S.D. Cal., Local Rule 83.10

United States District Court, S.D. Ill., Appendix 1

United States District Court, D. Kan., Rule 38.1(B)(1).

Virginia Canons of Judicial Conduct

Wyoming Code of Judicial Conduct

Index

AARP, 31

Achenbaum, W. Andrew, 25

Adams, William E., 100, 109–10, 237n104, 242nn154–55

Adult education, 166n9

Age: Americans with Disabilities Act, as correlated with views regarding, 262n48; attitudes, influence on, 7; authoritarian tendencies, as correlated with, 261n42; categorization by, 6, 7; crime, as related to (*see* Crime); conduct, influence on, 7; courts, as correlated with confidence in, 258n3; criminal defendants, factor in sentencing of, 120–23; demographics, 165nn2,6,7; discrimination, as basis for (*see* Ageism; Age discrimination in employment; Discrimination); Discrimination in employment (*see* Age discrimination in employment; Age Discrimination in Employment Act); as efficiency device, use of, 7, 22; federal judgeships, factor in appointment to, 129–30; gay rights, as correlated with views regarding, 261–62n44; grading, 6, 172n1, 175n23; happiness, as correlated with, 204n98; intellectual decline, as correlated with, 37–38 (*see also* Capacity, intellectual and decision-making); judicial behavior, as affecting, 245n8; juries, as related to composition of, 155–60; jurors, as correlated with performance as, 140–49; legal treatment of (*see* Age Discrimination in Employment Act; Constitution, United States; Discrimination); litigants, 58–71; opinions re issues, as correlated with, 261n37; responsibilities, as basis for allocation of, 6, 7; rights, as basis for allocation of, 6, 7; sexual activity, as correlated with, 184–85n10; significance of, 6, 65, 174n21

Age bias: difficulty in identifying, 187n34; legal treatment of (*see* Age Discrimination in Employment Act; Constitution, United States; Discrimination); nature of, 15–19, 24. *See also* Ageism

Age Discrimination Act of 1975, 21

Age discrimination in employment: statistics, 187n34. *See also* Age Discrimination in Employment Act

Age Discrimination in Employment Act, 20, 57–59, 63–64, 68, 144, 180–81n42, 188n44, 189n51, 194n27, 213n174, 264n66; discrimination, statistics regarding charges of, 215–16n16; law firm partners, applicability to, 229n11; TV personalities, cases involving, 180n42. *See also* Age discrimination in employment

Age proxies, 249n65

Age stratification, 6, 172n1, 175n23

Ageism, 4–5; attorneys, on part of (*see* Chapter 6); authors as victims of, 180–81n42; cognitive processes as explaining, 40–42; compared to other *-isms,* 18–19, 54–55; constitutionally based attacks on (*see* Constitution, United States); cultural conditioning as explanation for, 24–27; defined, 10, 177n33; distinctiveness of, 18–19, 54–55; education as means to eradicate, 111, 137–38, 243–44n165 (*see also* Law School); elders' reduced productivity as explanation for, 27–29; frustration-aggression hypothesis as explanation for, 45–46; history as explanation for, 24–27; judges, on part of, 133–36; Marxist analysis as explanation for, 195n38; modernization theory, 24; nature of, 23–24; sociobiology as explanation for, 47–49, 50–53; sources of (*see* Chapter 4); TV personalities as victims of, 180n42. *See generally* Chapter 4

Aging: natural selection as related to, 209–10n157, 210–11nn160–61; physical causes of, 49–50. *See also* Age; Elders

Alexander, George, 246n20

Alfini, James J., 136, 254n108, 256nn134–35

Allison, Meredith, 72, 224n95

Allport, Gordon W., 23, 42–43, 205n114

Alpert, Geoffrey P., 146, 261n43

Howard Eglit is a professor of law at Chicago-Kent College of Law, Illinois Institute of Technology. He is the author of a three-volume treatise, *Age Discrimination* (1994). He has chaired the American Association of Law Schools' Section on Aging and the Law and has served as a member of the board of the American Civil Liberties Union, Illinois Division; the Alliance for Aging; the National Academy of Elder Law Attorneys, Inc., Illinois chapter; and Terra Nova Films. He is a member of the Advisory Board of the Buehler Center on Aging, The Feinberg School of Medicine, Northwestern University.